PENGUIN BOOKS

THE CANDY MACHINE

Tom Feiling spent ten years struggling to make documentaries for television. Exasperated by the declining fortunes of the genre, he went to Colombia in 2001, hoping to learn Spanish and open a hotel. Realizing that he had neither the money nor the stomach for the Colombian hotel trade, he instead made a documentary, *Resistencia: Hip-Hop in Colombia*, which went on to screen at film festivals around the world. He came back to London where he became Campaigns Director of Justice for Colombia, a TUC group that defends trade union rights of Colombians. He is a graduate of the London School of Economics. *The Candy Machine* is his first book.

TOM FEILING

The Candy Machine

How Cocaine Took Over the World

PENGUIN BOOKS

PENGUIN BOOKS

Published by the Penguin Group
Penguin Books Ltd, 80 Strand, London WC2R ORL, England
Penguin Group (USA) Inc., 375 Hudson Street, New York, New York 10014, USA
Penguin Group (Canada), 90 Eglinton Avenue East, Suite 700, Toronto, Ontario, Canada M4P 2Y3
(a division of Pearson Penguin Canada Inc.)
Penguin Ireland, 25 St Stephen's Green, Dublin 2, Ireland
(a division of Penguin Books Ltd)
Penguin Group (Australia), 250 Camberwell Road, Camberwell, Victoria 3124, Australia
(a division of Pearson Australia Group Pty Ltd)
Penguin Books India Pvt Ltd, 11 Community Centre, Panchsheel Park, New Delhi – 110 017, India
Penguin Group (NZ), 67 Apollo Drive, Rosedale, North Shore 0632, New Zealand
(a division of Pearson New Zealand Ltd)
Penguin Books (South Africa) (Pty) Ltd, 24 Sturdee Avenue, Rosebank, Johannesburg 2196, South Africa

Penguin Books Ltd, Registered Offices: 80 Strand, London WC2R ORL, England

www.penguin.com

First published in Penguin Books 2009
1

Copyright © Tom Feiling, 2009
All rights reserved

The moral right of the author has been asserted

Set in 9.25/12.5 pt Linotype Sabon
Typeset by Rowland Phototypesetting Ltd, Bury St Edmunds, Suffolk
Printed in England by Clays Ltd, St Ives plc

ISBN: 978-0-141-03446-1

www.greenpenguin.co.uk

Penguin Books is committed to a sustainable future
for our business, our readers and our planet.
The book in your hands is made from paper
certified by the Forest Stewardship Council.

Contents

CONTENTS

PART THREE
Where Do We Go From Here?

Acknowledgements

In the UK, I'd like to thank Julia Vellacott and Becky Swift for their advice when I first started looking for a publisher. Thanks too to my agent Broo Doherty and my editor at Allen Lane, Margaret Bluman, for taking a chance on a first-time writer. Sir Keith Morris, Danny Kushlick and Axel Klein are critics of the current handling of the cocaine trade. They made me aware of the main players in the debate, and I am grateful for the encouragement they gave me when I was in the early stages of researching this book.

Liam Craig Best of Justice for Colombia and Jenny Pearce of Bradford University advised me on who best to approach in Colombia. In the United States, the experience and analysis of John Walsh at the Washington Office on Latin America, Sanho Tree at the Institute for Policy Studies, and Adam Isaacson at the Center for International Policy were invaluable. In Bogotá, my friends Nick Perkins, Rusty Young and Ricardo Sanchez helped me a great deal with my research. Tiziana Laudato and Angelica Ibarra helped with translations. Journalists and film-makers Françoise Nieto Fong, Ricardo Restrepo, Daniel Coronell, Steve Ambrus, Romeo Langlois, Pascale Mariani and Carlos Lozano all had interesting things to say about the drugs trade in Colombia, and supplied me with plentiful leads. I'd especially like to thank the many people who agreed to meet and discuss the subject with me, especially since many of them will not share my methods or conclusions: Aldo Lale-Demoz, Rodolfo Llinas and Hugo Javier Bustos at the UNODC (United Nations Office on Drugs and Crime); Juan Carlos Montero at DIRAN (Colombian Anti-Narcotics Police); Carlos Medina at the Observatorio de Drogas of the Dirección

Nacional de Estupefacientes; Nick Eliades in the DEA (Drug Enforcement Administration) Public Affairs Office; Than Christie in the Narcotics Affairs Section of the US Embassy; Luis 'Lucho' Salamanca, Kevin Higgins, Chris Feistl, Colombian Vice-President Francisco Santos, Malcolm Deas of Oxford University and David Hutchinson. My thanks, too, go to Dan Scott-Lea, Yaneth Pachón, David Curtidor, Daniel Maestre, Adelaida Moreno at the farmworkers' union Fensuagro, Congressman Luis Fernando Almario Rojas, Congressman Wilson Borja, Alberto Rueda, Markus Schultze-Kraft at the International Crisis Group, Ricardo Vargas at Acción Andina, Gustavo Duncan, Luis Eduardo Cellis Mendez at the Fundación Nuevo Arco Iris, and Omar Gutierrez at the Centre for Investigation and Popular Education (CINEP).

In Jamaica, I'd like to thank Geraldine O'Callaghan and Andy MacLean for letting me stay with them while I was on the island. Marta Shaw, Flip Fraser, Sarah Manley, Lois Grant and Paul Burke gave me plentiful insights and pointed me in the right direction. Thanks also to local law enforcement officers Inspector Michael Simpson, ACP Carl Williams and Carlton Wilson; and to the British police officers working in Jamaica as part of Operation Kingfish: Les Green, Paul Robinson and John McLean. I'm particularly grateful to journalists Anthony Barrett, Glenroy Sinclair and Mark Wignall, and to Bobby Sephestine and Olga Heaven at the prison charity Hibiscus. Lloyd Evans and Gordon Brown helped me to better understand the political situation. I'd also like to thank Barry Chevannes, Horace Levy and Donna Hope at the University of the West Indies at Mona.

In the United States, I'd like to extend my thanks to Marcela Guerrero for help in finding places to stay in various cities, and to Chris Robinson, David Russell, Carlos Tovar and Neerav Kingsland for putting me up as I travelled from city to city. Bruce Johnson, Doris Randolph, the late Dr John Morgan, Elizabeth Mendez Berry, Kym Clark, Larry Miller, James Peterson, Mark Mauer at the Sentencing Project, Clarence Lusane, Professor Peter Reuter and Steven Robertson at the DEA Public Information Office allowed me to pick their brains. The US chapters owe a great deal to ethnographies of drug users and dealers written by John M. Hagedorn, Rick Curtis, Travis Wendell and Philippe Bourgois. My special thanks to all of them. Alex Sanchez of Homies Unidos, Luis Rodriguez, Jeff Chang, Father Tom Hereford and Bruce George all shed precious light on the cocaine economy. Ethan Nadelmann, Tony Newman, Ed Kirtz, Gabriel Sayegh, Tony Papa and Margaret Dooley-Sammuli at the Drug Policy Alliance were supportive and helpful. Rusty White, Jack Cole, Celerino Castillo III, David Doderidge, and Russ Jones of Law Enforcement Against Prohibition provided an invaluable critique of the war on drugs from the point of view of those who have prosecuted it, as did Judge James Gray, Kurt Schmoke and Eric Sterling. My thanks also to Jon Veit, David Lewis, Julienne Gage, John Maass, Samuel Wilcher and Jacob Sullum at *Reason* magazine. Tom Horvath of Practical Recovery Services, Susan Burton of the 'A New Way of Life' re-entry project, Marqueece Harris Dawson of the Community Coalition, Lou Martinez at The Effort Community Health Center and Kenny Glasgow of the Ordinary People Society work with compulsive drug users. The conversations I had with them improved my understanding of addiction and social deprivation in the United States.

For help in investigating cross-border smuggling and the drugs trade in Mexico, I'd like to thank Elijah Wald, Jon Forrest Little, David Fry and Leticia Zamarripa at El Paso Immigration and Customs Enforcement, Sam Quiñones, Rafael Nuñez, Jaime Hervella, Howard Campbell, Tony Payan, Richard Cockett, John Dickie, Sam Logan, Dudley Althaus and Jorge Chabat. For insights into the street drug culture of Mexico City, Benito Azcano Roldán, Alfonso Hernandez at the Centro de Estudios Tepiteños, Carlos Zamudio, Ricardo Sala and Mister Hunter deserve special mention.

I'd like to thank friends who helped me out in one way or another in the writing of the book: Lauren Ferreira, Erin Howley, Mike Sadler and Anna Wilkinson, Chris Walker and Jordan Ethe in the United States. In Mexico, that means Elizabeth Clark, Danielle Savage, Ed Peterson and Jonathan Barbieri, who all helped to make breaks from the writing process more enjoyable. Back in London, when I wondered how to turn such a welter of information into a good read, Sharon Kinsella, Slawek Dorosz, Daniel Wilson, Bryony Morrison, Sam Low, Richard Garner and Michael Ryan offered valuable feedback on early drafts. Maribel Lozano and Nelson Diaz helped with translations and kept Colombia on my mind. Finally, I'd especially like to thank four writers whose insights into the drugs issue most inspired me: Harry Levine, Anthony Henman, Alonso Salazar and Francisco Thoumi.

Unless otherwise indicated, the Colombian interviews were conducted in September 2007, the Jamaican interviews in October 2007, the American interviews in November and December 2007, and the British interviews in May 2008. I would like to thank all the interviewees, particularly those who have chosen to remain anonymous, for investing their time and trust in me.

Introduction

In March 2008, the United Nations' World Drug Report confirmed that the price of cocaine in Europe had fallen to a record low, fuelling record levels of cocaine use. 'Celebrity drug offenders can profoundly influence attitudes, values and behaviour towards drug abuse, particularly among young people,' the report warned. The United Nations blamed this on 'celebrity culture' and even accused the police of turning a blind eye to rich and famous misusers of the drug.[1]

High-profile drug casualties, like the singers Pete Doherty and Amy Winehouse, and the model Kate Moss, vie for space on the front pages of Britain's tabloids and broadsheets alike with ever-larger drug seizures. In writing this book, I didn't want to get swept up in the all-too-familiar mix of nosiness, envy and sanctimony that masquerades as the 'public interest', or the ritual inflation and deflation of mediocrity that passes for 'celebrity news'. I have not sought the opinions of commentators, politicians or the drug-taking anecdotes of high-rollers. Instead, I wanted to hear from those who work day to day on the cocaine trade routes that run from London and New York via Miami, Kingston and Tijuana to Colombia. I wanted to see the impact of the war on drugs on the consumers, traders and producers of cocaine, and the impact they have on the soldiers, police officers, customs officials and doctors charged with prosecuting the war. I wanted to bring the tight-lipped mechanics who keep the cocaine economy ticking over on to the stage.

In 2002, I spent a year working in Colombia, at the end of which I made a documentary called *Resistencia: Hip-Hop in Colombia*. After a screening at a film festival in Bogotá, a Colombian told me that she was surprised but glad to see that a foreigner had made a film about her country that made no mention of the cocaine trade. Cocaine seemed to be the only thing that outsiders knew or wanted to know about Colombia, she told me, and their depictions of the business invariably ended up trading in stereotypes. Colombia is a fascinating and beautiful country and its tourist board will no doubt be happy to read that I would recommend a holiday there to anyone. But they probably won't enjoy reading anything else I have to say about their country in this book. Colombians argue that their country is not the only cocaine-producing country in the Andes, that the business exists only because of strong demand for cocaine in Europe and the United States and that no country has paid such a high price for cocaine as theirs. But no other country is as well suited to cocaine production as Colombia. Most commentators never consider why this might be, for while the cocaine business, the war on drugs and Colombia's civil conflict are tangled and confusing, once prised apart, it is shocking how oblivious each player is to the others. Attitudes, policies and institutions seem to function quite independently of one another. This incoherence is not particular to Colombia: it is characteristic of anti-drug strategies worldwide.

When I moved back to London from Bogotá, everybody seemed to be complaining about stress, information overload and how expensive everything had become. Why then, I wondered, did sizeable numbers of Londoners regard the strongest stimulant known to mankind as suitable Friday-night entertainment? Expensive, energizing, esteem-boosting, inclining its users to delusions of grandeur and paranoia in equal measure, cocaine seemed to have become the perfect accompaniment to twenty-first-century life. In 1903, the British Committee on the Acquirement of Drug Habits described cocaine users as typically 'bohemians, gamblers, high and low-class prostitutes, night porters, bell-boys, burglars, racketeers, pimps and casual labourers'.[2] By 2008, cocaine had become ordinary. Indeed, its ordinariness was what most perturbed the authorities. According to *The Times*, 'police say privately that cocaine is becoming as acceptable in middle-class Britain as cannabis was a generation ago and that they are losing their battle against the drug'.[3] On his first day as Commissioner of the Metropolitan Police in February 2005, Sir Ian Blair informed the waiting press pack that 'people are having dinner parties where they drink less wine and snort more cocaine'.[4] In fact, they were drinking more wine *and* snorting more cocaine. The exotic newcomer cocaine is more often than not consumed in conjunction with alcohol. The two combine in the liver to produce coca-ethanol, a whole new buzz which stays active for twice as long as cocaine.

'I'm not interested in what harm it is doing to them personally,' the new Commissioner of Police went on, 'but the price of that cocaine is misery on the streets of London's estates and blood on the roads to Colombia and Afghanistan.'[5] The Commissioner's words echoed those of Nancy Reagan, who in 1988 warned that 'if you're a casual drug user, you're an accomplice to murder'.[6] Critics of recreational drug use find themselves in a quandary. Without a social problem to crack down on or helpless victims to whom they might extend their help and compassion, they can only articulate their objections to certain mind-altering substances by invoking the misery that has been caused by driving drug use underground. The source of the problem, it would seem, is the desire for luxury. Cocaine has long been familiar and acceptable to the wealthy and famous. Young British people, aspiring to both wealth and fame, are paying for and enjoying cocaine as never before. Cocaine consumers, whether middle class, working class or lower upper middle class take flack for being uncaring and self-congratulatory, but office work, profligate consumption and a weekly mash-up to make sense of it all have become defining features of life and style up and down the country.

If the likes of Sir Ian Blair and Nancy Reagan were looking for a social problem, why didn't they target the daily use of crack by the destitute? Unlike the prostitutes of 1903, most of today's sex workers are in the business only to raise money to pay for their expensive, compulsive crack and/or heroin use. Casualties of crack cocaine have become part of the street life of my neighbourhood in London and several friends of mine have become compulsive users of heroin and crack. Why are there still so many 'problematic' drug users? Why do some people succumb to addiction, while others seem able to treat cocaine as mere ornamentation? And why is 'addiction' suddenly being bandied about to explain overeating? If we are all junkies of one potentially harmful substance and/or activity or another, does that mean that double espressos and excessive use of Play Station can also be addictive?

In 2004, a kilogram of cocaine typically sold for £655 in Colombia. Once smuggled north into Mexico, it was worth £3,940. Once over the border and into the United States, it would sell for £11,750.[7] Once divided into a thousand one-gram bags, it would be worth £18,500. Had you adulterated or cut the kilo with 200 grams of laxative powder or glucose, you could increase its value to £22,200. If, on the other hand, you took that wholesale kilo of cocaine to Europe, you'd be able to sell it for an average of £23,845, more than twice the price it would have fetched in the United States.[8] These figures come from a book by Sandro Calvani, one-time head of the Colombian branch of the United Nations Office on Drugs and Crime. They sound credible to me, but it should be understood at the outset that when describing any facet of the cocaine economy, supposition can all too easily take the place of fact. Writing objectively about an illegal activity is difficult at the best of times and most observers seem happy to err on the side of wild exaggeration: figures such as $500 billion for world drug sales are thrown around quite glibly.[9] You can't blame harried journalists, since this figure originated in a press release issued by the United Nations. The Colombian economist Francisco Thoumi has since discovered that 'the $500 billion figure was the result of "research" attempted by the United Nations agency responsible for coordinating the global assault on drug trafficking, when the boss was desperate for a quick number before a press conference'.

Such laxity is not unusual. The Financial Action Task Force, a multinational organization set up to tackle money-laundering by drugs traffickers, also commissioned a study to calculate the size of the illegal drugs business. When its author reported back that the global trade in illegal drugs was probably worth between $45 billion and $280 billion a year, his employers decided not to publish his findings because 'some country members expected a larger figure'.[10] When even international agencies set more store by what they expect to be true than by what they find to be true, it is no surprise that non-specialists follow suit. The writer of a popular book on the world drug trade claimed that illegal drugs provided Colombia with 36 per cent of its GDP. In fact the cocaine trade has never been responsible for more than 5 per cent of Colombian GDP.[11] The United States State Department is required by statute to produce data on the scale of the drugs business, but given the lack of scrutiny of drugs policy by Congress, there is not much incentive to make that data plausible. Perhaps the need to appear authoritative in public discussions is sufficient motivation to produce the numbers, but not reason enough to do the job properly. In 'The Vitality of Mythical Numbers', an article published in 1971, Max Singer showed that if one tallied the official figures for the number of heroin addicts in New York City with the price of a heroin habit and an habitué's dependence on theft to support that habit, New York City did not exist any more – it had been stolen by junkies.[12]

Opponents of the international war on drugs are also prone to exaggerating the size of the drugs trade. Colombia's FARC (Revolutionary Armed Forces of Colombia) guerrillas, who generally regard the United States as a nation of gluttonous savages and hopeless drug addicts, say that the drugs trade constitutes between 20 and 30 per cent of the world economy.[13] Other critics are convinced that the US economy is a net beneficiary of the drugs business, and that the war on drugs is no more than a façade behind which Wall Street banks enjoy the fruits of prohibition. But there is no reason for US banks and corporations to prefer drugs money over any other kind of money. If people spend their money on drugs, it can only mean that they're not spending it on something else. Francisco Thoumi has pointed out that if it were true that the illegal drugs business contributed to economic growth in the United States, canny economists would recommend that Colombia declare tobacco illegal, thereby raising cigarette prices and increasing smuggling, which would then generate revenue to buoy the country's national income. Corporations pay taxes to governments; cocaine dealers do not. Corrupt people and tax havens benefit from the trade in illegal drugs, but a country's economic system does not.

Thankfully, there are trustworthy sources of information on the size of the drugs economy. Whatever its size, the economics of the drugs business clearly favours its practitioners. There are thought to be about 300 major drug importers into Britain, 3,000 wholesalers and 70,000 street dealers. Approximately one in 500 Britons works in the business of buying and selling illegal drugs.[14] Between them, they turn over sales of £7–8 billion a year, which is about a third of the size of Britain's tobacco market and two fifths of its trade in alcohol. Annual imports of cocaine have recently been estimated at 33 tons. Given that a gram typically sells for £50, we can safely assume that the retail cocaine market in the United Kingdom turns over 33 million grams of cocaine, worth £1.6 billion a year.[15] To put this figure in some perspective, sales of footwear in the UK were worth £5.7 billion in 2005 and soft drinks sales were worth £6.2 billion.

In the United States, the total value of illegal drug sales is likely to be around £25 billion a year, which amounts to less than 1 per cent of America's GDP and less than 2 per cent of Americans' total personal consumption. Given that the United States is far and away the biggest market for nearly all illegal drugs, the global figure is unlikely to be more than twice this. A £50 billion-a-year market is a big market, but in the context of total global trade flows of almost $3 trillion or £1.5 trillion a year, it is a very modest share indeed. The drugs trade's share of total world trade declines to the trivial when you consider that most of the trade's value is added only when the drugs cross the United States' borders. Valuing the drugs trade at import prices reduces its overall value to no more than £10 billion. Besides, there are much bigger illegal businesses than the drugs business. Americans made roughly £350 billion from illegal activities in 1998, equivalent to about 8 per cent of the country's GDP. The biggest earner was tax evasion, which was worth £131 billion a year, making the £25 billion a year drugs-trafficking business look paltry by comparison.[16]

I crunch these numbers to demonstrate that the subject of drugs is replete with inaccuracies. As we will see in Chapter 1, the first restrictions on cocaine use were imposed by politicians with moral objections to drug use, but their objections were informed by ignorance, prejudice and caricature. I urge the reader to proceed with an open mind. By giving airtime to those involved in the cocaine business, I hope to

puncture some of those stereotypes and draw the reader's attention to
the motives and rewards that sustain both the supply of and demand
for cocaine. A drugs policy fit for the twenty-first century will only
emerge when these hidden stories are revealed, read and acted on.

PART ONE

How Did We Get Here?

PART THREE

How Did We Get Here?

I

From Soft Drink to Hard Drug

*The only answer to increased crime is increased punishment:
as long as there are witches, enchanters and sorcerers in the
world, there must be fire! fire! fire!*
        Hugh Trevor-Roper, *The European Witch-Craze of the
                                16th and 17th Centuries*[1]

In a scene from a documentary film entitled *Coca Mama* (2001), an
indigenous Peruvian gives a telling introduction to the story of how
the coca plant became the subject of an American war. 'When the
whites came, our ancestors consulted the Sun God,' he tells the viewer.
'He told them to trust in the coca leaf. "The coca will feed and cure
you", he said, "and will give you the strength to survive."' He also
said that the white men would discover its magic force, but that they
wouldn't know how to make use of coca. The Sun God told our
ancestors that coca would turn the white men into brutes and idiots.'[2]
    An excerpt from the journal of the Italian explorer Amerigo Ves-
pucci indicates that the white men held a similarly low opinion of the
coca chewers. It describes an encounter that took place in 1499, off
the coast of what is today Venezuela.

We descried an island that lay about 15 leagues from the coast and decided
to go there to see if it was inhabited. We found there the most bestial and
ugly people we had ever seen: very ugly of face and expression, and all of
them had their cheeks full of a green herb that they chewed constantly like
beasts, so that they could barely speak. Each one carried around his neck

two gourds, one of them full of that herb and the other of a white powder that looked like pulverized plaster. They dipped a stick into the powder, and then put the stick in the mouth, in order to apply powder to the herb that they chewed; they did this very frequently. We were amazed at this and could not understand its secret or why they did it.[3]

The green leaf Vespucci saw the natives chew was coca. The repression and prohibition of the derivatives of the coca bush is just one of a host of measures that served to banish specific peoples and cultures from Latin America. The conquistadores arrived in the New World fresh from a pan-European campaign of witch-burning, and had few qualms about putting what they considered demonic customs to the torch. Many of those customs, including use of the coca leaf, have only in the past twenty years begun to recover from the assault those first Europeans launched. Cocaine was invented by a European chemist 140 years ago, but the leaves of the coca bush from which cocaine is extracted have been chewed by Americans from Chile to Guatemala since 2100 BC.[4] Coca was one of the first plants to be cultivated by the peoples of the Americas. The architects and workers who built Machu Picchu chewed coca leaves, as did the builders of the lines in the desert at Nazca, the incredible terraced agricultural laboratory at Moray, near Cuzco in Peru, and the 3,500-year-old temple at Kalassassaya in Bolivia.[5]

In the seventeenth century, European explorers brought back many mild psychoactive substances from the New World, including such staples of modern stimulation as coffee, tobacco and chocolate. The first Spanish settlers of the Andes had noticed how the Inca people used coca to suppress hunger and fatigue, and derived 'great contentment' from it. So why wasn't coca part of that first wave? Europeans were not accustomed to smoking plants, but they took to smoking tobacco with gusto, perhaps because the habit was genuinely strange to them. The prevailing opinion of coca seems to have been akin to that of Amerigo Vespucci: the chewing of a wad of coca leaves reminded them of their cows.

Not only did the new masters of Peru not take to coca-chewing, the first Catholic missionaries saw that the practice was a key obstacle to converting the natives from paganism to Christianity because coca was the gateway to the native pantheon. The missionaries did, however, recognize the importance of coca to their new subjects, and how useful it might be to their mission in the New World. Coca offered physical as well as spiritual benefits to its users: it warded off hunger and tiredness, so the colonists supplied it to the miners who extracted silver from the mountains. Indigenous tradition had it that buying and selling coca leaves was sacrilegious; none the less, the coca plantations soon became the mainstay of the Peruvian colony, and many Spanish colonists paid their workers in coca. In the seventeenth century, the coca market of the silver-mining city of Potosí had a turnover twice that of the markets for food and clothing.[6]

With the commercialization of coca cultivation, a sacred plant became a tool to exploit the native workforce. This exploitation of Indian workers by Creole landowners, who were the proxies of the Catholic kings of Spain, created the American continent's first drug dealers. As one contemporary wrote, 'Our fair-minded masters do not want the poor to recognize their tragedy, and wish instead that they should die without realizing their hunger and their ignorance; that the bitter taste of coca might dull the instinct to rebel, and that they might live in an artificial paradise.'[7] Seeing coca in its economic context – as a sacred plant made to serve the commercial interests of a distant empire – supplies us with an important lesson in how innocuous plants can become dangerous drugs.

Well into the twentieth century, Andean landowners paid their indigenous workers in coca leaves, a practice that resulted in malnutrition and supplied the case studies for a novel theory of drug addiction. In the 1940s, a Peruvian pharmacologist called Carlos Gutierrez Noriega developed a theory of 'cocaism', largely based on his observation of the coca-chewing habits of prison inmates. He assumed that indigenous Peruvians had been enslaved by coca, and that it was their coca-chewing that had landed them in prison. Noriega argued that the natives chewed coca leaves instead of eating, and that this was the cause of the malnutrition they were suffering. He called coca 'the factor of greatest importance opposed to the improvement of the Indian's health and social condition'. The Colombian government maintained that coca-chewing was physically debilitating, slowed the educational development of children, caused behaviour 'incompatible with civilization and Christian tradition', and 'exacerbated sexual instincts'.[8] Notwithstanding the fact that Gutierrez Noriega's only experience of Indian culture was the time he spent in the prisons of Lima, whose inmates he used as the subjects for his experiments, he became the world's foremost authority on the use of coca. In the years that followed, his critique of 'cocaism' became the standard interpretation of both coca and Indian poverty.

After 1938, the Colombian government restricted the sale of coca leaves to pharmacies. In 1947, it became illegal to pay salaries in coca leaves, or to cultivate or distribute coca. In 1952 the United Nations banned a practice going back thousands of years in the name of combating the very modern disease of 'drug addiction'. The ban was only lifted in 1988, when the drug conventions were revised to make some allowance for traditional use of psychotropic substances such as coca and opium. Sandro Calvani, the former Colombian representative of the United Nations Office on Drugs and Crime, wrote in 2007 that 'these days there is sufficient empirical and scientific evidence to demonstrate that it is absurd to continue regarding the coca leaf as a dangerous drug or psychotropic, or the consumption of coca tea as evidence of "drug addiction".'

The coca leaf contains B vitamins, and more iron and calcium than any other food crop indigenous to the high Andes. It relaxes the bronchial air passages in the lungs, which makes it easier to breathe at high altitudes, where oxygen is scarce. Chewing coca is also said to ward off the cold, and to have unrivalled anaesthetic effects. As its effects are short-lasting, it produces neither over-stimulation nor sleeplessness. About 8 million people in the Andean region chew coca regularly, which means that there are more coca-chewers in Latin America than there are cocaine users in North America.[9]

I met Daniel Maestre at the offices of the National Indigenous Organization (ONIC) in Bogotá. I had gone there hoping to talk to somebody about the ancestral use of coca and had been directed to where Daniel was quietly chewing coca as he waited for a friend to come out of a meeting. I asked him to what extent coca's enduring appeal lay in its physical effects. 'We say that the coca bush is an intelligent plant,' he told me. 'When you first chew it, it might make your tongue numb, but soon your body relaxes, so when you see someone who is used to chewing coca, you see how peaceful his face is. Coca is a relaxant, but more because of the slow and steady movement of the jaw than its chemical effects. The physical effects of chewing coca are barely perceptible.'

About 0.5 per cent of the chemical content of a coca leaf is cocaine. An Andean coca-chewer might get through 30 grams of leaves in a day, which yields the equivalent of 150 milligrams, or an average-sized line of cocaine. Just as anyone mainlining caffeine would experience physical effects quite distinct from those enjoyed by drinking a few cups of coffee in the course of the day, snorting 150 mg of cocaine has effects hard to compare with those attained by the slow, steady absorption of coca through the mouth and stomach. Today, even the American Embassy in the Bolivian capital of La Paz advises recent arrivals to sip coca tea until they get used to being 12,000 feet above sea level.

But the difference between coca and cocaine is not just one of intensity. Their users ascribe very different meanings to each. The Páez live in the Colombian province of Cauca. They are one of many indigenous communities that chew coca daily, but traditional Páez doctors also use coca in cleansing ceremonies. Every six months, a family will gather under a tree, and the doctor will chew a wad of coca leaves while swilling *aguardiente* (the local fire water) around his mouth. Then he'll spit the wad on to the family's pastures to keep the animals healthy and ward off evil spirits. When night falls, he'll chew some more coca until he is able to distinguish those fireflies that are carrying good luck from those that are carrying bad luck. The latter he catches, bundles up with twigs and douses with coca leaves and *aguardiente*, before burying them in the ground.

Coca, myth and the rituals of daily life are intimately bound, as Daniel Maestre went on to explain. 'My grandfather told me that the coca bush was once a very pretty woman. She was so pretty that everybody fought over her. Since not everybody could have her, the elders turned her into a plant, so that she could be enjoyed by everyone.

What began as a source of division became a source of unity. When you get to puberty, the elders start preparing you to receive your *poporo* (a gourd). You mix the coca with ground-up seashells in the *poporo*. As you chew, the calcium from the shells releases all the beneficial chemicals and alkaloids from the leaves, and you start dreaming, thinking, remembering, listening and seeing. Coca represents the word of my grandmother, and the *poporo* the word of my wife. Coca is sweet like a woman, and it sweetens the words that come out of your mouth. It gives harmony to your words, and it makes conversation well balanced and meaningful. You feel a great sense of harmonious energy. You spend all your life with your *poporo*, just as you do with your wife, and, just as nobody likes to see another man touch his wife, so you don't let other people touch your *poporo*.'

The prohibition of recreational drugs like cocaine, heroin and cannabis is a relatively recent departure from a tradition in which European and North American societies tolerated the use of a wide range of psychoactive substances. Until a hundred years ago, opium was a popular psychoactive on both sides of the Atlantic. America's colonists regarded low doses of opium as a familiar resource for pain relief. Benjamin Franklin regularly took laudanum (opium in alcohol extract) to alleviate the pain of kidney stones during the last years of his life.[10] Identifying and isolating the active ingredients of the opium poppy and the coca leaf was a vital first step in developing a mass market for these drugs. Nineteenth-century chemists busied themselves with decoding all kinds of previously 'magical' substances: codeine in 1832, caffeine in 1841, and then cocaine in 1859. But this isolation was not only a chemical process: it also sheared psychoactive substances from their specific cultural context. They could now be packaged as commodities, and sold to anyone with the money to buy them. Since these substances were no longer dispensed by healers, or reserved for special ceremonies, people had to learn how to take drugs all over again.

Initially at least, it seemed that Europeans and Americans were fast learners. In the last quarter of the nineteenth century, expanding overseas markets fuelled the growth of manufacturing industries. A new class of white-collar workers, known as 'brain workers', struggled to keep pace with the demands of this economic boom. Brain workers needed stimulants to keep them going, but until the 1880s, the only stimulant available was caffeine. Cocaine filled this gap. It hit the mass market in two forms: patent and ethical. Patent preparations came from general food and grocery suppliers and typically contained unspecified amounts of coca leaf extract. Most coca products were tonics, and most contained relatively small doses of the active ingredient. Coca extracts and mild cocaine solutions immediately found favour as 'pick-me-ups' rather like the espresso coffees and energy drinks of today. The manufacturers ran slogans such as 'Don't lose time, be happy! If you're feeling run down and fed-up, ask for cocaine,' and 'Strengthens and refreshes body and mind.' One such concoction was coca wine, an infusion of coca leaves in red wine. The first person to buy coca wine in the United States was Abraham Lincoln, who paid 50 cents for a bottle of 'Cocaine' in 1860, a month before he was elected President of the United States. The most popular brand of coca wine was 'Mariani wine', created by an Italian chemist called Angelo Mariani. He was called to the bedside of another American President, Ulysses Grant, who was suffering from cancer of the throat. Mariani found Grant being nursed by the writer Mark Twain, who was determined to keep Grant alive long enough to collect his memories of the American Civil War for his latest book. Mariani suggested that Twain encourage Grant to take coca wine for his condition. Grant soon affirmed that the enormous quantities of coca wine that he ingested daily were a great help, though he admitted finding it very hard to stop drinking it.

Mariani wine went on to become the most popular prescribed remedy in the world, lauded by the likes of H. G. Wells, Thomas Edison, Emile Zola, the Tsar of Russia and even Pope Leo XIII, who sent a gold medal to Angelo Mariani by way of thanks.[11] Jules Verne, author of *Twenty Thousand Leagues under the Sea*, enthused that 'since a single bottle of Mariani's extraordinary coca wine guarantees a lifetime of a hundred years, I shall be obliged to live until the year 2700!' Vin Mariani is produced in the Bolivian capital La Paz to this day, though its aficionados are much reduced in number and renown.[12]

Coca-Cola was another triumph of this first wave of cocaphilia, one of the many fruits of nineteenth-century globalization. It was also the zippiest beverage imaginable, widely available from soda fountains and popularly used as an antidote to hangovers. It started out as an attempt to side-step the nay-sayers of the city of Atlanta, who had ordained the prohibition of alcohol in 1886. The beverage then known as Peruvian Wine Cola emerged divested of its alcohol content, as a therapeutic combination of coca, caffeine and an extract of the African cola nut, the invigorating qualities of which had been celebrated by the Scottish explorer David Livingstone. With the passage of the Harrison Narcotics Tax Act in the United States in 1914, however, the Coca-Cola Company was forced to remove the cocaine from their secret 7X formula, and the company stopped touting it as a tonic.[13] The modern-day can's red and white livery, taken from the colours of the Peruvian flag, is the only reminder of Coca-Cola's Andean origins.

Aside from the patent preparations, the ethical coca preparations were supplied by Merck of Germany and Parke-Davis and Burroughs Wellcome of the United States, and the cocaine content of their preparations was clear and explicit. Between them, these pharmaceutical giants helped make cocaine one of the great pharmaceutical success stories of the late nineteenth century.[14] By 1900, pure cocaine was selling for 25 cents a gram in the United States, and had become one of the nation's top five best-selling pharmaceutical products.[15] It was used as the principal active ingredient in everything from toothache drops to haemorrhoid plasters, inhalers, ointments, and even cigars. It was touted as a remedy for dyspepsia, an appetite suppressant, a cure for shyness in children and a general panacea for the sick and the listless. Cocaine, Parke-Davis proudly announced, 'can supply the place of food, make the coward brave, the silent eloquent and render the sufferer insensitive to pain.'[16] It seemed to offer a cure for everything except rational scepticism. Readers of the Sears Roebuck catalogue in the 1890s were even offered, for a mere $1.50, a handy Parke-Davis cocaine kit, which came with its own hypodermic syringe.

In 1900, pharmacies around the world stocked 70,000 substances that contained psychoactive ingredients of one kind or another.[17] Until 1907, practically any drug could be bought from chemists in the United States. The trade was legal, unregulated and unlicensed and the demand for coca leaves grew exponentially. Peru was the world's biggest supplier of coca products: in 1900 its growers exported 10 tons of cocaine (today, annual exports of cocaine from Peru, Bolivia and Colombia are thought to be closer to 1,000 tons a year). Commercial coca plantations were sown by Dutch colonizers far from the Andes, in the coffee-growing highlands of Java, where coca plants yielded higher cocaine content than anything ever seen in the Andes. Plantations were also sown by the Japanese in Taiwan, and by the British in what was then Ceylon. Some consumers chose to take cocaine in its most concentrated form, but it is important to recognize that most preferred to enjoy it as a soft drink. Cocaine's origins as an ingredient in legal preparations have been obscured as twenty-first-century aficionados and prohibitionists alike have focused their attention on the drug in its most potent form. In the late nineteenth century, there was no drug scene. There were no coke-heads, drug dealers or crack-addicted prostitutes. Drug-taking was not commonly regarded as an escape from day-to-day life, nor was it a rite of passage into the glitterati, the literati or the cognoscenti. It was neither high class, low class or under class. Drugs were not a matter for the courts, politicians or educationalists, and they hardly ever warranted a mention in the papers, except as copy for advertisements.

The most worrisome mind-altering substance at the turn of the century was not cocaine or opium, but alcohol. Alcoholic drinks had been popular in the United States since the founding of the Republic, but from the eighteenth century onwards, drinkers had to contend with a strong temperance movement. American newspapers were chock-a-block with the yellow journalism of zealous moral entrepreneurs, who regularly claimed that booze lay at the root of most of the crime, insanity, poverty, divorce, illegitimacy and business failures in the United States. So when cocaine use was banned, it was as a small part of a much broader movement against all kinds of intoxication.

The prohibition of potentially dangerous substances like alcohol, heroin and cocaine had its progressive as well as its reactionary champions. On the one hand, the campaign to ban drugs and alcohol was part of a programme of social and economic reforms that was supposed to improve the lives of the downtrodden. They included the end of slavery, free public education and women's suffrage. But the temperance movement was also bolstered by the support of more self-interested Americans. Recent immigrants from Ireland, Italy and the Jewish communities of Eastern Europe were bringing boozier habits into the United States. Suspicion of their customs was bound up with worries about rapid urban growth, overcrowding, violence and the waning power of white Anglo-Saxon Protestants in American cities.[18]

The smoking of opium, for example, was a habit that Chinese immigrants had brought with them when they came to the United States to build the railroads. Anti-opium campaigns only gathered steam when white workers in San Francisco started to protest at the competition they faced from Chinese labour. No sooner had the Chinese completed the Pacific railroad and been made redundant than they were collectively made the scapegoat for an anti-opium scare. In the Southern states too, mention of problematic cocaine use followed on the heels of redundancy. The sharecropping cotton economy of the Southern United States was in decline when whites first started hollering about cocaine-addled Negroes. The police complained that their .32 pistols weren't powerful enough to stop a black man on cocaine. 'Ordinary shootin' don't kill him,' as one Southern police officer put it.[19]

Heroin and cocaine were undoubtedly causing health problems in the United States. The first cocaine users had been predominantly middle-class professionals – a third were either physicians or dentists – and it was from this group that the first cases of abuse appeared.[20] These 'cocainomaniacs' were mostly injecting cocaine, and were few in number. As the press became more critical of the unregulated drug industry, and the harm that cocaine and opiates could do became clear, the public became warier of using them, and use of both fell by up to half long before they were prohibited. But as cocaine use spread to other communities, white politicians found that drug scares offered them an opportunity to bond with their white electors, especially in times of recession or redundancy. The political gains to be made by scaremongering invariably outweighed whatever concerns over public health they might have had.

The first scare stories about cocaine in American newspapers focused on its appeal to those thought least able to handle it. This was the era of the first full segregation laws, and the high point of the lynching of black men in the Southern United States. Much of the cocaine in the United States arrived on ships sailing north from the Pacific coast of Latin America, through the Panama Canal and north to New Orleans, where it seems to have found favour with the city's dock-workers, as it helped them to work long hours with little sustenance, a habit their employers were keen to foster. In 1912, Dr Charles B. Towns opined that 'When an overseer in the South will deliberately put cocaine into the rations of his Negro labourers in order to get more work out of them to meet a sudden emergency, it is time to have some policy of accounting for the sale of a drug like cocaine.'[21] Nothing struck panic into Southern white Americans quite like the threat of black violence. Since cocaine use also led to binges and brawls, Southern voters were soon calling for cocaine to be banned outright. Dr Christopher Koch of the State Pharmacy Board of Pennsylvania testified before Congress that 'most of the attacks upon the white women of the South are the direct result of a cocaine-crazed Negro brain'. America's first drug Tsar, Dr Hamilton Wright, alleged that drugs made black men uncontrollable, and that they encouraged them to rebel against the authority of white people.[22]

The United States Pure Food and Drug Act of 1906 required that the inclusion of certain drugs in patent medicines be clearly indicated on the label, so that consumers would know what they were taking. Manufacturers had extensive ranges of products that they could not afford to see compromised by negative publicity over cocaine. Consumers could still buy pure cocaine, but most consumers of mild coca and cocaine-infused preparations simply stopped buying them, or switched to de-cocainized versions of Vin Mariani and Coca-Cola. Unfortunately, the authorities made little distinction between coca and cocaine, or between problematic and unproblematic drug use. As a result, legitimate concerns over public health and misleading advertising were hijacked by imaginary fears and generalizations.

This tangled combination of high-mindedness and bigotry also informed the government's policy on opium use. By 1900, British merchants were supplying opium to 27 per cent of the people of China, a trade in narcotics on a scale never rivalled before or since. American Christians were revolted by the way the British turned the drug dependency of their colonial subjects to their commercial advantage. When the Americans bought the Philippine islands after the Spanish American War, they found opium smoking to be widespread there too. Charles Henry Brent, the first Episcopal bishop of the Philippines, was determined to put an end to the opium trade, and led the anti-opium movement in the United States. State Department officials concurred with people like Brent for their own reasons, principally their desire to appease the Chinese government. Hamilton Wright, the department's Opium Commissioner, thought the anti-opium movement could be used 'as oil to smooth the troubled water of our aggressive commercial policy there'.

Restricting opium and coca production would require worldwide agreement, so in 1911 Charles Henry Brent presided over an international conference in The Hague. The twelve nations represented signed a convention which gave the producing and consuming nations control over their boundaries, while requiring each to enact domestic legislation to control the drugs trade. The goal was a world in which drugs would be restricted to medicinal use.[23] The campaign to ban these drugs was framed in terms of protecting public health, but the medical profession in the United States was slow to put its weight behind it. Doctors saw what excellent medicines opium and cocaine were for the treatment of pain. Laudanum was widely prescribed for all kinds of ailments, and cocaine was recognized to be an effective local anaesthetic, as well as a stimulant, albeit one with potential for abuse. Most drug addicts at the time were opiate users, but doctors recognized that most of them were productive citizens with jobs and homes.

However, the medical profession's attitude to intoxication was turned on its head by changes in the perceived purpose of medicine itself at the end of the nineteenth century. Many doctors were keen to expand their original mission of healing the sick to become the defenders of physical and mental health, the priest class of a modern, secular civilization, which turned 'good health' into a moral and political imperative. The psychiatrists, meanwhile, saw cocaine use not just as deviancy, but as a disease, on which they foisted their exciting new theory of addiction. This theory of 'addiction', allied to the legislation passed in the wake of the conference in The Hague, forms the bedrock of drug policy around the world to this day.

There has been no better popular exposé of the failure of drugs policy in the United States than the HBO television series *The Wire*. Set entirely in Baltimore, Maryland, the series was devised by a former journalist with the *Baltimore Sun* and a former narcotics detective with the city's police department. Its storylines are grounded in the writers' shared experience of the crack epidemic that swept through the East Coast cities of the United States in the 1980s. Kurt Schmoke, who has a cameo role in the series, was mayor of Baltimore from 1987 to 1999. When I met him in November 2007, he told me that he shared the writers' frustration at the state of local and national policy-making on the issue of drugs. 'One of the things I had noticed as mayor is that for a city of 750,000 people we had a significant homicide problem that was related to drug sales and distribution. I had been a prosecutor for five years, throwing people in jail, and fighting the war on drugs as a traditional drug warrior, but the more we prosecuted and incarcerated, the less impact we seemed to be having on the problem. Unfortunately for me, the crack epidemic had hit Baltimore just about the time that I came into office. The homicide rate hit 300 a year and a lot of that had to do with crack. I started to look at the problem from the economic side. We had a whole lot of people who were hooked not on drugs, but on drug money. I thought about the era of alcohol prohibition in the United States and this era of drug prohibition, and it led me to think that prohibition, in the way that we were going about it, was doing more harm than good.'

Eric Sterling was a legal counsel to Congress in 1986 and was instrumental in drafting that year's Anti-Drug Abuse Act, the corner-stone of Ronald Reagan's war on drugs. He too has gone on to become a trenchant critic of how the law has been manipulated to serve the war on drugs. 'Historically, federal law enforcement was limited to smuggling, robbery of the mails, and counterfeiting money,' he told me. 'The Harrison Narcotics Tax Act of 1914 was the first federal drug law. It was styled as a tax law. It created a tax of $1,000 per ounce of drugs, and if you didn't have the tax stamp, you were violating the law.' The 1914 Act permitted the presence of opiates, including heroin, in small amounts in non-prescription remedies such as cough medicines, but forbade any trace of cocaine in patent remedies. This was the most severe restriction on any drug to date. Nevertheless, the Act never proposed that drug users should be dealt with in the criminal justice system. 'It assumed that there would be government regulation,' Kurt Schmoke told me, 'but not blanket prohibition. It assumed that states would be allowed to let physicians distribute drugs. But it was changed over time by the forces of politics and the courts, by J. Edgar Hoover and the early heads of the Bureau of Narcotics.'

In the wake of the First World War, the United States acquired a much greater presence on the world stage, and it used this power to put pressure on other governments to extend the limits of the existing legislation against opium. The stage was set for an international drug-control regime, based not on regulation but outright prohibition. Banning drugs also seemed logical to other governments struggling to impose some order in the aftermath of the First World War. During the war, it had been alleged that imperial Germany was promoting the distribution of cocaine, a charge based on Germany's pioneering role in manufacturing cocaine since the 1880s.[24] Despite the tiny number of cocaine users in the UK, the British government worried that its fighting ability would be undermined by imports of foreign drugs, so it amended the Defence of the Realm Act in 1916, to prohibit the use of drugs during wartime. This was the United Kingdom's first anti-drugs law. The same emergency provisions limited pub opening hours to two hours at lunchtime and three in the evening, watered down the beer, and jacked up prices three-fold, as a result of which alcohol consumption fell by half and convictions for drunkenness by three quarters.

Britain won the war, but emerged from it an exhausted nation, more suspicious of alien influences than ever. In 1920, Parliament amended the Aliens Act of 1914, which for the first time required visitors to Britain to fill in landing and embarkation cards. With the passing of the Dangerous Drugs Act 1920, the wartime ban on drugs was made permanent, as were the restrictions on pub opening hours, which were not lifted for another eighty-five years. Cocaine had been popular among London's nascent *demi-monde*, as noted by the columnist 'Guinevere' in the *Daily Mail* in July 1901. 'The habit grows rapidly: a mild 10 per cent solution obtained at a chemist's to cure a tooth-ache has given many people a first taste of the joys and horrors of cocaine. The first effect of a dose is extreme exhilaration and mental brilliancy. The imagination becomes aflame. The after-effects – reaction, utter loss of moral responsibility, a blotched complexion, and the lunatic asylum or death. Yet any chemist will tell you that it has been increasingly in demand by women of late years.'[25]

In 1922, a Chinese Londoner by the name of 'Brilliant' Chang became the first drug dealer to make the headlines of a British newspaper. The press revelled in the story of how Chang had enchanted an actress called Freda Kempton with cocaine powder, which promptly killed her. According to an article in the *World's Pictorial News*, Chang was a purveyor of exotic sexual practices as well as of drugs. It described how 'half a dozen drug-frenzied women joined him in wild orgies'.[26] Seduction by an exotic foreigner is a long-established source of fear and fantasy in British literature. In Shakespeare's *Othello*, when the Senator Brabantio discovers that his daughter Desdemona has eloped with the black general from Morocco, he says that Othello must have lured his daughter with 'charms', by which he refers not to Othello's charisma or good looks, but to what we would today call drugs. In 1894, George du Maurier's best-selling novel *Trilby* had introduced British readers to Svengali, a musician of purportedly Hungarian Jewish origin, who exercised his sinister prowess over the young heroine. The popular press was happy to hitch the threat posed by new, still more exotic potions to these popular tales. The post-war generation was uncomfortable in many regards, not least in regard to pleasures. Many believed that feminine pleasures in particular had to be kept under a watchful eye. In 1920, a British woman wasn't allowed to vote until she was twenty-seven; it was hoped that, by then, she would be able to count on the good counsel of her husband to navigate the complexities of adult life. Until such time, she was judged to be too prone to the sway of emotion to take charge of such responsibilities. This unease with the freedom that many British women found during and after the First World War is evident from an article that appeared in the *Daily Express* in 1922, which described the 'predominating type' of female cocaine user as 'young, thin, underdressed, and perpetually seized with hysterical laughter'.[27]

On the other side of the Atlantic, the US government was as confident in its belief that alcohol posed a terrible threat to its citizens as it was in its ability to drive alcohol consumption out of existence. In 1919, Congress passed the Eighteenth Amendment and then the Volstead Act, which prohibited the production, sale and consumption of alcoholic drinks. Initially at least, it seemed that supplies of alcohol could be curtailed: alcohol consumption fell sharply at the beginning of the Prohibition Era, to about a third of its pre-1919 level. But as Americans learnt to circumvent the new laws, illegal supplies rose to meet the demand, and alcohol consumption rates went back up, to about 70 per cent of what they had been before the Volstead Act was passed. Dismayed but not deterred, pragmatists then argued that if supplies could not be entirely cut off, at least they might be made sufficiently scarce to drive prices up, which would put the booze out of the reach of those intent on consuming it. In the Prohibition years, drinks prices shot up to three times their pre-1919 levels. But this only made the business more lucrative. Having passed from the hands of legal brewers and distillers into those of illegal bootleggers and gangsters, the trade in alcoholic drinks became the subject of a vicious struggle for dominance which the authorities proved unable to quash. The homicide rate in the United States went through the roof, peaking at 9.7 per 100,000 people in 1933. Such high murder rates wouldn't be seen again until 1980, when at the height of the 'war on drugs' homicides in the United States hit 10 per 100,000.[28]

The inability of the federal government to contain either the illegal trade in alcohol, or the violence and corruption of officialdom that it created, led to widespread public disenchantment with Prohibition.

Ultimately, neither higher prices, respect for the law, social pressure, nor the muck that passed for alcohol had put people off drinking, and the Dry Law was repealed in 1933. Many feared that the nation would drown in a torrent of cheap legal alcohol, but the repeal of Prohibitionist laws had a surprisingly mild slight on how much the public drank. Consumption levels remained virtually the same immediately after the era of Prohibition was brought to an end, although they gradually returned to their pre-Prohibition level in the course of the following decade.[29] With the restoration of standardization to the trade, drinkers were better able to gauge what and how much they were drinking, and the death rate from alcohol poisoning, which had increased sharply during Prohibition, fell back.[30] Murder rates fell sharply too, as disputes between rival traders could now be settled in court, instead of on the street.

The parallels between the Prohibition Era and today's war on drugs are instructive. Both demonstrate how difficult it is to ban intoxicating substances, the resilience of demand for them and the violence that stirs when highly profitable trades are made illegal. The Prohibition Era also had a huge social impact. It cast immigrants as criminals, not just in the imagination of newspaper editors, but in reality. Communities of recent arrivals were the first to lose their jobs when the legal economy went into a tailspin in the late 1920s, and the first to latch on to illegal sales of alcohol as an alternative. Prohibition Era mobsters like Al Capone, Bugsy Siegel and Meyer Lansky had struggled to get by in a new country in the face of constant prejudice from locals. They saw bootlegging as a good opportunity and were not daunted by the fact that it was illegal. Discrimination, powerlessness and recourse to illegality defined the working lives of other ethnic groups too. The numbers game was an illegal lottery in which money was wagered on a certain combination of digits appearing at the beginning of a series of numbers published in a newspaper, such as share prices or sports results. In the 1940s, the numbers game in Chicago employed more African-American men than any other industry.[31]

Mike Jay, author of *Emperors of Dreams: Drugs in the Nineteenth Century* (2000), calls the Prohibition Era 'the irrational aberration of a young and immature country under the sway of fanatical religious impulses and an intolerant zeal for racial purity'. Prohibition failed because it stoked the very fires it was intent on quenching.[32] The prohibition of popular vices creates gangsters, whose existence in turn justifies the incessant appeal for a return to order and authority, and provides the bedrock for relations between politicians and white voters. Instead of defusing this conflict, the press and politicians feel compelled to turn it into a theatre piece, in which caricatures of good and evil do battle. Questions of public policy are dramatized and become plot-shifts that strive for public approval on the nightly news instalments. Once away from the public gaze, politicians have had to be much more level-headed in how they deal with gangsters, sometimes accommodating the very criminals that their laws have created, and on occasion being corrupted by them.

The United States government never tried to export its prohibition of alcohol policy. In retrospect, it might be argued that what most sapped the confidence of the prohibitionists was the Great Depression, just as their victory in the First World War had inspired it. Prohibiting alcohol was not a rational policy. It was a moral crusade, an idealistic flourish, and an expression of confidence in America's power to reform the world from the ground up. As for the booze addicts that Prohibition was supposed to dry out, the return to a legal, commercial market in alcoholic drinks forced American Christians to develop new ways of tending their flock. Since they couldn't make alcohol go away, the temptation to drink it had to be resisted. By 1934, Bill Wilson had ruined a promising Wall Street career because of his constant drunkenness. Wilson was treated at the Charles B. Towns hospital by Dr William Silkworth, who argued that alcoholism had to be treated as a disease. While in hospital, Bill Wilson underwent what he believed to be a spiritual experience and, convinced of the existence of a healing higher power, he was able to stop drinking. Alcoholics Anonymous, which he co-founded, is based on abstention, in which spiritual awakening replaces dependence on alcohol, and the support of one's peers replaces the isolation of alcoholism. AA is still the first port of call for people around the world who want help to stop drinking.[33]

For many years the ban on drugs was much more successful than the one on alcohol. Although the press continued to revel in occasionally scandalous use of cocaine in Hollywood, the drug gradually went out of fashion. In 1930, the New York City Mayor's Committee on Drug Addiction reported that 'during the last twenty years cocaine as an addiction has ceased to be a problem'. The laws probably hastened the trend. Fear of what prolonged cocaine use could do certainly reduced demand for recreational stimulants, which was now met by amphetamines, a new class of synthetic drugs which soon became cheaper and more widely available than cocaine.

Notwithstanding the near invisibility of drug addicts, the press and politicians still used popular fear of drugs to mobilize witch-hunts against those deemed undesirable. 'The anti-marijuana laws were passed during the Great Depression, when an enormous drought in the dustbowl states caused internal migration to California,' Eric Sterling, the former legal counsel to Congress, told me. 'California had been Spanish from the sixteenth century until the 1840s, when the United States effectively took it after gold was discovered. A new narrative was constructed, in which the Californians were somehow foreigners, using a foreign drug that made them homicidal.' Newspapers repeated unsubstantiated claims that 'the killer weed' led users, particularly Mexican users, to commit terrible acts of violence, particularly against Anglo-Saxon women. Harry J. Anslinger, the first head of the US Bureau of Narcotics, said that 'reefer makes darkies think that they're as good as white men'. In a context of land hunger, the press's demonization of marijuana users served to justify the robbery and imprisonment of Spanish speakers across California. As Eric Sterling pointed out, it was judged 'better to employ the good Christian whites who have fled the Great Depression to California, who need jobs'.

The censors also pandered to ignorance and prejudice. From 1934, the Motion Picture Association of America refused a seal of approval for any film that depicted the use of narcotics, a ban that lasted until 1956, when *The Man with the Golden Arm*, in which Frank Sinatra plays a musician struggling to overcome an addiction to heroin, was successfully exhibited without a seal.[34] Even in the hermetically contained, vice-free vacuum that the authorities hoped to create, drug scares still flared on occasion. In the 1950s, the media jumped on a

story of how two teenagers in Colorado had suffered terrible hallucinations after accidentally inhaling model airplane glue. This led to
another well-meaning nationwide panic, as well as turning a lot of
bored and curious young people on to glue-sniffing.

The United States' first genuine drug epidemic spread through New
York City. One of its participants remembered just how discreet heroin
use was when it first found favour. 'In 1959, you didn't see heroin
being sold on the streets. The dope addicts hung out in the park – that
was it! It wasn't like they were out to bother people hanging out
in front of their buildings. I tell you, the dope addicts then were
well-dressed people. The only reason you knew they were dope addicts
was because they were always falling over from being doped up. And
they worked, they had jobs. True, they took from their own – from
their mother or wife – but to go out and mug people, you hardly ever
saw that.'[35]

The year 1961 marked a turning point in the story of drugs in
New York City. A shortage of heroin sent once-discreet heroin users
ricocheting around the city in search of drugs, and made public what
had until then been a very private vice.[36] In the same year, the United
Nations, in session in New York City, passed the Single Convention
on Narcotic Drugs. Most, but certainly not all, of the most ardent
prohibitionists were Americans. Such was the power of the United
States, the Convention was basically drawn up by Americans and
signed by the other United Nations member states. The Convention
committed its signatories to restrict the supply of illicit drugs still
further, treat and rehabilitate addicts and punish traffickers. The range
of banned substances was expanded to include cannabis and coca
leaves. Peru and Bolivia were expected to phase out coca leaf production within twenty-five years. The world would rely on the products of Western pharmaceutical companies for their aspirin and
paracetamol, and on Western confectioners for their Coca-Cola and
Nescafé. 'Drugs', whether for pleasure or the relief of pain, would
now become commercial medicines. This was supposed to be the
definitive conclusion to the struggle to define and contain magical
potions, which had been waged since the mid-nineteenth century.

So it was that a policy principally aimed at combating the use of

heroin by a very small minority of Americans inadvertently criminalized several million Andean coca-chewers, who had been chewing
coca unhindered for thousands of years. In 1961, heroin seizures in
the United States were running at about 1 kg a year. Only 4 million
Americans had even tried an illegal drug. By 2003, 74 million Americans had done so.[37] The Single Convention has not put an end to drug
use. Nevertheless, it has remained in place to this day, with some
amendments, apparently clad in iron. Harry Levine, co-editor of *Crack
in America: Demon Drugs and Social Justice* (1997), has phrased the
universal appeal of prohibition thus: 'Over the course of the twentieth
century, drug prohibition received support from liberal prime ministers, moderate monarchs, military strongmen, and Maoists. It was
supported by prominent archbishops and radical priests; by nationalist
heroes and imperialists' puppets; by labour union leaders and sweat-
shop owners; by socialists, social workers, social scientists and social-
ites – by all variety of politicians practising all brands of politics in all
political systems.'[38] The Single Convention is dependent for its survival
on the commitment of the United States, but it gives the United Nations
enormous clout too, and all governments seem to benefit from the
additional police and military powers that the attempt to prohibit
drug use requires. In the United States, there are more undercover
narcotics police than there are in any other branch of police work.
Policing the drugs trade requires intelligence and surveillance operatives who can be diverted into other lines of work. The Watergate
burglary, for example, was conducted by former CIA agents from
Richard Nixon's own special anti-drugs team.

There was a dramatic increase in drug use in the late 1960s. Eric
Sterling remembers that it took place in a context of enormous social
conflict, dislocation and fear. 'By the mid-60s you had riots, bus
burnings, the assassination of President Kennedy in '63, the assassination of Martin Luther King and Senator Bobby Kennedy in '68, and
the shooting in '72 of George Wallace, the presidential candidate. You
had hundreds of thousands of people marching and sitting in, burning
draft cards and burning flags. You had mass events like Woodstock,
men no longer wearing their hair short, but wearing it long, all the

women waving their brassieres at the 1968 Democratic Convention. There was a sense that society had run off the tracks, and drugs were perceived as this agent that was driving the youth insane. Drug control was part of an effort to put the lid back on.'

As drug consumption went from being an esoteric and marginal activity to one intimately associated with the nascent youth culture, the supposedly comprehensive ban on drug use proved ineffective in controlling the supply of drugs. One fine day in Palm Springs, Elvis Presley fell into conversation with Vice President Spiro Agnew. Elvis wanted to know how he might use his celebrity status to promote the Nixon administration's anti-drug campaign. So it was that on 21 December 1970, Elvis went to the White House to meet President Richard Nixon. The day before the meeting, Elvis and two of his bodyguards went to the gates of the White House, where Presley handed the guard a handwritten letter addressed to the President, in which he made clear his opposition to the 'drug culture, hippy elements and Black Panthers' who, he wrote, hated America. He declared that he wanted nothing but to 'help the country out', and asked to be designated a 'federal agent-at-large'. The next day, Elvis went to meet the President and made him a gift of a Second World War-era Colt .45 pistol. A photograph was taken, in which the two men can be seen shaking hands, Nixon in a suit and tie, Elvis in tight purple velvet trousers, a purple velvet cape slung over his shoulders and an enormous belt buckle. They agreed that 'those who use drugs are in the vanguard of American protest'. On New Year's Eve, Nixon wrote a note to Elvis, thanking him for his gift of the pistol, but making no mention of enlisting his aid in the war on drugs. The administration's ambivalence about engaging 'the King' in its anti-drugs campaign is apparent from the correspondence of Nixon's aides. In an inter-office memo dashed off on the morning of Presley's visit, Nixon aide Dwight Chapin had suggested that if the President wanted to meet 'bright young people outside the government, Presley might be the one to start with'. Aide H. R. Haldeman responded, 'you must be kidding'.

Elvis Presley died from heart failure in 1977. The coroner put his death down to 'undetermined causes', but some speculated that Elvis's obesity and the ten drugs found in his bloodstream at the time of his death may have played a part. Elvis was known to have tried Dilaudid, Percodan, Placidyl, Dexedrine, Biphetamine, Tuinal, Desbutal, Escatrol, Amytal, Quaaludes, Carbrital, Seconal, methadone and Ritalin. What help could such a prolific drug user possibly offer to anyone waging a 'war on drugs'? Elvis's love of drugs and his hatred of 'drug culture' shows that the distinction between legal and illegal drugs can't be explained in terms of their chemical properties. Of much greater importance than the drug itself in determining the response of officialdom is the social position of the drug user. In the 1960s the press ran stories of how LSD dissolved human chromosomes and produced two-headed babies. In the 1970s, journalists warned their readers that PCP, better known as Angel Dust, gave its users superhuman strength, and was so powerful that the police needed super-strength stun guns to subdue them. None of the drugs that Elvis chose to use and abuse was made the subject of such scare stories.

Despite the scare stories, the civil rights movement, the Vietnam War protests, and the threat of riots had drawn the police away from drug law enforcement. The Knapp Commission Report of 1973, which was written in response to the shooting of an undercover narcotics officer in Williamsburg, New York, revealed the shocking extent to which the city's police had been corrupted by the drugs business. Thereafter, the police concentrated their resources on high-level sellers, which took the heat off street dealers and users. A third factor favouring drug users was that in the 1970s the government of New York City was practically bankrupt. Police officers were laid off, and the lack of street-level drug law enforcement gave drug dealers the run of almost every park in the city.

Then a congressional delegation returned from Vietnam, warning that as many as 40,000 US troops had become addicted to heroin. Celerino Castillo III, a former Drug Enforcement Administration agent from Texas, remembers the extent of the epidemic well. 'If the soldier was well liked, someone would pump a bullet in his body, and the family would be told he'd died a hero's death. If the consensus was that the dead soldier had been an asshole, he would be sent home with nothing more than needle pricks in his arms.'[39] 'The Vietnam War had a big impact on our communities,' a former gang member called Luis Rodriguez told me when I travelled to Los Angeles to look into the origins of the prison crisis in California. 'A lot of poor working-class kids were sent to war, and many came back traumatized, addicted to heroin, and knowing how to kill people. And they contributed to the gangs, making them better organized, and probably a little nuttier.'

The post-Vietnam heroin epidemic in the US was a genuine problem that demanded a comprehensive response from public health authorities, but the matter was subsumed by President Nixon's broader fight against hippy culture. Nixon's war on drugs started out as an assertion on the part of nominally abstemious, white, Christian America against opponents of the establishment, for whom drug use had become emblematic over the course of the 1960s. Jack Cole is the executive director of Law Enforcement Against Prohibition, an organization of police officers disillusioned by their inability to enforce drugs laws effectively. 'I joined the narcotics unit of the New Jersey State Police in 1970, at the beginning of the war on drugs,' he told me. 'The term "war on drugs" was coined by Richard Nixon, but it had nothing to do with drugs, and everything to do with the fact that he was running for the Presidency for the second time and he thought that it would be nice if this time he won. He knew that if he was a strong anti-crime guy that would get him a lot of votes. But boy, if he could be in charge of a war, how those votes would pour in! He went to campaign for the Presidency in New Hampshire, and while he was up there he wrote a letter to his mentor Dwight Eisenhower. "Ike," he wrote, "it's just amazing how much you can get done through fear. All I talk about in New Hampshire is crime and drugs, and everyone wants to vote for me – and they don't even have any black people up here."' After a briefing with Nixon in 1969, H. R. Haldeman, by now the President's top aide, noted in his diary that 'Nixon emphasized that you have to face the fact that the whole problem is really the blacks. The key is to devise a system that recognizes that, while not appearing to do so.'[40]

Tony Papa served a life sentence for cocaine trafficking before joining the Drug Policy Alliance, the principal organization campaigning for an end to America's war on drugs. He experienced at first hand the punitive drug policies introduced by Nelson Rockefeller, the then governor of New York. 'Rockefeller aspired to be President. He wanted to look really tough on crime, because he figured it would appeal to the Republicans, so he created what became known as the Rockefeller drug laws in 1973. The idea was to capture the drug kingpins and curb the drug epidemic that supposedly existed in New York at that time. He made the toughest laws in the nation. Fifteen years to life for sales of two ounces [approximately 60 grams] of coke or possession of four ounces.'

Nixon's war on drugs was politically expedient, as it turned attention away from the disastrous escapade in Vietnam, while preserving the military culture that had inspired the war in the first place. Despite its appeal, it was flawed from the start, not only by its disregard for the epidemiology of drug use, but also by the instability of the core values animating America's Christian soldiers. In 1972, Richard Nixon appointed the Shafer Commission to look into America's drug control policies. Among the issues it raised, the commission's report pointed out that 'the national religious community has failed to address its most important task: the elaboration of values upon which individual choice could rest. The decline of moral certitude regarding drug consumption has left a void. The religious community has a major responsibility to confront the profound philosophical, moral and spiritual questions raised by the drug problem.'[41] The Shafer report went on to assert that there was no link between marijuana and crime; that alcohol was far more dangerous than marijuana; and that personal use of marijuana should be decriminalized. This was not what the good Christian Richard Nixon wanted to hear. 'Every one of the bastards that are out for legalizing marijuana is Jewish,' he raged.[42]

The United Kingdom's Misuse of Drugs Act of 1971 was also coloured by the politicians' backlash against the popular culture of the 1960s. In the parliamentary debates prior to the passage of the Act, British MPs gave vent to their indignation at 'youth culture' and the new moral values it championed. But in the backrooms, talk was of a national identity crisis rather than the health risks associated with drug use. Britain had been withdrawing from its colonies one by one since 1945, a humiliating experience only made worse by the devaluation of the pound, and Franco-German domination of the European Common Market. National Front supporters were marching in the streets, with their own ideas of who was to blame for Britain's loss of standing in the world. Before the passage of the Act, the UK had had a relatively liberal drugs policy. Heroin addicts could be prescribed enough of the drug to manage their addiction without being forced to buy from the black market. But MPs felt that a stand had to be made. On the face of it, cracking down on drug use ruffled few feathers and threatened no vested interests. The only illegal drug that most people had even heard of was cannabis, and only hippies and Rastafarians were likely to object to a toughening of sentencing guidelines.

MP Peter Jackson tried to table an amendment which would have included nicotine on the list of dangerous drugs enshrined in the Misuse of Drugs Act. The outright rejection of the Jackson amendment in Parliament showed that the dangers to health posed by drugs were a relatively minor consideration. Far more important was the government's assertion of its right to make distinctions between good and bad drugs, irrespective of the harm they caused, or the opinion of scientists, teachers or doctors. In other contentious debates about matters of personal behaviour and individual choice, like pre-marital sex, abortion and homosexuality, the state was ceding ground to popular pressure to institutionalize more liberal attitudes. In passing the Misuse of Drugs Act in 1971, Britain's politicians drew a line in the sand, asserting that when it came to drug use, the government had every right to intervene in the private lives of its citizens.

2

Building a Hard Drug Economy

> *I know thy works, and where thou dwellest, even where*
> *Satan's seat is . . . To him that overcometh will I give to eat*
> *of the hidden manna, and will give him a white stone, and*
> *in the stone a new name written, which no man knoweth,*
> *saving he that receiveth it.*   Revelation 2: 13, 17

Cocaine, in crack form, was to become the principal target of the war
on drugs in the 1980s, but as we have seen, the war had been declared
with quite distinct enemies in mind. Demand for cocaine only revived
when narcotics law enforcement agencies began cracking down on the
black market in amphetamines in the 1960s.[1] Cocaine made its return
appearance in the American public eye in 1969, in a scene in the film
Easy Rider in which Dennis Hopper and Peter Fonda can be seen
stuffing large bags of cocaine into the gas tanks of their motorcycles.
Like Sherlock Holmes and his habit of injecting himself with cocaine,
this was not a fiction intended to reflect reality. The film's writers
had felt that bags of marijuana would not be sufficiently dramatic,
and heroin was too dangerous; cocaine was chosen because it was
unfamiliar, exotic and fun. For small groups of cocaine users in
Europe, Latin America and the United States, that was the way it
stayed for the first half of the 1970s.

In the second half of the decade, people became more familiar with
cocaine. It was an adman's dream, brought into the marketplace as a
luxury product available only to the affluent. In 1977, a cover story
in *Newsweek* magazine likened cocaine to Dom Pérignon champagne,

a sign of the sophisticated good taste of the upper echelons of society. Initially, that meant the executive class of Hollywood and the music business, whose operators were typically young, highly paid and obliged to work for long hours in pampered but high-pressure environments. But cocaine soon became every ambitious young American's favourite accessory. Like Dom Pérignon, cocaine was a mass market product with bona fide upper-class cachet. *Time* magazine called it 'the drug of choice for perhaps millions of solid, conventional, and often upwardly mobile citizens'. Unlike a lot of other drugs, cocaine was regarded as a fitting accompaniment to both work and leisure. It had none of the counter-cultural connotations or mind-bending potential of LSD or cannabis and it was too expensive to be more than an occasional treat for all but a small constituency of wealthy acolytes. Poor people couldn't afford it, and cocaine addicts were non-existent in 1975. It was the drug for people who didn't like drugs.

American politicians didn't seem to have a problem with cocaine either. In 1975, the White House, under the presidency of Gerald Ford, issued a White Paper which, without challenging the Single Convention of 1961, insisted that 'cocaine is not physically addictive, and does not usually result in serious social consequences, such as crime, hospital emergency room admissions or death'. In 1977 Jimmy Carter ran for election on a manifesto which included the decriminalization of marijuana. He duly won the election and though his plans to decriminalize marijuana were soon scuppered, his drugs policy adviser, Peter Bourne, described cocaine as 'benign'.

By 1979, illegal imports of cocaine had become Florida's biggest source of income, said to be worth $10 billion a year at wholesale prices. This was the heyday not just for cocaine traffickers, but for the drug users of the United States more generally. There were 25,000 'head-shops' across the nation, selling drug paraphernalia worth $3 billion a year. One in ten eighteen-year-olds was getting stoned on marijuana every day. Two thirds of eighteen- to twenty-five-year-olds admitted having tried some kind of illegal drug, and the number of Americans who had tried cocaine hit 22 million.[2] As illegal recreational drugs became big business, large-scale criminal cartels stepped up their operations, processing and exporting cocaine to the United States in such volumes that wholesale prices began to fall, which further stimulated demand for their product. Drug warriors have since come to regard the Democrats' initially lax response to rising cocaine use as having eased the way for the Colombian cartels to get a foothold in the United States.

The problem, initially at least, was not the drug, but the drugs trade. The huge profits to be made selling cocaine had stoked fierce competition between Colombian and Cuban traffickers, few of whom could have been described as easy riders. By 1979, there was a drug-related murder a day in Miami.

The trade was lucrative, but cocaine was illegal, so the profits made were always vulnerable to confiscation, depending on the political mood. At the end of the 1970s, the United States was still a bitterly divided nation, one half of which saw drugs as emblems for all that had gone wrong in their country in the 1960s. Parents who had avoided the clutches of the drug culture watched their children inherit not their own attitudes to drugs, but those of the drug culture. The violence of Latino immigrants, the perceived permissiveness of cocaine users, and the threat to the innocence of American children galvanized conservatives into a firm rebuttal of liberal America. In 1980, Ronald Reagan was elected President, and in the autumn the Republicans also took control of the Senate for the first time since 1952. In 1981, then Vice-President George Bush Sr launched a special task force to take on the traffickers, firing the first salvo in an invigorated war on drugs. In the decade that followed, the political agenda was defined by 'culture wars' between liberals and conservatives. The latter emphasized moral renewal and respect for the law. But as it pertained to the growing market for illegal drugs, Ronald Reagan's crusading zeal was to have many unforeseen consequences. Drug use is cultural and drug markets are driven by economics, so it was unclear how a moral crusade might affect either, however strong the temptation to launch one.

Whatever the resolutions of ambitious politicians, day-to-day government runs on a course which is only sometimes in tandem with official policy. The response to events early in the Reagan Presidency showed the official stance on drugs to be less than robust. The Contras were a group of Nicaraguans who had launched a guerrilla war against the left-wing Sandinista government that had taken over the Central American country in 1979. The Reagan administration saw the Contras as its allies in the global fight against communist subversion: the President even went as far as to describe them as the latter-day equivalents of the founding fathers. The United States Congress was less gung-ho in its support for the Contras, however, and passed amendments which prohibited the use of government funds 'for the purpose of overthrowing the government of Nicaragua'. This meant that the Contras were strapped for cash to buy weapons.

The Iran-Contra scandal is a well-known blot on Ronald Reagan's copybook. Colonel Oliver North was found to have sold weapons to the Iranian government, supposedly an enemy of the White House, in order to raise money for the Contras. A lesser known chapter in the story, and one that throws the integrity of the Republicans' war on drugs into real doubt, is that the CIA also approved and supported the Contras' trafficking of cocaine into the United States. Key state operatives later testified that the Contras would take delivery of planeloads of military apparel that had been sent to El Salvador by Nicaraguans living in the United States. For the return flight north they would load the empty planes with cocaine. 'It was coming up through Los Angeles,' Russ, a former secret service operative from San Jose, California, told me. 'There were boatloads of it coming up through San Francisco. A lot of it was going into Mena, Arkansas. The money that they were making was then filtered back to support the Contras in their fight in Nicaragua.' Former Drug Enforcement Administration (DEA) agent Celerino Castillo III, who was the special agent in charge of El Salvador at the time, takes up the story. 'They gave all the coke to Norwin Meneses and Danilo Blandon, who was a CIA asset. He in turn fronted all that stuff to Ricky Ross. Ross became the Walmart of crack, distributing to the Bloods and the Crips and everybody else all over the country. They fucked up all of California with the crack epidemic.' Thanks to his Nicaraguan connection, Ricky Ross became America's first and most successful crack cocaine seller. He was coming to the end of a twenty-year sentence at the Federal Correctional Institute in Texarkana, Texas, when I spoke to him. 'Me and Danilo

Blandon were really tight. I knew from earlier that he was backing some war, and I knew that he was from Nicaragua, but I had no idea about the Contras. I was illiterate at that time, you know? I never read a newspaper or listened to the news. They say that Danilo was protected, and you can assume from the Feds that I was being protected too, but I never knew that. I was just in it for the money, trying to get out of the ghetto.'

'Hangars 4 and 5 at Ilopango airport in San Salvador were used as a trampoline for drugs coming in from Colombia and Costa Rica,' explained Celerino. 'Oliver North and a Cuban exile named Felix Rodriguez were running one of them, and the other one was owned by the CIA.' Rodriguez was on the CIA pay-roll and had been present at the killing of Che Guevara in Bolivia in 1967. 'Rodriguez and North used a plane called the Fat Lady, which was also owned by the CIA, to load up with arms at Ilopango and then airdrop to the Contras in the jungle. Then the Fat Lady got shot down by the Sandinistas. The only survivor was the pilot Gene Hasenfus, who was also working for the CIA. He was captured and said that it was a covert operation being run by the White House, and that's when the story broke that the US government was supporting the Contras.'

Under the shelter provided by the umbrella of national security doctrines, the CIA hurriedly intervened to protect its allies from the Drug Enforcement Administration. In June 1986, Congress submitted to pressure from the Reagan administration, and approved a $100 million aid package to the Contras. As soon as the flow of legal aid resumed, the Contras and the CIA severed their connections to the cocaine business. The Contras' small fleet of aeroplanes at Ilopango was flown to a remote airstrip and destroyed. Senator John Kerry chaired a congressional committee that looked into the affair. 'There is no question in my mind,' his report concluded, 'that people connected with the CIA were involved in drug trafficking while in support of the Contras.'[3] 'The shit hit the fan, and everybody ran for cover trying to deny it. Even Reagan tried to deny it,' Celerino told me. 'Then I started getting calls from the DEA saying, "Don't close the Contra files." I asked why, and they said that once the file was closed, congressional investigators would have access to it. So when Senator

John Kerry had his hearings, I wasn't called because he hadn't seen my report.' Castillo told the authors of *White Out: The CIA, Drugs and the Press* that 'they never contacted me. The special prosecutor for the Iran-Contra case was Lawrence Walsh, but he came to an agreement with the government that the only thing he was going to investigate was Oliver North's sale of the missiles to Iran.'[4]

Despite this unequivocal indictment of government collusion with cocaine smugglers, the cocaine-Contra scandal remained on the margins of the debate as the White House went to war on drugs from 1985. Reporter Lawrence Zuckerman recalls returning from Central America laden with stories of cocaine-running by the Contras, only to be told by his editor that 'if this story was about the Sandinistas and drugs you'd have no trouble getting it in the magazine, but *Time* is institutionally behind the Contras'.[5] Between 1982 and 1985, concurrent with the CIA's protection of the Contras' cocaine shipments into the United States, wholesale cocaine prices in Miami, Los Angeles and Baltimore dropped by half.[6] To what extent the Contras' cocaine shipments were responsible for this drop in price is a matter for speculation. What is beyond doubt is that it put cocaine within the reach of many more Americans, and paved the way for the crack epidemic that swept through the inner cities of the United States in the 1980s.

The cocaine-Contra scandal might have undermined the United States' determination to scupper the cocaine trade, but it also brings to mind earlier cases in which the US government has allowed drug traffickers to sell drugs in the United States, usually in pursuit of the same anti-communist goals that animated their strategy in Nicaragua. The Italian-American Mafioso Lucky Luciano was the first beneficiary of collusion between the US government's spies and its gangsters, as the government turned to the Italian Mafia for help in invading Sicily in 1943. United States intelligence agencies not only arranged for Luciano, then the world's pre-eminent heroin dealer, to be released from prison; they also allowed him to rebuild his drug-smuggling business, watched as heroin flowed into New York and Washington DC, and then lied about what they had done. The CIA later facilitated opium and heroin trafficking to the United States by their allies in Southeast Asia during the Vietnam War. They turned a blind eye to heroin trafficking by Mujahidin rebels in Afghanistan, because trafficking paid for Afghan resistance to the Soviet Union's occupation of the country in the 1980s. Prior to the Israeli invasion of Lebanon in 1982, Israel's only allies in the country were the Christian Phalangists. Knowing this, the CIA deliberately scuppered the DEA investigations of the Phalangists' smuggling of heroin into New York City so as to allow them to raise funds for their assault on the PLO in Beirut. Each of these drug-trafficking operations had a direct and significant impact on heroin and cocaine markets in the United States. Nevertheless, they were all protected by the CIA, and by extension, the US government.

This collusion is shocking, yet widely overlooked. So too are the deep roots that drug-fuelled crime has sunk in American soil. The most systematic estimate of the number of Americans selling drugs, either full-time or part-time, is 1.8 million.[7] How have drug markets become such big employers in so many cities of the United States? Since the turn of the twentieth century, the country's most criminalized, and hence most profitable, enterprises have been those that have fed Americans' desire to get rich, get drunk and get laid: illicit gambling and the numbers game, bootlegging and prostitution. Yet until the 1980s, the drugs business was shunned by many figures in organized crime, with the exception of a small but lucrative heroin-smuggling business in New York City. In the 1960s, drug-selling had been handled by discreet, family-run operations, but in the early 1970s, tougher law enforcement tactics weeded out these small-time ventures, most of which had neither the funds to buy off policemen, nor the gall to kill them. As penalties grew harsher, the risks incurred by dealers became higher. Prices were raised and profits went up, which attracted the attention of the Mafia. Organized crime moved into the drugs business because it was the only entity able to absorb the rising human and financial costs of dealing in illegal drugs in New York City.[8]

Several developments in the 1980s made the drugs business more attractive to newcomers and encouraged them to join criminal organizations. First were the enormous changes in industry and employment in the United States. De-industrialization, a rusting process which had been gnawing its way through the inner cities since the 1960s, was gathering speed. Between 1967 and 1987, Chicago lost 60 per cent,

New York City 58 per cent and Philadelphia 64 per cent of their manufacturing jobs.[9] Employers left the cities for the suburbs, other parts of the United States, or overseas; others just disappeared. As inner-city steel mills, factories and car plants closed down, the neighbourhoods that had been built to house their workers were reduced to pools of low-wage or unemployed labour, what have been described as 'warehouses for the poor'. In New York City neighbourhoods such as Bedford-Stuyvesant and the South Bronx, more than half their young people were jobless in the late 1980s. A study of gang finances in one gang's neighbourhood in 1990 found that the unemployment rate in the gang's neighbourhood was over 35 per cent, a rate six times higher than the national average.[10] Most of the children lived in poverty, and 60 per cent of them were growing up on welfare. The community had wasted away, both literally and figuratively: in 1990, it had only half the population it had had in 1950, and just one in five of its children lived with both their parents. Atrophy left city halls with a much smaller tax base from which to raise the money needed to pay for the welfare services that their people now depended on. Republican party politicians didn't want to pump money into urban communities, partly because the inner cities had always voted Democrat, and partly because Republicans proved unable to solve social problems they had played a large part in creating. Instead, President Ronald Reagan responded to de-industrialization by dramatically cutting back the very programmes that had alleviated some of the resultant poverty, as well as those that were training people to make the transition to any new jobs that were available.

Baltimore is the last resting place of Edgar Allan Poe, America's finest gothic fabulist. It also provides the setting for *The Wire*, an equally haunting depiction of American vice. In 1950, the biggest employer in Baltimore was Bethlehem Steel. Jobs for the unskilled were easy to come by, and thriving communities grew up around the steel plants. Today, the biggest employer in Baltimore is Johns Hopkins Hospital, a leader in health services, education and technology. The rise of Johns Hopkins has brought employment opportunities for some, but it has never been able to absorb the numbers thrown out of work by the decline of heavy industry in the city. It is grimly ironic that a hospital should become a major city's principal employer, and that the treatment of the sick has become such a huge employer in the United States as a whole. Ironic, too, that so many Americans should be taking drugs of one kind, while their government fights a war on drugs of another kind. But the greatest irony of Johns Hopkins is that one of the hospital's founders, Dr William Stewart Halsted – to this day considered the single most innovative and influential surgeon the United States has ever produced – was a clandestine drug addict for forty years. Halsted depended on a daily fix of 180 mg of morphine, a habit he inadvertently acquired while trying to overcome an addiction to cocaine. He was able to maintain his addiction to heroin while building one of the best hospitals in the US, firstly because he had better access to quality morphine than anyone else in Baltimore, and secondly because he also had a real stake in conventional society, a vocational calling which helped to keep his drug habit within some bounds. By 1989, one hundred years after Halsted helped found Johns Hopkins Hospital, one in eight adults in Baltimore had a serious drug abuse problem, a rate unmatched by any other city in the United States. Unlike Halsted, most of them had neither a stake nor a vocation to temper their compulsive drug use.[11]

The destruction wrought by hard drugs in cities like Baltimore met with little resistance. Growing divisions in the black community weakened unity and resolve at a time when both qualities were in short supply. In 1968, the poorest fifth of black households was getting by on an average of $10,600 a year. By 1995, this figure had actually dropped, to $10,200. The richest fifth of black households, meanwhile, had seen their average annual income go from $60,000 to $84,000, and many had used that money to move to the suburbs. In better times, the children of the poor have had opportunities to make their way up and out through the education system, but this is not what has happened in Baltimore. In 1990, one in five high school seniors dropped out of school before they even graduated.[12] One parent was very often a single woman, with few skills to trade and laden with childcare responsibilities. Many young people grew up without the support of their parents, the encouragement of their peers and elders, or reasonable educational opportunities.

The new jobs created by the information-driven economy often passed inner-city residents by. In response to what was politely termed 'economic restructuring', the unemployed went back to school, enrolled in what training programmes they could find, found good jobs and struggled to keep them, or settled for temporary jobs in service industries. Some moved to other states or other countries, looking for work or an easier life elsewhere. Others resorted to what James Scott has called 'the ordinary weapons of relatively powerless groups: foot dragging, dissimulation, desertion, false compliance, pilfering, and feigned ignorance'.[13] Growing numbers fell out of the legal economy altogether. Many sought solace in alcohol or drugs.

I sat out one freezing Sunday afternoon talking to Ted in a diner near his house in Williamsburg, New York. Ted had spent the past twenty years selling cocaine, and was adamant that, for his customers at least, cocaine use was unproblematic. I asked him why he thought he and his friends had been able to take cocaine for so long without significant problems, whereas crack cocaine had been the undoing of so many people. 'Discovering drugs is a part of adolescent risk-taking. By the time I was twenty-five I had done every drug you could name ten times. You don't want someone to discover drugs as an adult. By the time I had any money at all, I was pretty much inoculated against becoming an out-of-control drug addict. The person who is going to become an out-of-control cocaine user is going to be someone who is naive about drugs. In the 1980s you had a whole lot of poor, minority folks who were naive, at least about crack. "Studies show that poor people are often depressed?" No fucking shit. In the '80s, New York was really fucked up. There were no jobs. All of a sudden crack comes along, and you get to be poor and feel great. Of course you're going to get out of control with that shit.'

Hopeless poverty goes a long way to explain why so many people developed crack habits; it also accounts for there being so many willing suppliers. Ricky Ross, who benefited from the Contras' cocaine-smuggling and went on to become the first and biggest crack dealer in the United States, told me how he first got involved in selling drugs. 'I was a youngster. Uneducated, uninformed, unemployed . . . I mean, you could just keep going on with the "uns". I was looking for opportunities. I wanted to be important in the world, somebody who was respected. Basically I wanted the American dream, so I guess I was ripe for the picking. The opportunity came in the form of drugs, and I latched on to it.' Marc started selling crack cocaine in South Jamaica, New York City, at the age of sixteen. Like most of those I talked to about their drug-selling careers, he had served a prison sentence, which had given him ample time to consider how and why he had become a cocaine seller. 'There's a song by Jay-Z, and he says, "even righteous minds go through this". You can be a good kid, and just get caught up. It's the fast money disease. Say you need the money for something. Back when things were popping on the streets, it was nothing to double your money up. People do it for all kinds of reasons. Personally, I was doing it to belong, and to prove that I could do it better than my brother. For some, it's just the law of the streets, you know? But like this guy Andre I knew used to say, "you can't do the right thing the wrong way". There were people out there who had good intentions, but ultimately that didn't solve the problem.'[14]

The fall-out from economic restructuring was one factor animating the growth of the crack economy. The second was an economic crisis in the Caribbean and Latin America, which soon came to transform many of America's inner cities. The farming economies of countries such as Colombia and Peru were shrinking, feeding a stream of unemployed farmers and labourers who gravitated towards the biggest cities in search of work. They ensconced themselves as best they could in the shanty towns that sprang up on the peripheries of cities like Lima, Caracas and Kingston. For millions, their first experience of urban life also gave them their first taste of what it meant to be illegal. They worked, if they worked at all, in the informal economy, where their wages went untaxed. They often had no access to basic services, and found themselves maligned by mainstream society and unable to count on the protection of the law. Many of these migrants from countryside to city kept going until they arrived in the United States. In the space of twenty years, traditional village-based societies in countries like the Dominican Republic, Haiti and Guatemala, whose members had been schooled to have strong moral objections to drugs and criminality by the Catholic Church, were uprooted and transplanted into urban milieux. Once there, the attitudes to drugs and crime of many of them became more pragmatic. Alex Sanchez runs an organization called 'Homies Unidos' in Santa Cruz, California, which tries to act as a counterweight to the forces pulling young people into the cocaine economy. 'I came to Santa Cruz as a kid because of the United States' war in El Salvador. We didn't have a lot of things in my community. The alley, with the broken glass and the smell of urine, was my backyard. The community wasn't there for me, and my parents weren't either because they were both working two jobs. Other people were selling drugs to feed themselves, or to feed their craving for drugs. The drugs and the alcohol were just a dose to reduce the pain that we were going through, and the hunger that we felt. It was the gang that gave me shelter.'

Economic and political change dislocated many Americans, both north and south of the Rio Grande, but several additional factors ensured that the cocaine economy became a key employer of the surplus labour. One was the launch of the legal lotteries that many states set up as a way of increasing tax revenues, which all but wiped out the numbers game. Players who had been accustomed to spending a good part of their day standing on street corners, running from the police and living on their wits, started to look elsewhere for a hustle. Another factor was cheap cocaine. A host of policies introduced by American free marketeers unintentionally made cocaine production more profitable than ever. In 1981, the Reagan administration decided on a tough-sounding programme to wipe out the Mexican marijuana crop, which was then the main source of the cannabis smoked in the United States. Herbicides were sprayed from light aircraft on to the marijuana fields, a tactic also deployed in Jamaica and Colombia at various times in the early 1980s. In response, plenty of Colombian cannabis farmers switched to coca cultivation. Almost simultaneously, the USAID programme of building highways in the interior of Colombia and Bolivia, which was intended to boost legal exports and provide alternatives to drug production, inadvertently made cocaine exporting easier.

Former legal counsel Eric Sterling takes up the story. 'The US, by its subsidy of domestic sugar production, lowered the global price of sugar, so sugar cultivation in Peru became unprofitable. You had

Peruvian sugar farmers, desperate for work, moving up the valleys to grow coca. In the early '80s we had legislation, that I helped to write, that gave the Department of Defense the authority to put law enforcement detachments on naval vessels. We started using AWACS aircraft to fly over the Caribbean and monitor ship traffic. Marijuana now started going up in price. If you're a Colombian marijuana smuggler you say "they're stopping my boat traffic. I have a million dollars to invest. I'm not going to invest it in a pot shipment that's bulky and pungent, that's going to creep along by boat and get intercepted. There is a market for cocaine that is continuing to grow, so I'll invest it in cocaine, put it in an airplane, and drop it somewhere off the coast of Florida." So at the very time that the powder cocaine market has peaked, you've got more cocaine than ever coming into the country.' This inevitably led to a big fall in the wholesale price of cocaine in the United States.

In the early 1980s, Wall Street executives, most of whom had no history of drug or psychiatric problems, started to show up at drug treatment clinics asking for help in overcoming their cocaine habits, only to be turned away on the grounds that cocaine wasn't addictive. Then several high-profile cases began to challenge the prevalent belief that cocaine was risk-free. The comedian Richard Pryor almost died from burns sustained after his hair caught fire while he was free-basing cocaine in 1980.[15] The actor John Belushi died of a cocaine-heroin speedball overdose in 1982.[16] By 1984, *Rolling Stone* magazine was running articles telling its readers how to get off cocaine. As people wised up to the risks inherent in habitual cocaine use, the drug started to lose its cachet and Colombian exporters began to open up new markets for what was by now a much more affordable drug. Consequently, once cocaine made land in the United States, it was increasingly sent into the inner cities rather than the wealthier suburbs.

But cocaine's journey into the inner city was also aided by changes in the policing of the drugs trade, particularly in New York City. In 1983, Mayor Ed Koch launched Operation Pressure Point in a determined attempt to put a dent in drug-selling operations on Manhattan's Lower East Side. The police ensnared drug dealers in 'buy and bust' operations, and the building and fire departments worked together to condemn and bulldoze abandoned buildings. Pressure Point was deemed a great success in Manhattan, where it paved the way for the gentrification of the Lower East Side, but the pressure the authorities exerted only pushed heroin and cocaine users and their dealers across the Hudson River into Brooklyn, where many of New York's recent immigrants lived. 'I started copping at Alphabet City, on the Lower East Side,' Robert, a cocaine user from Newark, New Jersey, told drug ethnographer Rick Curtis.[17] 'When Operation Pressure Point started, the boys told me things had moved over to Williamsburg. Then they cracked down over there because of the new housing, and the place was virtually cleaned up apart from a few bodegas [off-licences] up and down Broadway that you could buy cocaine from. So the whole scene closed down and I started coming down to Bushwick.'

In the mid 1980s the neighbourhood of Bushwick in Brooklyn, New York, was near the bottom of any property developer's wish list. It had lost its manufacturing jobs, and house prices had slumped. So many people wanted to sell houses in Bushwick, and so few wanted to buy them, that many home-owners resorted to torching their properties to cash in on their insurance policies. The vista of abandoned shop-fronts and burnt-out houses in Brooklyn neighbourhoods like Bushwick, Crown Heights and Flatbush was only brightened by the little buoyancy the marijuana business could provide. Rastafarians in Brooklyn had been selling marijuana imported from the Caribbean in their grocery stores since the 1960s, and many small businesses had been financed by money made from selling ganja. But the spraying of the ganja fields of Mexico caused a drought in Bushwick, and raised the price of marijuana across New York City. Marijuana smokers started casting around for alternatives, and many found it in cheap cocaine.

When a drug user snorts powdered cocaine the active ingredient takes effect in three minutes. Injecting cocaine in solution, the drug takes effect in fourteen seconds. The fastest way to feel the cocaine high is to smoke it, but in powdered form cocaine decomposes before it reaches the temperature required to turn it to vapour. The solution, albeit a dangerous and technically challenging one, was free-basing.

To 'free' the 'base' drug in the form of a vapour, cocaine is heated with ether over an open flame, and then inhaled. With no ganja to sell, but lots of cocaine, the dealers of Bushwick held free-base parties to encourage their regulars to switch from smoking marijuana to inhaling free-base cocaine.[18] Free-basing was largely confined to New York City, where it was initially consumed in unobtrusive settings by an inner circle of drug dealers, and mainly white, middle-class people who were familiar with cocaine and keen to try it in a new way.[19]

One who was there was Lance, a cocaine wholesaler from South Jamaica, Queens, who was rumoured to have given many of the best-known crack dealers in New York City their break into the business. 'In the Reagan era, cocaine was considered to be a rich man's high,' he told me. 'From 1974 to 1984, a kilo of cocaine cost anywhere from $42,000 to $44,000. But from the summer of 1984, the price of coke dropped dramatically to about $16,000. A lot of actors and stars were free-basing. Me and my brothers were the connects, selling cocaine on a large scale. It was coming in through the Bahamas. Back then, there wasn't no terrorist threat, you were able to just put cocaine in your suitcase, get on the plane, and bring it in.' Ricky Ross told me about the cocaine scene he found when he first started selling the drug in Los Angeles. 'At that time, the only people that were doing cocaine were very up-class. In my neighbourhood that meant pimps, PCP dealers, doctors, and entertainers. My first customer was a friend of mine, who was a pimp. He came back a second time, and it snowballed from there. Next thing I know, I know all the pimps in LA.'

Not only was cocaine getting cheaper – it was also getting stronger. Street-level gram purity went from an average of 25 per cent in 1981 to 70 per cent by 1988. Widely available, cheap and powerful cocaine wrong-footed everyone, including its dealers, many of whom soon learnt how naive they had been in thinking they could control their free-base consumption. Wealthy marijuana dealers who had until then regarded drug addicts with incomprehension or disdain found them-selves selling everything they owned to buy cocaine. Doris was a cocaine addict for twenty years. She told me what she remembered of the time. 'Here in Harlem, we had a lot of big-time cocaine dealers we'd buy our coke from. I'd ask, "Hey, where's so-and-so?" And people started saying, "Oh, he's up in the base-house." I didn't know what they were talking about, but three or four months later, you'd see the same big-time dealer who'd always dressed so nice looking completely unkempt, with runned-over shoes and his hair undone. He had gotten caught up in this free-base, and he was in the grips of it.

'Making free-base was a long process,' Doris went on. 'There were two or three pages of instructions, and unfortunately, the solvent tended to ignite. Then someone discovered that all you really needed was some baking soda and some water, and you could bring that cocaine powder back to a rock form.' This variety of cocaine makes a cracking sound when it is heated, hence its name. Crack cocaine began as a rescue plan for drug dealers intent on recuperating the money they had lost to their free-base habits.[20] Preparation and packaging of the drug was done in-house, and the drug was sold at prices that people were accustomed to paying for marijuana. By selling $10 vials of crack instead of $50 bags of cocaine powder, dealers could market their product to people who'd previously thought of cocaine as being out of their reach. 'So they started putting it into vials, with a coloured cap to distinguish its source, putting it out on the street, and making it commercial. That's how crack was born.'

In Williamsburg, New York, Ted watched as crack cocaine ruined what he assured me had previously been a 'civilized' cocaine scene. 'Crack is not a drug. It's a marketing scheme. It's like the McDonald's of cocaine. It's cocaine for poor people. It's the same high as coke, but in a different setting. I might be selling coke out of my apartment, but I'd take great care not to bother my neighbours. I'd call the police on the guys selling crack on my street. They had no class to them. They didn't give a fuck.' Crack was not a new drug. It was just an easy way to take cocaine in its most powerful, inhalable form. However it is taken, high doses of cocaine can have damaging cardiovascular, respiratory and neurological effects, as well as cause gastrointestinal complications like abdominal pain and nausea. Though the effects of the drug on the heart are still not clear, cocaine has been associated with heart attacks. Large doses can also lead to disinhibition, impaired judgement, grandiosity, impulsiveness, hypersexuality, hypervigilance, compulsively repeated actions, and extreme psychomotor activation.[21]

A peculiar characteristic of this cocaine-induced psychosis is formication: the hallucination that ants, insects or snakes are crawling under the skin.

Aficionados of powdered cocaine can experience these problems, but the urge to take large doses is more pronounced in crack users, and this stems from the incredible rush that the crack user feels. Groping for words, crack-takers describe the ascent as akin to a whole-body orgasm, the most intense sense of being alive the user will ever enjoy. Someone using cocaine in powder form might feel something similar, albeit less intensely, since the drug takes effect more slowly when it is snorted, and there is a limit to how much cocaine the membranes in the nose can absorb. In crack form, there is no such limit, which means that users tend to binge on the drug for hours or even days, repeating the dose every twenty minutes or so, until either their funds or their ability to remain awake are exhausted.

It is an uncomfortable truth that the most pleasurable drugs are also the most dangerous. As a Canadian crack user put it, 'a drug which induces a secular parody of Heaven commonly leads the user into a biological counterpart of Hell'.[22] But this oscillation between bliss and bedlam was made still more dramatic by the setting in which cocaine was increasingly being taken. In the 1970s, cocaine had epitomized the ease and wealth of middle-class America. As it fell out of favour with its first mass market in the 1980s, it was repackaged as crack for the move downmarket. The backdrop changed from poolside parties and upscale nightclubs to abandoned lots and burnt-out cars. Taking cocaine was no longer an accessory or an adjunct to wealth and ease, but an end in itself. Where the rich had shared it, now the poor jealously guarded it. Once it had lubricated communication and dissolved barriers. Now it made people self-conscious to the point of paranoia. Regular crack users might buy a $10 vial four times a day, and binge without sleeping for days on end. They would go on 'missions', a term borrowed from *Star Trek* (another American vision of blissful escape from the present), to raise money, whether by robbery, fraud or prostitution. Then they would buy crack and 'beam up'. Between raising the money, finding and then buying from a dealer, and securing a place to smoke in peace, crack users had little time for

idleness. Lurching from euphoria to dysphoria, from slavish submission to aggressive isolation, crack kept its users frantically busy,
and many of them were soon making more money than ever to support
their drug habits. To onlookers, these new cocaine users seemed as
irredeemable as they were unrepentant, lost in a wilderness of their
own making. But crack was also a great motivator, unleashing enormous energy and productivity wherever it went.

Ted told me how he had first realized what a different beast crack
was from cocaine. 'I would work from time to time as a bicycle courier
with this Puerto Rican kid called Jose. He was a hard-core messenger
who looked like he went to the gym every night. He was a universally
respected guy, but Jose started smoking crack and just went downhill
so fast. It was like "he borrowed $5 from you too?" In six months his
reputation went from golden to complete fucking shit.' Cocaine's
reputation fared no better. In 1985, the number of people using the
drug on a routine basis soared from 4.2 million to 5.8 million. The
following year, cocaine-related emergency room admissions went up
by 110 per cent.[23]

Crack users were a dealer's dream customers. In the mid-1980s,
traditional organized crime groups controlled only a quarter of the
drug-trafficking business of New York City.[24] Until then, Colombian
traffickers had been shipping cocaine mainly into Miami, but with
word of the discovery of crack and the huge sums to be made by
selling it, they moved into New York in a big way too. Since the
Colombians were too small in number to manage the transition from
elite to street distribution, they recruited Dominican groups to handle
street sales. To this day Dominicans dominate cocaine wholesaling in
New York, Boston and Philadelphia, working closely with Colombian
suppliers and local street gangs.

A booming market for crack cocaine, largely kept within the con-
fines of poor communities with high unemployment and plentiful new
arrivals also attracted the attention of Jamaican posses. Delroy 'Uzi'
Edwards was one of the first Jamaicans to start selling crack in Bedford-
Stuyvesant, New York. From 1985, his Renkers gang branched out to
Philadelphia, Baltimore and Washington DC. By 1989, Jamaican
gangs were supplying crack to forty-seven cities across the United

States, and even to small rural towns in Iowa, Kentucky and South Dakota. Jamaican criminal gangs are still New York City's most prominent wholesale and mid-level cannabis distributors. They are also active in cocaine markets across the Northeast, though their dominance has been reduced as smuggling routes have moved west from the Caribbean into Mexico.[25]

On the East Coast, crack-houses were supplied by Jamaicans, Colombians and Cubans. West Coast crack-houses were mainly run by the Bloods and Crips, gangs that had started out in the early 1970s as hybrids of the street gangs and revolutionary political groups of the previous decade. Their political aspirations were suffocated by a general lack of leadership and had been completely subsumed by the 1980s, as both gangs became obsessed with protecting themselves from rivals and enriching themselves through the drugs trade. Crack-houses in the Midwest were supplied by the Young Boys Incorporated and the Chambers Brothers. Billy Chambers was one of many grocery store owners in Detroit who used to sell marijuana to supplement their legal earnings. In 1984, the state of Michigan revoked his liquor licence, and Chambers cast around for an income to replace what he had once generated selling alcohol. He wasted no time in 'rocking it up' as the customer waited, with Chambers and a brother running their crack business 'like a couple of frazzled short order cooks'. He started to buy from two wholesalers who epitomized the transition from cocaine for the rich to crack for the poor. The first partner was white, had sold cocaine in the 1970s to a well-heeled crowd, and still had connections to a Colombian in Miami who worked for the Cali cartel. The second partner was black, and had the contacts needed to sell drugs in the most deprived neighbourhoods of Detroit. Together they built a staggeringly successful business that pulled in $100,000 a day for two years. At its height the Chambers Brothers' crack-selling venture was reputed to be the most profitable privately owned business in the city.

This rags to riches story was repeated with local variations across the country, by people like Ricky Ross in Los Angeles. 'I couldn't come into the house with new shoes or new clothes or my mom would have a fit – she didn't know that I was selling cocaine until I was rich. So I just kept saving my money, and buying more drugs. My childhood friends would all be walking, but I'd be driving a nice car, and they'd want to know how I got the car. "Oh, I'm selling cocaine now," I'd say. "Teach *me* how to sell cocaine," they'd say. So my friends started to get involved, and before long we're making a lot of money, and I'm eating at McDonald's whenever I want to. At our height, some days a million dollars would come through our hands in a single day. Next thing I know, the whole neighbourhood is selling.'

William Adler, the biographer of the Chambers brothers of Detroit, ascribes the crack whirlwind to 'the head-on collision during the 1980s of the cultures of greed and need'. Even the local DEA office in Detroit admitted that 'kids in the ghetto who couldn't get jobs or couldn't get to jobs because they didn't have transportation out to the suburbs could rock up cocaine and sell it on any street corner'.[26] On the one hand, the Chambers brothers were the lead characters in an archetypal American story of entrepreneurial success. They had identified a niche market, studied and overcame barriers to entry, bought wholesale, tracked inventory, managed cash flow, analysed risk and expanded aggressively until they cornered the market. Plenty of those involved in the upper echelons of the cocaine business, such as Lance in South Jamaica, Queens, craved the respect granted to their counterparts in the legal economy and regarded themselves as successful businessmen whose stock-in-trade happened to be illegal. 'The structure of the business is like a Fortune 500. We'd have different titles for different positions, but it all basically remains the same as in corporate America. You have your CEO, your supervisor, your treasurer. You might be the captain; you have your lieutenants, your soldiers. We were responsible for feeding over five hundred families in twenty-three states.' By 1988, people in all the big cities of the United States were making 'crazy money' by selling crack cocaine. Ricky Ross told me that 'when we went to restaurants, our tips would be so big that they'd give us the food for free'.

On the other hand, cocaine dealing was against the law, and any financial success its practitioners enjoyed was the fruit of ruthlessness, violence or intimidation. Their entrepreneurial zeal might have been respected by their peers, but it was anathema to wider society, and was disowned as a perverse parody of the American dream. In some neighbourhoods, entire blocks became outdoor markets, with up to a hundred sellers competing for trade on less than friendly terms. Drug dealers became the favourite targets for robbers: they were among the few people who still had money in their pockets in poor neighbourhoods. Being aggressive and threatening became the only way to avoid being robbed. Teenagers entered the business, and soon learnt the value of a reputation for 'acting crazy'. Marc, who once worked as a crack cocaine seller in South Jamaica, Queens, was under no illusion that selling crack cocaine was easy. 'It was the hardest job I've ever had. It's pure capitalism, you know? Say you're selling drugs in the South Bronx, say at 138th and 3rd Avenue, and another crew of guys is selling the same drugs as you two blocks away. The block they're on is making about $2,000 a day, and the block you're on is making about $2,000 a day. They decide, "You know what? You're a punk. You're a pussy." So they move you. If people feel that they can take stuff off you and not have to pay you, you might as well go and get a job. What are you going to do? Who do you get now? You can't call the police. That's a complete no-no up in these parts. It's pretty much you and your gun.' Ricky Ross explained that 'people were already gang-banging, but now we were able to afford more expensive weapons, more expensive cars, and better houses and the police started noticing it more. Gang-bangers [gang members] driving Rolls-Royces and Ferraris is more newsworthy than a gang member getting caught with a rusty .22 pistol that barely works, you know?'

The chaos engendered by the rush for 'crazy money' and the wider public's disgust at this terrible parody of entrepreneurial success prompted a resolute whack on the head from the local police. Manuel had been unemployed for a long time when his then-eighteen-year-old son Mano started selling crack. Mano quickly became the main breadwinner in the family. 'I try to keep my eye on him,' Manuel told ethnographer Rick Curtis in 1996. 'They don't steal it from nobody, that's one thing. The guys that work out here work hard in a way, but it's still wrong. I got my own opinions. Nobody puts a gun to nobody to use drugs. But the law says that's a law. The only thing I say to the police is "take him if he's done something wrong". But you don't have to beat on him, knock him all silly.'[27]

Older, more senior dealers like Lance saw how dangerous the business had become. 'Ninety-five per cent of those who get involved with selling drugs on the streets have a three- or four-year run, at most. It's a rude awakening. You're either paralysed and in a wheelchair for life, or you're in jail for twenty years or better. Or you just straight meet your Maker. That's it, end of story, dead. Three outcomes.' Between 1985 and 1992, the murder rate in New York City doubled, largely because of the anarchy of the crack market.[28] But still business boomed. As more of the Latino drug sellers who had pioneered street sales went to jail, more blacks, whites and heavy drug users took their place. In 1990, police in Detroit found that 60 per cent of those they arrested for selling cocaine were crack users who sold the drug to fund their own drug habit.[29] These user-sellers would invariably flit between two concurrent fantasies: the first was to become a millionaire by selling crack; the second was to have an endless supply of crack to 'smoke lovely'. One fantasy or the other impelled them to the end of each day, when they would more often than not find themselves as broke as they had been at its start, having pushed crack on anyone who happened to be passing by and antagonized plenty of people in their neighbourhood in the process. Because these street-level dealers were wont to smoke their consignments, and often absconded with the money they had made selling crack, they were regular victims of brutal 'beatdowns' from their supervisors.

As more people spent more money on more crack, whole communities started to come apart at the seams. Crack made prostitutes of most of the women who used the drug, and transformed the world's oldest profession, with the drug dealer replacing the pimp. Many women lost custody of their children, and spent the rest of their increasingly short lives trying to escape life on the streets and get their children back from relatives or child protection services. One response to the chaos of the streets was the rise of the 'freak-house', usually the apartment of an elderly single crack user who traded his lodgings for free crack and sex from five or six crack-abusing women. In return, the women got a place to cook, sleep and bring paying customers who would come to have sex with all of the women, a practice known as 'flipping the freaks'.

Even the drug users and sellers of Bushwick in Brooklyn welcomed the police crackdown when it first came. In the four years that followed passage of the Anti-Drug Abuse Act of 1986, the police arrested over 8,000 people in Bushwick. The prison on Rikers Island, where thousands of crack dealers served time for possession with intent to supply, was said to resemble a Bushwick block party. However, by 1992 when 10 per cent of local people reported having been physically assaulted by a police officer, it was clear that police tactics were alienating whatever popular support they might once have garnered, as well as having precious little impact on street sales. Bushwick was ready to riot, and for the next eighteen months the neighbourhood was virtually occupied by a small army of police officers.

It has been speculated that a quarter of the street price of drugs compensates the seller for the risk he runs of being caught and sent to jail; in the late 1980s, the average American street dealer stood a one in four chance of going to jail for selling cocaine.[30] A further third of the price compensates for the risk of being physically harmed.[31] Unsurprisingly, many drug dealers joined a gang to minimize those risks and gangs have grown as the war on drugs has intensified. There are said to be 2,000 gangs in Los Angeles today, most of which derive a sizeable portion of their income from the drugs trade.[32] The gangs of Chicago are thought to have 70,000 members.[33] In the Colombian city of Medellín, another city struggling with industrial redundancy and a booming illegal drug economy, there were 6,300 gangs in 2003.[34]

Violent, clandestine drug-dealing gangs made life in the inner cities still more complicated. 'I was involved in gangs in east LA from the age of eleven,' Luis Rodriguez told me. 'I became a hard-core gang member by the early '70s, and then eventually I got into drugs. I became an addict, and spent seven years on heroin. I got involved with the violence, shooting people. LA and Chicago were the two gang capitals of the United States. Gangs make sense for drug sales because they're an organized force. You can get a large number of young people out there doing sales. Many of the gangs that they're dealing with almost everywhere in the country in 2008 have roots in Chicago or LA – Sur-13, the Latin Kings, the Gangster Disciples, the Vice Lords, the Latin Disciples, the Bloods and the Crips. By the '90s,

Mara-Salvatrucha had started spreading out too. Drugs were always involved in Chicago and LA, but to the side. By the '80s they were central, and I saw the change in the gangs, going from being a group of guys who had a camaraderie, who were willing to love and care about each other, to becoming more connected with drugs in the '80s.'

The rise of these gangs made calls for a tough response even shriller, but as Alex Sanchez of Homies Unidos in Santa Cruz, California, told me, it has become all too easy to imagine criminal masterminds and conspiracies in lieu of real knowledge about how the drug economy works. 'The gangs don't have the capacity or the funding to deal with all that organized crime stuff. You have higher level activity, but it's mainly territorial or to survive the prison system. They're not real strategic organizations that can get involved at those high levels of trafficking, but the immigrant gangs are easier to target than organized crime. We had a raid in November 2007, when they arrested thirty-two members of Mara-Salvatrucha, and they're getting ten-year terms just for conspiracy.' As we will see in the next chapter, the Republicans' crusade against drugs and vice has long been stymied by their fondness for easy answers to difficult questions.

3

A Rush to Punish

The Constitution is not an instrument for the government to restrain the people. It is an instrument for the people to restrain the government, lest it come to dominate our lives and interests.

Patrick Henry, American colonial revolutionary

By 1986, crack cocaine was creating huge problems of abuse, neglect and self-destruction for its users. Their dealers seemed to be driven by just as insatiable an appetite for money and power. But the press showed little interest in covering the story. To make 'news', journalists need sources, people to whom authoritative statements can be attributed. Both needs dispose them to reproduce the line taken by the police and government, for news is often made by the passage of a law or by a public statement in the wake of a bizarre murder or suicide. Few news stories can simultaneously please newspaper editors, advertisers and politicians, while attracting readers in droves, quite like the death of a star from a drug overdose. Public discussion of drug use thus tends to centre on the most dramatic examples of drug use, a tendency intensified by the journalist's desire to tell a dramatic story.[1]

Eric Sterling was legal counsel to Congress in 1986 and told me about the background to the death of basketball star Len Bias. 'Members of Congress are very aggressive, competitive men and women. They play basketball, and they have a court in the House gym. In June 1986, the lead college team was from the University of Maryland, right outside Washington DC, and the star of the team was a gifted athlete named Len Bias. The best professional team was the Boston Celtics. At the end of the NBA season, Len Bias gets hired by the Boston Celtics, so the best collegiate player in the country goes with the best professional team in the country. He flies back from Boston to his dormitory at the University of Maryland, and celebrates his million-dollar contract by drinking and snorting cocaine, and he dies.'

Len Bias has been called 'the Archduke Ferdinand of the Total War on Drugs'.[2] Although the coroner's report concluded that there was no clear link between Bias's drug use and his heart failure, this precious detail was lost on the press. In the month following his death, the news networks of the United States aired seventy-four evening news items about crack and cocaine, routinely confusing the two forms of the drug, and often stating that it was crack that had killed Len Bias. The crack scare that followed set the benchmark for every irrational, hysterical and moralizing panic the American media has cooked up since. The advertising industry and the main broadcasters even donated a billion dollars' worth of ads and airtime to the anti-drugs movement, saying that 'on this issue we're ready to go over the top!'[3] As the head of the DEA office in New York put it, 'crack is the hottest combat-reporting story to come along since the end of the Vietnam War'.[4] Police footage of their raids on alleged drug dealers' homes appeared in a quarter of all drug stories over the following two years. The police and the DEA encouraged the use of their footage because it was dramatic, and by its very nature it put the viewer in the place of the raiders as they went 'over the top'. Though the raiders' point of view was only one among many, the press adopted it as their own.

Selective or erroneous coverage of drug-related stories was nothing new. A good example of how the press created stories to fit the demand for a drug scare is 'Jimmy's World', the title of an article published in the *Washington Post* in September 1980, which described the life of an eight-year-old heroin addict who lived in a housing project in Washington DC with his drug-addicted parents. Jimmy's mother was quoted as saying, 'I don't really like to see him fire up. But, you know, he would have got into it one day anyway. When you live in the ghetto, it's all a matter of survival. Drugs and black folks been together a long time.'⁵ This stew of youth, drugs and the hopelessness of the inner city was sufficiently compelling for the writer of the article, a black journalist by the name of Janet Cooke, to win the Pulitzer Prize for Feature Writing for her story the following year. So embarrassing was 'Jimmy's World' that Marion Barry, the then mayor of Washington DC, sent out search parties to look for child drug addicts. A $10,000 reward was offered to anyone who could find one, but it went uncollected. Then it emerged that there was no Jimmy. Janet Cooke had made the whole thing up. The Pulitzer Board had had its doubts about the 'Jimmy's World' story, but had been persuaded of its veracity by Roger Wilkins, a distinguished black journalist who had said that he could easily find pre-teen drug addicts within ten blocks of where the Pulitzer Board sat at Columbia University in Manhattan. With press and politicians united in fear of a drug epidemic that they barely understood, and many black journalists as keen to stoke those fears as their white colleagues, the facts had been sacrificed to a convenient fiction.

Six years later, evidence of a drug epidemic was again twisted to suit the perceived expectations of readers. This time the press's *wunderkind* was the crack baby. Both *Time* and *Newsweek* magazines ran stories in which paediatricians were quoted as saying that 'the part of the brain that makes us human' had been 'wiped out' in babies born to crack-addicted mothers. Each crack baby born, they reported, would cost a million dollars to bring to adulthood. The prospect of a generation of (mainly black) babies born addicted to cocaine, and destined to become an intellectually and emotionally stunted 'biological underclass' had newspaper editors across the country clamouring for copy. Eric Sterling watched as panic gripped the politicians. 'Senator Chiles of Florida said "I seriously wonder if America can survive crack cocaine." I mean, we survived Pearl Harbor! But that was the level of hyperbole that was going on. And of course, part of this was that "they're all black". It was perceived and reported as a black phenomenon.' Like Jimmy, the eight-year-old lead in what might be termed 'Janet's World', the crack baby didn't exist. Taking cocaine while pregnant, like smoking cigarettes, increases the risk of low birth weight and premature delivery, but it is not associated with any pattern of birth defects.[6] Heavy drinking during pregnancy causes foetal alcohol syndrome, but nobody wanted to hear about the dangers of drinking while pregnant. They wanted to hear, read and talk about how crack was 'instantly addictive' and how it was spreading from city to suburb on a tide of poor black ignorance and apathy.

Thanks to this panic in the press, the stereotypical cocaine user was no longer rich, white and tragically misguided. She was poor, black or Hispanic, and criminally negligent of herself and her children. This invited intervention, not by service providers, but by what can best be described as a secular priesthood. The epidemic of problematic drug use sweeping across the US was regarded as akin to mass demonic possession. 'Drug tsars' urged 'crusades' against 'drug barons' and the 'plague' of drug use that they had unleashed. Journalists fulminate about drugs in such medieval language because they consider drug use to be a sin not a vice; they certainly don't see it as an essentially social or medical problem. Most American Christians consider drug-taking to be morally wrong. They regard the human body as the vessel for the God-given soul, of which the bearer has only temporary custody. Human consciousness is a gift from God, and God and his gift can only be appreciated by a sober and drug-free vessel. Wrestling with the crack epidemic took many Christians back to a time when most Americans believed that the devil really was a supernatural being intent on tempting stray souls into hell. Christians had to practise endless vigilance, to defend their mortal souls from temptation by the devil, against whom they had to marshal all their reserves of goodness. If they succumbed to temptation, they might be possessed, leaving exorcism as a last resort. When the crack economy took root in the inner city, the official response seemed to be much influenced by these notions of an untended flock that had been led astray.

American history provides another example of resolute defiance of the forces of evil, one invoked by Ronald Reagan in 1986. 'My generation will remember how America swung into action when we were attacked in World War Two. The war was not just fought by the fellows flying the planes or driving the tanks, but also at home by a mobilized nation. Well, now we're in another war for our freedom, and it's time for all of us to pull together again.'[7] Reagan issued a

Presidential Directive, which called drugs 'a national security concern'. George Bush Sr was still calling for vigilance three years later, when he told reporters 'all of us agree that the gravest domestic threat facing our nation today is drugs'.[8] By 2002, George W. Bush deemed the threat posed by drugs to be all-encompassing, warning Americans that 'drug use threatens everything. Everything.'[9] Eternal vigilance was the aim of the 'Just Say No' campaign too, which succeeded in reducing the debate over how best to deal with mass drug abuse in the United States to a single word.[10] At a Just Say No rally in 1984, Nancy Reagan led the kids in yelling 'No!' to drugs. 'That's wonderful,' the First Lady said of this collective exorcism of moral corruption. 'That will keep the drugs away.'

'It's a deadly and poisonous activity,' former drug tsar William Bennett said of drug-taking. 'People should be in prison for a long time for doing it. It's a matter of right and wrong.'[11] The harm that drugs can cause is obvious to users and non-users alike. It can be measured, and steps can be taken to minimize harm. But right and wrong cannot be measured by doctors, or evaluated by social workers. Ignorance and moralizing combined to ensure that the debate over how best to deal with widespread, dangerous and destructive behaviour soon succumbed to blind panic. A barrage of scare stories in the press had the whole country scared witless by crack cocaine. A poll conducted in 1986 found that 54 per cent of Americans believed that drugs were the single greatest problem facing the nation. Just 4 per cent cited unemployment.[12] In 1980, 53 per cent of Americans had favoured the legalization of small amounts of marijuana for personal use. By 1986, only 27 per cent held that view.[13] In 1989, ten years after the heyday of the American drug culture, and in spite of the cocaine-Contra scandal, the Republicans seemed to have been validated in their rebuttal of liberal America.

In communities where drug abuse and drug sales were causing catastrophic harm, the conservatives' Manichaean simplifications carried less weight. Kurt Schmoke, the former mayor of Baltimore, became a pariah after suggesting that the crack epidemic in the city might be better tackled by decriminalizing drug use. 'I once had the dubious distinction of debating the subject with drug tsar William

Bennett at, of all places, the Ronald Reagan Library in Simi Valley, California,' Schmoke told me. 'Sitting in front of me was Mrs Reagan. Most of the audience was upper-income, white and Republican. It dawned on me that friends of theirs have had problems with alcohol, and friends of theirs have recovered from addiction. Alcohol is something that they are familiar with. But most of their friends don't take cocaine, at least not to their knowledge. Substance abuse is something done by "those" people, as opposed to "our" people. So I asked a rhetorical question. "If you found that your grand-daughter was addicted to cocaine, would you call the police or would you call a doctor?" I bet that most of you would call a doctor. You'd want her to get help to get off this stuff. But if you heard that two miles away, in the heart of the city, there's a black kid or a Hispanic kid who has dropped out of school because he's using cocaine, what would you think the intervention should be? Most of you would probably say "call the police."'

Jack Cole spent twenty-six years working as a narcotics police officer for the New Jersey state police before becoming executive director of Law Enforcement Against Prohibition. When I met him he too questioned the distinction made between those drug problems that require the intervention of a doctor, those that require the intervention of the police, and those deemed to require no intervention at all. 'I was raised on movies like *Reefer Madness* and *The Man with the Golden Arm*, and I believed all that. I didn't think that we had a drug problem in Wichita, Kansas. But of course we did. I had major drug problems. I used to get falling-down drunk with my friends when I was fourteen years old! I smoked two packs of cigarettes a day for fifteen years! We had major drug problems. We just didn't acknowledge them as drugs, that's all.'

For most Americans, the panic over the crack epidemic stemmed from their ignorance of illegal drugs and their latent fear of inner-city violence. But more level-headed politicians saw that a sensationalistic drug scare could be turned to their advantage. By making caricatures appear real and exceptions appear normal, the crack scare invited politicians to take a strong stand on a safe issue, and goaded the police into 'getting tough'. Conservatives showed the public what they were defending them from, but also what they expected in return. They stressed individual responsibility for health and economic success, respect for the police, and resistance to peer-group pressure. They highlighted the importance of belief in God in recovering from drug abuse, and of sports and healthy activities as alternatives to drug-taking. They stressed the need for everybody to set good examples to children, the importance of children getting good grades in school and the threat drugs posed to those grades.

Drug scares have lasting value for authoritarians of all stripes because they make pariahs of drug addicts, while flattering the credulous and the ignorant. The idea that a heroin addict might inject drugs into her eight-year-old son becomes credible, while the idea that the press might fabricate stories to sell more newspapers seems outlandish, or even 'un-American'. Irrespective of the intoxicants flowing through their blood on any given day, every American could rally around ritualistic campaigns against drug users and their dealers, and the promise to deliver them a society cleansed of evil. Harry Levine, co-editor of *Crack in America*, has written that 'the worsening of almost any social problem can be blamed on drugs. Theft, robbery, rape, malingering, fraud, corruption, physical violence, shoplifting, juvenile delinquency, sloth, sloppiness, sexual promiscuity, low productivity, and all-round irresponsibility can be, and has been, blamed on "drugs".'[14]

Blame is at the heart of the war on drugs. In retrospect, one can't help but conclude from the politicians' reactions to economic restructuring and the closure of many of America's biggest factories in the 1970s and 1980s, that the crack scare obviated the need to develop effective policies to tackle mass unemployment. As long as the focus stayed on drug sales and drug abuse, inner-city residents could be blamed for the poverty they had been driven into. Endless scare stories about crack cocaine eased the passage of laws that restricted welfare payments to the unemployed and allowed penalties to be dressed up as incentives. Denying welfare to the unemployed only fuelled the drug economy, but that was deemed to be incidental, which in a sense it was. The inner cities were going to be abandoned either way; what the politicians had to do was convince the American public that the inner cities deserved to be abandoned.[15]

Drug abuse has been a huge social problem in many parts of Europe and the United States for almost forty years, yet stories of how poverty, neglect and racism can cause depression and despair, and sometimes lead to self-destructive drug use still make for uncomfortable reading. At the same time, stories blaming drug addicts for a myriad of social problems are newsworthy because they chime with a broader perspective according to which the poor have only themselves to blame for their poverty. The political scientist James Q. Wilson is regarded as a 'drug warrior' by many, but he too has expressed shock at popular indifference towards the crack epidemic's health effects. 'What are the lives of would-be addicts worth? I recall some people saying to me "let them kill themselves". I was appalled.' In 1998, a study of probation officers found that the US probation service typically viewed crimes committed by black people as caused by personal failure, but treated crimes committed by white people as caused by external forces.[16] The poor, particularly the black and brown poor, were regarded as being blinkered by 'a culture of poverty' which led them to seek, enjoy and perpetuate destructive lifestyles. Inevitably, such a dim view of inner-city dwellers encouraged the reader to champion the authorities charged with administering the inner cities, however brutal that administration might be.

In this climate of recrimination, policing the inner cities was always likely to be harsh, but the very nature of drug laws made policing arbitrary as well. Between 1985 and 2002, the number of arrests made for drug offences in the United States more than doubled.[17] In 2006, the police made 1.88 million such arrests, equivalent to one every twenty seconds, the highest rate ever.[18] The annual budget of the DEA more than doubled between 1985 and 1990, and by 1994 it topped $1 billion.[19] Since it was not physically possible to lock up the 19.5 million Americans who took illegal drugs in 2002, and the prison system would have been hard pushed to accommodate the 1.8 million Americans thought to be selling drugs, the drugs laws could only be enforced selectively. So the police had to pick and choose their targets.

I spoke to a former police officer called David about his experience of street-level policing of the drugs business. 'In 1990, I went from the detective tables to work South Bureau Narcotics, 77th Street, right in the middle of South Central Los Angeles. Our supervisor pulled us together and he said, "There's only one thing that matters here, and that's D.O.T. – dope on the table."' The focus was on arrests, confiscation and incarceration. Typically, arrests of drug dealers would be made by an undercover police officer as part of a 'buy-bust' operation, using 'pre-recorded marked buy money [PRMB]', while his fellow officers acted as 'ghosts', waiting nearby to arrest the dealer in possession of PRMB cash. 'Were we effective at putting a dent in the narcotics trade? No. We were effective at putting dope on the table, and we were effective at arresting people. It didn't matter how many people you arrested. For every one you arrested, there were two fighting to take his place. It was there, it was going to stay there, and it was coming in all the time.'

The more impotent the police felt, the more aggressive their response became. Many police officers concluded that if a dent couldn't be made in the trade, at least they could strike some fear into the brazen, and recoup some sense of control. In 1997, a member of a police unit recounted their tactics to a researcher. 'We're into saturation patrols in hot spots. We do a lot of our work with the Special Weapons and Tactics unit because we have bigger guns. We send out two-to-four-men cars, we look for minor violations and do jump-outs, either on people on the street or automobiles. After we jump out, the second car provides periphery cover with an ostentatious display of weaponry. We're sending a clear message: if the shootings don't stop, we'll shoot someone.'[20] Another member of the same unit boasted: 'When the soldiers ride in, you should see those blacks scatter.'[21]

Jack Cole told me that after joining the New Jersey State narcotics unit in 1970, he watched as drug warriors increasingly pushed for military tactics and training to be used to police the inner cities. 'It used to be that the ten largest cities had Special Weapons and Tactics teams, but we now have something like 4,500 SWAT teams in the United States. Every little village has its own SWAT team. I hate SWAT teams. I don't mind them for what they were created for, which is a barricaded hostage situation, but what are they using them for? To serve warrants on somebody that got arrested for smoking pot!' The war on drugs, like any war, needs soldiers, and soldiers wield force to subjugate the enemy. Policing fell hostage to a clumsy metaphor, but the militarization of policing was fuelled by more than belligerence, racism and the culture of blame. It gained further momentum with the end of the Cold War in 1989. The United States had been in a state of war readiness for half a century. Bound by bureaucratic inertia, it felt impelled to find new enemies, and turning on itself, it found them.

Chasing drug dealers from pillar to post made for good footage for the nightly news and might have reassured Americans looking for a resolute response to social breakdown. But police detectives knew that only long-term intelligence-led operations would allow them to pierce the inner workings of drug-dealing organizations. Another way to do this was by creating profiles of likely drug suspects. Police drug teams have repeatedly said that they don't stop and search Americans on the basis of their race. Today, the word 'profile' isn't even officially mentioned by the police because prosecutors and defence lawyers know that the racial implications can raise constitutional challenges.[22]

Interstate highway 95 is a crucial drug-trafficking corridor connecting the major cities of the East Coast. Between 1995 and 1997, racial profiling of potential drugs couriers created a situation in which 70 per cent of the drivers stopped by police on I-95 were African-Americans, even though African-Americans made up only 17 per cent of the drivers on the road.[23] Yet the instances in which drugs were actually discovered were the same per capita for black and white motorists. I asked Jack Cole about how they went about creating drug courier profiles in the early 1970s, when the war on drugs first got underway. 'If we didn't create racial profiling, we certainly raised it to a high art form,' he told me. 'Road troopers on the New Jersey turnpike would back their cars up on the side of the road at night, so their headlights were shining perpendicular across the highway and they could see all the cars going by. Whenever a car with brown people in it went past, out they'd go. The thinking was that since all the cocaine is in the brown community, if I stop Colombians and Cubans, I'll wipe out the cocaine.'

Guidelines for DEA agents give conflicting advice on when police officers should become suspicious. In Tennessee, a DEA agent told a judge that he was leery of a man because he 'walked quickly through the airport'. Six weeks later, in another affidavit, the same agent said his suspicions were aroused because the suspect 'walked with intentional slowness after getting off the bus'. One Maryland state trooper said he was wary because the subject 'deliberately did not look at me when he drove by'. Yet a second Maryland trooper testified that he stopped a man because 'the driver stared at me when he passed'.

If police methodology seems opaque, their target was not. A review of federal court cases in which drug courier profiles were used between 1990 and 1995 revealed that in all but three of sixty-three cases, the suspects were members of an ethnic minority.[24] To this day, African-Americans are twice as likely to be arrested for drug law violations as non-African-Americans. In Texas, they're three times more likely to be arrested, and in the town of Hearne, Texas, they're sixteen times more likely to be arrested. In November 2000, the local narcotics task force raided Hearne's only public housing complex. They found no drugs, but they did arrest 15 per cent of the town's young black males, charging twenty-seven of them with selling cocaine. The District Attorney's case rested on information provided by Derrick Megress, a convicted thief and crack user. As the cases began to crumble in court, it transpired that the police had given Megress a list of the names of young black men in Hearne, and had asked him to indicate which of them had sold him crack. In court, the DA admitted that he 'might' have warned Megress that he would be raped in prison, and that the best way to avoid doing time was to testify against those who had sold him drugs.

There are forty-five narcotics task forces in Texas alone. They are subject to no federal scrutiny, and their budgets are allocated according to the number of arrestees each force can proffer. Derrick Megress's arrest in Hearne coincided with the annual budget round and the local task force needed to get their numbers up. This focus on numbers encourages the police to focus on the quantity, rather than the quality, of the arrests they make. Because black people in Hearne generally don't have the money to hire a lawyer, they get whatever legal representation they're given, and are deemed to be ripe for the picking.[25] Russ, a former narcotics detective from San Jose, California, told me that 'a lot of times you wouldn't make any progress up the line, you were just running around laterally. You know, "hey, we made fifteen arrests!" Very rarely did we get to the real head person, the person supplying the cocaine, because he never touches it. He just gets on the phone and says, "Sally, I want you to deliver this cocaine to this guy."'

Another reason why drug laws are hard to enforce is that the transaction between buyer and seller is willed by both. Because there is no victim, the police become dependent on informants. 'Ninety-five per cent of federal indictments are put together starting with informants,' Lance, the former cocaine wholesaler from South Jamaica, New York, told me. 'Our business was all family-oriented, and even the outsiders were considered family because we'd been together for twenty years. If it wasn't for informants we'd have never got arrested.' Russ explained how he found those informants, and the dangers he ran in doing so. 'The under-the-influence team would arrest someone for being under the influence, or the buy team would arrest someone at a party for having a small amount of cocaine. The guy didn't want to go to jail, so he'd give evidence on who he was buying his cocaine from. They would pass that person to me. My job was to go after the big dealers, the guys who were making the big bucks. So we would go to meet his dealer, and the guy would pass me off as one of his buddies who wanted to make a large purchase, and the dealer would sell me two or three ounces. The next time, I'd try to buy half a pound. If he couldn't get me a half pound, he'd introduce me to his supplier. I'd dress fancy, pretend that I had flown in from who-knows-where and I'd take everyone to dinner. I might be doing a $120,000 buy. Things start to get real dangerous at that point. What's to stop them pulling a gun and stealing your money? And of course, they're afraid that you're going to pull your gun and steal their cocaine.'

The police's dependence on informers also means that those with information to trade are able to negotiate with the police over the charges they'll face in court. As a result, the courts are full of the drug trade's 'foot soldiers', who generally have nothing to trade. Tony Papa's story is telling. 'I had been showing up late for the league at the alley where I bowled in Yonkers, and this guy asked me why. I told him that my car had broken down. He asked me why I didn't fix it, and I told him that I didn't have the money. So he introduced me to somebody who dealt coke in Westchester County, a big spender, and this guy asked me if I wanted to make a quick buck. I turned him down, but some time later, I think it was January, a blizzard hit. I owed rent, I had no money, and I was desperate. The guy approached me again with his carrot on a stick and this time I went for it. I took an envelope containing four and a half ounces of cocaine to Mount Vernon, New York. But I walked into a police sting operation. Twenty cops came at me out of nowhere. The guy I had met had three sealed indictments, and he was facing life imprisonment. The cops had said, "If you get us other people, you'll do less time," so he'd turned informant. That moment changed my life for ever.'

Sometimes, informants supply enough credible evidence to indict the senior members of a drug-trafficking organization. But it is often a Pyrrhic victory, as Russ explained. 'We'd have a nine-month investigation, and eventually all the search warrants would get signed, and at four in the morning I would have all these police officers from Santa Clara and Cupertino here. Homes would be searched, cocaine would be seized, and a bunch of people would go to jail. Later that morning the District Attorney would have all the drugs and the guns on a table, and he and the police chief would talk about how the cocaine community had been dealt a terrible blow. Of course we narcotics officers knew that what was really going to happen was that someone was going to take this dealer's place and we would start on another investigation.'

This 'terrible blow' invariably fell in the form of a prison sentence, but the police know that many drug dealers consider prison time an inevitable cost of doing business. When a drug dealer is sent to jail, a subordinate will most likely take his place and keep the operation going. If, however, the police can seize the dealer's assets and working capital, they can shut down his business for good. In the words of Cary Copeland, Director of the Department of Justice's asset forfeiture unit, 'asset forfeiture can be to modern law enforcement what air power is to modern warfare'.[26] Before being elected Mayor of Baltimore in 1987, Kurt Schmoke was the public prosecutor for the state of Maryland. 'I was, in the parlance of our time, a drug warrior, and a very aggressive and successful one. Year after year our arrest numbers went up, our conviction rates increased, and our drug seizures multiplied. My office seized so many vehicles from drug dealers that many joked that I was the largest used car dealer in the city. In the war on drugs, this is how success is measured.'

Once the government had established that a property was subject to forfeiture, the burden of proof was reversed. There was no presumption of innocence, and no right to an attorney. The property owner had to prove that his or her property did *not* belong to the government. Goods could be forfeited even if their owner was acquitted. Jury trials could be refused, illegal searches condoned and rules of evidence ignored. With no right to appeal, it is not surprising that almost 90 per cent of cash forfeitures went uncontested.[27]

Such was the booty yielded by the asset forfeiture laws that by 1987 the DEA was paying for itself, and by 1996, the Justice Department's asset forfeiture fund was raking in $2.7 billion a year.[28] The prospect of a self-financing law enforcement branch, largely able to set its own agenda and accountable to no one, had sceptics echoing the words of George Mason, one of the framers of the American Constitution, who had warned that 'the purse and the sword ought never to get into the same hands'.[29] Before long, police departments were arresting drug buyers over drug dealers because buyers were sure to have cash with them, even though targeting buyers did little to reduce the supply of drugs. Patrick Murphy, the former Police Commissioner of New York City, told Congress that police had a financial incentive to impose roadblocks on the southbound lanes of highway I-95, which carried the buyers and their cash into the city, rather than the northbound lanes, which carried the drugs back up into New England, because seized cash would be forfeited to the police department, while seized drugs could only be destroyed.[30]

Even when the police were able to arrest senior members of drug-dealing organizations, the forfeiture laws allowed kingpins to buy their freedom. Those with the most assets to forfeit served shorter prison sentences and sometimes no prison sentence at all. In New Jersey, for example, a defendant facing twenty-five years to life on drug kingpin charges negotiated a dismissal of that charge and parole eligibility in five years on a lesser conviction, by agreeing to hand over $1 million in assets. In Massachusetts, agreements to forfeit $10,000 or more bought elimination or reduction of trafficking charges in 70 per cent of such cases.[31]

Back in 1988, an article published in the *University of Chicago Law Review* warned that 'The law enforcement agenda that targets assets rather than crime, the 80 per cent of seizures that are unaccompanied by any criminal prosecution, the plea bargains that favour drug kingpins and penalize the "mules" without assets to trade, the reverse stings that target drug buyers rather than drug sellers, the overkill in agencies involved in even minor arrests, the massive shift in resources towards federal jurisdiction over local law enforcement – is largely the unplanned by-product of this economic incentive structure.'[32] The Justice Department boasted about the big fish they caught, but threw a cloak of secrecy over the many innocent people swept up in the same net; most of the items seized weren't the playthings of drug barons, but the modest homes, cars and savings of ordinary people.[33] Worst of all, the aggressive use of forfeiture laws had no impact on drugs trafficking. The $730 million obtained by federal authorities in 1994 was never going to shut down America's $50 billion a year drugs trade, but it was enough to show some appreciation to the police and government officials for their efforts in the war on drugs.

Drugs law enforcement is hampered by the nature of the crime and the self-preservation instinct of bureaucracies, but also by the nature of some police officers. Trying to enforce drugs laws exposes police officers to large amounts of cash and drugs held by individuals who are not likely to complain about police corruption. The Knapp Commission, appointed in 1972 to investigate corruption in the New York City Police Department, had found that the most prevalent form of corruption among police officers was taking money to overlook illegal activities such as bookmaking. The war on drugs transformed this venality. Cynicism grew more pervasive among rank and file officers as the militarized response to inner-city drugs markets proved ineffectual. The Mollen Commission of 1994 found that the most prevalent form of police corruption in New York City was police officers actively committing crimes, especially in connection with the drugs trade. The Commission found that police corruption and brutality were prevalent in *every* police precinct with an active drugs trade that it studied. It found that police officers had stolen from drug dealers, sold and used drugs, and indiscriminately beaten the innocent and the guilty alike.[34] Lance, the former cocaine wholesaler from South Jamaica, Queens, told me that 'If they don't have enough evidence to build a case against you, they just try to hurt your business. They'll try and catch you going in to stores to buy furniture or whatever and they just take your money from you. Then they get so used to taking your money that they acquire expensive tastes. It's free money, you know?' Enforcing drug laws also made explicit the latent racism rife in police departments, as Daryl Gates, the former head of the Los Angeles Police Department, unwittingly revealed when he defended his officers against accusations of using excessive force on black suspects. 'We may be finding that in some blacks, when the choke-hold is applied, the veins or the arteries do not open as fast as they do on normal people.'[35]

Since 1995, ten police officers from Philadelphia's 39th District have been charged with planting drugs on suspects, shaking down drug dealers for hundreds of thousands of dollars, and breaking into homes to steal drugs and cash. David, the former police officer with South Bureau Narcotics in Los Angeles, told me that planting drugs on suspects was common. 'Sometimes when we stopped a guy, we'd search him thoroughly but couldn't find any drugs. So we figured that he must have dropped them when he saw us, and we'd go back and check the pathway. When we couldn't find anything, one of my partners would say, "Hey, *here* it is!" Well, after that I went to the Filing Team, where we used to take all the drug arrests to the District Attorney to be filed. We used to get a lot of reports that said "saw cop, dropped rock". We'd smile when we saw those reports.'

In 1998, forty-four officers from five law enforcement agencies in Cleveland were charged with taking money to protect cocaine-trafficking operations. There have also been cases of drug-related police corruption in Atlanta, Chicago, Detroit, Los Angeles and New Orleans. This corruption feeds on police officers' cynicism about the criminal justice system, their contempt for suspects, and their unquestioned loyalty to other officers. 'When you work dope, it's a whole different mental environment within the police department,' said David. 'You've got all kinds of cool cars. You've got lots of money so you can pay snitches to go out and work for you, and your time is pretty much your own. A lot of dope cops felt like they were a class above everybody else. You're working together and you have to be able to trust each other.'

Jack Cole freely admits that narcotics policing was brutal, corrupt, racist and ineffective. 'I knew it was bullshit, but I had my own addictions. I was addicted to the adrenaline rush of working these jobs. As you go up the ladder, you catch all the useless ones, but going up, you're getting to some really smart people. Had they been in a legitimate business, they'd have gone right to the top. Me and my partner worked our way up from an eighth of an ounce cocaine buy in a little bar in Union City, New Jersey, to a billion-dollar cocaine ring, what was at the time the largest cocaine-trafficking organization in the world. It was exciting.'

It was so exciting that the police became wholly engrossed by the primordial conflict between good and evil that they believed they were waging. In 2002, Detroit's Chief of Police Jerry Oliver admitted that 75 per cent of his department's budget was spent on fighting the drugs trade.[36] This has had important ramifications for other branches of law enforcement. In cities where police agencies commit the most resources to arresting their way out of their drug problems, the arrest rates for violent crime such as murder, rape and aggravated assault have declined. In Baltimore, drug arrests have skyrocketed over the past three decades, but arrest rates for murder have gone from 90 per cent to half that. Younger police officers are no longer capable of investigating crime properly, having learnt only to make meaningless drug arrests at the nearest corner.[37]

By 1989, three quarters of all cases heard in the criminal courts of Los Angeles were drug-related.[38] James Gray is the presiding judge of the Superior Court of Orange County, California, and has seen how counter-productive this narrow focus on policing the drugs trade has been. 'I'd have five or six members of the Santa Ana police department sitting outside my courtroom, waiting to testify in a case where they had a $20 purchase of cocaine from some schmuck who is basically an addict selling drugs to support his habit. You look at all the back-up for these undercover officers, the people surveilling them to make sure that they're safe, all the wiretaps, and then all of the reports. We're spending so much time and energy prosecuting low-level, non-violent drug offences that we don't have the resources to prosecute the really heavy-weight offences.'

Those arrested for violation of US drug laws find judges to be no less draconian than police officers. A genuine drug epidemic, combined with simple-mindedness, blind ignorance and an unrestrained rush to punish, ensured that a compulsive urge to pass new drug laws gripped the Congress that gathered in 1986. Eric Sterling described the passage of the $6 billion Anti-Drug Abuse Act that soon followed. 'At the beginning of July, the Speaker of the House, Tip O'Neill, the top elected Democrat in Washington, called the Steering and Policy Committee of the Democrats together and said, "We control the House. We are the chairs of every House committee. If we use this drug issue the right way, perhaps we can take the Senate in '86. I want the House to report out a comprehensive anti-drug bill." The first federal crack law was passed in 1986. I helped write it when I was counsel to the judiciary sub-committee on crime.'

The Anti-Drug Abuse Act 1986 stipulated that defendants would no longer be eligible for bail or parole. Prosecutors would be able to appeal sentences, a right that had previously been reserved for the defence. Congress also made twenty-six crimes, all related to drug sales and distribution, punishable by a mandatory minimum sentence. This proved to be the single most dramatic change ushered in by the anti-drugs legislation of 1986, one that inadvertently sent a generation of black American men to prison. Mandatory minimum sentences had first been passed by Congress for the crime of piracy in 1790. The fifty-eight mandatory minimum sentencing laws passed between then and 1986 are an indicator of the crimes most feared and loathed in their day, from 'the practise of pharmacy in China' in 1915, to 'treason and sedition' in the McCarthy era, to 'skyjacking' in the 1970s. After 1986, anyone found in possession of more than five grams of crack cocaine – even first-time offenders – was sent to prison for at least five years. The same defendant would have to have sold half a kilogram of cocaine powder to receive the same sentence. Bill Clinton's older brother Roger was sentenced to two years in prison in 1984 for selling cocaine. Had his case come to court after the mandatory minimums for crack- and cocaine-selling were made law, he would have received a ten-year term without parole. Had he sold the same quantity in crack form, he would have been looking at a life sentence.

There had been a clear need to set a benchmark because until 1986 judges had handed down wildly varying sentences for drug offences, usually according to the judges' political sympathies. But mandatory minimum sentences effectively took all power of discretion away from the judges. Mitigating factors such as a defendant's role in the crime, and the likelihood of recidivism were deemed unimportant. All power now rested with the prosecutor, who decided which charge to bring to court. Mandatory minimums were further encouragement for law enforcement agencies' targeting of the low-level foot soldiers of the cocaine economy instead of the major crime syndicates: less than 2 per cent of federal crack defendants were high-level suppliers of cocaine.[39] Thanks to this discrepancy in sentencing, small-time crack dealers regularly go to prison for longer than wholesale suppliers of cocaine powder. This has had a disproportionate impact on black drug sellers, because 88 per cent of those sentenced for crack distribution are black, whereas blacks make up only 27 per cent of those who go to jail for powder cocaine distribution. Mandatory minimums turned small-time drug dealers into lifers.

'I went to Sing Sing, a maximum security prison in upstate New York,' said Tony Papa, who was convicted on charges of distributing cocaine in the early 1970s. 'It was a total madhouse. I didn't know how I was going to survive. But I did, and in time I became a jailhouse attorney. Most of the guys were doing fifteen years to life, and they were either murderers or drug dealers. I thought, "This is crazy. This murderer got the same sentence as me." I met hundreds and hundreds of people that had been involved in drug activity, but I never met a kingpin or a high-end drug dealer. I just met a lot of pawns, who had been juggling to put food on the table for their families.'

Former Congressman Daniel Rostenkowski was given an insight into the effects of the mandatory minimum sentences that he had voted for in 1986, when he began a term in federal prison for mail fraud. 'I asked this young man, "What did you do that was so bad?" "Oh, I transported drugs," he said. I said, "Why would you do such a thing?" and he said, "Well, I was going to school, and I needed the money." "OK. And what was the price you sought for moving these drugs?" And he said, "$10,000." And I said, "What was your sentence?" and he said, "Seventeen years." And I said "My gosh!" The whole thing is a sham in my opinion. It's this "get 'em" idea. I was swept along by the rhetoric about getting tough on crime. Few of us had the patience or the courage to point out to the public that there was relatively little that changes in federal laws could do to reduce the violent crime in their neighbourhoods. So we acted, took our low bows and went on to other topics.'[40]

In 1993, the United States Sentencing Commission, which administers federal prison sentencing guidelines, tried to get Congress to return to the topic of mandatory minimums, when it proposed reducing the discrepancy between the prison terms given to crack sellers and the terms given to powder cocaine sellers. The Commission argued that crack was not appreciably different to cocaine powder in either its chemical composition or the physical reactions of its users. But for the first time in its history, Congress overrode the Commission's recommendation. Bill Clinton, who was President at the time, has since admitted his regret at not having done more to end the disparity in sentencing of powder and crack cocaine offenders, and has even said that he would be prepared to spend a significant portion of his life trying to make amends.[41] Not until 2007 did the Supreme Court rule that federal judges could impose shorter sentences for crack cocaine offences.[42] In an appeal case that came to court that year, Justice Ruth Bader Ginsburg said that a fifteen-year jail term given to Derrick Kimbrough, an African-American veteran of the first Gulf War, was acceptable, even though mandatory minimum sentencing guidelines called for Kimbrough to serve between nineteen and twenty-two years behind bars for his role in a crack-dealing operation. In the second case decided by the court, which did not involve cocaine, the justices upheld a sentence of probation for Brian Gall, who was white, for his role in a conspiracy to sell 10,000 ecstasy pills. There are no mandatory minimums for the possession or sale of ecstasy.[43]

Even without the system of mandatory minimum sentences, this inconsistency in the way the police and judges treat cocaine and crack cocaine dealers is apparent in the United Kingdom too. Julian de Vere Whiteway-Wilkinson was sent to prison for twelve years in 2004 for running a cocaine dealership from the old Truman's brewery in east London with three of his friends. Their computer records showed that they spent £7.6 million on cocaine in the course of a year. At their trial, the court heard that Whiteway-Wilkinson came from a prominent Devon family which had made its money in clay mines. Although he part-owned a plane, which he used to fly drugs into the UK, and drove a BMW, his declared earnings for 2002 were just £24,267. One of his partners, Milroy Nadarajah, told the Inland Revenue that he earned just £7,943 that year, despite having bought a £1.2 million house which the prosecution described as 'palatial', in front of which he parked his Porsche and his Jeep. Nadarajah owned a record label, and two recording studios where the theme tune for a James Bond film was recorded, set up with financial backing from Warner Brothers. In the house of the third partner, James Long, police found £1,000 in banknotes scattered over the floor; Long was said to find coins vulgar. Outside court, Detective Sergeant Mark Chapman said it was 'quite extraordinary' for men from such salubrious backgrounds to have become so deeply involved in the drugs trade.

Then you have the drug dealers whose involvement in the drugs trade the police do not find 'quite extraordinary'. In 2006, fourteen members of the 'Bling Bling' gang were jailed for smuggling about £50 million worth of cocaine into the UK in just two years.[44] The gang's members were mostly of Guyanese and Caribbean descent, but, as befitting their moniker, they had bases in London, Paris and New York. The gang brought the cocaine into the UK from the Caribbean, with the aid of either an accomplice working for DHL courier services or drug mules on passenger flights. Their mules used specially adapted shampoo or perfume containers and bottles of rum to smuggle the cocaine into Britain. Around three mules would be sent on each assignment; if one was picked up, the gang could still profit from the successful passage of the other two. Then they smuggled tens of thousands of pounds back to the Caribbean. The gang used their profits to fund a lavish lifestyle, buying diamond jewellery, designer cars and clothes, and villas in the Caribbean and West Africa. Police said that they had recovered receipts for goods totalling £450,000. Sixty-five of the gang's members around the world were imprisoned, including seventeen in the United Kingdom, twenty-five in France, thirteen in Guyana and ten in the United States. Ian 'Bowfoot' Dundas-Jones, judged to be the ringleader of the operation, was given a twenty-seven-year sentence and recommended for deportation. Judge Timothy King said the gang was part of a 'global conspiracy motivated by greed' that had created 'untold misery and human degradation'.

The explosive growth in the number of prisons in the United States is not the result of a campaign against misery and degradation, however, but of a rush to punish the poor. In 1990, the House Armed Services Committee demonstrated some of the vindictiveness that drives the war on drugs when it came up with the idea of shipping convicted drug offenders to the tiny Pacific islands of Medway and Wake. Citing the 'shortage of space available for convicted drug offenders', the committee proposed that the islands be turned into drug prisons where inmates could be put to work. 'There's not much chance they're going to get anything but rehabilitated on two small islands like these,' said Richard Ray, the Democrat Congressman who first floated the idea. 'They won't be interrupted by families coming to visit every weekend.'[45]

In the early 1970s there were 200,000 Americans in jail. Today there are 1.8 million,[46] and another 5 million are either on probation or parole. This makes the American penal system the largest in the world, and indeed, the largest in history.[47] Twenty-five per cent of the world's prisoners are American, even though Americans only make up 5 per cent of the world's population. Half a million Americans are in prison on drugs-related charges, which exceeds the number of people serving sentences in European prisons for all crimes – and Europe has 90 million more people than the United States. In cities like El Paso, where cocaine trafficking is rife, the proportion of prisoners serving time for drugs offences rises to 70 per cent.[48]

The combination of police anti-drug operations focused on the inner city, and long mandatory sentences for those found guilty of crack distribution offences, has ensured that nearly all of the drug prisoners in the state of New York are black or Latino.[49] By the millennium, a third of all African-American men in the US were in prison, on probation or parole or under some other form of criminal justice system supervision.[50] The proportion of black Americans behind bars is larger than the proportion of black South Africans imprisoned by the apartheid regime in South Africa. In 2008, more black men in their twenties were under the control of the nation's criminal justice system than the total number in higher education.

More than half of the United States' prisons have been built in the last twenty years and the prison system has developed its own peculiar self-perpetuating dynamic as it has grown to become a major employer. One of America's best-known crack dealers is Kenneth 'Supreme' McGriff. McGriff is held in ADX Florence prison in Colorado, a maximum security facility that was opened in 1994, at a cost of $60 million. Although Fremont County already had nine prisons, hundreds attended the ground-breaking. The lure of 900 permanent jobs, in addition to another 1,000 temporary jobs to be had in building the prison, encouraged local residents to set the ball rolling by raising $160,000 to purchase 600 acres for the new facility. 'Some of those upstate New York towns like Clinton Dannemora are built around the prison,' Tony Papa told me. 'You know, the prison came first, then the town. They were built mainly in Republican territories, and you have generations of prison guards in those towns. So they fed their communities by filling the prisons with people from the inner cities. It became their cash cow and politicians used to fight each other to build the next prison. That's why the laws are very hard to change.'

Incarceration might satisfy the punitive zeal of American politicians. It certainly provides employment to plenty of their electors. But it does not deter people from using drugs. Doris was a daily cocaine user in Harlem, New York City, for twenty years. 'I hear stories of people sitting on the bar-stool, with their pinky up in the air, or of how cocaine was glamorous at first but then it changed, but I never had a glamorous drug story. Mine started out in the basement with hard-core junkies. From the age of nineteen to the age of thirty-nine, I was a daily user, shop-lifting, going in and out of detoxes, treatment centres and jail, doing what we call skid bids. If the last one was four months, the judge would say, "this time you're getting six months!" I'd get out of jail, and go right out and get high again.'

Nor does incarceration seem likely to deter people from selling drugs. When the breadwinner goes to prison, families are broken up. Single-parent families find it particularly hard to avoid falling into poverty: as bills go unpaid and debts mount, people move house, resulting in less cohesive neighbourhoods.[51] Children whose parents are in prison often feel shame, humiliation and a loss of social status. Many of those children begin to act up in school or distrust authority figures, who represent the people who took their parent away.[52] The negative consequences of high incarceration rates in some communities may actually lead to increases in crime in those communities as the children of the incarcerated join the next generation of offenders.

I asked Luis Rodriguez, a former gang member from Los Angeles, about how the mania for incarceration had affected his neighbourhood. 'The prison system just seems to be a boot on the neck of these poor communities. Drugs continue. You can get drugs anywhere, any time. The law doesn't stop that. It just puts away a lot of people who shouldn't be in prison. There's no rehabilitation, no training, no real education for the most part, so these guys just get trained to become even better at the drug trade. Our tax dollars are just going to the training of more sophisticated criminals!'

'You can get over an addiction, but you'll never get over a conviction,' Jack Cole of Law Enforcement Against Prohibition told me. 'Every time you go for a job, it's hanging over your head like a big ugly cloud. The only place that wants you is right back in the drug culture, the very group that we say we're trying to save you from!' Three and a half million people will be released from prisons in the United States between 2000 and 2010, and an additional 500,000 each year thereafter. Such large-scale releases of prisoners, many of whom are unskilled, some of whom cannot even read and write, is bound to have a negative impact on wages. Wages are already low in deprived urban areas since reform of the welfare system in 1996 severely reduced former felons' access to welfare money.[53] By sustaining poverty, marginalization and neglect, the war on drugs perpetuates the very problems it was supposed to alleviate.

'I joined the Department of Corrections in Florence, Arizona, in 1973,' Rusty told me. 'Then I went out and worked the oilfields, but I went back into the system in 1988 to run the narc dog team and the track attack dogs. The dogs were there to try and keep the drugs out of the prison. My mind was good with that – you've already made a mistake, you're in prison, and you're not allowed those things. Now, we had forty-foot walls, gun towers, every technology known to mankind, but drugs were still the number one problem we had in the joint. If you can't keep them out of a totally controlled environment, how realistic is it to tell the American people that we can keep them out of the country? That's straight-up bullshit.'

Yet that is the fundamental premise of the war on drugs. President Nixon spent $16 million a year on his war on drugs in the early 1970s. In 2007, President George W. Bush's government spent more than $18 billion fighting the same war.[54] Spending on anti-drugs policies increased by a third under the Bush administration, and half of that was spent on domestic law enforcement. Combined expenditure by federal, state and local governments on counter-drugs programmes currently exceeds $30 billion a year, and that doesn't include the cost of incarcerating drug offenders.[55] All told, over the past thirty-five years, the United States has spent approximately $500 billion fighting its war on drugs.[56]

The highest cost of the war on drugs, however, is not economic but political. Once out of prison, felons find themselves politically as well as economically marginalized because the United States is the only industrial democracy that denies ex-prisoners the right to vote. In Southern states, as many as 30 per cent of black men are barred from voting. This has ensured that arch-conservative candidates have won successive elections in the south. Felony disenfranchisement was the key to George W. Bush's victory in the presidential elections of 2000, which hinged on a recount of 537 disputed votes in the state of Florida.

Two hundred thousand Floridians had been denied the vote that year. Most of them were black, and most of them would in all likelihood have voted for the Democrats' candidate, Al Gore.[57] Had so many Democrats been denied the vote in 1961, J. F. Kennedy would not have been elected President. 'It's modern-day slavery,' Kenneth, a former crack seller from Dothan, Alabama, told me. 'I don't care how they cook it, slice it, bake it, sauté or simmer it, that's what it is.'

The Anti-Drug Abuse Act of 1986 gave the police and the courts licence to prosecute a war on the suppliers of drugs. But it also sidelined doctors and teachers from the making of drug policies and replaced them with 'drug warrior' politicians. The mundane job of educating drug users about the risks they incur when they take drugs was deemed to 'send the wrong message'. The 'right message' was the one carried by Parents Against Drugs, whose head, Dr Donald Ian MacDonald, went on to head the Alcohol, Drug Abuse and Mental Health Administration. MacDonald was a staunch drug warrior with no training in or experience of drug treatment, who was nevertheless made drug tsar in 1987. Like many conservatives of his generation, he saw drug use as a cultural affliction, part of a wider challenge to authority inculcated at Woodstock. This outdated and simplistic explanation of the demand for drugs did little to address problematic drug use while making teenagers with any experience of drugs even more mistrustful of the little drug education they received. Very often, that education extended no further than a repetition of the 'Just Say No' mantra.

Those who said 'yes' to drug use would be punished. As the punishment failed to deter the crime, it became still more draconian. In 1998, Congressman Mark Souder tabled an amendment to the Higher Education Act of 1965, which had provided grants and loans to students who otherwise wouldn't be able to afford higher education. The Souder amendment denied financial aid to any student with a drug conviction. Since 2000, 200,000 students have been denied financial assistance because of prior drug felonies.[58] Rapists, muggers and murderers were not affected by the amendment, nor were those found guilty of crimes committed while under the influence of alcohol. After a lot of criticism, Souder amended his amendment in 2006; today it applies only to those who have violated drug laws while enrolled as students.

The anti-drugs message was carried from schools into the workplace. In 1995, 78 per cent of America's employers did some sort of testing for illegal drugs; by 2004, the percentage had dropped to 62 per cent. Many companies now admit that they drug-test their employees not because they want to, but because the government mandates them to do so.[59] The United States still spends $1 billion a year to drug-test about 20 million of its workers.[60] As well as being expensive, drug tests can have unintended consequences, as Rusty, the former Department of Corrections narcotics officer, told me. 'In the Dallas area, we've lost twenty-two kids to "cheese". It's a mixture of heroin and Tylenol. One of the reasons that kids are doing cheese is that the authorities are testing for pot in schools. Pot is bulky and it smells, but this stuff is about the size of an aspirin. The kids can snort it, some of the older ones mainline it, and it's killing them.' Drug warriors might argue that such deaths are the unfortunate but inevitable price to be paid for sending 'the right message'.

4

Cutting off the Lizard's Tail

*Woe unto them that . . . follow strong drink; that continue
until night, till wine inflame them!*   Isaiah 5: 11

The crack epidemic seemed to be both completely destructive and
completely resistant to intervention. Marc spent his teenage years
selling crack cocaine in South Jamaica, Queens: 'As a child growing
up there was no way to escape being around drugs. It was just something that the adults in the community did. You were a child and you
stayed in a child's place. Sadly, the streets become a rite of passage,
so when it's time to become a man, that's how it gets established in
our community.'

At the start of 1995, leading experts predicted an explosion in crime
in the years to come. The rate at which young people were killing
one another was expected to double by the millennium, prompting
Professor James Alan Fox, one of the most widely quoted criminol-
ogists in the popular press, to say that 'the next crime wave will get
so bad that it will make 1995 look like the good old days'.[1] President
Clinton sounded equally pessimistic when he said, 'we've got about
six years to turn this juvenile crime thing around, or our country is
going to be living with chaos.'[2]

But instead, and quite without warning, crime fell sharply in the
United States in the late 1990s, in all categories and all over the
nation. Homicide rates fell to their lowest levels for thirty-five years.
Wrong-footed by the sudden onslaught of peace on American streets,
the pundits struggled for explanations. Some cited the ageing of the

population, others the new and tougher gun control laws, and still others the strong economy. Steven Levitt, author of *Freakonomics*, has looked at the relative merits of the explanations given, and found that most do not hold water. He found that there is in fact little relationship between unemployment rates and property crimes. Nor is widespread gun ownership a determining factor in the number of crimes committed. There are approximately 65 million handguns in the United States, but only one in 10,000 of them was used to kill somebody in 1999. Many Americans like to think that the death penalty is an effective crime deterrent, and the evidence suggests that to some extent it is, but even on death row, the probability of being executed in any given year is only 2 per cent. Members of the Chicago street gang that Steven Levitt studied before writing *Freakonomics* had a 7 per cent chance of being killed while selling drugs in any given year, which didn't seem to deter them from going into the crack game.[3]

Increases in the number of police officers and the number of people sent to jail certainly played a significant role in reducing crime in the United States in the 1990s. New York City led the list of cities experiencing this 'crime drop', with a 73 per cent decline in the number of homicides between 1991 and 2001.[4] The New York City Police Department grew in size by 45 per cent over the same period, an increase three times greater than the national average. But neither was likely to affect drug sales or drug use.[5]

Levitt found an interesting and frequently overlooked factor that went a long way to explain falling crime rates: the legalization of abortion in 1973. Children born because their mothers were denied an abortion are substantially more likely to be involved in crime, even when taking account of the income, age, education and health of the mother. After 1973, far fewer unwanted children were born, as more women chose to have abortions. Between 1985 (when an unwanted child born in 1973 would have turned twelve) and 1997 (when he or she would have turned twenty-four), homicide rates fell by a quarter in states with high rates of abortion but *increased* by 4 per cent in states with low rates of abortion.

But the development that accounts for the largest part of the decline in crime rates is the one that seems to have elicited least comment, and that is the maturation of the crack economy and the sheer exhaustion resulting from ten years of extreme criminal violence. 'We don't understand a lot of things until they affect us,' Ricky Ross told me. 'Around '86, I started to question myself. Until then, I had been so far removed from the streets. I was selling to dealers with $400,000 of their own, so I really didn't see the suffering. But I started to see my cousins getting strung out, and then my aunties, my baby-mama, you know, people that I cared about, and it started to affect me.'

For twenty years, Doris's life had been ruled by her craving for cocaine. She told me that she was part of the generation of drug users in Harlem that graduated from heroin to cheap, widely available cocaine in the early 1980s. 'Most of my friends are dead. A lot of them died from AIDS, from shooting up. A lot of them just died from the street life. It destroyed so many families. I know so many people whose children are in the prison system because of crack, because they put the drug ahead of their kids. I adopted my niece's son because she was so cracked out that she couldn't keep her kids.'

Young people like Marc, who had been selling crack in South Jamaica, Queens, since he was a child, reacted to the violence of the crack business, the personal devastation wrought and the incarceration of whole communities by turning their backs on crack.[6] 'In 1990 I was sixteen years old. That was the height of the crack epidemic. New York was knee-deep in crack vials. I saw my older cousins, who were fourteen or fifteen years older than me, doing it. We were the first generation to see what this shit was really about. For us, it was completely off-limits, and it is to this day. We were like "smoking that shit? Are you crazy?"'

Many young people had spent the late 1980s living with unremitting hedonism, violence and fatalism. Almost a third of Bushwick's eighteen to twenty-one year olds reported having been caught in a random shoot-out, and almost a quarter said that they had been shot at or threatened with a gun. Some young people reacted to the violence by staying off the streets entirely. Javier, from Bushwick, was sixteen in 1993. 'About ten of the people I grew up with got killed and I think I grew up ahead of my time. Most of the time you find me with people who are like mid-thirties, forty years old. I feel safer, you know? I don't have to deal with what's going on in the street. Once in a while I'll hang out with one of the fellas I grew up with, but then you try and draw back, 'cause you don't want to get caught up in what he's doing, especially if the police are looking for him.'[7]

'He takes it hard,' Doris said of her nephew. 'You love your mother, even if she is sleeping in a basement and smoking crack. These children have seen their parents be called crack-heads, they've seen the devastation, and they don't want any part of it. For them, it's heavy, heavy marijuana smoking.' Neither the rise of the crack economy, nor the war on drugs could put young people off drug-taking for good. In 1999, more than half the students of the United States had tried an illegal drug of some kind. The marijuana drought that kick-started the crack economy had not lasted long, and by the late 1990s, marijuana was cheaper and more readily available than ever; 82 per cent of high school seniors said that they found it easy to get their hands on marijuana.[8] Teenage marijuana smokers began cussing crack users for their compulsiveness and even assaulting them out of sheer spite. Young crack users weaned themselves off the drug by smoking first wulla joints, a regular marijuana joint laced with crack cocaine, and then the Philly blunt, a joint rolled in the tobacco casing of a cigar, which became the sanitized offspring of the wulla joint.

Most of the big crack-selling organizations had completely disregarded the welfare of the people they employed and the customers they served. Many teenagers had served sentences for crack distribution, during which time their employers had not bailed them out, hired lawyers to defend them, or looked after their families. Ariel had been selling crack in New York City when he was arrested. While in prison on Rikers Island, he reflected on the business. 'My foster mother spoke to the owner and asked if he could bail me out. My bail was only $5,000. At that time, I had $10,000 out in the streets that different people owed me. He said "Well, whoever works for me and gets arrested has got to be a man. Do the crime, do the time." That right there pissed me off. Five thousand dollars? You're telling me that you couldn't bail me out? I don't want to hear that.'[9]

Abandoned to the criminal justice system, many young crack sellers formed gangs to protect one another from violence in prison. Aside from the protection they offered their members, many of these gangs highlighted the importance of family and community, the destructive effects of violence and drugs, and the urgent need to foster some pride in their communities. From 1993, young Puerto Ricans in New York City underwent something of a rebirth. 'Before I was a Latin King, I used to sell drugs a lot in school,' said Ariel. 'During my time on Rikers Island, I started seeing the light more and wanted to follow a more spiritual path. It's not all about selling drugs any more. It's about giving back to the community. I want to stay in the young tribe to help my younger brothers, to let them know that gang-banging is not the way of life. Believe me, I know it, and it's time for another path.'[10] Gangs have been cited as justification for the tough law enforcement approach to dealing with participants in the crack economy, but gangs such as the Latin Kings and the Ñetas were instrumental in encouraging their young members to 'uplift' their communities on their return. Many gangs struggled to impose some semblance of order on what had become an unmanageable situation, as part of a return to the values of 'brown pride' that drugs and the war on drugs had done so much to corrode.

Luis Rodriguez's memories of the spirit of community organization that had animated Latino barrios in the 1970s encouraged him to reconsider the purpose of the gangs. 'Many of the gangs now refuse to call themselves gangs. They are street associations. They're trying to eliminate drugs from the communities, which is very difficult when the dealers are their padres and soldiers from the streets, and drugs are still often the only way to pay the rent.' Hence the Bloods and the Crips, two of the most feared gangs in the United States, have been renamed 'Brotherly Love Over-riding Oppressive Destruction' and 'Community Revolution In Progress' respectively by members determined to salvage something of worth from the havoc wreaked by the drug economy. This revival of popular self-help organizations, led by older gang members and adopted by younger members, explains why gangs became more powerful just as violent crime started to fall.

As the epidemic stabilized and crack cocaine stories fell off the front pages, a rapprochement of sorts was reached between the legal and the illegal economies. Many drug sellers were in prison and many drug users were in shelters for vagrants. Others left the city, were hospitalized or died. The process of collapse that had begun when the inner-city neighbourhoods lost their industrial base, reached a frantic and gory end as the unemployed stripped everything that could be sold to buy crack. The takings were hoovered up by crack dealers and ultimately reinvested in more productive parts of the country. An expensive Italian restaurant built in what had until then been a drugs market near the waterfront in Williamsburg, New York City, speaks volumes about the processes at work. It was financed by a loan from the Bank of Commerce and Credit International (BCCI), now defunct but renowned at the time for offering a safe haven to fortunes made from the drugs business. The Panama City branch of BCCI had been the principal repository for money raised by the Nicaraguan Contras through sales of crack cocaine on the streets of Los Angeles.[11] The restaurant soon became a beacon for developers looking to exploit sky-high property prices in Lower Manhattan. Sales of crack cocaine on the West Coast inadvertently paid for the redevelopment of what had been a prime crack-selling site on the East Coast.

Selling crack is still a daily operation in the United States. Even with the waning of the crack epidemic in the early 1990s, police forces kept a tight lid on inner-city communities by implementing zero tolerance policies. Between 1993 and 1996, arrests for serious crimes in New York City rose just 5 per cent, but arrests for minor offences such as marijuana smoking, jaywalking, riding a bicycle on the pavement and drinking in public almost doubled, and young drug offenders were sent to prison in ever greater numbers.[12]

Zero tolerance policies have not put an end to drug dealing. Instead, drug markets have become more discreet, integrating themselves further into local communities as the police have regained control of the streets. Today, most drugs in most markets are sold through closed systems: drug sales are less likely to be conducted on street corners or in drug-houses, and more likely to be arranged by mobile phone, with runners making deliveries to private houses. The gentrification of inner-city neighbourhoods proceeds apace in cities across the United

States, but the appearance of sobriety is deceptive, as a bar worker in New York City's Lower East Side attested. 'There's richer people living in this neighbourhood, where ten years ago you still had the arty farty freaks who could sort of afford to live here. Now, you don't have that much of a street style, you know? What you have now is a gated community that lives in their apartments and that totally caters to a delivery clientele. I would say that the availability of drugs is higher than it was.'[13]

In Williamsburg, New York City's archetypal derelict-turned-hip neighbourhood, cocaine dealers like Rico have had to move with the times. 'The police made my business. They created it. Before, there was a line of people standing on the street, waiting to cop out of the door of a building. You could buy it like it was a supermarket. Who'd bother to call me on the beeper? But when the police destroyed them, they created my business.'[14]

The key drivers of the cocaine economy have not changed since the early 1980s. When neither the public nor the private sector will provide jobs, people have to create work for themselves. In Milwaukee, Wisconsin, for example, 40 per cent of adult men have been self-employed at some point in their working lives, and start-up companies account for almost a quarter of all new jobs.[15] Some are legal ventures, but in poor neighbourhoods most new businesses stay off the books. Streetside car repairs, hairdressing, babysitting, and house painting are usually too insecure a way of making a livelihood for their practitioners to survive without other family income. Nearly all of them are hindered by low incomes, inadequate training, paltry social networks linking them to market opportunities, and problems securing loans.

These new enterprises include the business of selling drugs. The cocaine business has proved to be a lifeline for plenty of Americans who would otherwise be without a job. In Milwaukee, at least 10 per cent of all young male Latinos and African-Americans make money from the drug economy, and the rate is higher in bigger cities. Bolo, a cocaine seller from Bushwick, attests to the sheer ordinariness of selling drugs for a living. 'Most of the fellas who work for me need the money. I mean, I'll be honest with you, I'm not going to bring in a kid who just needs money to buy a pair of sneakers. I'll bring a guy with me who has to support his family. I told everybody, "nobody here is getting rich. All we are doing is surviving." '[16]

Talk of the 'crazy money' to be made selling crack cocaine was wearing thin even in 1988, when crack selling was at its height. That year, the average earnings of retail drug dealers in Washington DC were estimated to be no more than $28,000 a year.[17] Street-level sellers earn roughly the federal minimum wage, which at the time of writing stood at $6.55 per hour, so most of them have low-paid legal jobs too. Even among senior dealers, more than a quarter also have legitimate jobs to make ends meet, a third report gross receipts from drug sales of less than $500 a month, and just one in six reports receipts of more than $5,000 a month. The stereotypical 'drug baron' and the outlandish fantasies of enrichment that created him are the staple fare of tabloid leader writers, but the personification of wealth and vice in one individual masks the reality of widespread, low-level drug dealing. More than 60 per cent of the revenues from America's drug economy go to the low-level wholesalers and retailers who make up the bulk of the drug economy's workforce.[18] Senior members of drug-dealing organizations generally take no more than 25 per cent of total revenues.

Despite the gap between the mythical wealth of the cocaine kingpin and the average earnings of an ordinary drug dealer, the drugs business is an equal opportunity employer that offers relatively good pay to the unskilled. Driving a car loaded with cocaine from El Paso to Chicago can earn the driver $10,000.[19] Plenty of young city dwellers prefer the crack game to stacking shelves, flipping burgers, or travelling to work in outlying areas populated mainly by people perceived to be unfriendly.[20] This reluctance to engage in menial labour has been one cause of a profound generational split. Young white men in the nineteenth century were urged to 'go west, young man' to seek their fortunes. During much of the last thirty years circumstances seemed to be urging young black and Hispanic men to 'go bad, young man' in pursuit of the same goal.[21] 'When I was young, all I was told was that I was going to end up dead or in jail,' Marc, who had sold crack cocaine in South Jamaica, Queens, in his teenage years, told me. 'That was the extent of the conversation. I was a teenager, I was struggling emotionally, all of that stuff, and I was like "Fuck you very much, and let whatever's going to happen, happen." '

The violence of the cocaine economy has waned as the war on drugs has evolved to become a war of attrition. In the early 1990s, drug gangs would often resort to gun-fights with their rivals, but as the most efficient operators came to the fore, relations between suppliers stabilized. A dealer from Chicago told Steven Levitt: 'We try to tell these shorties that they belong to a serious organization. It ain't all about killing. They see these movies and they think it's all about running around tearing shit up. But it's not. You gotta learn how to be part of an organization, you can't be fighting all the time. It's bad for business.'[22] A study of Milwaukee's drug entrepreneurs found that none reported having daily problems with violence. More than a quarter of all the drug businesses in the city see no violence at all.

Most of them have problems with the police no more than once a month and a quarter reported no problems with police at all. Lance, also from South Jamaica, Queens, had a twenty-five-year run as a cocaine wholesaler. 'Of course there's a lot of risk involved, and if you live the fast-money life, being real flamboyant, wearing a lot of loud jewellery and driving the most expensive car you can find, you're drawing attention to yourself. But if you carry yourself like the average nine to five working person, not dressing extravagantly or wearing Rolexes, you can have your home, your nice car in the garage and your run-around car, and you can remain under the radar.'

As drug dealers slip under the radar, prohibition has become harder to enforce than ever, but its advocates remain undeterred. In 1973, the Nixon administration declared that the nation had 'turned the corner on addiction and drug use'. In 1990, drug tsar William Bennett claimed that it was 'on the road to victory' over drug abuse.[23] An article written by John Burnham and published in the *Columbus Dispatch* in 2006 went a step further, arguing that the war on drugs had been won. At a reunion on the thirty-fifth anniversary of the appointment of the United States' first drug tsar in 1971, 'the seven former tsars held remarkably unanimous views, though they included Democrats and Republicans, and had worked for five very different presidents. The main conclusion – that we won the war on drugs –

was the biggest surprise, because advocates of illegal drugs have in recent years filled the media with rhetoric about "the failed war on drugs".[24] When asked for his reaction to the article, Lee Brown, who served as Bill Clinton's drug tsar, said, 'I do not recall anyone, especially me, reaching the conclusion that we have won the war on drugs.' In response to the article, one columnist wrote: 'If drug warriors want to declare victory and go home, I'm all for it. But to claim that you've won, and maintain the same policy that spends billions and locks up millions and has virtually no effect on either drug use rates, drug-related harm or addiction rates? What have you been smoking?'

In reality, cocaine, whether in powder or crack form, remains widely available all over the United States. A stable cocaine market, a nascent market in methamphetamines, increasing abuse of prescription drugs, and millions of Americans smoking marijuana grown in the United States, show the war on drugs to have failed on its own terms. Yet the battle goes on. The country's police officers remain on a war footing, partly because of the onus politicians have put on a militarized response to the inner-city drug economy, and partly because after two decades spent building up armies of paramilitary squads, the police have an apparatus to maintain. Moral crusades lead to wars on abstractions. Once displaced from the ground to the ether, they can be spun to suggest that they have been won, dragged out indefinitely or even that they never existed.

I have focused on the rise of cocaine in the United States because its government's influence at the United Nations has ensured that the American experience of cocaine has had an overwhelming influence on how the drug is regarded in other countries around the world. The question of how best to manage recreational and problematic drug use in the United Kingdom rarely inspires the messianic zeal characteristic of the debate in the United States. Unofficially, opinion among the New Labour establishment is blasé about recreational drug use, though official disapproval is as strong as ever. When Cabinet Minister Clare Short suggested a debate over the legal status of cannabis, she was severely rebuked by then Prime Minister Tony Blair, who sensed the public mood rather better: a Mori poll of 1997 found that only

21 per cent of Britons favoured the legalization of marijuana. *Tackling Drugs to Build a Better Britain*, a policy document published in 1998, remains at the core of the UK's drug policy. It set clear numerical targets, including, for example, a 50 per cent reduction in drug use among young people by 2008.[25] It also established four strategic objectives: to reduce the availability of drugs at street level in the UK; to reduce the prevalence of the use of illegal drugs, particularly among young people; to reduce the crime committed by drug users to fund their purchases; and to increase the number of people receiving treatment for drug problems.

The purpose of drug policy in the United Kingdom has changed as more drugs are consumed, and the public's objections to drug use have become less moralistic and more driven by public health concerns. This puts great strain on the existing legislation, precisely because it has so little grounding in science or medicine. The public is increasingly tolerant of all kinds of 'lifestyle choices', including the use of soft drugs. The criminalization of drug consumption is taken by growing numbers of people to be counter-productive and ineffectual, notwithstanding their opposition to drug legalization. Once away from the glare of publicity, the prevailing attitude of the authorities in the UK seems to be one of resignation. 'We manage the drugs problem,' a local policeman told the authors of a Home Office survey of drug dealing in deprived neighbourhoods. 'We will never clear this country of drugs, ever. We manage what we've got. We tend to react to it so that we can keep a lid on it and it doesn't get any worse than it already is because it is pretty damn bad now. And we do, we just manage it.'

The British police enforce the drug laws in an environment of low public confidence. All over the UK, local residents demonstrate a reluctance to trust, an unwillingness to engage with, and a general dissatisfaction with the performance of the police. The situation is worse in the big cities, where the targeting of black people has rebounded on the police, and the police are too timorous to deal with the issues as they relate to black people, having taken a hammering in the Stephen Lawrence Inquiry report and then from critical media coverage of racism in the police force.[26]

British counter-drugs operations are also hampered, as in the United States, by the practice of allocating resources according to the police's success in meeting performance targets. Numerical targets for tackling drug offences are easier to achieve than those for burglary, robbery and car crime, but whereas the arrest of a burglar might lead to a reduction in burglary, the arrest of a drug dealer doesn't necessarily lead to a reduction in the availability of illegal drugs. In only one in eight neighbourhoods known to have a drugs problem has police activity been found to have reduced the supply of drugs.

The global prohibition of drugs like cocaine rests on a simple theory: by making the supply and possession of a drug illegal, it becomes less available, so prices rise, thereby putting it out of the reach of most consumers. Blind faith in this theory is the only explanation for the United States' National Drug Control Strategy, which proposed to reduce illegal drug use and availability by 50 per cent over the ten years up to 2007.[27] Drug use *did* fall during the 1980s and 1990s, despite the fact that the drugs were getting cheaper. By 2005, however, Americans were consuming drugs in much the same quantities they were when Nancy Reagan first exhorted them to 'Just Say No' in 1984.[28] What has changed is not the overall level of drug use, but the drugs Americans choose to take.

Tougher sanctions have little deterrent effect on those who choose to use or sell illegal drugs.[29] Harsher drug law enforcement just increases property crime by hard-core drug users, as the inflated cost of drugs drives their hunger for money, while the marginalization of drug users and ex-offenders keeps them out of the legal job market. The simple, bitter truth is that wherever the demand for illicit drugs has remained constant, the market has adapted to and then overcome law enforcement.[30] For example, a large-scale police crackdown on a very public drug market in Vancouver, Canada, led to no reduction in the availability or prices of drugs in the city. Initially, the increase in the number of police officers on the street made it more difficult to buy drugs, but the trade soon moved to other neighbourhoods, where it quickly re-established itself. A study of cannabis users in Amsterdam, Bremen and San Francisco found that cannabis use was very similar in these three cities, despite the local police having radically different drugs policies. In none was the chance of being arrested for smoking cannabis estimated to be very high.[31] This finding goes a long way in explaining why so few drug users actively oppose drugs policy in the Netherlands, Germany or the United States. Most cannabis users would welcome a relaxation of the laws regarding cannabis use, but the majority does not think that the law really matters. Anti-drugs laws have had little impact on their drug use, which in all three countries seems to have peaked in the 1970s, declined in the late 1980s, and been on the rise again since the mid-1990s.

In 1936, August Vollmer, former President of the National Association of Chiefs of Police in the United States, said that 'drug addiction never has been, and never can be solved by policemen. It is first and last a medical problem, and if there is a solution it will be discovered not by policemen, but by competently trained medical experts whose sole objective will be the reduction and possible eradication of this devastating appetite.'[32] A survey of 22,000 chiefs of police in the United States conducted in 2004 found that 67 per cent of them believed that their drug enforcement efforts 'have been unsuccessful in reducing the drug problem', and 37 per cent of them called for a 'fundamental overhaul' of those policies.[33] 'If you get them off by themselves, about 80 per cent of cops will agree that it ain't working and that we need to do something else,' Rusty, the former Department of Corrections narcotics officer told me. 'But they can't stand up and say that because it would be political suicide.'

Agencies trying to describe and address drug use have succumbed to the vocabulary of war, with its enemies, allies, resolutions and victories.[34] But there can be no *war* on drugs, because drug users and sellers are not an army. They cannot win, nor can they be defeated. Successive governments have prided themselves on what can be seen in hindsight to be no more than shifts in the arrangement of players in the drugs trade. Lee Dogoloff, who was President Carter's principal drug policy adviser, has echoed Vollmer's assessment. 'Despite repeated demonstrations that comprehensive treatment-on-demand programs reduce the demand for drugs, we fail to translate that learning into the federal drug strategy budget. Isn't it time to make drug abuse and mental health treatment available to all who seek it?'

Suffice it to say, police officers found to have a drug problem are not criminalized. In Chicago, a police officer who tests positive for drug use is regarded as having a medical problem and treated as such. In New York City, an officer who fails a drug test is dismissed. In no police department is a positive drug test result treated as a criminal offence. Politicians and their families have also largely escaped prosecution for using illegal drugs. George W. Bush and Bill Clinton have admitted using illegal drugs, and Barack Obama trumped them both when he admitted that he used marijuana and cocaine as a student. What none will admit is that they tried an illegal drug and enjoyed it. An exception to the rule was the late Betty Ford, the wife of former President Gerald Ford. 'I liked alcohol. It made me feel warm. And I loved pills. They took away my tension and my pain,' Ford wrote in her 1987 memoir *Betty: A Glad Awakening*. In 1978, the Ford family staged an intervention and forced Betty to confront her alcoholism and her addiction to opioid analgesics that had first been prescribed for a pinched nerve in the early 1960s. Betty Ford went on to establish the Betty Ford Center, probably the world's best-known centre for the treatment of substance abuse.

Despite these admissions, the privately held opinions of police officers charged with prosecuting this war on drugs and the drug policy reforms adopted at state level, ending the extreme penalization of drug use in the United States has become a 'third-rail' issue, one deemed to be too sensitive to broach by any politician. The budget afforded the war on drugs seems to escape any rational scrutiny. Its aims and methods go unquestioned, the roots of illicit drug consumption and distribution are wilfully ignored, and alternatives to the criminalization of drug users are routinely dismissed out of hand. In the run-up to the presidential election of 2008, the Democratic Party leadership made it clear that the party would 'govern from the centre'. Real change, and the imagination and conviction needed to realize it, was not on the agenda. Neither Barack Obama nor John McCain campaigned for changes in sentencing disparity, the use of marijuana for medical purposes, or US policy towards Colombia, Mexico, Jamaica, or anywhere else affected by the drugs trade.

Twenty-five years ago, illegal drugs were usually first or second and certainly never lower than fourth in polls of public concerns in the United States. Now the drugs issue trails many others. The country's political agenda is dominated by the wars in Iraq and Afghanistan and the measures introduced to manage the recession. The only other domestic issues likely to intrude are healthcare reform and illegal immigration. Scare stories about drugs have passed their sell-by dates. In New York City, the crack scare that so gripped the press in the 1980s came to a swift end once the police had been granted the resources to take back the city's streets. That done, coverage of drug use and drug markets became onerous and unhelpful. After then Mayor Rudy Giuliani adopted a policy of withholding information about drug-related homicides and counter-drugs operations from the press, drug stories fell off the front pages.

If cocaine is no longer the cause for concern it once was, it is because the ritual punishment of the guilty is complete, the government has run out of ideas to curtail the supply of cocaine, and too many people like things the way they are. I asked Judge James Gray who he thought benefited from the war on drugs. 'I have five groups. The first is the big-time drug dealers. They're making billions of dollars a year, tax-free. The second is law enforcement, who are in effect paid huge tax money to fight the first group. It's unbelievable, but the good guys and the bad guys have a mutual interest in the perpetuation of the status quo. The third group that is winning is the politicians, who talk tough about the war on drugs – which gets them elected and re-elected. The fourth group is those in the private sector who make money from increased crime – the people that build and staff prisons, the people that sell burglar alarms and security services. There's big money in all of that. And the fifth group is the terrorists, because almost all of the primary funding for terrorism around the world comes from the sale of illegal drugs.'

Whilst waiting to meet a DEA press officer in the lobby of their headquarters in Washington DC, I happened across a guide to 'Target America: Traffickers, Terrorists and You', an exhibition curated by the DEA Museum in 2002. 'The exhibit opens with a sculpture composed of rubble and artefacts from the World Trade Center and the Pentagon. It uses the events of September 11th as a starting point for the historic story of the connection between the violent drug trade and terror from the Silk Road in the eleventh century to the present.' This elision of two very distinct phenomena seems strange, until you consider the inertia and instinct for self-preservation of the huge bureaucracies involved. Drugs policy is no longer a matter for politicians. It is handled by an army of bureaucrats, in jealous defence of their enormous budgets. There are fifty government agencies fighting the war on drugs in the United States.[35] The DEA has 227 offices in the United States, and a further eighty-six offices in sixty-three countries around the world. Among the biggest intelligence-gathering agencies are the National Security Agency, the CIA, the State Department, the White House intelligence tsar, and the Defense Intelligence Agency, all of which vaulted from Cold War to War on Terror by making themselves indispensable to the prosecution of the war on drugs.

The young people of the United States have been raised on a war footing. Both drugs and terror make suspicion and the need for surveillance eternal, because both are nigh on impossible to police, which becomes the very reason for surveillance. Permanent warrant-less wiretaps, one of George W. Bush's last and most controversial policy proposals, are the fruit of the war on drugs. Blackwater, a company of mercenaries which won its first big contracts from the Department of Defense for operations in Iraq, is now competing for indefinite-delivery, indefinite-quantity contracts for drug law enforcement in the United States.[36]

It is ironic that the main threat to the war on drugs has come, not from its resounding inability to tackle the demand for or supply of drugs, but rather, from another war on another abstraction. The war on terror shares with the war on drugs the promise of open-ended commitment and fuzzy parameters that provide little by which victory or defeat might be judged. Drug warriors concerned that the White House's attention is being distracted by the threat posed by foreign terrorists will do all they can to ensure that drugs too are defined as a foreign terror threat. Improved counter-drug efforts, they say, contribute to improved security against other threats. A slight decline in drug use is taken as evidence that government policies are finally working. A slight increase is taken to mean that not enough is being done. Both scenarios demand more funding. The war on drugs has become a war without end.

PART TWO

Supply and the Third World

5

Smugglers

Who give the guns, who give the crack?
No one to take the blame
And a who import the guns and cocaine
And a who inoculate the ghetto youths brain?
An mobilize dem inna this bloodsport game
Say if you want to be rich, you haffi kill Shane
And wicked enough to kill him mother Miss Jane
Mek dem say you a di wickedest man pon the lane
And if you want yu respect fi long like a train
Well you better make shot fall like a rain
Yu haffi put one foot pon them Concord plane
Hey, you better sell twenty kilo cocaine.

Bounty Killer, 'Down in the Ghetto'

In 2006, 492 metric tons of cocaine were impounded by law enforcement around the world. This was the second highest total ever seized after the 588 metric tons seized in 2004, which was in turn the fifth consecutive record-setting bust.[1] If supply-side interdiction isn't working, it's clearly not for want of trying. Yet the United Nations says that the profit margin on sales of illegal drugs is so inflated that the authorities would have to intercept 75 per cent of the cocaine produced to have any serious impact on the viability of the illegal drugs business. Despite years of eye-wateringly large interdictions, current efforts intercept no more than 40 per cent of cocaine shipments.[2]

Sir Keith Morris was the UK's ambassador to Colombia between 1990 and 1994, and his experience of the war on drugs as it has been conducted on Colombian soil has made him a trenchant critic of the very idea that supplies of cocaine can be effectively disrupted. Reflecting on the cocaine wars that gripped Colombia during his term, Sir Keith told me that 'the war on drugs briefings that the Americans were pumping out were basically "My God, we've got to go on . . ." It's a classic law enforcement thing around the world. They're always winning battles but losing the war, and needing more resources. When I discovered that HM Customs and Excise, God bless their cotton socks, had calculated that they were getting 9 per cent of the cocaine or the heroin coming into the country. 9 per cent? Why 9 per cent? You begin to realize that these things are so fictitious, in a way.'

This is not to belittle the notable impact that some multinational operations have had on the cocaine business. Operation Purple was launched by the DEA to coordinate seizures of potassium permanganate, a widely used disinfecting agent which is also one of the precursor chemicals used in the manufacture of cocaine. The operation was effective in drying up supplies from Europe and the United States, but a lack of international cooperation has stymied a water-tight prohibition. Almost half of potassium permanganate shipments are destined for Asian and African countries that do not participate in Operation Purple. Once docked, these shipments can be diverted to Venezuela or Ecuador, where the lists of controlled substances are much shorter, and then smuggled into Colombia.[3]

A British cocaine wholesaler told a Home Office prison survey that, prior to his arrest, he was buying and selling 60 kilograms of cocaine a week. He would buy from Colombian suppliers in Spain for £18,000 a kilo, and sell in the United Kingdom for £22,000 a kilo. Once broken down into grams for retail sale, that kilo would most likely have netted him £50,000, but, like most importers, he preferred to sell in bulk. His consignment would then pass through several pairs of hands, with the profit being distributed along the way. The difference between the wholesale and retail price of cocaine in the UK is about the same as that of most legal agricultural crops. The trickiest part of the smuggling operation, and hence the most profitable, is getting it into the European

Union in the first place. It accounts for the largest part of the 15,800 per cent mark-up in price enjoyed by a gram of cocaine between the laboratory in Colombia and its retail sale in the UK. By way of comparison, the difference in the price of coffee beans between source and sale is just 223 per cent.[4]

The same Home Office survey of cocaine smugglers and wholesalers found that attempts to disrupt the supply of cocaine into the UK have had an impact on local markets and local prices, but not at a national level, and not enough to deter dealers or importers. A major importer told the survey that he had used drug 'mules' to import cocaine from the Caribbean; he estimated that one in four of his couriers would not get through customs. An international haulier who had been importing cocaine into the UK by road estimated that four out of ten of his consignments did not get through, but despite losing half of his merchandise, he was still able to keep a healthy balance sheet.[5]

Most of those without a drug problem don't find it hard to get into the cocaine trade once they know a dealer, and are able to rise through the ranks once they have proven themselves to be honest and reliable.[6] The more dealers, the more competition, which keeps prices down. The majority of dealers consider the risk of arrest to be low and the threat of imprisonment not a serious deterrent, but a low-risk occupational hazard. If they are arrested and convicted, they hand the business to a colleague while they serve their term. The only real threat comes when the police take action to seize the dealer's assets.

Importing drugs is always likely to be monopolized by those with ties to countries where drugs can be bought cheaply. Until recently, Jamaican groups were most prominent in importing cocaine, cooking it into crack, and then distributing it around the UK, because Jamaica is an ideal transit point for cocaine bound for Europe from Colombia. But as more Europeans have developed a taste for cocaine, and more cocaine comes into the EU through Spanish and Dutch ports, there have been opportunities for other nationalities to become involved. Four out of every ten drug dealers in British prisons were born outside the UK, and they hail from any one of thirty-four countries.[7]

Up to 250 tons of cocaine enters the European Union every year.

Some European wholesalers get their cocaine directly from Central American and Caribbean suppliers, and work in concert with Colombian and local traffickers to bring it home. Most of it is hidden aboard large container ships that ply the sea lanes between the Caribbean and Spain and Portugal. As the European market for cocaine has burgeoned in recent years, pressure on one link in the supply chain has sent Colombian smugglers scrambling for suitable entrepôts. These days, a third of Europe's cocaine comes via West African countries such as Ghana, Senegal and Guinea-Bissau.[8] From West Africa cocaine can be flown to clandestine landing strips in Spain or Portugal, or smuggled aboard commercial shipping containers bound for Barcelona, Rotterdam or Antwerp. In many West African countries cocaine seizures have gone up six-fold in as many years. In Tema, Ghana, half a ton of cocaine was seized in January 2004; another half-ton load was seized in the capital, Accra, in November 2005 and 1.9 tons was seized off the Ghanaian coast in May 2006. Ghanaian police also recorded the continent's biggest ever cocaine bust that year, arresting the Ghanaian and Nigerian drivers of a van loaded with two tons of the drug concealed in boxes of fish. A ton was seized in Kenya in late 2004, three tons were seized off Cape Verde in February 2006 and in June of the same year, more than 14 tons of a mixture of cocaine and white cement was seized in Lagos, Nigeria.[9] African seizures still account for less than 1 per cent of global cocaine seizures, which suggests that only a tiny proportion of the cocaine transiting the African continent is actually intercepted.[10] Karen Tandy, the former head of the DEA, has said that 'Africa will become, in terms of a drugs hot-bed, one of our worst nightmares if we do not get ahead of that curve now.'[11] Intent on doing just that, in 2007 the UK led eight European nations in setting up a Maritime Analysis Operations Centre, a task force of navy, police and customs officials to target cocaine traffic from Africa.

'Among the destitute locals are scores of wealthy, gaudy Colombian drug barons in their immodest cars, flaunting their hi-tech luxury lifestyle, with beautiful women on their arms,' wrote a journalist in the *Observer*.[12] He went on to describe how 'the seizure of West Africa by Colombian and other drug cartels has happened with lightning speed'. This po-faced depiction of hapless Africans at the behest of unscrupulous drugs traffickers was reiterated by the Executive Director of the United Nations Office on Drugs and Crime (UNODC), Antonio Maria Costa. 'In the nineteenth century, Europe's hunger for slaves devastated West Africa. Two hundred years later, its growing appetite for cocaine could do the same. When I went to Guinea-Bissau, the drug wealth was everywhere. From the air, you can see that the Spanish hacienda villas and the obligatory black four-wheel-drives are everywhere, with the obligatory scantily clad girl, James Bond style. There were certain hotels I was advised not to stay in.'[13] Few locals have been privy to the view from the air that so appalled the head of the UNODC. But I would venture that many of them would regard it as an improvement on what their country looked like before the arrival of the drug barons. The average income in Guinea-Bissau is $600 a year. The barons' development plan for Guinea-Bissau may not tally with that of the United Nations, but which is more likely to alleviate the poverty its people live in?

I met a Cuban-American called Juan Pablo by chance while having a late-night drink in a cheap bar in the old part of Bogotá. When I told him that I was keen to talk to those with first-hand experience of the cocaine business, he gave me an indulgent wink, and pulled up a chair. 'The factory is usually out in the suburbs,' he told me. 'It's a sweathouse, eight or ten people just sitting at tables and cutting up coke that's come in directly from the farms and the labs in the provinces. When I was last there $100 got you about 100 grams, and it's 95 per cent pure.' Juan Pablo then told me how he went about smuggling the cocaine back to the United States. 'You make it about grape-size. Compact it as much as possible. Then you coat it with wax, wrap it two or three times in the plastic, dip it in the wax again, wrap it in the plastic again. You don't want it breaking open. That's trouble. Three and a half ounces is about 15 grapes. Then you swallow them. Don't fly out of Colombia in any way, shape or form. I took the land border to Venezuela, and from there I flew to Guatemala. Eat guava seeds. They make you constipated. You don't want to be shitting on the plane. Every time I stopped, I shit, washed the grapes, took off the outer layer and replaced that. Then I swallowed them again, and flew to the United States. That's the nerve-racking one. Going through customs, you've just got to wholeheartedly believe that you're not doing anything wrong. If you're not doing anything wrong, people don't think you're doing anything wrong. So you make yourself the typical asshole American. "Fucking foreigners, I can't believe their customs. I had this bad thing happen to me, but now I'm home, thank God." You know, acting friendly. They search your luggage. "Oh sure, I understand, you're just doing your job." And you get through. Then you really shit yourself, which comes out good anyway, because you know that you just pulled off something fucking major. I can buy a kilo here in Bogotá for 1.5 million pesos, which is $700. That's probably $20,000 profit if you take it to the States, but that's when it gets dangerous. The key is not to get greedy. Swallowing 100 grapes is going to hurt, and there's a lot more chance that they'll rupture, but twelve grapes is just not that much to have in your stomach. Miami, South Beach, I sold it for about $50 to $70 a gram. That's a really nice little profit.'

Juan Pablo was a lone drugs 'mule'. Most mules work for the smaller drug-smuggling operations, and are driven by cash not glory. Thirty tons of cocaine is thought to enter Europe on commercial flights every year. HM Revenue & Customs and the Ghanaian authorities set up Operation Westbridge in November 2006 to catch drug smugglers who were using Accra as a gateway to the UK. It covered the installation of surveillance equipment, X-ray machines, swab tests and urine tests. In November 2007, two teenagers were seized with nearly four kilos of cocaine ingested in around sixteen condoms, en route for London Gatwick. The boys, one aged sixteen and the other nineteen, were from Lithuanian families living in south London. As many as sixty mules are thought to arrive in Britain from West Africa every week; in 2007, a single flight from Ghana to Amsterdam was found to be carrying thirty-two drugs mules.

Since November 2006, Westbridge has seized 356 kg of cocaine, 2,275 kg of cannabis and 1.3 kg of heroin. These operations make good copy for press releases, but they are short-term measures. As soon as the British police left Accra airport, the traffickers were able to bribe the baggage handlers to take bags past the scanning machines and straight on to the planes bound for Europe. 'We don't have sniffer dogs. We don't have enough scanners. It's all about profiling and gathering intelligence and we need the British to attain that, not just temporary assistance,' a Ghanaian customs officer said.

Westbridge followed the lead of Operation Airbridge, a UK–Jamaican initiative launched in 2002 to catch mules before they boarded planes from Jamaica. Airbridge was set up after police at London's Heathrow Airport found that 25 per cent of passengers arriving from Jamaica were carrying cocaine. Most mules are recruited from the poorest neighbourhoods of Kingston and the city's 'dungles' (rubbish dumps and empty plots of land squatted by recent migrants from the countryside). Muling is also fuelled by the fact that a lot of Jamaicans who work for Colombian smugglers are paid in cocaine: since there is only a small local market for cocaine, it makes good commercial sense to pay a mule to carry the cocaine to New York or London, where there are Jamaicans willing to sell it and locals willing to buy it.

By 2002, 400 Jamaican women were serving sentences in British prisons for bringing cocaine into the UK.[14] I met Sharon at the Kingston office of Hibiscus, an organization set up to help drug mules serving sentences in foreign prisons, most of whom are poor women duped into carrying drugs by unscrupulous traffickers. 'I was a business person, buying footwear and clothing to sell in the market,' she told me. 'I wanted to get more money to put into the business to buy things to sell. I borrowed some money from the small loans office to upgrade, but unfortunately, the bigger stores were selling clothes cheaper than we could sell, and I couldn't make enough money to repay the loan. I had put my furniture and my TV up as collateral for the loan and the office was threatening to repossess them. Then a friend introduced me to a man who said that he could make me a loan to pay back the first. But I realized that he wasn't a loans man. He was a drugs man. He said that if I made a trip to the UK I could make more than I needed. I said I didn't want to take that chance. What if I go to prison? "No man," he said. "You have a nice appearance. They won't stop and check you." He was offering me £2,500. We went to a hotel in the resort area, and I swallowed about fifty pellets, about 200 grams of cocaine. But at the airport in England they checked the entire flight. They made us do a urine test and then an X-ray, and I got caught. The judge gave me five years.'

When a mule carries cocaine to Britain, she might expect to be home in a couple of weeks. But if she is arrested, her children can spend up to five years without their mother. The luckier ones will be brought up by friends or relatives, but many children have to fend for themselves as 'barrel children', dependent on the arrival of a barrel of goods from relatives overseas. Even if a drug mule evades detection, she faces other dangers: several cocaine couriers have died in London, after being ripped off and killed by traffickers or overdosing on cocaine when the condoms they were carrying ruptured.

'I got three years nine months in Cookham Prison in Kent, and me do half. One year, ten month and two week,' a cocaine courier called Angela told me. 'I went to prison and me seen nuff people who me know from Kingston. Me called the drug-men back in Kingston to tell them that they lock me up, and the person said "We don't want to hear nothing from you. Your brother's going to go down for this, and when you come over Jamaica, you're going to go down for it too." The thing that was puzzling me brain was me children, sweating that they was going to kill them off. Me come in to Cookham on suicide watch, but me get work folding and packing textiles, and me find meself start a get happy. Me get £18 a week, and me save and me send money back home to give me children. But when I called my mother a couple of months later she said, "It looks like the drugmen killed your brother Steve." The year following, me return to Jamaica. Soon after, they light me house a fire. Me didn't tarry, me just leave immediately, and ended up living in the burnt-down market by Harris Street. Me haffi wait til the people selling in the market pack up and gone by ten at night before me can go a bed and lay down. Me can't have me children around me – me go a bed a night time, and me don't know which part they are pon di road. Last week me look pon me mother and me say me sorry the judge never give me a bigger sentence, where me had somewhere comfortable to put down me head.'

When the Colombian authorities cracked down on cocaine-smuggling through their seaports, traffickers started to move more cocaine through Venezuela to the Netherlands Antilles, a self-governing region of the Netherlands in the Caribbean whose people carry EU passports. In 2000, four tons of cocaine was seized at Amsterdam's Schipol International Airport.[15] The Dutch authorities responded to the increase in muling from the Antilles by implementing a novel strategy that they termed '100 per cent Control'. Passengers were subject to extensive searches; when cocaine was found, it was confiscated, and the mule had his or her passport confiscated for up to three years. They were then deported, but not arrested. The authorities reasoned that the threat of incarceration in a European prison would be scant deterrent to potential drug mules, most of whom are desperate for money. But by increasing the rate at which the authorities intercepted cocaine shipments, they could make smuggling unprofitable. In 2003, eighty couriers were thought to pass through Schipol airport every day, but by 2005, this had been cut to just ten a month.[16]

In response to these crackdowns, smugglers have switched their tactics again. These days, mules are more likely to be British, Dutch or Spanish residents who get paid for the loan of their stomach and get a free holiday in the Caribbean to boot.[17] The authorities are reluctant to admit it, but their airport interception efforts are also hampered by local corruption, as Humberto told me when we met to talk about his time as an anti-drugs police officer in Bogotá. 'We infiltrated a group of eight guys who were trafficking cocaine out of the airport in Bogotá. I'd filmed the whole thing, and one day my boss asked to look at the tapes. I thought he was straight, so I handed them over, but he erased everything I'd shot, so when we went to the public prosecutor with the case, we found that we had no evidence. Then the smugglers started sending funeral wreaths to my house. Who had the address of my house? I ended up working up the case by myself. In the end their operation was busted, and the traffickers were charged with smuggling 360 kilos of cocaine through the airport. My boss, who'd protected their operation right the way through, got a medal. I just got more funeral wreaths.'

*

In 2007, the Jamaicans declared 'yet another significant victory in the war against drugs' when the British Navy seized twelve bales of cocaine, said to be worth almost £50 million.[18] In June 2008, a headline in the *Daily Telegraph* ran: 'Prince William set for showdown with drugs baron on Royal Navy patrol in Caribbean'.[19] Despite these flourishes of bombast, in reality cocaine shipments heading north across the Caribbean have been diverted, rather than diminished, by law enforcement. Traffickers have learnt to evade interception by leap-frogging from island to island. Puerto Rican authorities seized a record 10 tons of cocaine in 1998; Jamaica seized a record 3.7 tons in 2002; the following year it was the turn of the Dutch Antilles, where the authorities seized a record 9 tons, and the Bahamas, which seized a record 4.3 tons.[20] The Dominican Republic has become a command, control and communications centre for cocaine movement through the Caribbean, used to store cocaine before onward shipment to Puerto Rico and the United States.[21] Much of the construction business in the Dominican capital Santo Domingo is believed to be financed by drug money as a way of laundering revenue.[22] Nearly all of the cocaine entering the Dominican Republic comes over the mountains from Haiti, its neighbour to the west.[23] The Haitian anti-drugs police have only forty members.[24]

The focus on supply-side interception is not only ineffectual; it is also destructive. As the North American market for cocaine took off in the early 1980s, Colombian traffickers cast around for a base in the Caribbean through which they could move their product. Jamaica quickly became one of the main transhipment points for cocaine between Colombia and the United States. The island lies 550 miles north of the Colombian coast and 550 miles south-west of Miami. Consignments could be flown from clandestine airstrips on the north coast of Colombia to Jamaica, where the planes were refuelled for the second leg up to Miami. With the help of their British counterparts, the Jamaican authorities responded by building a radar station to track aircraft coming into Jamaican airspace. So the traffickers switched from air to sea. Kingston wharf is the biggest transhipment port in the Caribbean, full of ships bound for ports all over the world. The Americans have installed container-scanning equipment at great cost, but the cocaine trade is driven by poverty and a disdain for legal niceties that no amount of machinery can entirely quash. The port has plenty of low-paid dockhands and security guards keen to supplement their wages by smuggling cocaine on to the container ships.

Colombian traffickers also began to move their product in 'go-fast' boats that they stole from Caribbean and Latin American ports. 'Big Colombian speed fucking boats,' Jah Runnings told me, gesturing from the bright blue sea to the little coastal village of Bluefields where he lives. 'It usually come in at Crab Pond Point up there, two times a month. Big raas clot engine, you understand me? They're very fast – they let off and they go. The coastguard is in Montego Bay and Negril, but they're not in their channel. Sometimes they intercept, but not all the while. In 2000, a Jamaica Defence Force helicopter intercepted one of the boats, but they didn't find any cocaine. They'd thrown it overboard, stashed it down the road. They've been doing it for years.' The go-fast boats are typically stripped of all but their cargo and fuel tanks, run red at 60 knots an hour and are abandoned once they make land. Jamaica's 600 miles of coastline has plentiful mangrove swamps to hide boats in and see few patrols by the authorities. The Jamaican government recently bought three new go-fasts, at a cost of £750,000 a piece. Until 2005, Jamaica's Marine Unit was completely dependent on the six or seven worn-out boats that they were able to recover from cocaine smugglers every year, which they then refitted as police boats. The new boats provide a visual deterrent, but in private officials admit that the entire Jamaican police force would have to be put to sea for the authorities to stand any chance of stopping the go-fasts from getting through.

According to Jah Runnings, the main suppliers of the cocaine that came through Jamaica were Colombian paramilitaries formerly affiliated to the Autodefensas Unidas de Colombia (United Self-Defence Forces of Colombia), but he was understandably hazy about the details. 'Colombians mostly stay up in Montego Bay, Ocho Rios. They're so sceptic, they live indoors, so you don't know them. Those guys are real mafia, they're hard to study, you know? You can't mess with those guys. They'll kill you. The big Jamaican dons work along with the Colombian dons, but the Colombians are the more don because they have the merchandise.' Jah Runnings explained that Colombian suppliers employ locals to unload the boats, stockpile the drugs and send them out again from the north coast of the island, usually bound for the Bahamas. 'My friend used to work with the Colombians, unloading the boats on to big trucks. He got 750,000 Jamaican [about £5,300] for taking 1,500 kilos from Colombia to here. A two-day run. It's small money, man. They'd have a couple of guys drive along with them to clear the way up to Montego Bay. From there it leaves to America and England, or sometimes to Cayman Islands, and link from there. Then one time, the boat come in, but intercept by the coastguard, so they take off the drugs and come hide it up in the bush. A bale of cocaine went missing, so they come back and killed my friend. Shoot him three times in his head.'

Before going to Kingston, I had read that 64 per cent of Jamaicans believe crime to be the most pressing problem facing the country.[25] I wanted to find out what impact the cocaine trade had had on the island and to what extent it was responsible for Jamaica's notoriously high crime rate. Things had got so bad that in 2004, Jamaica's Minister of Tourism warned that violent crime threatened to derail the island's tourism industry.[26] In 2005, the Minister of National Security, Peter Phillips, spoke of 'a criminal elite whose activities are centred on the illegal trade in drugs, which constitute the tap root of violent crime in Jamaica'. Five years previously, Phillips had put the soaring crime rate down to 'narco-terrorism'. The Minister had requested assistance from 'friendly countries with experience in fighting urban terrorism', and ordered in armoured cars of the type the British pioneered for use on the streets of Belfast.[27]

Jamaican gangs have become notorious for their role in smuggling and selling cocaine and crack cocaine in the United States and the United Kingdom. I wanted to find out how they had become so successful and why crime seemed so resistant to law enforcement. It is not enough to point to the poverty of Jamaica's garrison communities, or the expatriate Jamaican populations in both countries. It seemed more significant that Colombian traffickers had found local criminal networks already in place thanks to the ganja-smuggling business, and that the island was accustomed to the high levels of violence that the cocaine trade requires to perpetuate itself. Wills O. Isaacs, one of the founders of the People's National Party (PNP), asked the presiding judge at the trial in which he stood accused of incitement to riot in 1949, 'what are a few broken bones in the birth of a nation?' Jamaican politicians have been fomenting gang violence for a long time. The gangs' lineage goes back to the war over West Kingston fought between the PNP and their rivals in the Jamaican Labour Party (JLP), which began in 1966 when the Back O'Wall slum was demolished by the JLP MP for West Kingston, Edward Seaga. As new tenement houses went up, JLP supporters got the construction jobs, and when the work was done, they got the tenancies too. PNP supporters were driven into the dungles. PNP leader Dudley 'Burning Spear' Thompson led the fightback, carving niches for his party's supporters in other West Kingston neighbourhoods, and setting up the 'Fighting 69' to defend PNP meetings from attack by JLP supporters.

It was during these tumultuous years following independence from British rule in 1962 that the 'rudeboys' came to the fore, the 'Johnny-Too-Bads', whose frustration at the lack of change was exacerbated and then exploited by the extreme partisanship that divided the island. Having drawn young people into politics, both parties distributed guns to their supporters and created Jamaica's first gangs. The JLP created the Phoenix gang. The PNP created the Spanglers and the Vikings (named after the rousing Kirk Douglas film of 1958). These gangs quickly colonized the rest of Kingston's downtown neighbourhoods, chasing out all political opponents and dividing the city into a patchwork of clearly defined and ruthlessly policed garrison communities. The gangs' leaders were charged with the task of mobilizing votes on election day, liaising between the local MP and his or her constituents and dispensing the jobs and houses that the MP brought back from meetings at Jamaica House. These leaders came to be known as 'dons'. Through their connections to the local MP, and thereby the ruling party, the dons became providers of employment, protection, and some measure of pride in the garrison communities. Whatever ideological loyalty the JLP or PNP has ever been able to inspire has always been tempered by the simple fact that if your party is out of power, you go hungry. As a result, Jamaica's gangs and its two political parties have dispensed terrible violence and acquired huge power. These are, in the words of the reggae singer Peter Tosh, the 'politricks' of the Jamaican 'shitstem'.

The present shape of both the parties and the gangs was cast by the events of the 1970s. In the run-up to the elections of 1972, the opposition PNP was quick to address the thwarted hopes and mobilize the latent violence of the 'sufferers', Jamaica's poor majority. Rastafarians, too, were at the forefront of what soon became a powerful movement for change. Bob Marley has long since been taken to the heart of the Jamaican establishment, but in the 1970s Marley and his Rastafarian brethren were despised by many members of the 'Afro-Saxon' mixed-race elite that had governed Jamaica since independence. Locals had to go to rum shops to hear reggae music because the island's radio stations wouldn't play it. The Rastafarians asserted an African identity, holding Emperor Haile Selassie of Ethiopia, not Queen Elizabeth II, to be their sovereign ruler. The Jamaican government showed great disdain for this challenge to its authority, well illustrated by the fact that they recognized Mormonism as an official religion of Jamaica before they afforded the same status to Rastafarianism, despite Mormonism's roots in white supremacist thinking.

In 1970, PNP leader Michael Manley returned to the island from a visit to Ethiopia with a ceremonial staff that he had been given by Emperor Haile Selassie. Hitting the campaign trail in 1972, Manley took his 'rod of correction' to every parish he visited, and in the general election of that year he was vaulted into power on a wave of pride in all things African. In 1974, Manley declared the PNP to be a socialist party. The Prime Minister was quoted as saying that there were five flights a day to Miami, and that anyone who didn't like his policies should take one. Many wealthy Jamaicans did just that, taking their families and their capital with them. Foreign investment soon dried up, and the Jamaican dollar plunged in value. Prices fell, and local merchants began hoarding goods, which led to food shortages and then riots. Jamaica was polarized between left and right, and in the face of rising violence Manley was forced to declare a state of emergency again. The Prime Minister imposed what he called 'heavy manners', temporarily locking up all 'top ranking' garrison dons in an attempt to put an end to the gun terror of the JLP gangs. Anyone found in possession of a firearm was sentenced to life imprisonment.

Against this background of economic crisis and political turmoil, Bob Marley and Peter Tosh's One Love Peace concert of 1978 assumed special importance. When Marley had Michael Manley and Edward Seaga join hands on stage it seemed that a peaceful solution to the strife was in sight, but behind the scenes the JLP was preparing for war. The boxes carrying the lighting equipment for the One Love concert from the United States had also been laden with guns. Rumours spread that the CIA was involved in importing guns to bolster the JLP's struggle with the Manley government, and cocaine to help fund it.[28] JLP gunmen began to use cocaine as well as trade in it, and the drug was widely blamed for 'the reign of the wall-eyed gunmen', a fit of violence in the weeks leading up to the general election of 1980, in which more than 800 Jamaicans were killed.[29] Manley lost the election to Seaga 'in a hail of bullets and a river of blood'.

Michael Manley was returned to power in 1989, but by then the man who had tried to plot an independent course for his country was resigned to an uneasy accommodation with the island's elite. He flew to Washington to tell George Bush Sr that socialism was dead and that the PNP was 'ready to do business'. Whatever political differences might once have justified the violence between the PNP and the JLP were now gone. As the demand for cocaine in the United States grew, increasing quantities of the drug passed through Jamaica, however. Jamaica's dons and politicians grew accustomed to laundering the profits they amassed from the cocaine business by sponsoring dancehall music productions. Reggae music seemed to lose its crusading message too, as it was eclipsed by dancehall music. In 1999, reggae singer Dennis Brown died of respiratory failure caused by his longrunning cocaine addiction.

Under Michael Manley's prime ministership Jamaica's economy had shrunk by a quarter. Exports of marijuana had played a big part in keeping the economy afloat, and the businessmen who ran the ganja business were among the first to get involved in the cocaine business. Much of the antagonism between criminal and legitimate enterprises in Jamaica today is between young and old, as young 'soldiers' know that many members of the business community, and even some government ministers, made their money from the ganja trade before graduating to the legislature or the island's chamber of commerce.[30]

'Ganja' is a Hindi word that entered the Jamaican language shortly after the first indentured Indian labourers landed in Jamaica aboard the *Blundell* in 1845. The Indians came to work in the sugar cane fields after the abolition of slavery had deprived their owners of cheap labour. Before long, the British colonial authorities were growing cannabis for their plantation workers, in the then-prevalent belief that it made them work harder. Hemp was also used to make rope, an industry vital to the maintenance of Britain's naval pre-eminence. A Royal Commission of 1901 had concluded that smoking cannabis was relatively harmless and not worth banning, but in the first two decades of the twentieth century, intoxication by cannabis, or anything else for that matter, was increasingly frowned upon by Americans and Europeans.[31]

By then it had become a firm favourite in Jamaica, but the authorities were not moved by its popularity. Rumours went around Jamaica House that people used ganja to prepare themselves for killing their wives. Until the 1960s, a Jamaican found in possession of ganja could expect to be sentenced to eighteen months' hard labour. In time, the mandatory sentences were repealed and discretion was restored to the judiciary, but as late as the 1970s, Peter Tosh was one of many Rastafarian singers to spend time in prison for smoking ganja. The politicians had always said that strict sentences were needed to protect the tourists, but as Rastafarianism and reggae music started to draw people to holiday in Jamaica in the 1980s, the criminalization of cannabis smokers came to look ever more outdated. Nonetheless, under Edward Seaga's government, dreadlocks and black pride were shuffled off-stage, and love of the United States and all things white, including the DEA's ganja eradication programmes, came to the fore.

This had unintended consequences in Jamaica, just as it had in New York City. When ganja traders suddenly found themselves bereft of a livelihood, many of them moved into cocaine smuggling.

The cocaine business thrives on the poverty, not just of individuals and communities, but of governments. Jamaica was close to bankruptcy when Edward Seaga became prime minister in 1980. By 1984, Jamaica's debt per head of population was the highest in the world. When the Colombian cartels started smuggling cocaine through Kingston harbour, they soon found that they would have to deal with the JLP-affiliated trade union that controlled the wharf. But since the new government was in no position to quibble over the provenance of foreign earnings, the island's banks were told to accept any deposits, regardless of provenance, and the government simply imposed a tax on anyone unable to prove where their money came from. The Americans were glad to see the back of Michael Manley, and, initially at least, were not overly concerned by the flow of cocaine through the island.

The bankruptcy of the Jamaican government ensured that austerity measures and collusion with gangsters became the orders of the day. Seaga boasted that he would 'lock down Jamaica tighter than a sardine can'. He brought food subsidies to an end, further devalued the Jamaican dollar and raised petrol prices. As unemployment rose and poverty deepened, the crime rate climbed still higher, prompting the government to get even tougher. By the mid-1980s, the Jamaican police were responsible for a third of the island's murders. Seaga's Caribbean Basin Initiative brought untaxed sweatshops to the island, the female workforce for which he supplied from JLP constituencies. The Prime Minister also launched a programme to revitalize Jamaican agriculture by supplying winter vegetables for the American market. The AGRO-21 programme was headed by Eli Tisona, an Israeli money-launderer for the Colombian Cali cartel. Its showcase farm was Spring Plains, whose head of security was Lester 'Jim Brown' Coke, leader of the Shower Posse, a JLP gang that was to pioneer cocaine smuggling from Jamaica to Miami and London.

Between 1980 and 1990, one in ten Jamaicans left the island for the United States.[32] Once there, the poorest and least educated had to 'juggle', to squeeze money from whatever opportunities came along. Very often, those opportunities were supplied by the gangs. They had been instrumental in mobilising voters in JLP-dominated garrison communities; their task complete, they now found themselves cast aside by the incoming government. Thus gangsterism became Jamaica's third principal export, after its labour and its music. Schooled in violence by their politicians, Jamaican gangsters soon found that the United States' booming cocaine economy supplied one of the few lines of work that actually required an ability to dispense violence. In New York, Miami and other East Coast cities, Jamaican gangsters became key players in the supply of ganja and cocaine. Between the early 1980s and 1995, Jamaican gangs killed 4,500 people in the United States, making them the most violent organized criminals in North America.[33]

The Shower Posse, so named for the shower of bullets they rained down on their rivals, was one of the first garrison gangs to move into the cocaine business in the United States. The Shower was based in Kingston's Tivoli Gardens, 'the mother of all garrisons' and the main distribution centre for cocaine and guns in Jamaica. It moved into Miami in 1984, and from there started running first ganja, then cocaine, and eventually heroin to New York City. The Shower Posse also moved into British drugs markets. When Pablo Escobar was killed in 1993, the Cali cartel took over many of the Medellín cartel's cocaine-smuggling routes and contacts. The Cali cartel wanted to open new markets for their product in Europe, so they recruited the Shower to sell their cocaine for them in the United Kingdom. With the money they earned, the Shower bought guns to send back to their affiliates in Kingston.

The Shower Posse was dependent for its success on the connivance of Jamaica's politicians. However, then as now, widespread corruption and impunity have ensured that most of those doing the conniving have escaped justice. In the absence of a criminal conviction, the illegal activities of the island's businessmen and politicians are the subject of incessant rumours, which the island's journalists find either too difficult or dangerous to substantiate. The leaders of the Shower were Vivian Blake and Lester 'Jim Brown' Coke. Coke took his nickname from the American football star Jim Brown, the only black cast member of the film *The Dirty Dozen*, which had been a big hit in Jamaica in 1967. 'Jim Brown' had set up the first cocaine smuggling routes with Colombian traffickers. But the startling success of the Shower Posse's cocaine smuggling operations was down to the complicity of senior Jamaican politicians. The story of how 'Jim Brown' shot and killed a minibus driver in Kingston in 1982 speaks volumes about the hidden relationship between Jamaica's politicians, police and garrison dons. 'Jim Brown' was wanted by both the FBI and his Colombian suppliers, but the Jamaican police regarded him as untouchable. When fellow bus drivers saw that the police were not going to do anything about the killing, they went on strike. The city ground to a halt, leaving the police with no option but to arrest 'Jim Brown'. His death is equally telling. While on remand in a Kingston prison cell awaiting extradition to Miami, 'Jim Brown' had vowed to testify about senior politicians' involvement in his drug-smuggling operations. He died just days later. The prison authorities said that Brown died in a prison fire while attempting to escape (as if one way to die wasn't enough).

A second Jamaican crew that went to New York to juggle was the Gullymen of McGregor Gully in Kingston, headed by Eric 'the Chinaman' Vassell. At its height, their network of crack houses in Crown Heights, Brooklyn, was taking in $60,000 a day. The Gullymen also ferried cocaine from New York to Texas, returning with dozens of handguns to ship back to Kingston, and supplied street-corner crack dealers in Crown Heights, who paid the Gullymen a tax. 'Vassell franchised his operation just like McDonald's,' said an FBI agent.[34] Feared criminals in New York, the Gullymen were regarded as benefactors back in Kingston because they were a steady source of US-dollar remittances and 'treats'. Treats date back to the days of slavery. Come Easter, owners would give their slaves a new article of clothing or a tiny ration of meat. Following this tradition, every Easter the Gullymen would spend thousands of dollars on treats for their communities back in Kingston. There would be toys and clothes for the children, and presents for their baby-mothers. In her book, *Born Fi' Dead* (1995), Laurie Gunst describes a beauty pageant held in

McGregor Gully, where each of the pre-teen contestants wore a sash bearing the name of the 'soldier' who had sponsored her. There was a Miss Sean, a Miss Jukie and a Miss Ever-Reds. Just before the winner was announced, a little girl stepped up to the microphone. 'This is the fifth year since the Schnectady Crew' – she had a hard time pronouncing the name of the Brooklyn avenue where the Gullymen were based – 'from the United States of America have shown their love and care for us citizens of McGregor settlement. Words cannot say how much we love and care for you.'[35]

The Jamaican gangs have become key players in an international trade. Recognizing the need for international aid to counter those gangs, in 2004 the Jamaican and British police launched Operation Kingfish to go after those running the cocaine trade in Jamaica. They dismantled two of Jamaica's fourteen major gangs, and disabled five clandestine landing strips used to fly cocaine to and from the island. In 2006, Donald 'Zekes' Phipps, the don of Mathews Lane, was jailed for life for a double murder. Since 2007, prominent businessmen like Norris 'Deedo' Nembhard, Leebert Ramcharan and Donovan 'Plucky' Williams have been extradited to the United States and convicted of cocaine trafficking.[36] News of the arrest of Robroy 'Spy' Williams was said to have struck such a blow to the business community of Montego Bay that supermarket sales in the town dropped 20 per cent.

Drug law enforcement efforts and the switch to overland smuggling through Mexico have ensured that today just 10 per cent of the cocaine bound for the American market passes through the Caribbean, and most of that moves through Venezuela, Trinidad and Barbados. Many Jamaican operators have returned to the marijuana business. The impact of Operation Kingfish, while it lasted, is not in question: a kilo of cocaine that cost £2,000 in Jamaica in 2004 cost £4,000 by 2007. But Kingfish dented rather than crushed the business. In 2003, 100 tons of cocaine was estimated to have passed through Jamaica.[37] Based on retail prices of $30,000 per kilo in the United States, that trade was worth at least $3 billion a year, which is three times more than Jamaica's earnings from tourism, its biggest legitimate exchange earner after remittances from abroad.[38] Since the last British police officer left, the arrests have dried up.

How long these small victories will last is doubtful. The Jamaican government's finances are in as parlous a state today as they were when the cocaine business first arrived. Sixty-five per cent of the government's expenditure is allocated to the servicing of the national debt. Eighty-five per cent of Jamaica's skilled labour emigrates, to the UK, Canada and above all the United States, where one in five Jamaicans now lives.[39] Older Jamaicans complain that 'easy money' from relatives living in London or New York has made the young idle. Not that there's much work to be done: the marketplaces are full of subsidized American farm produce, imported at prices that Jamaica's farmers can't compete with; the European Union has capped its preferential trade terms for Jamaican bananas and the sugar cane fields are on the wane. The island has deposits of bauxite, the main ore used in the making of aluminium, but all the processing plants are in foreign hands, so most of the profits go overseas. Officially, unemployment in Jamaica is running at 12 per cent, but in reality the rate is closer to 35 per cent. All of this bodes well for anyone considering running cocaine through Jamaica in the future.

There are said to be twelve big players in the Jamaican cocaine business today. In contrast to the first generation of traffickers, many of whom were garrison dons, today's traffickers are among the most prominent businessmen on the island.

After the financial crisis of 1997, many businesses in Jamaica went bankrupt and a lot of commercial property came on to the market, which only the cocaine traffickers had the money to buy. They have access to sizeable sums of money, which they launder through tax-free accounts in the Caymans and the Virgin Islands, or by buying up tourist spots on Montego Bay's Gloucester Avenue, car parts businesses, construction companies and the *casas de cambio* (bureaux de change). Until recently, the island's biggest *cambio* owner was rumoured to be Adrian 'Ruddy' Armstrong, a white Jamaican reported in the *Jamaican Gleaner* as 'facilitating the movement of billions of dollars from the US, Europe, Panama, Colombia and Jamaica for some of the big players in western Jamaica.'[40] Another major trafficker is Samuel 'Knighty' Knowles, a Bahamian reputedly worth £100 million, who gave many of the first generation of Jamaican cocaine traffickers their break into the business. Knowles invested his earnings in construction and shopping mall projects, and has lieutenants in the Montego Bay districts of Canterbury and Norwood. These businessmen-traffickers have used their wealth to ingratiate themselves with the police, politicians and the wider business community of Jamaica.

An investigation of police officers in Portland found they had stolen cocaine from smugglers; the corruption was judged to be so pervasive that the entire Portland police force had to be transferred from the parish. In 2005, all twelve members of the narcotics police unit in Montego Bay were also found to have accepted payments from local traffickers.[41]

It is safe to assume that most such cases go undetected or unpunished. Once corruption is seen to go unpunished, all public finances become potential sources of illicit enrichment and even the most principled public servants come to crowd the trough. In 2007, the International Narcotics Control Board acknowledged the arrests made as part of Operation Kingfish, but still warned that Jamaica risked becoming a 'kleptocracy' if the government didn't act against corruption by cocaine traffickers. So when JLP leader Bruce Golding won that year's general election, thereby putting an end to eighteen years of PNP rule, many Jamaicans hoped that the nefarious alliance of businessmen, politicians and cocaine traffickers might be broken.[42] Unfortunately, dismantling webs of corruption has turned out to be less than straightforward. The cocaine business is more lucrative than any other, and too many powerful people know too much about other powerful people's dalliances with it. While it would be unfair to call the JLP the cocaine traffickers' party, eighteen years in opposition made it the first port of call for anyone disgruntled by police crackdowns. JLP candidates are thought to have been given £650,000 to buy votes in Montego Bay alone, money said to have been made available by the town's businessmen-traffickers.

Both the PNP and the JLP have officially stated that they want to put an end to political tribalism and sever their alliances with the garrison dons, but partisan distribution of work, housing and 'scare benefits' still goes on. The politicians still rely on the gangs to mobilize voters come election day. The businessmen-traffickers still need the garrison dons and their shooters and still maintain close ties to Jamaican trafficking gangs in the United States – indeed, they are very often blood relatives of the government ministers vowing to wage war on 'narco-terrorists'.

But it is the change, rather than continuity, that is driving Jamaicans' fear of crime. The politicians have much less to offer the garrison communities these days, and the dons realize that they can fund themselves, either through the cocaine trade, or by extorting legal businesses. The dons of Flankers and Rose Heights in Montego Bay have effectively become the heads of parallel governments, which cover the school fees and medical expenses of people who would otherwise go without.

Before Operation Kingfish, there were about twenty-five dons in Kingston. Kingfish disrupted their control of the ghettos, but did nothing to tackle the deprivation that gave rise to that control in the first place. When the police arrested a don, his gang splintered and a leadership struggle among his lieutenants ensued, which only generated more violence. As the hierarchies of controlled violence have been dismantled, 100 'corner gangs' have sprung up in Kingston. These gangs have no ties to politicians, and are far more bloodthirsty than the traditional gangs. The degeneration of political violence into criminal violence is creating a generation of twelve- to thirty-year-old, near-illiterate hustlers whose idea of a job is to kill a policeman for his gun, so as to rob a gangster for the start-up capital for a cocaine deal. All of this goes on within spitting distance of the tourists of Montego Bay, who enjoy their holidays blissfully unaware of the 'daily burning' going on around them.

The shift from a ganja culture to a cocaine economy has also created a local market for crack cocaine on the island. Jah Runnings told me that every neighbourhood now has its resident crack user, often homeless, sometimes a thief, 'what is left after the cocaine has finished with the person', as he put it. 'There are crack houses all over Jamaica. People who use it always turn stupid idiots. Some are returning residents, some are retired, some man get kicked out from foreign. I know good people who get hooked by it and can't stop. Can you imagine, he has a little car, he has his family, but he's on crack, and he sells everything to maintain that thing. Jamaica start turn wicked since the coke get burst.'

At independence in 1962, there were six murders a year for every 100,000 Jamaicans.[43] By 1988, at the height of the crack era in the United States, Jamaica's murder rate was twice as high as that of the most violent American cities, and by 2005 the island had the highest murder rate in the world.[44] Most gun crime is confined to the garrison communities of downtown Kingston, which has fuelled a rush to the suburbs and made Kingston probably the only capital city in the Caribbean without a tourist trade. The cocaine trade has made crime Jamaica's most profitable enterprise and that trade has had knock-on effects. Prison authorities in the United States, the United Kingdom and Canada have been deporting Jamaicans who have completed (mostly drug-related) terms in their prisons. Between 2001 and 2004, Jamaica absorbed an average of 2,700 deported convicts a year, an influx equivalent to releasing half of Jamaica's prison population in the space of a year.[45]

Until recently, the principal way for poor Jamaicans to acquire power without resort to brute force was through education. Mass education was a keystone of post-independence government policy across the Caribbean, and parents did all they could to get their children schooled. But education no longer delivers jobs in Jamaica, so many of those who can, leave the island to look for work overseas. Political office offered a second route to empowerment, but politicians are more limited in what they can offer too.[46] The power to affect change has passed into the hands of the island's businessmen, who see few legal opportunities worth exploiting, but plenty of illegal ones.

For those without economic resources, dramatic change, albeit at a very local level, can be affected by the purchase of a gun. Until recently, downtown Kingstonians would ask relatives abroad to send books or food. These days they ask for a gun. Possession of a gun is as good as a job: it can be rented out, or used to rob what money there is, as well as to defend its owner from robbers. In 2003, a survey found that one in five Jamaican students had carried a weapon to school or college at some point in the previous month.[47] The gun exercises a sinister fascination: with a gun a young man can command fear and defend his fragile self-respect. The longer the causes of the violence go unaddressed, the more normal violence becomes. 'Street culture' has become synonymous with 'gun culture' within a very short period of time.

Successive Jamaican governments' emphasis on law and order in tackling violent crime has only made matters worse. It seems that everyone is clamouring for order, but no one for effective laws. There were 1,000 murders in Jamaica in 2004 but only forty murder convictions. Defence lawyers have too much power and the judiciary is slow and easily corrupted. The police force is underfunded; middle-ranking officers who resist bribery don't get promoted, and are regularly threatened by those involved in the cocaine business. Even discounting its corruption by the cocaine trade, the Jamaica Constabulary Force (JCF) is in no position to protect or serve the people of Jamaica. Per head of population, no country's police force kills as many of its citizens as does the JCF. The JCF was founded in the wake of the Morant Bay rebellion of 1865 to put down insurrection.[48] To this day, the JCF labours under the illusion that ranged against it is an enemy army of criminal combatants that parasitically draws shelter and sustenance from the civilian population, from which it must, in the words of Police Superintendent Reneto Adams, be 'flushed out into the open, where we can deal with it.' Adams has allegedly been involved in extra-judicial killings in which a total of thirty-eight Jamaicans have lost their lives, but he was tried and acquited of any offences. Away from the ghettos, the ruthlessness of the JCF has been widely applauded. Its apparent disregard for the law has come to be regarded as an entirely appropriate response to the breakdown in law and order.

Those most affected by violent crime are also those least likely to call the police. Where law enforcement is absent, it is in everyone's interest to recognize and submit to somebody's law as quickly as possible. This is why the dons have become the enforcers of order in the garrison communities. A garrison dweller whose daughter has been raped will get swifter justice by going to the area don than by going to the police. The dons' order may lack due process and procedure, and can be frighteningly swift, but that doesn't mean it is always unjust. Nor are criminal cultures always chaotic. Christopher 'Dudus' Coke, also known as 'the President', is the son of Lester 'Jim Brown' Coke, founder of the Shower Posse. 'Dudus' runs a highly organized criminal operation from Tivoli Gardens, a citadel that the Jamaican army and police tried and failed to take in 2001, in a stand-off that resulted in twenty-six deaths. Tivoli Gardens has an independent health care system and judiciary. Those hoping to tackle violent crime in Jamaica would do well to ask themselves why no politician has such tight control over his constituency, nor inspires the loyalty that 'Dudus' does. The dons may be ostracized by the mainstream, but the laws they break lost whatever respect people had for them when legal ways of earning a livelihood dried up, and politicians began colluding with criminals. In every poor country through which cocaine passes, corruption vies with violent crime for the top spot in the people's list of complaints. In explaining the relationship between the two, I have strayed some way from the subject of cocaine, but only to shed light on how and why the supply of cocaine is so resistant to law enforcement.

The national motto of Jamaica is 'Out of Many, One People'. It was foisted on the island by the mixed-race elite in preparation for the departure of the British in 1962. In fact Jamaica is 85 per cent black, and, far from being 'one people', any visitor can see that there are still two Jamaicas on the island. Away from the ghettos, Jamaica remains a small-minded place. Bernard Headley, a professor of sociology at the University of the West Indies, has written that 'our everyday crime concerns have more to do with monitoring the mango tree in the yard for barefaced thieves and remembering to take in clothes not quite dry off the clothes line. As long as the police keep violent crime in downtown Kingston, and prevent people from blocking Mountain View Road when we need to get to the airport in a hurry, crime is not for us a terribly big deal.'[49] Elite Jamaicans still talk about lower-class violence, but acknowledge no responsibility for it, and come up with no solutions to it. The cocaine business has made Jamaicans more impatient for change than ever, and has divested many of them of whatever scruples they once had (much as it has its users). But it has changed none of the fundamentals: Jamaica has few resources, and receives less today for the few that it has. The country needs a renewed sense of purpose, and the commitment to realize it. If the politicians cannot muster either, those confined to the margins of Jamaican society will find both in crime.

6

The Mexican Supply Chain

I live off three animals / that I love as I do my life / with
them I make my money / and I don't even buy them food /
They are stupid animals / my parakeet [cocaine], my rooster
[marijuana] and my goat [heroin].
Los Tucanes de Tijuana, 'Mis Tres Animales'[1]

The most famous drug smuggler of all time must be Pablo Escobar,
the founder of the Medellín cartel. But the cocaine-smuggling business
has changed beyond recognition since Escobar's day. 'In the mid-
1980s, Miami was the focal point for all the drugs coming in from
Colombia,' a former smuggler called Christian told me. 'The Medellín
cartel started the whole thing of flying it in on little Cessna planes,
throwing it in the water, and picking it up in speedboats.' Cocaine is
still flown over the US–Mexico border in light aircraft. In one case, a
road-building crew in Texas had to make a dash for cover when
a quick-thinking smuggler decided to use their freshly laid tarmac as
a landing strip. But once the Americans were able to monitor flights
over the Caribbean Sea effectively, most traffickers stopped using light
aircraft, and these days only a tenth of the cocaine entering the United
States comes in by air.[2] 'When the US government started cracking
down, we started using alternative routes, like Haiti,' Christian told
me. 'The Cali cartel took it to the next level, made it more like a
corporation, sending it in by the ton on boats. All the Colombian
ships were being searched up and down in the port of Miami, so they'd
ship it to another country and bring it in on a Panamanian ship or a

Guatemalan ship. We were hiding the stuff in concrete statues, or dissolving two or three kilos in water, soaking it into businessmen's suits, then drying them out and bringing it in that way. We were doing it the same way in plastic pipes.'

By 2004, 90 per cent of the US's cocaine wasn't even coming through the Caribbean. It was coming through Mexico.[3] The movement of cocaine through Mexico has been the source of some of the biggest fortunes yet accumulated in the history of cocaine smuggling, and the cause of bitter fighting between the country's rival trafficking cartels. Now the Mexican army is waging a war on those cartels that overshadows even the bloody cocaine wars that gripped Colombia in the 1980s. Over 2,400 Mexicans were killed in drug-related violence in 2007. By December 2008, a further 5,600 people had been killed and the death toll looks set to go still higher in 2009.[4]

Luis Rodriguez, the former gang member I had met in Los Angeles, told me how Mexico had become so important to the traffickers. 'The DEA made big efforts to destroy the trade routes through Florida, and the Colombians started to think, "Well, let's go through Mexico." At first, the Colombians didn't want to go through Mexico, because it had some of the oldest smuggling organizations on the continent, and they'd have to pay all these old drug lords who had been there for a long time. Back then, they had mainly been growing marijuana, but I used to go to Mexico to pick up heroin too. In the '90s, there was collaboration between the Mexican cartels and the Colombian cartels, and the business became very lucrative and very violent.'

There are several ways of getting cocaine from Colombia to the border between Mexico and the United States. A third of America's cocaine comes overland from Central America. A quarter comes directly from Colombia's Pacific coast ports like Tumaco and Buenaventura to Mexico's Pacific ports before it is smuggled north to the border. Another quarter leaves Colombia's Caribbean ports like Turbo, Santa Marta and Cartagena, hugging the coastline of Nicaragua and Honduras, before reaching ports on the Gulf of Mexico.[5] The scale of the shipments is staggering. In 2000, Colombian police seized a 100-foot submarine from a warehouse near Bogotá. Had it ever set to sea, it would have been capable of carrying 10-ton loads of cocaine, with a retail value of $500 million per load. In October 2007, Mexican police intercepted 11 tons of cocaine in the port of Tampico. The following month, they seized a ship carrying 23 tons of the drug in the Pacific port of Manzanillo.[6] Had it been sold in grams in the United States, the shipment would have been worth well over $1 billion.

The United States border with Mexico runs from San Ysidro, California, to Brownsville, Texas, a distance of almost 2,000 miles. At the side of the main road leading into the Mexican border city of Nuevo Laredo from the south stand two giant concrete skeletons wrapped in cloaks, with sickles in their hands. Behind them are several simple chapels, filled with candles, beer cans, packets of cigarettes, and other offerings to La Santa Muerte (Holy Death), the cult of Mexico's criminals and smugglers. Nuevo Laredo is the Mexican half of the Texan city of Laredo. Six thousand trucks cross the border at Laredo every day, making the city the single busiest crossing point for trade between the two countries. Once over the border, the trucks follow highway I-35 up to Dallas, and from there fan out across the United States. They carry 40 per cent of Mexico's exports, worth almost a billion dollars a day.

The gargantuan volume of legal commerce also makes Laredo the single most important point of entry for illegal drugs into the United States. Americans consume roughly 290 metric tons of cocaine a year. Imported in bulk, this load could be carried across the US–Mexican border in just thirteen trucks. Instead, it seeps in in thousands of ingenious disguises: dissolved in polystyrene and turned into pet bedding, sewn into children's nappies, or smuggled inside pineapples. Very often such complicated chicanery isn't even necessary: most of America's cocaine crosses the border hidden in private vehicles.

The shift to overland smuggling through Mexico is hugely problematic for the authorities trying to intercept cocaine shipments bound for the United States. Smugglers need to be able to lose themselves and their precious cargoes in a crowd, and the isthmus of Central America allows them to do just that. One of the reasons for the huge profitability of smuggling through Mexico is that the chances of being intercepted are so slim. The Colombian cartels had originally brought their Mexican counterparts onboard as transporters and smugglers, but the smuggling routes running north through Central America to the border with the United States proved so profitable that Mexican trafficking groups were able to charge the Colombians 50 per cent of the value of a shipment for running a consignment through their country. This was quite a rise from the 20 per cent that the Colombian cartels were accustomed to paying Dominican and Puerto Rican smugglers when the bulk of the trade moved through the Caribbean. But the new arrangement suited the Colombians, as many of them were facing extradition to the United States to stand trial for importing cocaine, and were happy to delegate the riskiest part of their operations to Mexican organizations.

The Mexican groups used their newfound leverage to build distribution networks of their own in the United States, relegating their Colombian suppliers to the role of wholesalers. They branched out from cities like Chicago and Detroit into the suburbs and the small towns beyond. In their wake, street gangs like the Gangster Disciples, the Vice Lords and the Latin Kings have formed new chapters in cities like Chicago, Cleveland and Detroit. Luis Rodriguez gave me an example. 'There's a family called the Herreras. They were from Mexico but they ended up in Chicago. When the Mexican cartels started controlling the business, the Herreras brought in a lot of drugs for the Chicago gangs, both Afro-American and Latino. In Los Angeles, the Mexican Mafia started making connections with the Mexican cartels, and brought in a lot of drugs from Mexico, which gave them more street credibility. Then all the gangs became drug-dealing organizations. Now the Guatemalan, Honduran and Salvadorean gangs are trying to get into taking cocaine through Mexico and into the United States.' As a result of this westwards shift from the Caribbean to Mexico, even the cocaine users of Miami, where nearly all of the cocaine for the American market used to come ashore, are now supplied from Mexico.

The weakness of the economy is a big driver of the cocaine business in Mexico, as it is in the United States and Jamaica. The devaluation of the peso after the financial crash of 1994, and the introduction of the North American Free Trade Agreement (NAFTA) the same year, forced thousands of Mexican farmers to sell up. Farming families have been pulled in opposite directions. Sons have crossed the border with the United States illegally to work as gardeners, kitchen porters and fruit pickers in California and other southern states. Daughters are often to be found working hundreds of miles away, in one of the thousands of *maquiladoras*, the assembly plants that sprang up along the border after 1994 to produce goods for the US market.

The invasion and occupation of Iraq might have dominated newspaper headlines in the United States for the past five years, but domestic politics in 2007 were notable for rising hostility towards Mexican immigrants. There have been calls for a 2,000-mile-long wall to be built along the border to keep them out. Groups of vigilante Minutemen patrol the border on the look-out for illegal migrants. In border cities such as El Paso–Ciudad Juárez, as much as 15 per cent of the population is living in the United States illegally, and many of them have suffered at the hands of officers from the US border patrol.[7] Many border town residents would doubtless argue that whatever their political differences, the economies of states north and south of the border are interdependent. For the businessmen of the United States to demand cheap labour, only for its politicians to score points by penalizing those who supply it, is senseless.

This is the backdrop to the rise of cocaine smuggling in Mexico, and explains why, despite the united front presented by the US and Mexican governments, in private, many Mexicans are reluctant to follow the United States' line on the war on drugs. Their scepticism finds expression in the *narcocorridos*, which offer a version of events at odds with the grandstanding of authorities on both sides of the border. The *corrido* is a genre of polka that became popular in Mexico over a hundred years ago. To the sound of the tuba and the accordion, the *corrido* singer would relate his stories of village feuds, the lives of the migrant labourers who worked the fields of California and the women they left behind when they headed north. After the Dry Law made alcohol illegal in the United States in 1919, *corridos prohibidos* (forbidden ballads) were written about the tequila smugglers and their outfoxing of US border patrol officers. One is the 'Corrido de los Bootleggers', written in 1935, which includes the verse: 'The crop has given us nothing / There's nothing else to say / Now the best harvest / is the one the barrels give us.' Another includes the lines: 'Here in San Antonio / and its surroundings / they never catch the bootleggers / only those who work for them.'[8]

Mexico has been producing and smuggling drugs into the United States since the late nineteenth century. Today the trade is bigger than ever. A large part of the heroin distributed in the United States is made in Mexico. Shutting down amphetamine laboratories in the United States has only displaced them south of the border, where they are even harder to locate, so Mexico also produces most of the methamphetamine consumed north of the border. In 2005, Mexico produced more than 10,000 tons of cannabis, making it the world's second largest marijuana producer.[9] Incredibly, around 30 per cent of Mexico's farmland is believed to be sown with either marijuana or opium poppies.[10]

Alcohol and marijuana are widely consumed in Mexico, but until recently, most Mexicans regarded the drug that smugglers like to call 'cola without the cola' with great suspicion. Cocaine smugglers met with the disapproval of the corrido singers, many of whose songs warned of the consequences of dabbling in what was regarded as a strictly gringo vice. The narcocorridos are a graphic illustration of how Mexican attitudes to cocaine have changed over the past fifteen years. Walk into any of the many record shops in downtown Los Angeles that cater to Mexican-Americans, and you can see how the corridos prohibidos have been revived and radicalized by large-scale cross-border cocaine smuggling.

The most famous singer of narcocorridos is Rosalino 'Chalino' Sanchez. In the early 1990s, Chalino migrated from a hill village in the northern state of Sinaloa, where the Mexican drug-smuggling tradition is strongest, to Los Angeles (where the American drug-taking tradition is strongest). Until Chalino came along, Mexicans born in California had usually taken their cultural cues from the native urban culture, listening to West Coast hip-hop and dressing like their black neighbours. Chalino was a reserved, stubborn man with a reedy voice, but his celebration of the exploits of a new generation of drug smugglers struck a chord with West Coast Latinos. They found Chalino's stories of how a cocaine trafficker evaded detection, made a fortune, and went back to his village to build himself a house with a pool cheering. If the trafficker then paid for a school to be built, he got added kudos for doing what the Mexican government had all too often failed to do.

Thanks to Chalino, Los Angelinos started to dress like Sinaloan drug traffickers. Out went the hip-hop gear, in came wide belts with engraved plate-metal buckles, lizard-skin boots and frilled jackets. This is not to say that drug smuggling became cool. To understand the *narcocorridos*, or the American offshoot of hip-hop known as 'crack music', as celebrations of criminality misses the point. Most of the young Mexican-Americans in the audience at a Chalino gig knew next to nothing about smuggling, but they responded to his *narcocorridos* because he didn't apologize for being a village-born Mexican. What Chalino celebrated was not the drugs trade, but the power the drugs trade has given to the powerless. For Mexicans who have had little choice but to leave their own country to work as second-class citizens in the United States, cocaine is the hero of the piece. It has given Mexicans something that Americans are happy to pay good money for, something that miraculously *gains* rather than loses value when it crosses the border.

In 1992, Chalino Sanchez was shot and killed after a gig in Culiacán, the state capital of Sinaloa. Following his death, the *narcocorrido* genre that he had pioneered went stellar. It remains big business to this day and *narcocorrido* singers have gone on to appropriate elements from gangsta rap, posing with bazookas and AK-47s on the covers of albums that sport titles like *Mi Oficio es Matar* (Killing is My Business). As the cartels have become more powerful and their violence more extravagant, the distinction between commentator and apologist has gradually been lost, with lethal consequences for the singers of *narcocorridos*. Valentin Elizalde's *A Mis Enemigos* (To My Enemies) became the signature tune of Sinaloa's drug-smuggling cartel, a tribute that rebounded in 2006, when gunmen from the rival Gulf cartel shot and killed Elizalde. In many cities of the United States, the authorities have asked radio stations not to play *narcocorridos*. The DEA has reportedly trailed the composers of the songs, as they have the composers of crack music. In some cases they have even taken singer-songwriters to court, charging them with complicity in the drug-smuggling offences they describe in their *corridos*.

Some of today's *narcocorridos* certainly celebrate the exploits of drugs traffickers, but most offer a more nuanced interpretation of the smuggling life, one more inclined towards the tragic than the epic. 'Los Tres de la Sierra' by Los Norteños de Ojinaga, for example, includes the lines: 'You damned Americans don't know what we go through / To get you the drugs you like so much.' Drug dealers can be simultaneously proud and ashamed of their actions, a sentiment apparent in much of the music about the drugs trade on both sides of the border. In border cities like El Paso-Ciudad Juárez, where drug smuggling is pervasive, most traffickers do not regard themselves as criminals, anti-heroes or victims of poverty, but as regular citizens trying to make a living. The services they provide may be welcomed and reviled in equal parts, but this contradiction, as familiar to the migrant as it is to the smuggler, is one that many residents see as just part of the rough-hewn fabric of border town life. Many have attitudes akin to those of the illegal poachers in Africa described by James Siegel. 'If a poor schmuck who is a subsistence hunter has bad luck outside a park area and then crosses into the national park hoping for better luck, he knows that he is breaking some central government law, but he doesn't see himself as a poacher per se. The common person sees the game warden as some stupid policeman for the state, not looking out for the community's interest at all. It becomes a game of cat and mouse, a silly and destructive contest.'[11]

Although there are nearly a dozen drug-trafficking organizations in Mexico, four are especially powerful. The biggest cartel is el Sindicato, the Sinaloa cartel, which is run by Joaquín 'el Chapo' Guzmán. The Sinaloa cartel operates cells in Guatemala, Nicaragua and El Salvador, and its leaders have also established a presence in Colombia and Peru.[12] Mexico's second largest cocaine-smuggling organization is the Gulf cartel, though its influence is on the wane. Its current *capo* is Osiel Cárdenas, who runs the business from the maximum-security La Palma prison near Mexico City. The Tijuana cartel, whose home city lies over the border from San Diego, California, has been run by the Arellano Félix family for many years, but its leaders are currently in prison in the United States, and it too is losing ground to the Sinaloa cartel. The fourth major drugs-trafficking organization is the Juárez cartel, based in El Paso-Ciudad Juárez.

Mexico's current wave of cocaine trafficking-related violence began when Osiel Cárdenas, the leader of the Gulf cartel, bribed his way out of a maximum security prison in 2001. He then bought himself an elite army regiment, known as the Zetas. This is not as hard to do as it might sound. Between 1994 and 2000, 114,000 conscripts deserted the Mexican army, and the cartels pay former soldiers much better wages than most legal employers. The Zetas were once a division of the GAFE (Grupo Aeromóvil de Fuerzas Especiales (Special Forces Airmobile Group)), where it is believed they received training in weaponry, intelligence gathering and surveillance techniques from the United States Army, before being sent to the border to combat drug trafficking. With the Gulf cartel's recruitment of the Zetas, acts of brutality usually not seen outside Colombia have become standard business practice for the Mexican cartels. Members of rival organizations have been tortured, executed and their corpses burnt in barrels. Severed heads have been set on stakes in front of public buildings and in one especially horrifying incident, the heads of five rival soldiers were sent rolling across the dance-floor of a nightclub in Michoacán.

In 2005, the ranks of the Zetas were augmented by soldiers from the Guatemalan Kaibiles, one of the most gruesome military forces in all Latin America, responsible for many of the massacres of civilians committed during Guatemala's thirty-six-year civil war. Inter-cartel violence has reached such levels that even in cities like Monterrey – one of the most affluent and, until 2006, one of the safest cities in Mexico – people talk of children's birthday parties having to be protected with metal detectors, and of security guards hired to inspect the guests' presents for explosives.

Former DEA agent Celerino Castillo III was a key witness of the cocaine-Contra affair described in chapter 2. He has become a keen observer of the drugs war since retiring to his border hometown of McAllen, Texas. He told me how extreme violence and good pay were drawing increasing numbers of mercenaries into the conflict. 'A few months ago, thirty US Iraq veterans came through from all over the country. They had just got out of the Army. They'd had two or three tours of Iraq so they're fucked up already, suffering from post-traumatic stress disorder. All they want to do is kill, so they just go out looking for a bullet with their name on it. They were hired by the Mexican government to kill members of the cartels. They went down there, and they got into big fire-fights. Every single one of them was killed and buried somewhere in Mexico. Now they've got another fifty going down.'

In July 2005, explosions and gunfire rocked downtown Nuevo Laredo's main shopping complex as drug traffickers spent half an hour battling each other with machine guns and grenade-launchers. The Gulf and Sinaloa cartels were fighting for control of the Nuevo Laredo *plaza*, a term that refers not to the city's main square, but to a cartel's right to smuggle drugs through a city. Since anything the security forces did that might have benefited one side would only have made them the target of the other, they did nothing. The laws against drug trafficking might just as well not have existed.

To defend such a lucrative business, traffickers have to be able to resort to terrific violence when necessary. The ability to dispense violence is an intrinsic part of running any illegal business that is both highly profitable and highly criminalized. Such lucrative cargoes, transiting such poor countries, generate fierce competition. Being illegal, and therefore unbound by any legally enforceable contract, that competition can all too easily turn vicious. Eliminating rivals and reaping the benefits can be preferable to dividing up territory and settling for less. Much of the violence of the cocaine trade through Mexico is caused by the fight for the right to run drugs through key border cities like Tijuana, Nogales, Ciudad Juárez and Nuevo Laredo. In the late 1990s, when the Tijuana cartel and the Juárez cartel were battling for dominance of Mexico's drugs trade, one of their main battlegrounds was Ciudad Juárez, and their war generated the same violence and corruption seen in Nuevo Laredo today. Ciudad Juárez is still a dangerous city, but nothing like it was when control of the drugs trade was being disputed.

Violence is also the product of personal vendettas between traffickers, who strike at each other's organizations to avenge the murders of family members or close associates. Once these reprisals get underway, they can quickly spiral out of control. The fight between the Gulf and Sinaloa cartels is a good example: Osiel Cárdenas was allegedly responsible for the murder of Chapo Guzmán's brother, and Guzmán's vengefulness set off a chain reaction of retaliatory killings.

Employees in the drug economy can only pray that they escape the violence. Some pray to Catholic saints, others to La Santa Muerte or Jesus Malverde, the patron saint of smugglers. Malverde was a railroad worker who was hanged in 1909 in Culiacán, the Mexican city most associated with the drugs business, after making a name for himself by robbing the rich to give to the poor. He has since become a sacred guide for all those skirting the edges of the law. The Roman Catholic Church doesn't recognize him as anything of the sort, but that has not diminished the esteem in which the 'narco-saint' is held. In 2007, a brewery in Guadalajara began producing a new beer for sale in northern Mexico's border states; they called it Malverde.

'This is not an easy task, nor will it be fast,' Mexican President Felipe Calderón told an assembly of army officers shortly after assuming office in December 2006. 'It will take a long time, requiring the use of enormous resources and even, unfortunately, the loss of human lives.'[13] In October 2007, US President George W. Bush offered President Calderón a $1.5 billion aid package to help his government in its struggle with the drugs traffickers over the next three years. There would be funding for a witness protection programme, sophisticated scanning equipment to be installed at the border crossings, and $500 million for transport and surveillance planes. This was in addition to the $7 billion that Mexico planned to spend on 'security measures' over the following three years.[14] Bush and Calderón's package still needs the approval of their respective Congresses, and is currently mired in Washington. Even if their aid package is approved, the Americans know that they can't count on the Mexicans to give them the kind of compliance they get from the Colombian government. For much of the 1990s, Mexico refused Washington's offers of assistance in tackling the cartels, and Calderón won't allow the United States armed forces, military advisers or private contractors to carry out operations on Mexican soil.

So for the time being at least, the Americans are dependent on the Mexican army and police to do the fighting. This reliance brings other problems. Violence might be the most eye-catching aspect of the drugs trade, but by and large it is only used when local officials and policemen won't accept the cartels' bribes. The drugs trade works so well in countries like Jamaica and Mexico because all too often the very people charged with fighting the drugs trade are corrupted by drugs money. In 2002, a corruption scandal in Tijuana revealed that key officials charged with fighting the traffickers, including the city's police chief and the assistant state attorney-general, were in the pay of the Tijuana cartel.[15] In 2005, prosecutors charged twenty-seven state, federal and city police officers in Cancún with running a drugs ring and murdering fellow officers. That year, the efforts of the city police in Nuevo Laredo were so corrupted by collusion with gangsters that the Mexican government suspended the city's entire police force and sent in the federal police to patrol the streets. Forty-one city policemen were later arrested for attacking the federal police when their units arrived in the city. Even with the city police in handcuffs, the federal police had no impact on the violence in Nuevo Laredo. The number of drug-related killings actually rose, as once again the delicate balance of power between the Gulf and Sinaloa cartels was upended.[16] The connections between police and criminals run so deep that many cartels have come to be seen as franchises of the Mexican police, and vice versa. To counter police corruption, the Mexican government has become more dependent on the army to go after the *capos*. But as soldiers have joined the front line, they too have succumbed to bribery. In 2002, more than 600 members of the Mexican army's 65th infantry battalion were found to have been protecting opium poppy and marijuana crops. Corruption was so pervasive that the authorities dissolved the entire battalion.

According to a report by Transparency International, an international non-governmental organization that monitors corruption around the world, Mexican judges are also particularly susceptible to bribery by drug traffickers. It cited a case from 2004, in which a group of eighteen hit men from the Sinaloa cartel was detained by soldiers in Nuevo Laredo. They were found to be carrying 28 long guns, 2 short guns, 223 cartridges, 10,000 rounds of ammunition, 12 grenade launchers, and 18 hand grenades, yet Judge Gómez Martínez set them free, ruling that they were innocent of charges of involvement with organized crime. A judge in Guadalajara, Amado López Morales, decided that Héctor Luis 'El Güero' Palma, one of Mexico's best-known drug traffickers, was in fact an 'agricultural producer', despite the fact that he too had been detained in possession of a battery of weapons. Another memorable judge is Humberto Ortega Zurita from the southern state of Oaxaca. In 1996, he presided over the case of two men detained in a car with six kilos of cocaine. The judge absolved them, declaring that no one could be sure that the cocaine was theirs. Hearing a case of a woman who had been stopped on a bus with three kilos of cocaine taped to her stomach, Ortega Zurita ordered that she be set free because 'she did not carry the drugs consciously'. Shortly afterwards, Judge Ortega Zurita 'committed suicide', by stabbing himself several times in the heart.[17]

There have even been allegations that the Catholic Church in Mexico has accepted contributions from drug traffickers. In 2005, Ramón Godinez, the bishop of the central state of Aguascalientes, caused uproar when he conceded that donations from traffickers were not unusual, but argued that it was not the Church's responsibility to investigate the source of donations. 'Just because the origin of the money is bad doesn't mean you have to burn it,' the bishop said. 'Instead, you have to transform it.' He insists that the money was 'purified' once it passed through the doors of his church.[18] In considering how best to tackle the cocaine trade, Bush and Calderón neglected to address the fundamental corruptibility of Mexico's institutions of state. They would have done well to heed the warning intoned by Mexico's biggest *narcocorrido* group, Los Tigres del Norte: 'Don't waste your money buying more radars / or tearing up my landing strips / I'm a nocturnal bird / that can land in any cornfield / And besides, the day I fall / plenty in high places will fall with me.'[19]

Since the earliest days of the drugs business in Mexico, official reports have linked drug traffickers to high-ranking politicians, who have long been suspected of being directly involved in the illegal trade and even of controlling it.[20] The monolithic Partido Revolucionario Institucional (PRI) ruled Mexico from 1928 until 2000, a reign quite unprecedented in what was, in name at least, a democracy. Under the PRI, politicians, police and intelligence agencies regulated, controlled and contained the drugs trade, as they did all aspects of business, protecting certain drug-trafficking groups from the law and mediating conflicts between them. To persist in seeing a neat division between legal state, society and economy, and illegal drugs cartels, counting on the former to support a war on the latter, is naive. The only governments that have ever been able to suppress the drugs trade effectively have been extremely authoritarian: the anti-drugs efforts of China and the Soviet Union spring to mind.[21]

An anonymous PRI official's lament to a journalist from the *Washington Post* illustrates the point well. 'In the old days, there were rules,' he told a reporter. 'We'd say, "you can't kill the police, we'll send in the army". We'd say, "you can't steal thirty Jeep Cherokees a month. You can only steal five." '[22] Impunity was granted to certain cartels, while others were persecuted to satisfy the politicians in Washington. In return, the cartels ensured a steady flow of cash remittances from abroad, and financed the election campaigns of prominent PRI politicians. One such grandee was Mario Ernesto Villanueva, who is currently serving a thirty-five-year prison sentence for cocaine smuggling. Between 1993 and 1999, while he was governor of the southern state of Quintana Roo, Villanueva helped the Juárez cartel smuggle between 17 and 27 tons of cocaine a month through his state. The Gulf cartel rose and fell with the fortunes of Raul Salinas, the elder brother of Mexico's then-president Carlos Salinas. Raul is suspected of shielding the cartel's former head, Juan Garcia Abrego, and his takings from the cocaine business, estimated to run to more than £5 billion a year.[23] Raul Salinas is thought to have made at least £500 million in the six years that his brother was president, though no wrong-doing on his part has ever been established.

For as long as anyone could remember, this collusion between Mexico's politicians and criminals was a *fait accompli*, but as the PRI began to lose political power, culminating in its defeat in the presidential elections of 2000, its grip on the smuggling business slackened. The election of Vicente Fox of the Partido Accion Nacional (PAN) as president in 2000 was hailed as a turning point in Mexico's development as a democracy. For years, the DEA had been telling the Mexican authorities that the root of the problem was the cartels and the official protection they enjoyed. Since the election of Vicente Fox as president in 2000, the Mexican authorities have arrested more than 36,000 drug traffickers, including senior members of nearly all the cartels.[24]

Fox was determined to reassure the Americans that he would be a dependable partner in their war on the drugs trade. Fox also wanted to show Mexicans that the cartels could and would be brought to book. He raised the military's profile in the anti-drug effort, gave more top soldiers positions in the judiciary, and extradited traffickers to face justice in US courts. Fox also made several valiant attempts to purge law enforcement agencies of corrupt officials, most notably the Agencia Federal de Investigación (AFI), the Mexican version of the CIA. Since its creation in 2001, more than 800 AFI agents have been investigated for drug trafficking, extortion, kidnapping, torture and murder.

Vicente Fox had swept aside the corrupt but cosy web spun by the PRI, but he failed to create a workable alternative. This became clear in the course of 2006, Fox's last year in office, when drug-related violence skyrocketed. Targeting the *capos* left a power vacuum; suddenly drug-trafficking corridors and territories worth billions of dollars were up for grabs, which the *capos*' lieutenants rushed to secure. The ensuing struggle for control unleashed terrible violence, which rival cartels vied to exploit and Fox's successors have proven unable to put an end to.[25] The problem is that aggressive drug enforcement only increases the violence it purports to put an end to. Yet such is the authorities' faith in the law and its enforcement that they see the disputes that their policies give rise to as a positive development, however counter-productive they prove to be.

The abject failure of Mexico's anti-drug policies has yet to be fully addressed because the truth about the drugs trade has been kept hidden. The complicity of Mexican police officers, judges and politicians and their corruption by the illegal trade in drugs are rarely discussed in public because the cartels bribe and intimidate journalists, much as they do the police and public officials. In both Colombia and Mexico, 'to disappear' has become a transitive verb, not something you do, but something that other people do to you. Those who don't toe the line laid down by the cartels face execution. As a result, Mexico is second only to Iraq as the most dangerous country in the world in which to work as a journalist. In 2006, nine Mexican journalists were murdered and three were disappeared. The following year was worse.[26] In February 2007, gunmen opened fire on the staff of the daily *El Mañana* in Nuevo Laredo, seriously wounding one person. Two journalists were killed in March for covering stories about the cocaine trade. In July, traffickers kidnapped Rafael Ortiz Martínez of the daily *Zócalo* in Moclova, a town in the northern state of Coahuila, after he reported on drug smuggling in the region. In August, Enrique Perea Quintanilla, editor of the monthly *Dos Caras, Una Verdad*, was shot dead in the northern state of Chihuahua after the Juárez cartel put a contract out on his life. In November, Misael Tamayo Hernández of the daily *El Despertar de la Costa* was found dead in a motel in the southern state of Guerrero, having been killed by a lethal injection. Later that month, Roberto Marcos García, deputy editor of the weekly *Testimonio* in the eastern state of Veracruz, another drug-trafficking centre, was shot dead in the street.[27]

In the climate of self-censorship that these killings have created, anyone hoping that the truth might make the light of day would have been heartened by an advertisement which appeared in a Mexico City daily in May 2006. It described the Gulf cartel's army of Zetas as 'narco-kidnappers and murderers of women and children', who had bought protection from agents in the Mexican Attorney-General's office. Unfortunately, the only person with the money and the courage to place the ad was Edgar 'La Barbie' Valdez, the head of the Negros. To counter the terror tactics of the Zetas, the Sinaloa cartel had raised its own army, known as the Negros. They had responded in kind, bribing police and other public officials, killing those who would not be bought, and waging a bloody street war with the Zetas.

*

Vicente Fox was succeeded to the Mexican presidency by Felipe Calderón in 2006. Just days after assuming the presidency, Calderón launched Operation Michoacán, despatching 6,500 soldiers and police to the central state of Michoacán to set up checkpoints, and execute search and arrest warrants of individuals linked to drug trafficking. Counter-drug operations have since been deployed in a further nine states, involving over 27,000 soldiers. From January to June 2007 they intercepted 928 tons of marijuana, over 5.5 tons of marijuana seeds, 192 kilos of opium gum and 3.6 tons of cocaine. They detained 10,000 people for drug crimes, including the leaders and operators of seven drug-trafficking organizations, seized money and arms, and eradicated 12,000 hectares of marijuana and 7,000 hectares of opium poppies. Drafting in soldiers to do the work of police officers was only supposed to be a temporary measure, but it has quickly taken on an air of permanence. Some legislators have even called for troops to be deployed to patrol the streets of Mexico City.

Corrupt officers are purged, new forces are created, and cocaine's kingpins are captured to be paraded before the cameras. Yet new traffickers and new organizations take the place of those killed or imprisoned, and the cartels' power and reach only seem to increase. In a single week in May 2008, they killed a hundred people, including Mexico's acting Chief of Police Edgar Millan Gomez, and the head of the federal police's organized crime division, Roberto Velasco Bravo. Were they targeted because they were doing their jobs, or because they were allied with a rival cartel?[28] Most journalists are too scared to even ask such a question. There is a growing sense of crisis in Mexico, as the solutions proffered seem to create new problems, without having the slightest impact on those they were designed to address. The cajoling and mollycoddling of the Mexican people into believing that victory is in sight is wearing thin. According to the Interior Ministry, public service announcements designed to combat drug trafficking and crime were broadcast on radio and television 732,000 times in just five months of 2007.

As the pill gets bitterer, politicians on both sides of the border insist that the medicine must be working. 'Why are we having all these homicides and all these crimes on the streets?' President Fox once asked.

'Because we've been winning the campaign. The more we destroy drug production and the more we catch drugs in transit, the more desperate the traffickers become and the more they challenge the authorities.'[29] President Bush's drug tsar, John Walters, made a similar claim about the rise in Mexico's drug-related murders when he said that 'unfortunately this is one of the possible signs of the efficacy of anti-drug efforts'.[30]

What to do but continue as before? Drug policy officials in Washington are genuinely worried about the escalation of the violence in Mexico. On the one hand, they had high hopes that President Fox would make significant headway against police corruption and ineptitude, and were confident that jailing top traffickers would have a lasting impact on the drugs trade. On the other hand, they view corruption as endemic to Mexico. When asked what should be done now that the army has been shown to be incapable of defeating the cartels, many throw up their hands in resignation.

Mexico's inability to control the drugs trade is already affecting the south-western states of the United States. Arizona and New Mexico both declared states of emergency in 2005. According to drug tsar John Walters, 'the killing of rival traffickers is already spilling across the border. Witnesses are being killed. We do not think the border is a shield.'[31] Worse, officials in the United States aren't immune to corruption either. Investigators have discovered that drug traffickers regularly pay off border authorities in exchange for the right to traffic drugs unmolested into the United States.[32] FBI probes have found instances of corruption in the US border patrol, as in the case of a senior agent and his brother who accepted $1.5 million in exchange for allowing truckloads of marijuana to pass through checkpoints near Hebronville, Texas.[33] Other undercover investigations by the FBI have revealed that US soldiers have conspired to traffic drugs through south-western states. One such probe nabbed thirteen current and former soldiers taking bribes in exchange for transporting cocaine between Texas and Oklahoma.[34] An operation called 'Lively Green' indicted fifty current and former soldiers and police officers in Arizona who pleaded guilty to similar charges.[35] The rewards on offer to those prepared to collude with the smugglers are sufficiently tempting to entice even the war on drugs' most loyal foot soldiers.

7

'Cocaine is the Atomic Bomb of Latin America'[1]

*She winds you up and reels you in / she's a sinner / take her
in your arms and she'll eat you up / you can't love Caine /
you can't believe in Caine / you think that you have her
under your thumb / but without her, you're nothing / you
just can't love Caine / you can't believe in Caine.*

Rubén Blades, 'La Caína'[2]

So much for trying to intercept cocaine shipments in transit. Anticipating the problems their law enforcement strategy was always likely to encounter in Mexico, the United States has spent most of the huge budget it has allocated to tackling the cocaine trade overseas in Colombia, as part of a determined effort to stop coca being turned into cocaine in the first place. 'Cocaine production means destruction here in Colombia,' Colombian Vice-President Francisco Santos assured me when I met him in Bogotá in October 2007. 'You can travel over the department of Putumayo in a helicopter for half an hour and all you see is barren land, where fifteen years ago it was one of the most pristine jungles in the world. Europeans don't like the moralistic perspective, so I hope the environmental one will have more of an impact on them,' Santos went on. 'You can't change their mindsets, but you can give them something to think about when they are snorting coke.'

'Shared Responsibility' is the title of a campaign rolled out by the Colombian government, which is designed to appeal to the eco-consciences of Western cocaine consumers. The premise of 'Shared Responsibility' is irrefutable. Since Western consumers have largely deemed the poverty, violence and injustice that the cocaine trade generates either irrelevant or inevitable, perhaps they will be prepared to listen to the environmentalists' perspective. Colombia covers a million square kilometres, which makes it the same size as California and Texas combined (or for Europeans, the same size as France and Spain combined). To evade detection, coca is grown in the most off-the-beaten-track parts of the country. As coca growers push further into the jungle, the soil quality gets worse, so growers use ten times more agrochemicals on their plots than do farmers raising legal crops in long-settled parts of the country. The average hectare of coca needs 550 kilos of pesticides, herbicides, fertilizers, gasoline, ammonia, cement and sulphuric acid to yield a crop and turn it into coca base (the first step in the process of making cocaine powder). That makes for 171,600 tons of chemical waste a year, dumped in the most remote parts of what is, after Brazil, the most bio-diverse country on Earth.[3] No other country has as many amphibians, or as many bird or frog species as Colombia. For each gram of cocaine produced, four square metres of tropical forest has to be cleared. Unfortunately, the Vice-President's 'Shared Responsibility' programme is a case of closing the gate after the horse has bolted. Most of the environmental damage caused by coca cultivation has already been done. Between 2000 and 2001, 55,000 hectares of forests were cleared to plant coca. Between 2005 and 2006, however, just 8,332 hectares were deforested for the same purpose.[4] After all, nobody enjoys clearing pristine rainforest. Most of the damage done to the Colombian rainforest today is the result not of coca cultivation, but of the fumigation of the coca crops with herbicides sprayed from American crop-duster planes.

In March 2006, the actor Bruce Willis gave a pithy assessment of who he considered responsible for the drug problem facing his country. 'The United States and everyone who cares about protecting the freedom that we have should do whatever it takes to end terrorism in the world. Not just in the Middle East. I'm talking also about going to Colombia and doing whatever it takes to end the cocaine trade. It's killing this country and all the countries that coke goes into.' Willis also gave vent to the frustration that many Americans feel at the failure to put an end to cocaine production at source. 'If they weren't making money on it, they would have stopped it. They could stop it in one day. These guys are growing it like it's corn or tobacco. It is a billion-dollar industry and I think that's a form of terrorism as well.'[5]

The cocaine business has fomented mutual recrimination between Colombia and the United States. After I had heard some of Humberto's stories from his time as a police officer with the Colombian anti-narcotics police in Bogotá, I told him about Willis's remarks. He gave me a wry smile. 'I was a policeman, and then a police captain for thirteen years. I lived in the States for two years, and I know that there isn't a strong anti-consumption campaign in the US. When I was there cocaine was in every disco. You'd hear them sniffing away in the bathrooms. I got pulled over by the police a lot when I was in the States, and when I said that I was from Colombia, they wanted to see everything I had. They thought I was a trafficker. Me! I've still got shrapnel in me from injuries I picked up when I was with the anti-narcotics police.'

Interestingly, Kevin Higgins, who works as a military adviser at the US Embassy in Bogotá, sees his role as one of stabilizing an ally beleaguered by its conflict with guerrilla insurgents, rather than of averting a threat to Americans. 'To me, cocaine is a mission. It is part of FARC [Revolutionary Armed Forces of Colombia] financing, and it is a security problem.' Vice-President Francisco Santos agreed that cocaine had become much more than just a problem for the gringos. 'The business finances the FARC guerrillas and the paramilitaries, so the survival of the Colombian state is at stake. In other countries it might be more manageable, but for us there is no option but to fight with all the tools and all the political will we can muster.' Than Christie is the coca eradication policy officer at the US Embassy in Bogotá. He assured me that 'the Colombians have a political will unlike any other country in the world. Every single day they have 6,500 people pulling up coca out in the fields. By comparison, on a good day, Peru has 150 people doing the same thing. There is a realization from the political class, the business sector, and the army that the drugs issue is Colombia's biggest problem. The corruption of politicians, the lack of economic opportunity, and the lack of invest-ment all stem from the drugs trade. It's the main source of funding for the FARC, and if there were no FARC and there were no kidnappings, international business would be here. Colombians wouldn't be sending all their capital abroad and their kids away to study. They would be investing back at home.'

Every drugs policy official that I spoke to in Colombia was at pains to stress the guerrillas' role in the cocaine trade. Since the Americans decreed that the FARC was 'the third cartel' and that the Colombian army lacked the strength needed to meet the threat they posed, an aid package was agreed on to wrest control of coca-growing regions from the guerrillas. In 2000, Bill Clinton gave his blessing to Plan Colombia, which has funnelled more than $5 billion into the Colombian treasury, making Colombia the world's third biggest recipient of US military aid after Israel and Egypt. Every day for the past eight years, the Colombian security forces have had $15 million to spend on weapons, helicopters, planes, boats, military training and intelligence-gathering, as well as the spraying of herbicides over two million hectares of Colombian land. The goal was to reduce Colombia's cultivation, processing and distribution of drugs by 50 per cent over the following six years.[6]

When cocaine came back into fashion in the United States in the 1970s, most coca bushes were cultivated in Bolivia and Peru. After each harvest, the leaves would be picked and then flown north to be processed into cocaine in laboratories in Colombia. As the Americans' eradication programmes took effect, and aerial surveillance made flying cargoes of coca leaves to Colombia riskier, coca cultivation also moved north. The traffickers moved down the Colombian tributaries of the River Amazon with their sacks of coca seeds, offering cheap credit to anyone who would grow coca for them. Belica is a *cocalero* (coca farmer) from a town called La Uribe, in the rural department of Meta. 'I started picking coca when I was eleven,' she told me. 'Back in 1986, some men came to La Uribe with their families. They brought coca seeds, and they started planting them. The plants grew very well and we started picking the coca leaves for them. They would pay us with coca seeds, so 300 or so of us went off and planted our own coca bushes, and before long there were really big coca fields around La

Uribe.' In the late 1980s, more than half a million Colombians moved into the remote eastern plains, hoping to enjoy the fruit of the coca boom. Though the fumigation planes have driven coca cultivation and coca pickers from the east to the south and now the west of the country, Colombia still produces 70 per cent of the world's coca leaves and has long been its biggest cocaine producer.[7]

To make a kilo and a half of cocaine, a cocaine chemist needs a kilo and a half of coca base. To make a kilo and a half of coca base, a *cocalero* needs a ton of coca leaves.[8] 'You have to do it by the book, or you'll end up with gum, which is completely useless,' Belica explained. 'First you chop up the leaves really well with a scythe, and put them in a tub. Add cement, ammonia, lime and a little bit of sulphuric acid. They're all easy enough to get. Get in there with your big knee-high rubber boots, and keep stirring the mixture until it goes completely black. Then transfer it all to a big steel drum, and fill it halfway up with petrol. Give that a good stir, and then let it sit for forty-five minutes. Then pour the petrol into a plastic bucket, add water and some more sulphuric acid. Drain off the petrol again. Add a bit more water to the petrol, stir it slowly for another forty-five minutes, then leave it for thirty minutes. Once the petrol has risen to the top, pour that off, and put what you're left with through a sieve. Then put it in a cloth and wring out the water. That's what we call the flour – coca base.'

By the 1990s, 80 per cent of the farmers of eastern departments like Vaupes, Meta and Guaviare were living off the coca business. More than half of them belonged to a floating population that with the vagaries of the coca harvests migrated across the vast jungle plains that run east from the Andes. Many local farmers didn't bother growing food crops like yucca or maize any more. They had their vegetables flown in from other parts of the country while they enjoyed a coca bonanza, drinking and whoring their way through their newfound wealth. Initially, they worked for big coca plantation owners, who owned coca fields of anywhere between 40 and 150 hectares. Luis 'Lucho' Salamanca has been spraying herbicides on the coca fields of Colombia from a tiny Turbo-Thrush crop-dusting plane for the past fifteen years. 'These days the number of large-scale coca fields is minimal, and that's because of our aggressive tactics. We've been spraying 150,000 or so hectares a year, hitting three or more areas in the country simultaneously every day. There are seven planes spraying every day, and most fields get sprayed twice a year.'

Fumigation might have put a stop to large-scale coca cultivation, but it has had less impact on small-scale cultivation. By 1998, total coca cultivation had mushroomed from 45,000 to 122,000 hectares. Figures from the United Nations Drug Control Programme (UNDCP) show that by the end of 2006, after six years of spraying herbicide in the department of Nariño, during which time almost 220,000 hectares of coca had been fumigated, total coca cultivation in the department was actually up by 6,000 hectares.[9] Despite sixteen years of ever more intense fumigation of coca fields from the air, Colombia produced 640 tons of cocaine in 2005.[10] Combine that with Bolivian and Peruvian production, and total global cocaine output tops 932 tons, which is about the same as it was in 1995.[11] Despite the failure to control the spread of coca, a White House report of 2001 asserted that attacking coca cultivation remained the most cost-effective way of reducing supplies of cocaine. 'In an ideal world,' the report said, 'drugs would be intercepted at source, and none would be able to enter the distribution chain.'[12]

And so an ideal world has trumped the real world. The United States government and the United Nations make wildly divergent estimates of Colombia's coca crop, never more so than in 2006, when the Americans estimated that there were 157,000 hectares of coca being grown in Colombia, which was more than double the UN's figure of 78,000 hectares.[13] The Americans admit that their estimate 'is subject to a 90 percent confidence interval of between 125,800 and 179,500 hectares'.

I asked the military adviser Kevin Higgins why eradication has had so little impact. 'There was a time when we said "well, this is the hectarage, this is world demand, this is how much cocaine can be made." But we had sprayed so much, and interdicted so much, that it seemed that there was some kind of warehousing system in Mexico or the States in anticipation of lean periods. Cocaine has a long shelf life. We don't have a good picture of what is going on there.' Than Christie, the coca eradication policy officer at the US Embassy in Bogotá, seemed equally stumped for an explanation. 'Maybe the laboratories are getting more efficient. Maybe they are using varieties of coca that produce more alkaloid. We're improving what we know about coca cultivation and farmer behaviour, but we are starting from a huge void of information.'

The United States and the United Nations don't really know how much coca is being grown in Colombia. Figures are slippery, partly because the entire cocaine economy is by its very nature hidden from scrutiny, and partly because governments and the United Nations make lowball estimates of cocaine production in order to make their war on drugs look like it is going somewhere. 'It's science fiction,' the estimable Colombian economist Francisco Thoumi, author of *Illegal Drugs, Society and Economy in the Andes* (2003) told me when I met him in Bogotá. 'In each of the past six years, Colombia has eradicated more coca than was thought to exist. By rights we should say that Colombia doesn't produce cocaine any more.'

In 2002 the United States Senate Appropriations Committee reported that Plan Colombia had 'fallen far short of expectations. Neither the Colombian government nor other international donors have lived up to their financial commitments, and the amount of coca and poppy under cultivation has increased. In addition, peace negotiations have collapsed, the armed conflict has intensified, and the country is preparing for a wider war which few observers believe can be won on the battlefield.'[14]

So why has fumigation failed? After all, fumigation of Colombia's marijuana fields proved very effective in the early 1980s (at least in the sense that cultivation was displaced from Colombia to the United States and Mexico). More recently, Lucho Salamanca and his colleagues in the fumigation programme successfully eradicated Colombia's opium crop. But coca has proven to be a very different beast. The coca bush is as fecund as it is hardy. It can grow for up to forty years in even the poorest soils and it has few natural predators, perhaps because the plant evolved its cocaine content precisely in order to ward them off.

But it is the Colombian farmer, rather than his crop, that accounts for the tenacity of coca cultivation. 'If the coca plants have been fumigated, the farmer will get a group of fifteen or so people together, and the next day they'll go out and cut off all the branches, right back to the trunk,' Belica explained. 'They'll grow back lovely. The chemicals only affect the leaves and the branches, not the root.' By pruning their bushes or washing the herbicide off the leaves, in 2004 three quarters of coca farmers saved their crops from the effects of aerial spraying.[15] Those that didn't move quickly enough invariably planted new bushes. For every hectare lost, the *cocalero* will replant two hectares: the first to recover his losses and repay the Mafioso who financed him, and the second to generate an income for himself.[16]

The fumigation strategy also seems to have failed because aerial spraying has simply reinforced Colombian farmers' reliance on coca, exacerbating the very problem it was supposed to solve. The short-term impact has been to raise prices paid for coca leaf, and reduce competition from the farmers of neighbouring regions. Coca cultivation collapses in some parts of the country, only to take off in other parts – what policy wonks call 'the balloon effect', much as squeezing a balloon only displaces the air inside to the other half of the balloon. Displacement looks good – the area under coca cultivation in Colombia in 2005 was 47 per cent lower than it had been in 2000 – but appearances were deceptive: the shortfall was compensated for by an 11 per cent increase in cultivation in Peru and a 74 per cent increase in Bolivia. I asked Luis Almario Rojas, member of Congress for the eastern department of Caquetá, why coca growing in his region was so resistant to fumigation. His answer was a stark one. 'There's no other way of making a living. We had 150,000 hectares under coca in Caquetá in 1996, and thanks to the balloon effect, today we still have 150,000 hectares.'

The long-term impact of fumigating the coca fields has been to drive Colombian coca farmers further down the Amazon and Orinoco rivers, and into the jungles bordering Peru, Ecuador and Venezuela. Alberto Rueda was working for the Colombian Ministry of National Defence when Plan Colombia was foisted on an unsuspecting public in 2000, and resigned in protest shortly afterwards. 'People talk about GM coca, but the resilience of coca has nothing to do with genetic improvements. It's just better techniques, more harvests, and cutting back or washing the plants after they've been sprayed. But to the United States none of this matters. They just want a budget and a military presence. The Colombians are afraid of aggravating the United States, and the rest of the world is asleep when it comes to drug policy.'

Military advisor Kevin Higgins has a long-term view of the problem. 'I have sat on hilltops with DEA agents, and they've said that this thing will always adapt, and pop up somewhere else. But that is not a signal for us to stop or give up. Colombia is not coca-free, but that doesn't mean that what we do is a failure. As the Army gets more control over the territory, it will make things more difficult for cocaine producers.' The authorities are certainly destroying more cocaine laboratories than ever: they claim to have put 200 out of use in 2006.[17] On the day that I met him, Kevin told me that he and his colleagues in the Colombian anti-narcotics police had just busted a lab in the eastern department of Vichada with a ton and a half of cocaine ready to be shipped. 'It's good to have busted it here, because tracking it down and interdicting it in smaller quantities in the States would be costly. The trade is too lucrative to obliterate. The trade will morph. We just have to make it as difficult as possible for them.'

Making things difficult for cocaine producers sounds laudable, but it is hardly a sustainable anti-drugs policy, and does nothing to address the destructive consequences of the illegal trade in cocaine. Cocaine base is usually made by the same *cocaleros* who grow the leaves. The base is then turned into cocaine in laboratories, which are run by the Mafia and are usually hidden deep in the jungle. Gato, an informants handler with the Colombian anti-narcotics police agreed that most of the foot soldiers of the Colombian cocaine trade make little money. 'The guys working in those jungle labs get paid fifty pence or so per kilo, which is nothing, but if unemployment is high even that sum seems good to them. Those responsible for stashing the product, the ones working in transport and security get paid better. A packer, for instance, might get £500 for a couple of weeks work. But even the bosses aren't always rich. They have a lot of outgoings, and if coca paste runs short, or they run out of chemicals, or the lab is raided, his finances are fucked. So if his boss only pays him £400, a packer has reason to be dissatisfied, which is when he might come to us. We had a call a few weeks ago from a guy in Tumaco who was ready to come in and tell us about the lab where he had been working, but his bosses killed him a couple of days later.'

Meanwhile, the 2.5 million litres of glyphosate that were sprayed over Colombia between 1992 and 1998, and the millions more that have been sprayed since then have had deleterious effects on the countryside. 'The wind picks up the chemicals and they go everywhere, so a lot of the maize, yucca and plantain turn sickly too,' Belica told me. 'The poison gets into the water, so a lot of people get ill. You get headaches and colic. It gets into your blood.' As of 2005, there have been 8,000 health-related complaints from people living in areas that have been sprayed with glyphosate.[18]

The United States government initially pooh-poohed these complaints, even accusing its critics of being in the pay of the cocaine traffickers. Eventually, it agreed to commission a study from the Organization of American States, which concluded that aerial fumigation did no harm to human health or the environment.[19] Critics then countered that the study wasn't valid because half the data used was supplied by Monsanto, which produces the herbicide, and that the OAS was a puppet of the United States anyway. 'Most of the people I know have left,' Belica told me. 'Some left because of the fumigation, others because of the army. If the army runs into coca pickers in the fields they'll grab them and beat them up. The army doesn't see us as human beings. They just see us all as guerrillas. Sometimes they'll kill a *cocalero*, dress him up in a guerrilla fighter's uniform, and make out he was in the FARC.'

Plan Colombia has few supporters among Colombia's neighbours either. As *cocaleros* are driven from the countryside, the United Nations has warned Ecuador and Peru to expect an influx of 30,000 refugees from Colombia. FARC guerrillas have criticized Ecuador's government for allowing the United States to despatch their crop-dusting planes from the airbase at Manta, and have threatened to strike targets in Ecuador in retaliation. The Brazilian government is worried that the chemicals sprayed from planes in Colombia will poison the Amazon and that the fumigation programme will eventually drive the cocaine trade into the Brazilian rainforest. The Venezuelans feel threatened by the military muscle being flexed by the Americans, and now by Colombian President Alvaro Uribe Velez himself.

Partly to placate those critics, the Colombian government has expanded programmes in which coca bushes are eradicated by hand. Police, army and demobilized combatants have been sent into coca-growing communities to pull up coca bushes under the slogan 'Every-body Against Coca', much as Nancy Reagan once urged America to 'Just Say No' to drugs. Plan Colombia has also started financing programmes that encourage the cultivation of alternative crops. War-weary commentators say that this programme of crop substitution is going very well: plenty of coffee bushes have been pulled up, and plenty of coca bushes have been planted. Alternative development programmes have been haphazardly planned and slow to arrive, but more importantly, the sums the Colombian government has invested in alternative development, relative to the hectares of coca sown, are among the paltriest of any of the Andean countries where coca is grown.[20] Aid of £500,000 to the remote, long-neglected, under-populated interior of Colombia is nothing compared to the £25 million that cocaine traffickers are prepared to invest in the coca crop of departments like Putumayo.

What most advocates of coca eradication fail to realize is that coca cultivation arrived in Colombia just as its farmers were looking for ways out of a profound crisis. Since the 1940s, Colombia's *campesinos* (peasant farmers) have responded to the chronic shortage of farmland by moving east on to the plains that run for hundreds of miles to the frontier with Venezuela and Brazil, or south towards the border with Peru and Ecuador. Once they found virgin land, these colonists would clear and farm it until its soils were exhausted. They would then sell up, more often than not to a cattle rancher, and move further into the jungle. As a result of this makeshift pattern of land clearance, much of Colombia's hinterland is without roads, almost half the rural population has no access to running water, and only one in ten country-dwellers has access to a sewer.[21]

The crisis in the Colombian countryside is rarely discussed in the press, perhaps because in the last thirty years Colombia's population has gone from being 70 per cent rural to 70 per cent urban. But it is the key driver of coca cultivation and it's getting worse. In 1990, Colombia's food imports were worth just 6 per cent of the country's GDP. Ten years later, this had risen to 46 per cent. Subsidies for Colombia's small farmers, which have long been available to farmers in the United States, are being eliminated to encourage the switch to large-scale production of export crops like African palm, pineapples and cocoa. 'It's difficult to get our legal produce to market because of the state of the roads, and the prices you get for them are really low,' Belica told me. 'We've always grown rice, yucca, maize and plantain. They give us enough to eat, but we need money to buy things like soap and clothes.' A farmer from Monterrey, in the northern department of Sucre, did the sums. 'Getting a sack of potatoes to market will cost a farmer between 3,000 and 5,000 pesos, and it will sell for between 10,000 and 12,000 pesos, depending on demand. Meanwhile, coca is a lot easier to sow and process, and doesn't need transporting because the traffickers come to the village to buy it. They pay 1,500,000 pesos for a kilo of coca paste.'[22]

Coca growers survive because there is a global demand for their crop, which is more than can be said for farmers of yucca, plantain and rubber, which are also plentiful and cheap, but increasingly imported. Higher coffee prices would reinvigorate Colombia's coffee farming sector and provide legal work for poor farmers, but no one is lobbying for higher coffee prices. In fact, the United States' Congress was instrumental in tearing up the International Coffee Pricing Agreement, which led to prices falling by almost two thirds between 1997 and 2000.[23]

A second, fundamental driver of rural impoverishment is that by and large Colombian farmers don't own the land they work on. Sixty per cent of Colombia's productive land is owned by just half a per cent of its people. In departments like Antioquia, Córdoba and Sucre, which are blessed with fertile flood plains by the rivers that run off the Andes, a huge amount of land is given over to cattle ranches. These benefit big landowners but supply little in the way of food or employment. This system of often unproductive *latifundios* (estates) has long proved resistant to change. Efforts towards a land reform programme were made in the 1960s, but all they achieved were some big irrigation projects in the north, and some resettlement programmes to areas that are today controlled by FARC guerrillas. The owners of the *latifundios* are increasingly likely to be paramilitary bosses, wealthy drugs traffickers, or both.[24]

'The European Union says that there should be investment instead of fumigation, which is a good idea, but they've done nothing,' Caquetá Congressman Luis Almario Rojas told me. 'They don't want to get involved in Plan Colombia, so they bow to the United States. Plan Colombia has financed some micro-budget projects, but they only employ 100 or so people. What we need here are funds to generate energy and build infrastructure. But who would invest in Caquetá? There is no business culture and people are worried about being kidnapped by the FARC.' A USAID study concluded that it was impossible to assist most coca-growers in rural Putumayo because of the security situation, the poor soil, and the region's isolation from markets.[25] Unsurprisingly, the study was hushed up by the US State Department shortly after being published in 2001. 'The root of the problem,' Luis Almario Rojas told me, 'is that there is no infrastructure for a legal local economy. If it existed, the *campesinos* would drop the illegal cultivation straight away. The farmers have become slaves of the Mafia. They're only getting $50 for a kilo of coca leaves. It's the traffickers of Colombia, Mexico and the United States that are making the money.'

The cocaine business is clearly more slippery than the policy wonks care to admit. If the lizard's head is said to be the cocaine consumers of Europe and the United States, one of its many tails is the Colombian coca farmer. You can cut it off as many times as you like, but it will always grow back. Former president Ernesto Samper gave the green light to Colombia's first fumigation programme, but he has since come to see the futility of trying to stem the supply of cocaine at source. 'We get 20 per cent of the profits and 100 per cent of the notoriety. We destroy the plots of our own peasants to satisfy electoral aspirations in the United States, and we pay for this with the corruption of our institutions and our armed forces. Within a few years, the only vestige of this debate will be the Marlboro marijuana cigarettes that we'll be importing by the million. And why not? We've been importing all kinds of dangerous substances: Agent Orange, pesticides that damage the ecological balance. Why don't we start thinking about importing another one in a few years time: marijuana? Everything seems to indicate that marijuana that comes from there isn't as harmful as marijuana that comes from here.'[26]

Virgilio Barco Vargas, who was Colombia's president between 1986 and 1990, claimed that drug trafficking was responsible for the majority of human rights abuses in the country, that it threatened democracy and national security, encouraged paramilitary groups and networks of paid killers and distorted the economy. His administration even contracted a firm of image consultants to show the world the high price Colombia paid for supplying the cocaine trade. That Colombia should be ripped to shreds by hypocritical Anglo-Saxons, flip-flopping between indulgence and self-reproach, seemed to be a tragedy that Colombia would have to bear alone. Responsibility for the chaos lies abroad, Colombia's politicians said, and no significant change could be made until the outside world changed.

Change came when the Americans started pumping cash into the Colombian treasury. But the idea that the myriad problems Colombia faces have been caused by the international cocaine trade is at best a half-truth. Even in 1989, when the 'cocaine wars' between traffickers and police were at their height, perhaps 200 people were killed and 800 injured in terrorist attacks carried out by Pablo Escobar's organization.[27] Almost three quarters of the 5,700 political killings committed that year were the responsibility of the Colombian army and police, often using resources supplied specifically for counter-drug operations.

It is a well-kept secret in Colombia that coca can grow in at least thirty countries. In the days before cocaine was prohibited, the biggest exporters of coca were the Indonesian islands of Java and Sumatra. Before the United Nations banned coca and cocaine, Colombia didn't export significant quantities of either. The demand for cocaine cannot explain why its main suppliers should be Colombians. Once an easy-to-grow crop is made illegal, cultivation is bound to concentrate in countries where it is easiest to do illegal things. Thereafter, illegal drug cultivation might exacerbate existing problems, but it doesn't explain them. Colombia is the only country in the world that produces cocaine, marijuana *and* heroin, and its proclivity to illegality isn't confined to the drugs trade. Colombia is the world's biggest producer of counterfeit US dollars. It has more *sicarios* (hit men) than any other country, and until Mexico took its place, saw more kidnappings. It has more landmines, exports more prostitutes, arms more children, and displaces more civilians through violence than any other Latin American country. Illegality is rampant in Colombia, yet the Colombian government chooses to blame Western drug consumers for the cocaine business.

Why do illegal activities find such a firm footing in Colombia? Poverty, inequality and corruption go some way to explaining Colombia's high rates of law-breaking, but none is unique to Colombia. So what is? A satisfactory answer can be had only by looking at the country's past. The Spanish colonists found vast, fertile lands in the north-western corner of South America, whose native population was small even before the arrival of European diseases. The Spanish found manual labour undignified, so they imported African slaves. But with so much of the country still unsettled, it was relatively easy for Africans and indentured indigenous labourers to run away and found their own settlements far from the reach of the Europeans. In Gabriel García Márquez's novel *One Hundred Years of Solitude* the tax-collecting *corregidor* is universally despised when he arrives in the imaginary town of Macondo. Its people had built the town without help from the state, so why should taxes be paid to it? For the people of Macondo, the government was a distant authority, its laws a game to be negotiated rather than an authority to be respected. It is a sentiment that many rural Colombians would endorse today.

Even before the Europeans came to Colombia, the north-western corner of the continent was one of the few with no central government and no empire. Mexico had its Aztecs and Mayas, Peru had its Incas, the southern cone its Guaranís, but the *chichas* of Colombia were a collection of chiefdoms, constantly warring with one another, and perennially divided. Colombian infighting is partly explicable by geography. The Andes divides into three huge mountain ranges at Colombia's southern border, from where they run north to the Caribbean Sea. The mountains have long hindered communications and trade within and beyond Colombia's borders. They also create great varieties of climate, from the valley savannah to deserts and high mountain plains, which support such a wide range of crops that until the twentieth century most cities didn't need to engage in trade with neighbouring cities because everything they needed could be grown locally.

So Colombia won its independence from Spain as a nation of regions, over which the state found it hard to impose its laws. The government has always had to negotiate with powerful regional elites. Until the 1920s, Colombia exported less than any other Latin American nation; since state coffers were dependent on taxes on trade, the central government was one of the poorest in Latin America. The capital that the Spanish settlers founded at Santa Fe de Bogotá has grown dramatically since the 1950s, but until that decade the city housed a much smaller proportion of the nation's people than other Latin American capitals. Go south or east from Bogotá and you soon find towns where roads, hospitals, schools and police stations have never existed (until recently, the same could be said for parts of Bogotá itself).

David Hutchinson is a British banker who was kidnapped by FARC guerrillas in 2002. He spent a year living in the forgotten hinterland of the country. 'We sit here in the middle of Bogotá and we can't see the FARC or the kidnap victims, but if you're out there in the hills, you can see the lights of Bogotá. You know where your house is, and what your people are doing. Your family can't see you but you can see them, so it's like a one-way mirror. Behind the mirror is over half the territory of Colombia, where the state can't see anything. Nobody ever saw us, and that's not at night. That's during the daytime. We walked over the Andes for day after day. No aeroplane came, no satellite saw us, nobody came and killed us. Nothing at all.'

For the government truly to exert its sovereignty throughout its territory, it would have to develop the many parts of Colombia where there are no viable concerns save the production of oxygen. Instead, the vacuum has been filled by private armies of paramilitaries (who collaborate with whoever makes up the local elite), or guerrillas (who do not). The remote areas these illegal armed groups run are often well suited to cocaine production, as well as gun-running, emerald smuggling and the massacre of obstructive miners and farmers. For many local honchos, accommodating paramilitary death squads and drug traffickers has been an acceptable price to pay for the pacification of the countryside and access to its goldmines, oilfields, forests and pastures.

Colombia has been plagued by violence since its inception. Because the state was always weak, Colombia's Liberal and Conservative Parties became the principal sources of authority, patronage and protection. Both parties mobilized all classes, and once in power catered only to their own. This pragmatic clientelism goes a long way to explain the conflicts of today. Prudence dictates that people try to get along with whoever is in charge, regardless of ideology, be it the FARC, the army or the paramilitaries.[28]

I asked Congressman Luis Almario Rojas about his day-to-day life in the department of Caquetá. 'The state has a presence in Caquetá, but people who work in local government have to put up with constant harassment from the guerrillas, and fire-fights between them and the paramilitaries as they struggle for territory. In 1995, the guerrillas created an underground Bolivarian political project, and they told the Mayor [of Florencia, the departmental capital] that anyone who didn't join them would have to leave town. That lost them a lot of support from the local people, and made for problems with both the Liberal Party under the Turbay family, and the Conservatives, under me. The leader of the Turbays was killed, and since then the guerrillas have tried to kill me more than ten times. It's a miracle that I've survived for this long. The paramilitaries and the drug traffickers have money down here, but they don't have any political power. That may change, as people say that they financed some politicians' electoral campaigns, in return for being allowed to do business.'

Laws passed in Bogotá don't carry much weight in places like Caquetá. Of course, lip service is paid to the law, but there is a huge gap between the formal rules laid out in the Constitution, and the informal web of money and power by which the country is actually run. Irrespective of the illegal drugs industry, Colombia has yet to build a society in which all its people can depend on the rule of law. The vitality of the guerrilla insurgency, paramilitarism and the cocaine business rests upon this fundamental disdain for the law.

'We saw Pablo Escobar gunned down on television,' US Republican Congressman Dan Burton said in an address he made to a congressional committee in 2002. 'Everybody applauded and said "that's the end of the Medellín cartel". But it wasn't the end. When they kill one, there are ten or twenty or fifty waiting to take his place. You know why? Because there's so much money to be made. We go into drug eradication and we go into rehabilitation and we go into education, and the drug problem continues to increase, and it continues to cost us not billions of dollars, but trillions. Trillions!'[29]

One of the traffickers waiting to step into Pablo Escobar's shoes was Juan Carlos Ramírez Abadia, alias 'Chupeta' (Lollipop). Reading the details of his career and eventual arrest, you can't help commiserating with exasperated Americans such as Bruce Willis and Dan Burton. Chupeta got his start in the cocaine business in 1985, while working as a jockey riding *paso fino* horses for the heads of the Cali cartel, Miguel and Gilberto Rodríguez Orejuela. By the time he was arrested in Brazil in August 2007, he had risen to become one of the leading members of the Norte del Valle cartel, with a personal fortune (probably under-) estimated at £900 million. Crucially, when the police arrested Chupeta, they also confiscated his laptop, which provided them with a remarkably clear picture of a contemporary large-scale cocaine-smuggling operation. Once the cocaine left Chupeta's jungle laboratories, it was taken to the coast under the protection of Autodefensas Unidas de Colombia (AUC) paramilitaries and loaded on to boats that carried an average of ten tons of cocaine per trip. The year 2004 was Chupeta's most successful: he exported 122 tons of cocaine, which means that he controlled a fifth of the Colombian cocaine business. Chupeta employed 400 people, often exporting in concert with family members or paramilitary chiefs such as Ramón Isaza, tellingly also known as 'Medio Tiempo' (Part-time). Chupeta cleared an average of £35 million in profits a month.

It has been estimated that Colombian cocaine cartels spend £50 million on bribes to officials each year.[30] The reach of Chupeta's bribes was quite amazing. Since the police relied on the Agustín Codazzi Geographic Institute for the maps they needed to raid Chupeta's jungle labs and stashes, Chupeta paid one of the Institute's functionaries £2,000 a month to be kept informed of any police enquiries.[31] He paid £2,500 a month to a mobile phone company engineer to let him know when his calls were being traced or intercepted. He typically paid £7,700 every time he needed to have a police roadblock lifted to allow his cocaine consignments to pass through. Once his merchandise was at sea, he had the benefit of dozens of maps showing the coordinates of the Navy vessels sent to intercept his shipments, secured thanks to a £35,000 bribe of a naval officer. In the run-up to Christmas 2004, Chupeta spent £1.4 million on presents, including gifts 'for our friends in the intelligence services'. No one seemed able to resist his bribes. 'Payment for dropping a news item and handing over video footage,' reads one entry in his computer records. He paid a district attorney £13,000 to drop a case against him, and £7,700 to a prison service functionary to have one of his friends transferred to another prison. When he needed to change his identity, he paid an official at his local registry office £78,000. Dozens of soldiers and sailors, senior officers and judges took his bribes, and one hundred state employees received regular monthly payments for their collusion in the smooth running of his business.

Chupeta was also murderous. At the end of 2003, his arch-rival Victor Patiño Fomeque was extradited to the United States. As part of the plea-bargaining process, Patiño Fomeque told the DEA all he knew about Chupeta's business. Over the eighteen months that followed, Chupeta had 150 people executed by any one of a team of 120 *sicarios*, who were paid a total of £779,000. The victims included thirty-five members of Patiño Fomeque's family, as well as the lawyers, business associates and *sicarios* who worked for him.

Still more shocking is that for twenty-two years Chupeta successfully evaded arrest. The case against him was hampered by the authorities' dependence on bribing informers, but even when they had him in their sights, their operations were constantly sabotaged by spies in the anti-narcotics police. It took a team of five 'bribe-proof' police officers a year to catch up with him. Once the police had arrested him and worked their way through his computer records, they found that Chupeta had laundered the proceeds of his cocaine smuggling through dozens of front companies. Once 'clean', the profits were invested in legal companies, including leading Colombian supermarkets and car dealerships, or simply paid into the accounts of prominent businessmen for safe-keeping. The police raided six huge stashes of cocaine in middle-class neighbourhoods of Cali, impounding £45 million in cash in the process. Three hundred of Chupeta's properties and front companies, with a value of over £200 million, were identified and confiscated. All this was only possible because Chupeta kept such comprehensive computer records, and because the police happened to find his laptop. Even with such unprecedented access to his records, the police have yet to recover £200 million in cash, believed to be buried somewhere in the jungle. Congressman Dan Burton will be galled to know that Chupeta will inevitably have been replaced and that his business will be alive and well under the leadership of another *capo*.[32]

Mafia culture has deep roots in Colombia, which is unsurprising given the country's long history of lawlessness. Mafia culture seems to thrive wherever the law is weak. In rural communities from Mexico to Pakistan, wherever the state is distant and strange, mafiosi are seen as protectors of the people and as dispensers of justice.[33] When local people refer to the local *capo* as 'an honourable man', they pay tribute to his role as an even-handed defender of public order. The *capo* does this not by arresting or imprisoning wrong-doers, but by intimidating and, when necessary, killing them. Outsiders will fear him, and call him a Mafioso, but those under his control and protection do not use the word. To them, it suggests delinquency and disorder, which is the polar opposite of what a true *capo* brings to his community.

The Colombian Mafia grew rich on contraband, which has been an important source of income since the days when the country was part of the Spanish Empire. The city of Medellín was made notorious by Pablo Escobar, but even in the 1950s the city's laboratories were

THE CANDY MACHINE

producing heroin, morphine and cocaine to be smuggled across the Caribbean to Cuba, where it would be sold to American mobsters like Meyer Lansky. In those days, drug distribution in the United States was entirely controlled by Cubans, but after the Cuban Revolution of 1959, the *paisas* (as natives of Medellín are called) moved the base of their operations from Havana to Miami, and from the late 1960s they came to control more of the distribution end too, muscling aside the Cubans, at times with great violence. More recently, the United States government has expressed fears that Cuba post-Castro might become a safe haven for drug traffickers. This seems a grim irony, since it was precisely Cuba's status as a playground for the rich and criminal of the United States that made its people so ready to support Fidel Castro's revolution. In publicly worrying about drug control in a future, presumably free-market Cuba, the United States implicitly acknowledges that the only government that has succeeded in quelling the smugglers, corrupters and gangsters that have become so powerful across the Caribbean since 1980 is the authoritarian one currently in power in Cuba.

In the 1970s, long before it started to make fortunes from cocaine, the Colombian Mafia got rich from *la bonanza marimbera* (the marijuana boom). The spur to growth was the pressure then US President Richard Nixon put on the Mexicans to spray herbicidal paraquat over the marijuana fields of Mexico. This pushed cultivation south: by the time the Mexican fumigation programme drew to a close, 75 per cent of the marijuana smoked in the United States was being grown on the north coast of Colombia.[34]

When demand for cocaine in the United States started to grow in the late 1970s, two cartels met it. The Medellín cartel was headed by Pablo Escobar, who was instrumental in bringing Mafia culture from the village to the *comunas* (shanty communities) of the city. *Capos* like Escobar took charge of communities that had until their arrival been completely lawless, imposing order and managing all types of criminal enterprise. Pablo Escobar built a neighbourhood for the poor of Medellín, which he named after himself, and football pitches for the children. On one occasion, he showered the residents of a poor neighbourhood in Medellín with dollar bills thrown from his

helicopter. For many of the millions of Colombians of Escobar's generation who had been uprooted from the countryside and transplanted to
the *comunas*, the cocaine traffickers were their only guardians. They
would cheer the *capos* as they railed against the indifference of the
patrician elite that ruled the city, the corruption of the politicians and the
duplicity of the gringos. Escobar is remembered with respect by many
people in the *comunas* of Medellín. They leave his graveside clutching
handfuls of earth, speaking of the 'miracles' Pablo performed for the
city, and praying that he continue to protect the poor from heaven.

Escobar's problems began when he tried to break the Mafioso mould
and join the ranks of the Colombian elite. He was treated as an
unwelcome step-child, and the patricians' rejection of the rising narco-
bourgeoisie goes some way towards explaining why Escobar launched
a wave of urban terrorism against them in the late 1980s. Escobar had
shown that he could bribe his way through any Colombian court, so
when the Americans started bringing pressure to bear, the government
resolved to extradite him to stand trial in the United States. For
Escobar, this was akin to excommunication. It provoked a bloody war
between a Medellín cartel front organization called Los Extraditables
(the Extraditables) and the Colombian army and police. Escobar made
bombings and assassinations everyday occurrences, borrowing from
the revenge tactics practised by the Sicilian Mafia, and the norms of
Colombia's long-running dirty war. In 1986, 3,500 people were killed
in Medellín, a city with just two million inhabitants: that year, Colombia had the highest murder rate in the world. The Justice Minister
Rodrigo Lara Bonilla had championed the extradition treaties, and he
was the first senior politician to be killed by Escobar's hitmen. In
1989, a *sicario* in the pay of Escobar killed Luis Carlos Galán, another
tough opponent of the traffickers, who had been widely tipped to
win the presidential elections. Under enormous pressure from the
Extraditables' bombing campaign, the Constitutional Court rejected
the extradition treaty in 1991.

Sir Keith Morris, who was British ambassador to Colombia at the
time of Pablo Escobar's death in 1993, described the moment when
he began to question his commitment to the war on drugs. 'I started
to have my doubts immediately after Escobar was killed, when the

American machine went into briefing us that "We've got rid of Escobar, but just as much cocaine is coming out of Colombia, so let's go on to Cali." All these people had died, and Escobar had been killed, but if that effort hadn't had any effect on the cocaine business, this suggested that it was all much more complicated.' The tactics of the Cali cartel were a novel departure from the Mafia tradition upheld by the *capos* of Medellín. Under the Rodríguez Orejuela brothers, the Cali cartel bought its way into the city's banks, using its money to ingratiate itself into the local business community. Before long, everyone in Cali seemed to be working for the *narcos*. Lawyers, accountants and bankers handled their proceeds; others supplied their retail services, worked on their construction projects or farmed their land. This put the people of Cali in a strange position, at once sufficiently removed from cocaine trafficking to escape the disapprobation of the DEA, yet wholly dependent on the rise of cocaine's buccaneering second generation of traffickers. Many *caleños* (as natives of Cali are known) approved of the Rodríguez Orejuelas' enlightened patronage of their city. Of course the cartel meted out violence, but it was of a discreet, functional kind, dictated by their need to control an illegal business, with few of the gruesome decorative flourishes indulged in by the Medellín cartel.

Yet both cartels had one foot in the past and another in the future, oscillating between ancestral and consumerist in their ostentatious displays of power. They indulged in the landowners' traditional love of *paso fino* horses and stud farms, but they also employed *narquitectos* to design their homes. Squandering money on fripperies, while seeking the blessing of the Catholic Church, was common to many Colombians who felt both ambitious and excluded. The money was wasted if it wasn't on display for all to see. The cartels were incredibly violent, not just because they had empires to defend, but because violence had become a way of announcing their arrival as new members of the elite.

Watching the way in which the Medellín cartel was brought down, the Cali cartel learnt not to take on the forces of the state. The whistle was also blown, though not for long, on the traffickers' funding of political candidates, a practice that had long been suspected, but which came to light only after Ernesto Samper was elected president in 1994. The pressure that the United States put on Samper after he was found to have received payments from the Cali cartel culminated in the United States' decertification of Colombia as a willing partner in their war on drugs. Samper could not afford to see his country classified as a narco-state; he pushed through a constitutional amendment that once again authorized the extradition of traffickers to stand trial in the United States.

After a concerted campaign led by the Americans, most of the first generation of Colombian *capos* had either been jailed or killed by 1997. But the cocaine business rebounded. 'Those who took over weren't going to advertise themselves,' Keith Morris told me. 'Nor were they going to try to build huge organizations, because they knew that that was very dangerous. There's been a lot of talk about the Norte del Valle cartel, but I think that's a hang-over. In general, there has been a multiplicity of small enterprises, run by people without any track record, which has made it much more difficult to tackle the top end of the business.' The 200 *cartelitos*, or mini-cartels, that run the cocaine business today have learnt to outsource operations to sub-contractors who have little knowledge of the rest of the organization. Breaking the monopoly held first by the Medellín cartel and then by the Cali cartel has also allowed Colombia's guerrillas and paramilitaries to become more closely involved in the cocaine business. Some traffickers have drawn closer to the paramilitaries, but others have no political affiliations. All too aware of the risk run by being flashy or defiant, the current generation of cocaine traffickers has adapted to survive. In doing so, they have become almost invisible.

Ordinary Colombians' attitudes to cocaine are contradictory. There have been plenty of laws passed to combat the drugs trade in Colombia, and yet there has never been a thorough debate about the drugs trade in the national Congress.[35] The government talks about how the trade funds the FARC guerrillas, but the endless public information announcements on Colombian television make little mention of the involvement of paramilitaries and politicians in the cocaine business. Colombians see cocaine as a dangerous drug when it is smoked as *basuco* (a crude by-product of coca paste, similar to crack) by homeless street children, but not when consumed in powder form by prominent newspaper editors. In this sense, perceptions of the drug differ little from those prevailing in London. Certain drug users should be punished and the FARC must be defeated, but few seem to realize just how intractable the cocaine trade has become.

Considering that Colombia is a leading producer of cocaine, marijuana and, until recently, heroin, and that the laws governing drug consumption are as selectively enforced as the rest of Colombia's laws, it comes as a surprise to find how few Colombians actually use drugs. Just 1.5 per cent of them have tried cocaine, largely because it's still too expensive for most of them, but also because it is widely regarded as a rich man's drug, strictly for export to the fantasy lands of Europe and the United States. For those left out of the fantasy, there are local hallucinogens, marijuana, legal prescription pills and *basuco*. About 5 per cent of Colombians use legal tranquillizers, sedatives and amphetamines, which is about the same proportion that use marijuana, the main difference being that two thirds of users of legal drugs are women. The most popular drug among young people in Medellín is Rohypnol, which is said to assuage the feelings of guilt that follow acts of violence, and is used by novices to ward off doubt and stiffen resolve. But Colombia's drug of choice is alcohol. Ninety per cent of Colombians have tried it, and 20 per cent of them are thought to be alcoholics.[36]

How much of a problem need the cocaine business be in Colombia, now that those engaged in it have learnt to stay 'under the radar'? In the 1980s, many Colombians regarded cocaine as a problem only for Americans, and as such, just deserts for a country that paid peanuts for legitimate Colombian exports. Proceeds from the cocaine trade buffered Colombia's economy from the worst of the external debt crisis that afflicted many Latin American countries in the 1980s. For the middle class at least, wages kept steady and living standards rose. The cocaine trade has also acted as an escape valve, absorbing some of the manpower left idle by the collapse of the coffee economy. Little wonder then, that plenty of city dwellers were initially happy to turn a blind eye to the traffickers.

In the course of a conversation with Nicolas, a former FARC

guerrilla, I asked him how he thought most Colombians felt about the cocaine business today. 'People in Colombia have got used to the drugs business. They don't openly criticize it, firstly for fear of the war lords, but secondly because unconsciously people know that narco-traffic plays a part in all aspects of economic life in Colombia. This is a subsistence economy, but even countries like Argentina and Brazil, which have some technology and benefit from more favourable trade treaties, don't have economies as strong as ours, because behind the legal economy, we have narco-traffic.'

Between 1987 and 1995, the sums entering the Colombian economy every year thanks to the cocaine trade were thought to oscillate between £588 million and £1.2 billion, which is about 50 per cent of the total sum invested in Colombia by foreign companies every year.[37] This would suggest that cocaine has become a mainstay of the Colombian economy, but in fact, even in the boom days of the late 1980s, income from drug sales was thought to be equivalent to just 5 per cent of Colombia's GDP, and had fallen to 2.3 per cent by 1998.[38] Whatever its legal status, cocaine is essentially a cheap agricultural commodity, and like many other cheap commodities produced for export, 75 per cent of the profits from cocaine production are invested abroad.[39] After all, illegal businesspeople invest their money with the same rationale as their legal counterparts, and the United States generally offers better returns on investments than does Colombia.

Cocaine is much cheaper and of much higher quality than it was when the war on drugs was launched.[40] As a result, proceeds from the drugs trade as a proportion of Colombian, Peruvian or Bolivian GDP are considerably lower than they were in the 1980s. Once the US dollar's fall in value is factored into the equation, the real fall in the value of the cocaine market to Latin American wholesalers is about 90 per cent. Just 1 per cent of the retail price of cocaine in the US goes to the coca farmer in Colombia. Four per cent goes to its cocaine producers and 20 per cent goes to its smugglers. The real winners are the distributors in the countries where cocaine is retailed, generally the United States or Europe.[41] Seventy-five per cent of the retail price of cocaine never leaves the country in which it was realized.

The little money that does make it back to Colombia has a destabilizing effect. Local economies become dependent on the fortunes of gangsters: Cali and Medellín both went into recession when their cartels were dismantled. Colombia imports more than it needs, because imports are a good way to launder ill-gotten gains. This undermines domestic producers who can't compete with cheap imports. The flow of dollars into the country also keeps the Colombian peso artificially high, which makes Colombian exports more expensive. Colombia has enormous tourist potential, but it remains unrealized because most governments advise their citizens against going there. The violence also puts off investors and has spurred the flight of domestic capital from Colombia to Miami. Moreover, Colombians who choose not to follow their money north have to spend vast amounts of money on private security, partly because the law is so ineffectual, and partly because the cocaine business is so violent.

Whatever economic benefits the cocaine business might bring to Colombia are outweighed by the deficits. It is all the more surprising then that although the Colombian government is committed to the fumigation of the coca fields, it seems less than willing to break the links between cocaine dollars and the legal economy. So-called San Andresito shopping complexes flourish in every Colombian city, selling contraband, paying no taxes, and often laundering millions of dollars derived from cocaine sales. Stories of how drugs money has been washed through legal businesses like Gino Pascalli, a big Colombian clothing company, and conglomerates like Grajales, the Sindicato Añtioqueno and Grupo Aval have made waves in the Colombian press. Yet the traffickers' infiltration of Colombia's financial system, banks and construction business has gone largely unchallenged. Proceeds from drug trafficking are often invested in real estate, yet the Dirección Nacional de Estupefacientes (the Colombian version of the DEA) is grossly underfunded, and functions at best as an incompetent estate agency. It took the DNE ten years to confiscate properties belonging to Pablo Escobar.

One of the first signs that there might be an ulterior motive to Plan Colombia has been the US State Department officials' glassy-eyed refusal to admit that they are failing to tackle coca production. 'For the first time in twenty years, we are on a path to realize dramatic reductions in cocaine production in Colombia, and a reduction in the world's supply of cocaine,' insisted the United States drug tsar John Walters in June 2004. 'This will contribute substantially to achieving the administration's goal of reducing US cocaine consumption by 25 per cent by 2006. The challenge before us is to stay the course.'[42] 'If support for fumigation collapse, and if we stopped spraying, cultivation would go up to 600,000 hectares, and we'd see a real worldwide problem,' fumigation pilot Lucho Salamanca told me. The governments of Colombia and the United States insist that without this aggressive law enforcement, demand for cocaine would explode. But this way of thinking side-steps the fact that world demand for cocaine is satisfied by about 200,000 hectares of coca, and has been, with little variation, since the late 1970s, in spite of the huge sums spent spraying the coca fields.[43] Coca cultivation has been unaffected by the fumigation programme. In response, the White House has done its level best to make sure that its fumigation programme is unaffected by coca cultivation.

Faced with uncomfortable facts, the governments of Colombia and the United States have found common cause in invoking a secular evil, intent on sabotaging what would otherwise be effective, rational policies. The term 'narco-guerrilla' was first coined by US ambassador to Colombia, Lewis Tambs. This elision of terms suits Colombian president Alvaro Uribe Velez, who would like the defeat of the FARC to be his legacy. 'With the FARC, the plan is to defeat them militarily, and then negotiate,' Vice-President Francisco Santos told me. 'But to do that you have to take away their main source of income, which is drugs traffic. It is part of the same fight.'

Colombia is the only large Latin American country that has never had a genuinely populist government. Once in power, such movements often prove to be financially disastrous, but at least they release some of the tensions that accumulate in societies as hierarchical as that of Colombia.[44] This lack of popular representation grows more pressing as the population increases – it has gone from 28 million in 1988 to 44 million today.[45] The FARC has been fighting the Colombian state with varying degrees of intensity since 1964. Theirs is a struggle for land, resources and power, fought to put an end to the impoverishment of the mass of the people and the political exclusion maintained by traditional political elites. But they have never secured widespread support. Joaquín Villalobos is a former Salvadorean guerrilla whose interpretation of the FARC has been widely quoted in the Colombian press. 'Since they were born with territory, they grew up to become more like a peasant self-defence force than an insurgency with a vision of political power,' he has said. 'For decades the FARC were a guerrilla force that was militarily and politically lazy, undoubtedly the most conservative insurgency on the whole continent, which has grown old in the depths of the Colombian countryside.'

What is the FARC's relationship to the cocaine business? Its guerrillas are active in two thirds of Colombia's coca-growing municipalities.[46] But most FARC fronts are active in municipalities where coca isn't even grown.[47] The party line on relations with the cocaine business hasn't changed since 1997: 'Our principles insist that we reject drug traffickers, because they are incompatible with democracy and the well-being of the Colombian people, and because drug trafficking generates corruption, impunity, criminality, and social breakdown, all of which have a particularly severe effect on the young people of the world.'[48] In 1978, when representatives from the Medellín cartel first travelled down the River Caguan, distributing sacks of coca seeds to poor farmers, the FARC was very much against the cultivation of coca. But theirs was an impoverished and militarily weak organization that was in no position to arrest such a powerful economic impulse.[49] Besides, the guerrillas are pragmatists; as they saw it, their role was to defend *campesinos* from landowners hungry for their land. In time, they saw that by defending the livelihoods of the *cocaleros* from the government and the United States, they could win a new base of support. In turn, many coca farmers welcomed the FARC's presence because coca-growing had brought plentiful violence, and the guerrillas imposed some order on the trade.

In the 1980s, the guerrillas flirted with joining the political mainstream, creating a new political party with the Colombian Communist Party, which they called the Unión Patriótica (Patriotic Union). At the same time, encouraged by their ability to kidnap and extort financing from landowners, the FARC also started building a fighting army. They moved into the regions where oil and mineral wealth or coca fields are concentrated, expelling what police presence they found, and dipping into municipal coffers. In response, local landowners turned to the Mafia for help in tackling the FARC.[50] The feud between the Mafia and the guerrillas was further aggravated when Gonzalo Rodríguez Gacha, a major Medellín cartel trafficker, refused to pay taxes to the FARC. The guerrillas burnt down some of his cocaine laboratories and in retaliation, Rodríguez Gacha set about killing activists from the Unión Patriótica.

The Colombian establishment was divided over how best to respond to the rise of the UP. For every Congressman who saw the party's electoral success as a sign that the guerrillas' insurgency might be coming to an end, there was an army general who saw the party as a Trojan horse, from which the FARC would eventually burst to take power. In October 1987, a shadowy alliance of politicians and cocaine traffickers had the UP's presidential candidate Jaime Pardo Leal killed. When the Communist Party's Bernardo Jaramillo ran for the presidency on a UP ticket in 1990, they had him killed too. In the same year they blew up a plane in mid-flight, killing Carlos Pizarro, a former M-19 guerrilla who was also running for the presidency.[51] Nobody has ever been prosecuted for these murders, or for the killing of any of the 3,500 UP members that followed.

The new Constitution of 1991 had brought left-wing insurgent groups into the fold of mainstream political life. The FARC too were invited to join the new Constituent Assembly, but the door was slammed shut when the armed forces, which certainly didn't want the guerrillas to join the mainstream, bombed the FARC's headquarters at the Casa Verde. The annihilation of the UP, the collapse of the Soviet Union, the FARC's split with the Colombian Communist Party and the bombing of its HQ all bolstered the FARC's military wing. With a negotiated settlement now more distant than ever, the guerrillas committed themselves to taking power by force of arms. To buy those arms they would need resources; their opening came in the mid-1990s, with the fall of first the Medellín and then the Cali cartels. 'These ageing Colombian insurgents found themselves living in the very areas that had the most coca production in the world,' says Joaquín Villa-lobos. 'Since even the CIA was getting involved in the business, they started financing themselves from the drugs trade, launching a new wave of violence as an army in the service of narco-traffic.' As the FARC's coffers swelled, their ranks began to grow. By the time Plan Colombia was launched in 2000, the guerrillas were 18,000 strong, making them the largest insurgent army in the world and a credible threat to the Colombian government.

In 1997, the DEA had reported that there was little evidence that the FARC were producing or trafficking in cocaine.[52] 'I asked these guys on the border who was financing the replanting,' Than Christie, coca eradication policy officer at the US Embassy in Bogotá, told me when I spoke to him in September 2007. 'They said that the FARC were paying them, and to a certain extent, telling them what to grow. Basically the FARC are charging taxes on the cultivation of coca and the production of coca base. But for the most part it's not FARC chemists who are turning the base into cocaine.'

Yet if the DEA, the Colombian press and government are to be believed, the FARC also own cocaine laboratories, trade processed cocaine for weapons and have been running drugs into the United States.[53] Since 2002, the DEA has indicted sixty-three members of the FARC on cocaine trafficking charges, and in 2006 it indicted a further fifty members, charging them with importing cocaine worth $25 billion into the United States.[54] The security forces believe that some of the larger Mexican cartels get over half of the cocaine they ship to the United States from the FARC directly or through intermediaries.[55]

Most observers, however, regard trafficking and foreign sales – the most profitable rungs of the cocaine production ladder – as being beyond the FARC's reach. They are more interested in protecting coca fields and trafficking routes, and using intimidation and violence to control people and institutions. Many of the smuggling corridors running east through the department of Casanare to the border with Venezuela, and onward to the European market, lie in FARC hands. Many of those running west to the Pacific port of Buenaventura and the North American market are in the hands of the paramilitaries. Both the FARC and their paramilitary rivals have become more involved in protection and control for fear of the power that dominance would give to the other. When the southern department of Putumayo came to replace the eastern department of Guaviare as Colombia's biggest coca-growing region, the paramilitaries followed the business, knowing that otherwise it would be entirely controlled by the FARC.

Cocaine has become currency for both the FARC and the AUC. An M-60 machine gun can be had for 10 kg of coca paste, or £6,000. The same corridors that carry cocaine down from the mountains to the ports are also used to carry arms to the guerrillas and paramilitaries battling for control of the trade. In 2005, Honduran authorities found a cache of Indonesian weaponry due to be smuggled to FARC operatives on the border with Brazil, and then onwards to the fronts in the south of Colombia where the fighting is fiercest.[56]

The cocaine business has allowed the FARC to become a self-sufficient, well-equipped army. But it has also kept the guerrillas on a permanent war footing and put their relations with the people they profess to defend under enormous strain. These days FARC policy runs in tandem not with poor farmers or *cocaleros*, but with the demands of a war economy. Indigenous communities in the *resguardos* (reservations) of Cauca complain that FARC units force them to grow coca. Farmers growing coca in areas controlled by paramilitaries are considered to be military targets by the guerrillas. Support for the FARC has fallen away as their terrorism targets even the most menial state officials, and FARC kidnappers target the middle class. 'The term "terrorist" was not foisted on the FARC by the Americans,' says Joaquín Villalobos. 'The FARC earned it by killing innocent civilians. The FARC are as hated as the paramilitaries, as proven by the millions who marched in protest at the FARC in February and March 2008. No Latin American government has ever been able to mobilize so many people against an insurgency. Usually it was the insurgents marching in the streets against the government.'[57]

But Villalobos has also said that none of this should detract from the FARC's fundamentally political purpose. He describes their involvement in the cocaine trade as 'a structural consequence of the Colombian conflict, one which has also contaminated the paramilitaries and much of Colombia's political class'. The simple bitter truth is that only illegal armies can control such a huge, lucrative business. In these circumstances, any organized political violence, whatever its intentions, ends up being corrupted by criminal violence.[58] By one account, the FARC make £10 million a year from taxes on legal businesses.[59]

Had Plan Colombia been able to put an end to coca production, it would also have dried up much of the pool from which the FARC sustains itself. Aerial fumigation of the coca fields has failed to do that, so the next best option is to drive the FARC from the coca fields. Plan Colombia insists on a southern push against the FARC, but even if it succeeds, it will still leave coca cultivation intact. There is no evidence that coca fields controlled by paramilitaries are any easier to destroy than those controlled by the FARC. More importantly, neither the failed fumigation strategy nor the southern push does anything to tackle cocaine production, most of which is not controlled by the FARC but the Mafia. They and their allies among Colombia's politicians, paramilitaries and army have escaped the attention of the architects of Plan Colombia. Both the United States' own agencies and the United Nations have consistently reported that the paramilitaries are far more deeply involved than the FARC in producing and shipping cocaine. In the latest chapter in the long-running struggle between foreign banana companies and their workers, the American banana-growing firm Chiquita Brands International was found to have paid paramilitaries $1.7 million for their help in putting down banana workers' unions on the Gulf of Urabá between 1997 and 2004.[60] Chiquita's banana transport ships have also been found to have been used to smuggle cocaine into Europe. More than a ton of cocaine was seized from seven Chiquita ships in 1997, though this was attributed to lax Colombian security rather than to Chiquita itself.

This begs the question why there isn't a war on narco-paramilitaries. US policy towards Colombia is marked by two contradictory trends. Although Colombia gets much less attention from the United States press and politicians than it did in the late 1990s, the size and purpose of the military aid provided are expanding rapidly. The question of just how much impact the Plan has had on the price, purity and availability of cocaine has been neatly side-stepped. Since, in truth, most of that impact has been absorbed by the drugs trade, the Americans have redefined just what it was they set out to do in Colombia. In a *Miami Herald* op-ed of April 2006, Nicholas Burns, then number three at the State Department, asserted that 'the United States' investment in Colombia is paying off. Colombia is clearly a better place than it was before we embarked on our joint undertaking to win Colombia back from the criminal gangs that were destroying the country.' Kevin Higgins, the military adviser at the US Embassy, also seemed happier talking about Plan Colombia's impact on the FARC than its impact on the cocaine trade. 'Kidnappings are down from 3,500 in 2001 to 180 in 2007. In 2001, the FARC attacked 120 towns, but so far this year only four towns have been attacked,' he told me.

The United States' support for the Colombian government in its struggle with rural guerrillas is not new. They supported Bogotá through much of the Cold War period, when communism was supposedly seeping into the Americans' backyard, starting with Plan Lazo, a military offensive against the FARC, launched in 1964. Sir Keith Morris watched the drug war escalate from the British Embassy in Bogotá. 'In 1989, when the Cold War came to an end, the different US agencies were fighting for budgets, and they suddenly became interested in the drug war. The Pentagon and the CIA moved into the drugs field, which had always been the DEA's remit. In my time, twelve different US agencies started running anti-narcotics programmes, until Mr Osama bin Laden came along and gave them something rather more urgent to do.' The war on drugs has become entwined with broader aims, one of which is to keep a heavy lid on a simmering conflict, another of which is to keep the US military in the style to which it has grown accustomed.

Alberto Rueda, one-time consultant to the Colombian Ministry of Defence, told me what he remembers of American thinking before 9/11. 'In 1999, the Pentagon was talking about the American arms industry being in crisis. Clinton pushed through the biggest defence budget the country had seen since the days of Ronald Reagan. It was an enormous budget, and Plan Colombia was part of it.' Stipulating that only US defence contractors could supply the equipment needed to beef up the Colombian army ensured that 70 per cent of the budget for Plan Colombia never left the United States.[61] It was a much-needed shot in the arm to the big arms suppliers. 'The defence lobby is superlatively important to the politics of the United States,' Rueda went on. 'Any contract worth upwards of $100 million is worth fighting for, so of course they want to maintain their Colombian contract. Colombia has become an unofficial US military air base.'

After 9/11, Congress passed legislation which allowed anti-drug budgets to be used for anti-terrorist operations in Colombia. So when the Colombian government's peace talks with the FARC collapsed in February 2002, army generals in Colombia and the United States were given the green light for the Americans to beef up Colombia's armed forces in preparation for a final showdown with the FARC. The Americans appear torn between their belated recognition of the extent to which poverty and instability in Latin America impact on life in the United States, and their instinct for military solutions to social problems. In 2003, the Organization of American States redefined the concept of national security to mean 'human security', to which poverty, gang violence, terrorism and natural disasters could all be considered threats, and in defence of which the US military can legitimately argue for intervention. As one US soldier put it, 'when the best tool you have is a hammer, every problem starts to look like a nail'.

The Colombian government's defenders in Washington and London admit that terrible abuses have been committed against the population in the name of maintaining the status quo, but argue that those responsible have usually been illegal paramilitaries. Now that the Americans are building up the Colombian army and the paramilitaries are being reined in, the army is committing more of those abuses.

The army is full of earnest young Colombians determined to rescue their country's tarnished reputation, but their valiance is all too often skewed by their officers' murderous hatred of communists, or by plain corruption. In 2007, there were nineteen cases of possible extra-judicial executions committed by the 15th Mobile Brigade alone. In 2008, Sergeant Alexander Rodríguez of the 15th Mobile Brigade told the Colombian weekly *Semana* that 'at the beginning of November

2007, Sergeant Ordóñez went around getting 20,000 pesos from each soldier, to pay for the pistol that they had planted on the guy they'd shot. Ordóñez said to them "if you pay up, well and good, if not, we'll leave it at that, but I'll give five days off to anyone who does".[62]

When the *cartelitos* fight one another, rogue elements of the army, local politicians and paramilitaries will often take the side of whoever happens to pay better. In Guaitarilla in the south-western department of Nariño, the army wiped out an entire unit of the anti-narcotics police in 2004, supposedly because they mistook them for FARC guerrillas, but actually because the army was working for one of the small cartels. As coca cultivation and cocaine production have moved into the south-western departments of Nariño, Valle and Cauca, the Third Brigade of the army has been corrupted by Diego Montoya of the Norte del Valle cartel. Whatever the size of the bone 'Don Diego' tossed to the brigade's commanding officers, it must have been sufficiently succulent for them to ignore the $5 million bounty on the don's head. The same might be surmised from the case of Colonel Bayron Carvajal of the High Mountain Brigade, whose connivance has ensured that the trafficking corridor between Norte del Valle and the port of Buenaventura stays in Diego Montoya's hands. The High Mountain Brigade has received training from the British Ministry of Defence, supposedly to improve their human rights record.[63]

Paramilitarism is the Janus face of the Colombian army: it grows stronger when the army hierarchy sees government policy towards the guerrilla insurgency as tremulous or irresolute. Like Colombia's Mafia and guerrillas, its private armies pre-date the arrival of the cocaine trade. Cattle-ranching families have long hired gunmen to defend their herds against rustlers, and their *paso fino* horses against extortionists. Before the cocaine trade took off, the FARC financed itself by kidnapping wealthy cattle-ranchers for ransom. In the mid-1980s, the FARC started kidnapping cocaine traffickers too, so landowners and traffickers organized 'self-defence forces', well-funded private armies that could count on the backing of the Colombian army. The AUC (United Self-Defence Forces of Colombia) was a loose confederation of these private armies that united around a programme of weeding out those they considered FARC sympathizers, which effectively meant anyone critical of the government, including communists, trade unionists, students and journalists. AUC paramilitaries also took a crypto-fascistic line on 'undesirables' such as drug users, petty thieves and street children.

Within two years of its formation in 1997, the AUC was an aggressive, fully fledged army, largely financed by cocaine traffickers. It went on the offensive against the guerrillas, and took control of most of the north of the country, at a terrible cost in human life and livelihoods. Like the Mafia, the AUC is part of a long tradition of private violence and ancestral conflicts, many of which go back to the birth of the Colombian nation in the early nineteenth century.[64] AUC members might venerate the Virgin Mary, but their sense of justice extends no further than vengeance. As the writer Gilles Lipotevsky has observed, 'it takes excessive pain, blood and flesh to abide by the code of vengeance'. In towns like Sincelejo in the northern department of Sucre, locals talk of *narco-paramili-polismo*: rule by an alliance of cocaine traffickers, paramilitaries and politicians.[65] In 2005, the remains of 500 victims of a local paramilitary boss known as 'Cadena' (Chain) were disinterred. Sincelejo had once been the centre of vibrant farmers' groups and community associations, but most of their leaders are now dead. 'There is no civil society here,' said a survivor.

Because the Colombian government shares the paramilitaries' hatred of the FARC, it turned a blind eye to the AUC's second motive, which was to get rich quick. AUC leader Carlos Castaño revealed that three quarters of the AUC's funds came from the production and trafficking of cocaine. Like the guerrillas, the paramilitaries went through bitter internal struggles over their relationship to the cocaine business. Castaño made his fortune working with the Norte del Valle cartel, but he was first and foremost an anti-communist, who saw the cocaine business as a means to a political end. When the AUC struck a deal with the government, by which the paramilitaries would leave the fighting to the regular armed forces, its political task was complete, and Castaño's card was marked. He was killed shortly afterwards by his brother Vicente.

The AUC was ready to demobilize. The battle to wrest control of the north of the country from the guerrillas had been won. In the course of the 1990s, AUC commanders and cocaine traffickers had acted as the advance guard for the return of the army and police to regions once held by the guerrillas. In the process, they had grown phenomenally rich, buying or stealing huge swathes of land in the Atlantic coast departments, the eastern plains that run to the border with Brazil and in the valley of the River Magdalena that flows from the Andes to the Caribbean Sea. A quarter of the agricultural land of Colombia is now thought to be in the hands of cocaine traffickers. Though valued at $2.4 billion, much of this land came cheap, because it had been controlled by guerrillas and only the cocaine barons had the private armies needed to resist extortion or kidnap by the FARC. This gargantuan land grab came at the expense of the peasant smallholders, who were expelled or reduced to penury, while much of the land they once owned today doubles as infrastructure for cocaine laboratories and landing strips.

Former cocaine trafficker Fabio Ochoa Vasco was particularly well placed to witness just what this demobilization of the AUC would mean: he was with Colombia's biggest cocaine trafficker at the time. 'I was with Salvatore Mancuso on his "05" farm when these two guys from Medellín showed up. They proposed a peace process. The AUC were very happy with it, and started to get everyone together so that they'd vote for Alvaro Uribe. They explained that they'd made some space for anyone who had problems in the United States, and that if you were accused of being in the AUC, they'd save you.'[66]

So former AUC heavyweights lent their support to Alvaro Uribe Velez's bid for the presidency, and after the 2002 elections a new political map emerged. Uribe Velez got the presidency and the AUC got the Justice and Peace Law of 2005, by which paramilitary fighters were to be 'reinserted' into civilian life and left to enjoy the gains they'd made through theft, plunder and cocaine trafficking.[67] Their senior commanders would have to do some jail time, but most of them would be free within five years. Many have already announced their intention to seek seats in Congress.

In January 2007, Salvatore Mancuso, the de facto leader of the AUC following the death of Carlos Castaño, became the first senior paramilitary commander to confess to kidnappings and mass murder.

Mancuso, who at the time of his arrest was thought to be exporting 10 tons of cocaine a month, confessed to only a fraction of his crimes and named only deceased collaborators, among them the head of the Army's Fourth Brigade.[68] Few of the victims of paramilitary violence are prepared to testify in court; even after demobilization, it is just too dangerous to do so. As a result, 90 per cent of the 30,000 ex-paramilitaries to have demobilized to date will escape all charges, and may even get to keep the land they stole.[69] Nevertheless, some victims have testified to rape, torture and murder by paramilitaries. Maria Helena of Ituango, Antioquia, described how, at the age of fifteen, she was raped for over a week by seven paramilitaries, despite being eight months pregnant, while her boyfriend was tied to a tree. After testifying she asked, 'what good will it do for me to have told you all this?'[70]

It was a question on the lips of many Colombians as the Justice and Peace law was debated in Congress. But when first the Constitutional Court and then the Supreme Court challenged the terms of the peace deal with the paramilitaries, the government was forced to backtrack, and the demobilized paramilitary leaders gradually realized that the deal they had struck with the government would not be fully honoured. This did not bode well for Uribe Velez's much-vaunted demobilization process. Evidence of the cosy alliance of cocaine traffickers and local politicians who backed the AUC and then negotiated their demobiliz-ation began to emerge in 2006, following the impounding of a laptop computer belonging to a senior paramilitary commander known as Jorge 40. His files contained records of the Ralito Accord, an agree-ment reached in 2001 between regional politicians and paramilitaries on the Atlantic Coast to preserve the paramilitary project even while officially demobilizing. The upshot of the accord was the assassination of 558 left-wing activists and trade unionists in the department of Atlantico between 2003 and 2005, and the systematic plundering of the department's budget, which was either pocketed or went to finance future paramilitary operations.[71]

The net kept widening: before long, more than sixty of Alvaro Uribe Velez's supporters in Congress were under investigation for collusion with paramilitaries. In 1987, when Pablo Escobar was busily trying to turn Colombia into a narco-state, a scandal broke when it was revealed that one in ten members of Congress had links to traffickers.[72] Today, it is thought that at least a third of the present Congress won their seats after making deals with paramilitaries and/or cocaine traffickers. In February 2007, Jorge Noguera, the former head of the DAS intelligence service, was arrested, accused of allowing paramilitaries to penetrate the service.[73] Then Foreign Secretary Maria Consuelo Araujo resigned, as it transpired that her brother was one of the imprisoned senators, her father was on trial for kidnapping and murdering indigenous leaders, and her cousin stood accused of winning a provincial governorship by intimidating voters with paramilitary violence.

It seems inconceivable that President Alvaro Uribe Velez, a key ally in the international war on drugs, was not aware of the relationship between his congressional supporters and cocaine-trafficking paramilitaries. But then, the President has long been suspected of ties to the cocaine business himself. His brother Santiago has been investigated on charges of cocaine trafficking, and has been associated with a paramilitary group known as the Twelve Apostles.[74] José Ortulio Gaviria, a nephew of Pablo Escobar, is one of the president's closest advisers. Alvaro Uribe Velez has brushed off all such talk as rumours and happenstance. What should we make, then, of a list of Colombian drug traffickers published by the Pentagon's Defense Intelligence Agency in 1991, in which one Alvaro Uribe Velez figures at number 82, described as 'a close personal friend of Pablo Escobar' and 'dedicated to collaboration with the Medellín cartel at high government levels'?[75]

The rhetoric of the war on drugs might suggest that the president should be extradited to Miami (many years ago, he was due to be extradited, but was ordered to be released by the governor of Antioquia's office).[76] But the reality is that Uribe Velez's shady past suits Washington because it makes him a hostage to American bidding in a region in which they have lost much of their ability to influence events. As if cognizant of this unwritten pact, President Uribe Velez has been jailing and extraditing cocaine-trafficking former AUC members in unprecedented numbers. In May 2008, Uribe Velez extradited fourteen top paramilitaries to the United States to stand trial on charges of

THE CANDY MACHINE

cocaine trafficking. Uribe Velez wanted to show Democrats in Washington that he meant what he said about breaking all links with paramilitaries who continue to murder trade unionists and other left-wingers. Democratic Congressional leaders and their trade union allies have cited those murders as grounds for holding back on a free-trade agreement with Colombia. But the extradition also served another purpose: to remove the most important witnesses in any future investigation of the president's dealings with Colombia's most notorious paramilitaries and cocaine traffickers.[77]

Uribe Velez's volte-face may well backfire on him yet. 'When Salvatore Mancuso sees that they are closing the doors that might have allowed him to be sentenced under the Justice and Peace laws, and then the pressure from the Americans, who know that he is Colombia's biggest *capo*, he's going to try to defend himself, and start talking about his alliances with President Uribe,' former cocaine trafficker Fabio Ochoa Vasco told a reporter from *Semana* magazine. 'All the AUC commanders that sat down at the negotiating table that first week know the truth. They know that to get where they are, they put down more than $10 million. Sooner or later somebody is going to spill the beans, because they feel betrayed by the government.'[78]

Even if the AUC can be successfully dismantled without leaving the government's drug war credentials in tatters, it is unclear what difference the demobilization of Colombia's paramilitary armies will make to cocaine trafficking in Colombia. Many paramilitaries sold the 'franchises' for their private armies to drugs traffickers before they turned themselves in.[79] In towns in Putumayo, the drug lords of Cali are back. They walk the streets guarded by 'demobilized' paramilitaries, impassively greeting those they meet and imposing prices for the purchase of coca base. As Diego Vecino, paramilitary commander of the Héroes de los Montes de Maria has said, 'The AUC is finished as a registered trademark. But paramilitarism goes on.'[80]

For most of the 1980s, Medellín was the most violent city in the world. Just as Eskimos are said to have forty words for snow, so the young *sicarios* of Medellín have thirty-seven words for a gun. They call it *tola, fierro, pepazo, pepinos, gaga, niño, tartamuda, changón, trabuco, balín*, *metra*, or *tote*. They have seventy-three words for death, forty-two words for violence and twenty-four words for a bullet. Though Catholic in name, their religion is one of 'warriors, not apostles'; it supplies not a code by which to live, but a talisman to protect them from the consequences of the crimes they commit.[81]

People have been coming to Medellín since the 1960s. Displaced by the violence in the countryside, the first arrivals built squatter settlements, warrens of steep stairways up the hillsides, and pirated their water and electricity. Today, residents of the *comunas* make up half of Medellín's population. Until 2003, police and soldiers dared not enter the *comunas* except in large numbers, so the residents grew accustomed to living under the control of street gangs, some of which were involved in organized crime. During the 1990s, as the effort to take down Pablo Escobar loosened the drug lords' grip on the *comunas*, the gang structure was taken over by the urban appendages of the guerrilla insurgency. These urban militia were soon challenged by the AUC. Flush with drug money and backed by the security forces, AUC units under the command of the renowned cocaine trafficker Diego Fernando Murillo Bejarano, better known as Don Berna, waged intense fire-fights in the neighbourhoods' lanes and alleys. Hundreds of people were executed on suspicion of collaborating with the other side, and the city's murder rate soared to nearly 200 per 100,000, numbers not seen since the last days of the Medellín cartel. By 2002, the paramilitaries had ejected the urban militia, taken over the gangs, and restored the police presence in the *comunas*. 'Don Berna does not control Medellín. He only controls criminality in Medellín,' said the writer and secretary of the city's government, Alonso Salazar. More than three quarters of Medellín's poor neighbourhoods were said to be under the control of Don Berna.[82]

Talks with the paramilitaries of Medellín were going nowhere when in November 2003 Don Berna unexpectedly announced the demobilization of his unit of the AUC, the Cacique Nutibara Bloc. In a gesture of extravagant goodwill, 868 purported members of the Bloc turned in less than half as many weapons, and were duly processed under the Justice and Peace laws. It would be the first of a long series of paramilitary demobilization ceremonies that took place throughout

Colombia over the next two and a half years, in which surprisingly large numbers of criminals claimed to be paramilitaries, and handed in surprisingly small numbers of weapons. None the less, the civilian population welcomed the lull that followed. For many, it was a relief to have to pay extortion money to only one group, and to be free of the threat of retribution for helping 'the other side'.

When I was in Bogotá in September 2007, Don Berna was in the Itagüí prison south of Medellín, accused of ordering the killing of a state legislator. But he still controlled the gangs in Medellín's *comunas*. Young men in plain-clothes kept quiet watch, though they no longer put up roadblocks and were more discreet in their killings. In 2008, the DEA discovered new evidence that Don Berna, the 'Pacifier of Medellín', was still sending cocaine to the United States, in violation of the Justice and Peace law. The US Embassy brought renewed pressure to extradite him, which President Uribe Velez found impossible to resist. Since Don Berna boarded his plane to Miami, the absence of both the *capo* and a well-established police presence has touched off another struggle for control of Medellín's ever buoyant cocaine business.

One night in Bogotá, I watched a television news story about a Russian serial killer who had murdered forty-six people. That same day, a demobilized paramilitary had confessed to killing 2,000 people, but no mention was made of him. Instead, the newsreader brought news from Montería of a government programme to teach demobilized paramilitaries how to use computers, part of their *reinserción* into the mainstream of Colombian life. This was followed by news that the singer Marilyn Manson, who was due to play a concert in Bogotá later that month, would have to fly out of the city the same night he played. The hoteliers of Bogotá found his pop videos offensive and were refusing to put him up for the night.

I had been surprised to see '*Bogotá Sin Indiferencia*' (Bogotá Without Indifference) plastered on the city's billboards. It was the new slogan of the mayor's office. If *bogotanos* are indifferent to life in the capital, it is because so many of them have been uprooted from their places of origin. Over the past ten years, a combination of para-military terror campaigns and fire-fights between the army, paramilitaries and the guerrillas has forced 3 million Colombians to flee their villages for the vagaries of city life. Only Sudan has a bigger population of internally displaced people than Colombia. Far from home, many of these families become isolated and individualistic, with scant regard for the community they live in. Colombia's 'violontology' specialists say that theirs is a nation of weak groups and strong individuals – or apparently strong individuals: millions of Colombians suffer from post-traumatic stress disorder and being a victim of FARC violence seems to be a prerequisite for any prospective government minister.

The only way to survive in such a violent, lawless place is by staying on the side of those apparently strong individuals. When Pablo Escobar was threatened with extradition to the United States, he went on a bombing spree and the threat was soon dropped. It was eventually restored, but Escobar's defiance chimed with the many Colombians who believe that might can only be met with might. People of all classes have suffered at the hands of the country's traffickers, urban militia, FARC kidnappers and paramilitaries, organizations that owe some or all of their power to the cocaine trade. The most desperate victims are those who have had to flee their homes in the countryside, often with no more than the clothes on their backs. Yet the plight of the displaced is roundly ignored by most Colombians. People have vengeance in mind, even if the talk is of respect, order and legality. Cocaine has paid for everyone to enjoy the fruits of violence. It has reduced the hide-bound elite of a staunchly traditionalist society to the status of ordinary men and women. The poor are no longer cowed by the elite, but neither has been able to affect any meaningful political or economic reforms to their country. In this climate of frustration and mistrust, cocaine has shown the poor that violence can be an effective weapon. It has democratized violence.

Supporters of Plan Colombia argue that the billions of dollars of US military aid have improved the Colombian army's fighting capacity. The FARC have been rolled back into the jungle and up the mountains; Colombians can once again travel between the main cities of the country without fear of kidnap, and the return of foreign investment has cheered the Bogotá stock market. In 2006, Alvaro Uribe Velez was re-elected to the presidency with 53 per cent of the popular vote (notwithstanding the fact that only 54 per cent of the electorate felt inspired to vote at all). Uribe Velez says that if Colombia didn't have drugs, it wouldn't have terrorists and has reaffirmed his commitment to fighting the Americans' war on drugs.[83] There is certainly a war on coca growers, the FARC and the drugs mules. But this is far from being a war on drugs. If the Colombian government was serious about tackling the cocaine trade, the Ministry of Agriculture would tackle the land reform issue, instead of chasing Colombian coca farmers around the country in fumigation planes. When the coca fields are sprayed, cultivation just moves on. Of course the coca fields finance the guerrillas, but Colombia had trafficking routes and mafiosi long before it had coca fields. The cocaine traffickers are unaffected by the fumigation programme. Even without the coca fields, the Colombian Mafia would source coca paste elsewhere and produce cocaine in the Colombian jungle, as it did in the 1980s. But Plan Colombia makes no mention of the big traffickers, and they aren't going to be brought to justice as long as they can buy politicians. That so few of the structural problems driving coca cultivation have been addressed suggests that, despite the rhetoric, drugs traffic per se is not seen as a big problem in Colombia.

The ills afflicting Colombia did not begin with the advent of the cocaine trade, yet the lack of effective solutions offered to date has made the drugs trade (and the violence, corruption and impunity it has fostered) wholly sustainable. The cocaine business has funded illegal armed groups to both left and right. By sustaining the paramilitarization of Colombian society, the cocaine trade has put paid to local democracy, civil society and any prospect of negotiations with the guerrillas. It has paid for a buy-out of what was a peasant economy, leading to a concentration of land in the hands of a few *capos*, which has only aggravated the agrarian crisis. Its financial reach and the impunity that it enjoys have undermined the authority and credibility of the law. It has also corrupted the political ideals of the FARC. Worse still, it has given AUC paramilitaries the financial muscle to corrupt thousands of politicians across the country, with the apparent complicity of the Colombian government, as well as its allies in the United States and the United Kingdom. The Colombian government's campaign to get western cocaine consumers to 'share responsibility' for the cocaine trade looks simplistic at best, duplicitous at worst.

8

Globalization

In reading the history of nations, we find that whole communities suddenly fix their minds upon one object, and go mad in its pursuit. We see one nation suddenly seized, from its highest to its lowest members, with a fierce desire of military glory; another as suddenly becoming crazed upon a religious scruple; and neither of them recovering its senses until it has shed rivers of blood and sowed a harvest of groans and tears, to be reaped by its posterity. Men, it has been well said, think in herds; it will be seen that they go mad in herds, while they only recover their senses slowly, and one by one.

C. Mackay, *Extraordinary Popular Delusions and the Madness of Crowds*, 1852[1]

Since the first Gulf War of 1991, the United States has moved to lessen its reliance on supplies of oil from the Middle East. Today, it gets more of its oil from Latin America than it does from the Middle East. But dependence on Latin American oil has brought its own problems. Its biggest Latin American supplier is Venezuela, but Venezuelan oil is in the hands of Hugo Chávez and his country's national oil company, which limits the Americans' scope for influence. Ecuador terminated a contract with the Occidental Petroleum Corporation of Los Angeles in 2006, thereby returning the right to exploit its reserves, thought to be worth $1 billion, to its state oil company. Brazil and Mexico also have nationalist policies governing their oil wealth, which limit the extent to which foreign companies can exploit their oil. So it should come as no surprise to find that since 2000, the Latin American presidential candidates keenest to invite investment from foreign oil companies have also been those that have received the keenest support of the United States. The first is Alan García of Peru, and the second is Alvaro Uribe Velez of Colombia.

Colombia has had to offer good incentives to the foreign oil companies because getting at Colombian oil is a risky business. Only a hundred years ago, Colombia's oil bubbled from the ground untapped; barrels of oil were carried to the coastal ports on the backs of mules, and oil workers had to watch for the arrows of resentful Indians. Today, Colombia is the seventh biggest supplier of oil to the United States and were it not for the FARC guerrillas, it would be among the most exciting sources of future oil reserves. The FARC's presence in remote parts of Colombia means that 80 per cent of the country has yet to be surveyed for potential oil reserves. Most of the existing oil infrastructure is in the north-east of the country, but there too foreign oil companies' pipelines are regularly sabotaged by the guerrillas, and their executives threatened with kidnap and extortion. 'Clearly we have an energy threat,' Congressman Mark Souder said in 2002. 'Colombia is either our seventh or eighth largest supplier of oil. Our economy depends on that. We already have instability in the Middle East. We have more compelling reasons to be involved in Colombia than almost anywhere else in the world.'[2]

The American army is thinking along similar lines, as Geoff Foreman, a Special Forces sergeant stationed in Colombia made clear in an interview he gave to oil policy researcher Daniel Scott-Lea in 2005. 'We never mentioned the words "coca" or "narco-trafficker" in our training. The objective of our operations was not to help the Colombians, but the Americans who pay taxes for the investment made in Colombia. The objective continues to be oil. Look where American forces are: Iraq, Afghanistan, Indochina, the Caspian Sea, Colombia, all places where we expect to find oil reserves.'[3] Stan Goff, another Special Forces trainer stationed in Colombia, confided to writer Doug Stokes that 'the American public was being told, if they were being told anything at all, that this was counter-narcotics training. The training I conducted was anything but that. It was pretty much updated, Vietnam-style counter-insurgency doctrine. We were advised to refer to it as counter-narcotics training, should anyone ask, but the only thing we talked about with the actual leaders of the training units was the guerrillas.'[4] Trace the principal battlelines on a map, and it becomes clear that the fiercest fighting between the army, the paramilitaries and the guerrillas is not for control of the drugs business, but of the areas in which Colombia's oil and mineral wealth is concentrated. Much is made of the guerrillas' dependence on the drugs trade, but when taken together, the FARC and the ELN (National Liberation Army, the second of Colombia's two guerrilla armies) actually make more money from the oil business.

When a multinational oil company agrees to invest in Colombia, it signs a security contract with the Colombian army, which undertakes to defend the company's operations from attack by the guerrillas. This has led to army collusion with paramilitaries to assassinate local trade union leaders, who are often assumed to be in cahoots with the insurgents. The Drummond Coal Company has been sued by the union that represents workers at its Colombian mines for conspiring with paramilitary groups to destroy the union.[5] Lawsuits have also been brought against Exxon, BP, Texaco, Occidental Petroleum and Conquistador Mines for their relationships with paramilitaries. The United States' publicly stated intention of tackling cocaine production at source has become a savvy façade for more primordial concerns: supporting governments that are 'ready to do business' and undermining their challengers; addressing America's need for cheap and reliable supplies of oil and protecting the considerable investments American companies have made in the region.

This is not to say that the war on drugs is disingenuous. America remains susceptible to irrational fears unbecoming such a powerful nation. The domino theory, according to which every Third World nation that aspired to some measure of autonomy was to be forced into submission before they fell to Soviet expansionism, informs America's anti-drugs policies too. Wasn't the United States once 'under siege from crack'? The paranoid fear of the Soviet Union that kept Americans onside during the Cold War seeped into their fear of America on drugs, and now their fear of Islamic terror. Once stoked, irrational fears can be manipulated to secure public support for policies that only sustain the original fear. However, the day-to-day work of US agencies prosecuting the war on drugs in Latin America is more prosaic, and more revealing, than the rhetoric of the country's politicians would suggest.

Faced with a case of high-level drug corruption in Latin America, the DEA will often find itself in conflict with the US State Department. Drug enforcement agents might want to arrest a high-ranking government minister who has been found to be colluding with cocaine traffickers, but the State Department may not want to destabilize a friendly government.[6] A federal inquiry into high-ranking PRI politicians in Mexico was halted, according to retired DEA agents Phil Jordan and Hector Berrellez, in the months leading up to the signing of the North American Free Trade Agreement.[7] The Guatemalan military is deeply involved in cocaine trafficking, but its officers are to all intents and purposes beyond prosecution, and have been since they secured the United States' backing to fight a dirty war against the country's communists. During the Cold War, more than 200,000 Guatemalans were killed in what became Central America's bloodiest twentieth-century conflict. But Marilyn McAfee, Bill Clinton's ambassador in Guatemala City, had bigger things to worry about than her host government's drugs trafficking, notably ongoing peace talks with the Guatemalan military. 'I am concerned over the potential decline in our relationship with the military,' she wrote to her superiors in 1994. 'The bottom line is we must carefully consider each of our actions toward the Guatemalan military, not only for how it plays in Washington, but for how it impacts here.' A couple of months later, Epaminondas González Dubón, Guatemala's most senior judge, was assassinated for ordering the extradition to the United States of Lieutenant Carlos Ochoa on charges of cocaine smuggling.

Since the murder of González Dubón, the DEA has been all but impotent in Guatemala. Guatemalans use the DEA to settle scores, traffickers use the agency to get one over the competition, and politicians pander to it in order to keep money from the United States' anti-drugs budget flowing. Colombian smugglers looking for a first stop on the route north to Mexico know that the impunity enjoyed by the Guatemalan military makes its officers perfect partners in crime. As a result, three quarters of the cocaine consumed in the United States is said to pass through Guatemala.[8]

The US government has shown itself to be happy to facilitate drugs traffickers when they share the Americans' broader foreign policy goals. Former DEA agent Celerino Castillo III has written that 'we spent billions trying to beat down an ideology in Central America, while the cartels rented nations as transit routes'.[9] Of course, there are limits to American indulgence of drug trafficking: the case of Manuel Noriega, the military dictator who ruled Panama between 1983 and 1989, shows what US agencies are prepared to do when anti-communist allies in Central America overstep the mark. Noriega had been trafficking drugs, and working for the CIA, since the late 1960s. The United States' security agencies had long overlooked Noriega's cocaine trafficking for the Medellín cartel because of the strategic role the Panamanian played in supporting the Contras in Nicaragua. But when Noriega took a hard line in negotiations with the Americans over the future of the Panama Canal, the CIA dropped him as an asset, and the White House decided to depose him. George Bush Sr, who as director of the CIA had paid Noriega $100,000 for services rendered in 1976, launched Operation Just Cause, and bombed Panama City in 1989.[10] Once in court, Noriega's lawyers tried to subpoena evidence that proved that their client had smuggled cocaine to fund the Contras in Nicaragua and that he had done so with the approval of the CIA. But the Americans outfoxed them. Citing reasons of national security, they made sure that the jury never got to see the relevant documents. Noriega's defence collapsed, and he was sentenced to serve forty years behind bars.

Carlos Lehder, one of Colombia's pioneering cocaine smugglers, amassed a personal fortune of £1.25 billion, but he made the same mistake of going political with the Americans. Lehder is currently contesting his prison sentence, alleging that the US authorities agreed to reduce his term in return for his testimony at the trial of Manuel Noriega. It has been suggested that the Americans reneged on this agreement because Lehder is privy to intimate details of the Contras' cocaine-smuggling operations that would incriminate the CIA.

Even when cocaine traffickers' operations have no bearing on the State Department's wider interests, the CIA has negotiated reduced sentences with Colombian drugs traffickers in exchange for the delivery of large sums of money to the United States government. As cocaine trafficker Fabio Ochoa pointed out, much of this money ends up funding paramilitarism in Colombia. Ochoa alleges that he was extradited to the United States shortly after he refused to give £15 million to the paramilitaries.

Even when the DEA is able to work without political interference from the State Department, the CIA or the FBI, it often finds that it doesn't have sufficient sway with its hosts to do the job it came to do. A DEA agent described his relationship with his counterpart in the Mexican Federal Judicial Police to Ethan Nadelmann, director of the Drug Policy Alliance, on condition that his anonymity was preserved, and what he said is worth quoting at length. 'When a new *comandante* arrives in town at the beginning of a new presidential term, he has a couple of incentives to cooperate with the DEA. First, he needs the DEA most then. Usually his predecessor will leave nothing but an empty filing cabinet, if that. So he relies on the DEA to find out who is who and what is what. Second, he has an interest in cracking down hard soon after his arrival to show who's in charge. Thus, during the first year or so, the DEA will get excellent cooperation from him. Some time during the first year, the traffickers will try to cut deals with the *comandante* to buy protection. So the *comandante* starts receiving offers: a car, an apartment, a house, women, and so on. He and the chosen traffickers will reach an understanding, usually involving a retainer. The traffickers understand that if they do anything stupid, the police will have to act. But there is also an understanding that the *comandante* will not pursue them too hard. He will stall and find ways to avoid cooperating with the DEA, and eventually the DEA agent will get the message. During the next three years, the DEA agent will get great cooperation in any operations not involving one of the *comandante*'s special relationships. In his last year or two, however, cooperation can really go downhill. Everyone is trying to make a killing before he leaves office. By that point, there is almost nothing the DEA can do. Probably 75 per cent of DEA–Federale relationships fit this model. Is this "corruption"? By US standards, sure, although the US has lots of corruption itself. But in Latin America, that's just the way the system works. Every cop goes along with it or he's out.'[11]

In Mexico, Bolivia, Colombia, Peru, Belize, Jamaica, Ecuador, Paraguay, Panama and the Bahamas – all, bar the last four, drug-producing countries – those charged with waging the war on drugs find themselves dependent on those corrupted by drugs money. All over Central and South America, drug corruption is widespread at all levels, and has been for years. In Ecuador, judges reportedly bid between themselves to hear drug cases, because they offer such lucrative opportunities for the stuffing of pockets. In Haiti, cocaine has utterly corrupted the upper echelons of former president Jean Bertrand Aristide's Lavalas party, including senators, senior police officials and (naturally) the head of the anti-drugs police. Aristide was overthrown in a military coup led by generals, many trained by the CIA, who once in power went deeper still into the pockets of the cocaine traffickers. This is unsurprising, as after the collapse of its coffee business and the evaporation of its offshore assembly plants, Haiti's top sources of foreign exchange today are whatever money Haitians abroad are able to send home, foreign aid and the drugs trade.[12]

In cases such as that of the Luis García Meza regime which came to power in Bolivia in the 'cocaine coup' of 1980, the United States' government has gone public with its protests, withdrawn its ambassador and shut down its DEA office, but this kind of zero tolerance is rare. Where it really matters, accommodation not confrontation is the norm. Ethan Nadelmann also interviewed a DEA agent who had worked in Paraguay and Panama, who told him that 'you can't dwell on drug involvement at the highest levels. There's nothing you can do about it. If you do, you just get depressed.'[13] So the focus turns to gathering intelligence, arresting drug mules, seizing vessels and airplanes transporting cocaine, and getting a few big traffickers extradited to the United States. Everything then, bar tackling the collusion and corruption on which cocaine trafficking depends.

Brazil's State Special Operations Battalion has a chant that goes: 'interrogation is very simple: grab the *favelado* [shanty dweller] and beat him til it hurts / Interrogation is very simple: grab the *favelado* and beat him til he's dead'. In June 2007, 1,350 police stormed the Alemão Complex *favela* (shanty town) in Rio de Janeiro, Brazil, killing nineteen people. There have been killings like these in Rio de Janeiro since the early 1990s: about 1,000 people are killed by the police in Rio every year.[14] Typically, the authorities blame vigilantes or rogue off-duty police officers, or say that they happened in 'confrontations' between the police and drugs traffickers. But the events in Alemão Complex marked a new approach to law enforcement. This time the Brazilian police offered no excuses. They admitted killing traffickers, regardless of the law.

The cocaine trade has drawn Brazilians into a real-life drama in which good purports to battle evil every day on the streets of Rio, a morality play every bit as captivating as the police footage of drug busts which held the attention of television viewers in the United States through much of the 1980s. Polls suggest that 85 per cent of the people of Rio approve of the police's operations, and agree that they should be rolled out in other *favelas*. They approve of the coercive methods because they blame *favelados* for the drugs trade. What is the point, they ask, of extending education, jobs and basic services to delinquents and criminals, who only squander the opportunities they are given? So the criminalized remain on the margins, quite powerless, and hence all the more enthralled by the power conferred by a gun. Their destiny is prison, a violent death, or both.

In fact, only 1 per cent of *favela* denizens work in the drugs business. Those that do invariably pay a high price for their involvement. Within two years of taking part in a study of young people working in the drugs trade in Rio, 46 of the 230 respondents were dead. The study had found that 60 per cent of them had got into the business before they turned fifteen. It is galling to think that the children of Brazil's least powerful citizens should shoulder the opprobrium of an entire society, or be considered a threat to security, rather than deserving of it.

In May 2007, while on a visit to the Farm of Hope drug rehabilitation centre near the Brazilian city of Aparecida, Pope Benedict railed against 'the hedonism of modern life' and warned the leaders of the cocaine cartels that they faced the wrath of God for what they were doing. Many of those who had gathered to hear the pontiff speak were recovering drug addicts, one of whom remarked that the Pope's speech was all well and good, but it made no mention of the corruption that allows the cocaine business to flourish.[15] The *favelados*' murderous struggle over crumbs is widely perceived to be the epitome of organized crime, but those profiting from the cocaine trade are obviously not *favela* dwellers. Nine recent federal police operations and four recent parliamentary inquiries have found state officials to be involved in drug-running.[16] But no matter: the police intelligence needed to penetrate the upper echelons of the drugs business is in short supply, as is the will to do so, and repression is easier to deploy than justice.

Those tempted to think that Brazil's *favelados* are dying to supply the cocaine habits of wealthy Westerners are mistaken. Increasingly, they're dying to supply the cocaine habits of wealthy Brazilians. Brazil is today the world's second-largest cocaine market after the United States. The long-standing division between the drug-producing countries of the South and the drug-consuming countries of the North has been blurred. Until recently, most Central and South American and Caribbean countries had low levels of cocaine use and abuse, but as cultures, populations and goods have become more mobile, borders of all kinds, including moral and cultural ones, have become harder to police.

Wherever cocaine moves, consignments are used as payment in kind. Local middlemen have created markets for hard drugs in towns where such things were once regarded as being strictly for export. The Mexican city of Tijuana, which lies across the border from San Diego, California, has 100,000 methamphetamine addicts; far more than you'd expect to find in a city of 1.4 million.[17] Mexico, Brazil and Argentina are all struggling to deal with growing numbers of cocaine users. The destitute have latched on to *paco*, which is made from leftovers from cocaine processing. There has also been an epidemic of crack use among the street children of Mexico City.

But to adduce increases in rates of drug use in Mexico to poverty would be to miss the real changes afoot. Most street children get food and shelter from charities and NGOs. They make money in the informal economy, guarding market stalls, picking up rubbish to sell, unloading trucks and the like, and that money goes on crack. More important than poverty in driving the rise in cocaine consumption in Third World countries is the fragility of the family. As more women go out to work, many *machista* men respond to their partners' newfound independence with violence. This leads to divorce and traumatizes children, who often flee the family home for a life on the street.[18] Once there, many children find that drugs offer the only respite to be had. Alex Sanchez from Homies Unidos in Santa Cruz, California, told me what he found when he was deported from the United States to El Salvador. 'Crack cocaine was not the drug of choice in Central America in '94. It was glue-sniffing. But once people who knew how to cook up rock cocaine were deported from the US, they started making profit distributing it down there.'

Since the late 1980s, cheap cocaine and heroin have fuelled a marked increase in drug use worldwide. Countries such as Russia, Ukraine, Thailand, Vietnam, Iran and India, where injection drug use was not common ten years ago, are now grappling with drug abuse on an even larger scale than that seen in European and American cities. Drug use made a comeback in China in the 1980s, prompting the Chinese government to announce a 'People's War on Drugs' in 2005. In recent years, Chinese and US authorities have stepped up cooperation, and the DEA quietly opened an office in Beijing about five years ago. In May 2006, they decommissioned 135 kilos of cocaine, by far the largest seizure of the drug ever made in China.

As cocaine traffickers have come to exploit the expanding global market for their product, drug warriors, frustrated at their inability to stem the flow of drugs from Colombia, have put great store by freezing the traffickers' assets. Few enterprises, legal or illegal, operate with such large and steady cashflows as the illegal drugs business. Prohibition Era mobster Meyer Lansky was famed for his skill in concealing the origin of the funds he used to buy real estate for the American Mafia. Latterday smugglers face the same challenge. In 1989, DEA agents working as part of Operation Polar Cap acted as distributors for the Medellín cartel so as to infiltrate the workings of the organization. This they did, but even the DEA didn't know what to do with the $1.5 million in small denominations that they were handling every week.

The easiest way to launder ill-gotten gains is to get the help of somebody working inside a financial institution. Bank employees can be coerced or bribed not to file the suspicious activity reports instituted to tackle money-laundering. In the United Kingdom, the most popular way of laundering cash is to make under-the-counter payments to an estate agent for the purchase of property, which can then be resold. Drug dealers also buy expensive cars, antiques and jewellery for cash, or buy holdings in companies in their accountants' name. Restaurants are a good front for money-laundering because they are accustomed to taking in large amounts of cash, and it's easy to overstate their takings or understate their costs. HM Revenue & Customs is not geared up to investigate over-reporting of taxable income, nor is it an offence to have unaccounted wealth.

Wholesale drugs traffickers in the United States are thought to generate and launder between £4 billion and £12 billion in proceeds from marijuana, methamphetamine, heroin and cocaine sales every year.[19] The Chicago Police Department estimates that in the three years up to 2007, gang members in the city laundered £90 million of their drug proceeds through fraudulent real estate transactions and mortgage fraud.[20] Christian, the former cocaine trafficker from Miami, told me about the methods used by Colombian traffickers to smuggle their proceeds south. 'Just the same way that the drugs come in, hidden under whatever it may be, the cash will go right back hidden in something else. One time, I went back to Colombia with $90,000 sewn into my pants. A lot of times they'll try to send large cash shipments back to Colombia, and every once in a while they'll get popped with $30 million in a container. Or the cash goes back in double-sided suitcases that can hold up to $200,000. Those one-dollar stores that you see popping up were started by the cartels. They'd get these cheap Chinese products that you buy for ten, fifteen cents a piece, and sell them for a dollar, but they'd report the earnings as much higher.'

Perhaps the simplest method is to get multiple payees, known as 'smurfs', to send sums up to £1,500 via Western Union Bank. Drug dealers are not the only ones that need money-laundering services.

There are plenty of white-collar offenders, Medicare fraudsters, recording pirates and tax evaders who need to hide the origins of their wealth. The former cocaine trafficker Fabio Ochoa described how Colombia's biggest *capo* laundered his takings. 'Salvatore Mancuso used to bring the money back to Colombia by different routes. He never used private planes. He'd bring the cash in through commercial airports, which meant that he had to buy off a lot of people. Mancuso's got a group of lawyers that set up companies and buy farms. Just in terms of land, he has more than 100,000 hectares. The guy's worth $500 million.'

Since 1989, international law enforcement agencies have developed increasingly intrusive measures to keep drug money out of the financial system. The control regime has extended from banks to car dealers, casinos, corner-shop money-transmission businesses, jewellers, pawn-brokers and insurance companies. Policing the international financial system has become harder because free trade zones, extra-territorial banking, electronic money transfers and smart cards have made the movement of capital much easier over the past twenty years. Every day, there are 70,000 international money transfers, shunting £1 trillion to and from accounts around the world. In 1979, there were seventy-five offshore tax havens. Today, there are more than 3,000, and nearly half of the world's money supply passes through them. These havens have institutionalized tax evasion by the world's greatest fortunes. They have also given money-launderers many more options.

The neo-liberal economic reforms that have been foisted on the Third World also favour the international drugs trade. The logic of neo-liberalism is to reduce governments' ability to withstand external market pressures, thereby forcing them to conform to the dictates of the international marketplace. Unfortunately, there is depressingly little the world market wants from countries like Peru and Bolivia other than coca. Despite wide-ranging economic reforms, the legal export sector is stagnant in both countries, and coca generates most of their reserves of foreign exchange, because it is the export commodity which provides both countries with the best returns in the global economy.

Since Peru and Bolivia are struggling to keep up with interest payments on their enormous foreign debts and face declining revenues from their traditional exports, both have welcomed the influx of US dollars from the cocaine business into the banking system. The Bolivian government approved a number of measures that eased the absorption of drugs money into the financial system, such as loosening the disclosure requirements of the Central Bank and declaring a tax amnesty on repatriated capital. Narco-dollars have financed Bolivia's debt repayments to foreign banks, an open secret since new laws prohibited official inquiries into the origins of any wealth brought into the country.

This puts the Peruvian and Bolivian governments in a tight spot, because the aid and diplomatic favour of the United States government are conditional on their compliance with the diktat of both neo-liberalism and anti-drugs policies.[21] Officially, Peru and Bolivia are loyal allies. As far as the World Bank is concerned, Peru's most important agricultural export is asparagus. Unofficially, both countries have defected from the war on drugs, while playing a delicate game of drug diplomacy. Since the war on drugs is one fought with resolutions and exhortations rather than facts or logic, there is plenty of room for what the CIA might call 'perception management'. Bolivian and Peruvian politicians blame their lack of progress in curbing drug production on corruption, bureaucratic mismanagement or inadequate resources. They make occasional high-profile drug seizures and arrests of drug traffickers, which have little impact on the cocaine trade, but appease policy-makers in Washington. Were Washington's drug warriors and neo-liberal economists to address one another instead of the governments of Peru and Bolivia, their rhetoric would surely lose its lustre. Since they don't, current economic policies and drug prohibition policies have shown a remarkable capacity to coexist, even when they operate at cross-purposes.

Why don't Latin American governments challenge this flawed anti-drugs strategy? Because the United States threatens any Latin American government that challenges their handling of the drugs trade with decertification. Decertification is the system enacted by the United States Congress in 1986 to punish foreign countries that don't toe the party line in the war on drugs. When US representatives in organizations such as the World Bank and the International Monetary Fund threaten to vote against loans to the offending country, impose tariffs on its exports and suspend air transport between it and the United States, the Americans can be sure of the offending government's undivided attention. When Colombia was decertified in 1996, it went into a recession from which it is only now emerging. Such is their fear of the big stick of decertification, countries like Mexico have thrown their military forces into battle with the cartels because at least they are cleaner than their police forces. But as the Mexican army has come face to face with the cocaine business, it too has succumbed to the traffickers' bribes. Reliance on the military also diverts attention and resources from the essential reforms of the police, intelligence apparatus and judiciary necessary to have any long-term impact on the drugs trade, or anything else for that matter. Perhaps in belated recognition of the negative effects of their big stick, in 2002 the US Congress modified the process by which their allies earn brownie points. Countries are now automatically certified as willing partners in the war on drugs unless their counter-drug efforts are toe-curlingly poor.

The threat of decertification also nips any hint of a challenge to prohibition in the bud. In 2001, Jamaican Prime Minister P. J. Patterson appointed a National Commission to look into the possible decriminalization of marijuana for personal use. The Commission's report concluded that 'the criminalization of thousands of people for simple possession does more harm than could be done by the use of ganja itself'. No mention was made of legalization, which would have contravened the 1961 United Nations Single Convention to which Jamaica is party. All the same, the US Embassy in Kingston made it plain that it would not tolerate the decriminalization of any drug in Jamaica, and issued a thinly veiled warning of decertification.[22] The Ganja Commission's recommendations, despite cross-party support in the Jamaican Parliament, have since been quietly shelved. The Jamaican ganja crop is still the target of government eradication squads, but this is widely regarded as window-dressing to keep the White House happy.[23]

The irony is that the United States government can more readily impose its will on small Third World nations than it can on states such as California, which has legalized the medical use of marijuana, in the face of staunch opposition from the federal government.[24] Many other states in the Union have passed legislation that permits the use of marijuana for the relief of severe pain, after glaucoma sufferers and AIDS patients sued the government for their right to use marijuana for medical purposes. In response, the federal government has cautioned the public against 'misplaced compassion'.

The law enforcement approach that has ingrained the drugs war into inner-city life across the Americas is based on tackling the supply of drugs. The supply-reduction strategy assumes that if enough coca fields are fumigated with herbicides, cocaine laboratories destroyed, shipments intercepted and traffickers arrested, less cocaine will be available to buy on the streets of the United States. If the authorities can thereby drive the purity of what is available down, and prices up, people will be dissuaded from buying cocaine and smugglers will give up trying to bring the drug to market.

This is not what has happened. In the ten years up to 2007, the United States government spent $31 billion on overseas drug control, which is almost twice the amount spent in the previous ten years.[25] In spite of this huge increase in resources, cocaine has only been getting purer. Street cocaine sold in New York City in 1970 was reported to contain just 6 per cent cocaine.[26] This rose to an average of 40 per cent purity in 1981 and to 63 per cent in 2003.[27] Cocaine prices fell over the decade leading up to 2003: in Western Europe by 45 per cent and in the United States by about 50 per cent.[28] The DEA counters that there has been a marked increase in retail cocaine prices in American cities since 2003. While this is true (the average price per gram went from $80 to $100 between 2003 and 2005), this is not necessarily good news for the DEA. To some extent, the price rise is due to stepped-up policing by the Mexican authorities and disputes between rival drug-trafficking organizations in Mexico. But more significant has been the increased demand for cocaine in Europe, where prices are higher and the value of the euro has risen against the dollar. The North American cocaine market has also lost out to growing demand for cocaine in transit countries such as Mexico, Brazil and Argentina. What appears at first sight to be the first signs of a long-awaited improvement proves on closer inspection to be quite the opposite. Cocaine is produced in quantities sufficient to supply the biggest markets, plus enough to cover anticipated government seizures, and has been for some time. The situation shows no sign of changing, however much money the United States throws at the problem.[29] Former US drug tsar Lee Dogoloff acknowledged as much when he said that 'everyone has agreed for the past twenty or thirty years that the only real improvements will come from demand reduction, not supply reduction'.

PART THREE

Where Do We Go
From Here?

9

The Demand for Cocaine

*All laws which can be violated without doing anyone any
injury are laughed at. Nay, so far are they from doing
anything to control the desires and passions of man that,
on the contrary, they direct and incite men's thoughts
toward these very objects; for we always strive toward what
is forbidden and desire the things we are not allowed to
have. And men of leisure are never deficient in the ingenuity
needed to enable them to outwit laws framed to regulate
things which cannot be entirely forbidden. He who tries to
determine everything by law will foment crime rather than
lessen it.*   Baruch Spinoza, *Political Treatise*, 1677

'You can have all sorts of successes in the war on drugs, as has
happened with heroin in Turkey, India and Thailand, where there
have been big successes, but as long as there is demand, the supply
will come from somewhere, and the war on drugs is just fuelling conflicts which will continue unabated.' I had asked Sir Keith Morris what
conclusion he had drawn about the war on drugs from his tenure as
British ambassador to Colombia between 1990 and 1994. Addressing
the demand for drugs seems obvious, and lip service has long been paid
to the need to reduce the demand for drugs. But drug-taking is illegal,
and so it is furtive, which makes it difficult to analyse. The gaps in official
understanding leave plenty of space for pontificating by people with
little knowledge of, and strong objections to drug-taking, which cannot be a good basis for analysing, let alone controlling, anything.

About 5 per cent of the world's adult population, equivalent to 200 million people, is thought to take illegal drugs. Cannabis remains far and away the most widely used drug: about 162 million people smoke it on a regular basis. Of the 13 million cocaine users around the world, two thirds live in the United States and a quarter live in Europe, where cocaine use has been rising for the past ten years. The American cocaine experience has played a pivotal role in determining the rest of the world's drug policies, but that experience and the poverty, racism and zealous law enforcement agenda that shaped it is far from typical. Arguably, a more representative scenario can be found in the United Kingdom. In the 1990s, growing numbers of British people were willing to try illegal drugs, culminating in 2000, when 34 per cent of British adults admitted having used an illicit drug at some time in their lives, up from 28 per cent in 1994.[1] Fourteen per cent of them, equivalent to 4.5 million people, have tried a 'class A' drug, the category to which the British government's medical scientists despatch the psychoactive substances they consider most dangerous, which includes cocaine, ecstasy and heroin. Most people used them occasionally, not habitually. Over the course of 2001, just over a million British adults used a class A drug at some point, and 500,000 of them had used a hard drug in the past month.

In the UK and Spain, more young adults now take cocaine than take ecstasy, and in both countries, cocaine is the second most popular drug after cannabis.[2] In 2000, 4 per cent of Spaniards admitted taking cocaine at some point in their lives.[3] While this is a sizeable portion of the adult population, one could just as easily extrapolate the conclusion that hard-drug use appeals to remarkably few people. Even allowing for the prodigious increase in cocaine use in the UK, Spain, Ireland and Italy, just over 1 per cent of teenagers and adults in Western Europe took cocaine last year. Even in the United States, the world's biggest cocaine market, the average rate is just 2.3 per cent.

Why such low numbers of people should be of such concern may be because drug use is more common among young people. Almost 6 per cent of the UK's sixteen to twenty-four-year olds – that's 350,000 people – took cocaine last year.[4] According to a report from Liverpool John Moores University, 50 per cent of young people in Liverpool took cocaine in 2008.[5] Whichever statistic comes closer to the truth, it leaves questions of why people take cocaine and to what extent it need be cause for concern unanswered. As long as cocaine enjoys a reputation among Europeans which, as the UN's World Drug Report of 2006 put it, 'is still not very negative', they can be expected to consume more of it in the future.[6] This makes a clear understanding of the demand for cocaine more important than ever.

Considering the terrible fear of 'instant addiction' that the American press indulged in throughout the 1980s, the first point to make is that few of those who try crack or powder cocaine become regular users, much less addicts, of either. In 2003, 35 million Americans admitted trying cocaine at some point in their lives, but less than 6 million of them had taken cocaine in the past year. Far from succumbing to cocaine addiction, most Americans who try cocaine never take it again. Almost 8 million Americans admit having tried crack at some time in their lives, but only 1.4 million of them had smoked it in the past year.[7] This is not to deny that plenty of people become dependent on cocaine and crack, but drug dependency cannot be explained by the inherent qualities of the drug itself. A more profitable line of enquiry would be to look at the difference between the 604,000 Americans who smoked crack in the past month and the 800,000 Americans who smoked crack in the past year but *not* in the past month. Why do some people run into problems with cocaine while others don't?

Interpreting drug use, like drug use itself, is subject to fashion. Young people have adopted a more relaxed attitude to class A drugs since the rise of ecstasy in the 1990s. Despite being categorized as a class A drug, nobody became addicted to ecstasy, and few people suffered ill-effects. Well-publicized exceptions only served to convince drug-takers that press and politicians were hysterical, hypocritical or possibly both. They became more suspicious of their teachers' and politicians' admonitions, less wary of ecstasy and more willing to take powerful stimulants in combination with other drugs. As the American experience shows, drug users have often been stigmatized as part of a wider culture war between liberals and conservatives, but Britain's ecstasy generation has largely escaped attempts to caricature it because ecstasy seemed to be a drug without political affiliation. It was certainly celebrated as a quest for unity after the divisive Thatcher years, but as such, it appealed to people on both sides of the divide. It was not a badge of exclusion or exclusivity, but an escapist attempt to transcend both.

As the quality of ecstasy pills has fallen over the past five years, many drug users have looked for the strong stimulation offered by ecstasy and found it in cocaine, which has become more afford-able. Britons were paying an average of £65 for a gram of cocaine for their Millennium Eve parties. By 2005, the average price had fallen below £50.[8]

One of those users was Bridget. 'I'm thirty-five,' she told me. 'When I was eighteen, the drug of choice was most definitely ecstasy. The parties were in fields and disused warehouses, but it wasn't as if the organizers were making loads of money on the bar, because although you might get a couple of bottles of water, ecstasy is not something that you drink with. As the acid house thing started to wind down, it pushed people into bar culture through the '90s. We had the rise of the style bars, and DJs playing in bars and that definitely goes hand in hand with cocaine. People wouldn't necessarily pay to get in, but they would stay all night to dance, and the bar would make its money on drinks. As cocaine began to get cheaper and there were more and more bars, you'd have a couple of lines and go bar-hopping. I used to run bars and it was so in our interest to have people on coke because they just drink and drink and drink. There would be big signs up saying that if you got caught doing drugs you'd be thrown out, but as long as people didn't start fighting, I didn't see there was a massive problem with there being some coke available.'

The British folk tradition of taking ecstasy in a field strewn with empty water bottles and high-wattage speakers lives on in the summer festivals. Just as festival-going has passed from the radical fringe to become an essential fixture in the social calendar of millions of young Britons, hard drugs have migrated from distinct sub-cultures into the mainstream. Alan is in his late thirties and works for an advertising agency in London. 'With the advent of the music festival crowd, it's become Guardian-cool, Channel Four-cool to get twatted. You might not do it all the time, but it's all right to do it every now and again.

In my company it is absolutely, 100 per cent acceptable to take cocaine. Dabbling in a bit of coke is not a taboo subject. You don't blurt it out in front of your managers, but that's what everyone does. It's like getting pissed in the '70s.'

Cocaine is no longer the preserve of the advertising executive. It is consumed by many successful, stable, otherwise law-abiding citizens, and it is this change in the drug-taking demographic that makes the laws governing drug use so out-dated. Studies have shown that American drug users' wages are 7 per cent higher than the national average, and that this increases to 20 per cent for users of hard drugs.[9] This may seem surprising, but the same holds true for drinkers. Use of alcohol and/or strong drugs is not associated with low productivity, or sloth. Both have become part of the lifestyles of those who are most productive and have passed into even the most respectable institutions. Every year, the British Army dismisses the equivalent of almost a battalion of soldiers for taking drugs. The numbers involved are still small: 769 soldiers tested positive for drug use in 2006, a rate of less than 1 per cent, compared with over 7 per cent in civilian workplace drug-testing schemes. But the number of positive tests for cocaine use by serving personnel has risen fourfold since 2003, and now outnumbers positive tests for cannabis use.[10] Sniffing cocaine is no longer the distinguishing feature, tag or signifier for young people that it once was. As it moves from the cultural niche in which it first found favour into the mainstream, it is likely to become more widely used and more widely acceptable.

Why do people want to take cocaine? Every era has its drug, its effects serving as a barometer of the prevailing mood of a time and a place. In some periods, people have been inclined towards relaxing, narcotic drugs such as opium; in others, people have chosen to take reality-warping, psychedelic concoctions. The spirit of the new century seems to respond best to stimulants, such as caffeine, cocaine and amphetamines. Throughout the 1970s, cocaine was available to a small and moneyed British market but it wasn't until the following decade that use of the drug spread to highly paid, highly pressurized professionals working in the media and the City of London. All drugs gain their first adherents among a small clique, but it is telling that cocaine use first became fashionable among members of the elite. In 1985, a doctor in La Paz, Bolivia, described the city's typical cocaine user. 'The majority of occasional cocaine users belong to the upper or upper middle class. Almost all of them are professionals, artists, businessmen or successful politicians. Generally, the quantity does not go over a couple of grams a month. Its use is usually limited to weekends, and it is generally used only at night. Daily use is extremely rare. The majority use cocaine with the same frequency that they use alcohol, as an antidote to drunkenness or to prolong the entertainment. A minimal percentage uses cocaine to increase their physical or intellectual output. A few young women use it to lose weight; others like its aphrodisiac powers.'

Cocaine is part of a wave of democratization of bourgeois taste in the United Kingdom. As access to holidays abroad, designer fashion and exotic cuisines has spread from the elite to the masses, so too has access to cocaine. Its use has become a gesture of extravagance, sophistication and conspicuous consumption, akin to drinking champagne. 'Cocaine is getting more popular with less affluent people because it's opening a gate for them,' a recreational cocaine user called Carl told me. 'It makes them feel a bit better about themselves, in the same way that people go to Tesco's and buy an organic carrot instead of a cheap carrot. We're in a consumer state now and people's self-esteem is boosted by what they can afford to buy.'

In 1924, two German doctors wrote that 'generally a cocaine user is a sociable personality'.[11] The UK might have become a politically and economically more conservative country in the past thirty years, but it has also become one whose mores are more permissive and whose people are more sociable. The Victorians first took bourgeois propriety to the masses. Today, the mantle has been almost entirely cast aside, as Britons revert to a pre-Victorian tradition of carefree pleasure-seeking.

Gabrielle works for Strathclyde police constabulary, but outside working hours she has found cocaine to be an effective social lubricant. 'Some of the best conversations I've ever had have been between close friends when we've had some charlie. You're on it, but there isn't that pressure to compete with other people for attention. You can have an earnest and honest chat about personal things. We were friends before, but the coke helped us to really open up to one another.' When I asked Alan from the advertising agency about the pleasure he got from cocaine, he described it as 'a tribal feeling, doing it with your friends, and all going off into a little story together. Coke amplifies your personality and makes your conversation that little bit more amusing and sparkly, if only for a short period of time. It's a subtle state of euphoria. It makes me lose my inhibitions without being out of control. Or at least you think you're in control. While you might be boring the shit out of the people you're talking to, you think you're being witty and intelligent.'

The sense of heightened awareness, combined with confidence and ease that cocaine users describe was recognized by the first Europeans to study its effects. According to his biographer, Sigmund Freud 'tried the effect of a twentieth of a gram and found it turned the bad mood he was in into cheerfulness, giving him the feeling of having dined well, "so that there is nothing at all one need bother about," but without robbing him of any energy for exercise or work'.[12] Under the influence of cocaine, Freud's intellectual output was much increased. On 21 April 1884, he was still only planning to secure some cocaine, but by 18 June, he had completed a veritable paean to the wonders of cocaine, an essay that was hurriedly published in the *Zentralblatt für die gesamte Therapie*. Freud's initial praise and eventual repudiation of cocaine has become a widely cited cautionary tale. After whole-heartedly recommending cocaine to his friend Ernst Fleischl von Marxow as a cure for his morphine addiction, Freud watched as Fleischl developed an all-consuming cocaine habit.

What most tellers of this tale omit to mention is that Fleischl was driven to daily use of morphine and then cocaine by recurring tumours that kept him in unremitting physical pain. For the average rec-reational cocaine user, Freud's experience of cocaine is more pertinent than that of his friend because it demonstrates that while cocaine has long been regarded as a drug for the sociable, it has other uses as well. As might be expected, British cocaine users are more likely to go to pubs and clubs than non-cocaine users. But 62 per cent of British people who have used cocaine in the past month are not frequent pub-goers and several of the users that I spoke to incorporated cocaine into their daily lives. 'I got a couple of grams for my birthday and it lasted me a month,' a recreational user called Paolo told me. 'I'd have a little line before I went to work and maybe one when I was at home with the kids. Last Sunday, I had a line at about 4 o'clock and I happily did the ironing. Today I had a Red Bull, and my heart was pounding, but I don't get that with coke. But it is expensive and I don't want to be in zippy mode all the time.'

The need and desire to be in 'zippy mode', to face the world with energy, optimism and fearlessness, provides a promising insight into cocaine's rise to fashionability. Pam is a former cocaine user from Detroit, who has long put her addiction to cocaine behind her. I asked her what she had got from cocaine. 'I grew up in a town in rural Michigan, so there weren't a lot of drugs, but I would do anything and everything I could get my hands on. I didn't have access to cocaine until I was fifteen. I had a boyfriend from Detroit who was a little bit older than me, and he brought cocaine on a date for us to snort. I liked it a lot. It suited my personality. I'm pretty hyperactive, and one of the things that I liked about cocaine was that I didn't have to sleep as much. I could stay up and get a lot done.'

In the course of the freezing Sunday afternoon I spent with Ted in Williamsburg, New York, I asked him about the reasons underlying his cocaine use. I was met with a look of befuddled frustration. 'I never thought about why I did coke. It's a central nervous stimulant. It makes you feel really good. It makes you want to talk and have sex and dance, and whatever else you normally do, only more so. I guess some people want to be more awake than others. You miss stuff if you go to sleep. I might have dozed off once or twice when I ran out of drugs, but I basically didn't sleep from 1979 to 1986.'

In the early years of the twentieth century, an artistic movement that came to be known as Futurism was notable for being the first to recognize high speed as the main, if not sole, contribution that modern civilization had made to the history of human pleasures. Life in the modern cities of the world is characterized by its speed: city dwellers in all the developed countries are in constant physical, mental and spiritual movement. Everything is subject to change, and we are constantly being encouraged to absorb and respond to those changes. In this context of incessant stimulation, we cannot afford to switch off because anyone tempted to passively observe change risks being left behind. The coordination, communication and efficiency that speed facilitates are among the greatest virtues of modern city dwellers. The hyperactivity, impatience and restlessness it produces are among our worst vices. The seductive capacity of cocaine resides in its promise of committed engagement with the present. Cocaine helps its users to maintain intense attention, even as it shortens its span. Indeed, cocaine promises its users little other than a fascinated engagement with the here and now. Perhaps the sensation of speed has eclipsed the origins and destination that once gave the journey its meaning. Even as the object and purpose of that engagement remain distressingly elusive, cocaine reminds the skittish of what complete engagement feels like.

Hard drug use was virtually unheard of in the United States in the period between the First and Second World Wars.[13] By contrast, drugs had a profound impact on the postwar period. There has been a generation of heroin users born between 1945 and 1954, a generation of crack users born between 1955 and 1969, and a generation of marijuana users born since 1970. Hysterical claims about drug use have abounded since the Industrial Revolution, but a more sober assessment now seems possible. Most people don't like most drugs. Most of those who do try cocaine do not go on to use it heavily. They don't even go on to use cannabis heavily.

Most recreational drug use is unproblematic. Studies have shown that young Americans who use drugs heavily and often are more likely to be emotionally insecure, less likely to be able to form healthy relationships, and were often emotionally distressed as children. But they have also shown that young people who abstain from all drug use tend to be equally maladjusted, described in one study as 'anxious, emotionally restricted and lacking in social skills'. Those who fared best were those young people who used drugs occasionally, engaging in what the authors of one study termed 'age-appropriate, developmentally understandable experimentation'. They went on to argue that heavy, frequent drug use among American adolescents is a symptom, rather than a cause of psychological problems, and that focusing on symptoms rather than the underlying causes is counter-productive.[14] Another study showed that the same holds true for American adults: life satisfaction is associated with moderate and occasional drug use. Dissatisfaction is associated with both heavy use *and* abstinence.[15]

Authorities charged with reducing the demand for cocaine might take some small solace from the fact that whereas in the UK, cocaine has risen in popularity as ecstasy's star has waned, in the United States there are more first-time users of ecstasy than of cocaine. Cocaine use among American high-school students is now 60 per cent lower than it was in 1985.[16] The all-time peak of cocaine use occurred in 1979, when about 20 per cent of eighteen to twenty-four year olds said they had used cocaine in the last year. It had never been that high before, and it has never been that high since.[17]

The popularity of a given drug is subject to the whims of fashion, like any other consumer good. But attitudes to drugs also evolve in tandem with the law, or the lack of it. The days when most of the cannabis smoked in the United Kingdom was imported from Morocco are long gone. The advent of widespread home-grown cannabis culti-vation has made it much harder for the British police to enforce the prohibition of cannabis. Acknowledging the limits of law enforcement, many European cities have instituted a de facto decriminalization of cannabis possession, even where official policies and rhetoric remain unchanged.[18]

British cocaine users face a less than 1 per cent chance of being apprehended by police in possession. Today's aesthetes take drugs because they can get away with it, but also because they have an almost politicized sense of pleasure. They jealously guard their right to define what their pleasures might be. Pleasure, having been har-nessed to the engine of commerce, carries its passengers to a utopia of endless shops. Goods and goodies have become indispensable to our personal happiness as well as that of the wider economy. As pleasure and profitability become paramount, and the global drug economy continues to thrive, the distinction between a chocolate cake, a fine single malt and a line of cocaine has become blurred. Many consumers

THE DEMAND FOR COCAINE

would argue that if they have the money to pay for all three, they have the right to buy all three.

Drug sub-cultures still exist. They are a way of life and an important part of the self-identity of some young people. Asking some teenagers to give up smoking cigarettes is tantamount to asking them to give up their credibility in the only peer support system they have. Drug use was so important to a specific sub-culture of the 1960s that it was regarded by friends and foes alike as an ideological statement. Today, however, there are multiple sub-cultures based on race, sexuality, music, even the food you choose to eat and the shops you choose to buy it in. It is no longer a question of being hip to drugs that mainstream society spurns. Instead, there is a grey area of generalized drug use, which most practitioners would file under 'occasional leisure activities'.

Cocaine is likely to remain popular because it works with rather than in opposition to Britain's drinking culture. As Alan the ad-man put it, 'once I've had a line, I'm in pintage mode. It's wet against dry. You need the wetness of a pint to match the dryness of the coke.' 'Teenagers today are incredibly blasé,' Ted assured me. 'They've been watching women getting fucked by horses on the internet since they were five. Everything that was counter-cultural or subversive has been co-opted, so drugs have become more normalized. They're an option. To worry about young people taking drugs is about as sensible as worrying about what kind of shoes they wear. What's the big deal? It's highly unlikely that they're going to take as many drugs as my generation did, and we didn't turn out that badly.'

A blasé attitude to cocaine is, however, no surer a guide to its effect than a fearful one. Understanding the risks inherent in using cocaine is a vital first step towards anticipating and dealing with compulsive cocaine use. Trying to figure out why cocaine becomes a problem for some but not for others, I started by asking recreational users what they considered to be cocaine's negative effects. Ricardo, who I had met while I was in Bogotá, wanted to talk about the contradictions inherent in taking cocaine to ease communication. 'One of the main effects of coke is that everyone wants to talk and talk and talk. But after a point you realize that the words aren't working. You find yourself trying to describe your need to talk, but realizing that the words to do so barely exist. Words become useless, despite your fluency with them.'

Back in London several months later, I met Mark, who told me that he had tried cocaine and decided that he didn't like it. Like Ricardo, he had found that far from easing conversation, the loquacity that cocaine gave him betrayed him in the end. 'I was out until five o'clock in the morning, having the most earnest conversation of my life. I felt a desperate urge to unburden myself, to reveal things. But then I asked myself, "am I only saying this because I'm on charlie?" That terrible double-edged paranoia was quite a horrible experience. The cocaine should have created some kind of bond between me and the person I was talking to, but your inhibitions are there for a reason and we hadn't loosened them organically. We'd caustically stripped them.'

'I went to a nightclub the other day,' he went on. 'Everyone was on charlie, but I'd arrived at the point where the coke had run out, and I had the feeling that the party was going on somewhere else, in some dark recess. Everyone was an island, like monkeys in some strange zoo. You couldn't talk to anyone, because they were all following the one guy with coke, like he was the Pied Piper of Hamelin. The desperation was frightening.'

Ted seemed to have a prosaic explanation for this. 'Coke turns you into an asshole just by being expensive and desirable. You've got to make sure that everybody doesn't find out that you've got coke, so you make your secretive trips off to the bathroom with your elite little club of buddies. Cocaine is an IQ test. If you're still doing it, you flunked. It's like masturbating. Masturbating is good fun, but in the end we probably want to do something else with our day, don't we?' Bridget agreed that the pleasure to be had from cocaine was self-limiting. 'In the run-up to one Christmas, I remember having quite a hard-partying agenda, and I got very bored of taking cocaine. If you're always artificially excited, how can you ever be genuinely excited? Most people work that out.'

'For me, the downside comes when I go to bed at four in the morning, and I say to myself, "I'm not going to be able to go to sleep",' Alan told me. 'When I do loads of coke I get a pain in my side, and I allow my brain to embark on a voyage of death. I start feeling paranoid, wondering if my heart is beating too fast. I read on the internet that when you get numb fingers or a numb shoulder you're in trouble, so I'm always looking for those signs.'

Whether bringing out its users' wit or their morbidity, cocaine seems to have none of the quasi-mystical connotations of other drugs. Indeed, the promise of a 'trip', an escape from or transcendence of reality, no longer appears to be a tempting one for most drug users. Cocaine has been described as 'the steel drug'.[19] It changes perception, not by making the world appear more wonderful or magical than the user had imagined, as might be said of cannabis or hallucinogens, but by making it seem even more stimulated than it really is. There hasn't been a cocaine movement, as there has been an ecstasy movement, or a heroin sub-culture, perhaps because cocaine makes people too self-conscious to listen to other people, let alone devise a collective plan. Sherlock Holmes was probably the first fictional cocaine user. His creator, Sir Arthur Conan Doyle, used Holmes's drug abuse to illustrate his character's restless intelligence, low tolerance for boredom and the ennui that they gave rise to. In *The Sign of Four*, the great detective says, 'I abhor the dull routine of existence. I crave for mental exaltation. That is why I have chosen my own particular profession, or rather created it, for I am the only one in the world.' As this suggests, among the risks of taking cocaine is that it can elevate the ego to airless heights, the better perhaps for the user to throw himself from. For misanthropes, it can make the world appear inane and people mechanical.

Though illuminating, these accounts tell us more about the context in which cocaine is used and the personality traits of its users than they do about the drug itself. The primary effects of any drug are physical, and stem from its natural properties. The pleasure experienced when taking cocaine is a result of the drug's effects on levels of dopamine in the brain. Dopamine plays a big part in rewarding us for experiences which promote reproduction and survival, which is why eating, having sex and fighting feel good. Cocaine blocks the re-uptake of dopamine at the nerve synapses in the brain, so the dopamine stays in the synaptic gap between axon and neuron a little bit longer, making the synaptic nerve endings especially sensitive. It is this heightened sensitivity which produces the euphoric feelings described by cocaine users. The Andean Indian chewing a mouthful of coca leaves, the stockbroker snorting a line of cocaine and the homeless prostitute smoking a crack-pipe are each getting high on that delayed re-uptake of dopamine in the brain. What they actually experience varies enormously, however, because a drug's effects also depend on how much you take and the way you ingest it.

Many substances can be both cure and poison, depending on the size of the dose. Discussing a local medicine, Aristotle recommended that doctors prescribe a *dragma* (measure) to enliven the patient and boost his confidence, but warned that two *dragmas* would make him delirious and start to hallucinate, three would drive him to permanent madness, and that four *dragmas* should only be administered if the doctor wanted to kill his patient. Can it be said that *dragmas* are dangerous? Not as long as Aristotle was able to measure the dosage. As Ted pointed out, 'even drinking the nicest Chardonnay, if you drink two cases you're going to be puking on your shoes. Similarly, if you take the most subtle, refined Peruvian vintages in sufficient quantities, you can find yourself committing some bizarre sex act that lasts for three days.'

One of the unintended consequences of driving drug use underground has been to make the accurate measurement of dosage much more difficult. Every year there are about 3,000 cocaine and heroin-related deaths in the United States. Eighty per cent of them are thought to occur either because the drug has been adulterated with harmful additives or because it hasn't, in which case the user runs the risk of injecting a much purer dose than he or she intended to.[20] In the days when the US government prohibited alcohol as well as drugs, drinkers ran similar risks and died in similar numbers.[21]

The cocaine experience depends on the form in which the drug happens to be available. Coca leaves, typically chewed or brewed as a tea, are a mild stimulant comparable to tea or coffee. The World Health Organization's investigation of coca and its derivatives found that coca consumption had beneficial effects on health, and produced no noticeable problems for the user's work, family or social life. But because all coca products are illegal, importers bring them into the UK in their most lucrative, concentrated and powerful form, as powdered cocaine. There is no market for coca leaves, coca tonics or the myriad milder forms that proved most popular with British consumers in the nineteenth century, when buying cocaine was as easy as buying tea. After all, why would a smuggler risk going to prison for a cheap, bulky product that offers its users only a mild high? Banning drugs has had a crucial effect on the demand for them. Nobody had even thought of smoking cocaine before it was banned.

The effects of any drug also depend on the setting in which it is taken and how it is regarded by others. If you can imagine a world in which alcohol was unknown, the slurring of words, the woozy stagger and clumsy bonhomie that characterize the drunk would be unrecognizable. Instead of being met with a knowing wink, he would have to contend with an uncomprehending stare. Put that drinker in the company of someone who has also had a drink, or has at least been drunk in the past, and he is much more likely to be able to relax. Anyone who has learned how to drink alcohol knows that his clumsiness is not permanent. It is a passing effect of the drug he has imbibed, for which sensible drinkers make allowance, and from which they can then derive amusement.

To some extent at least, the incidence of drug-related problems, including drug-induced psychoses, depends on a drug-using culture's stage of development. Marijuana first came into popular use in the United States in the 1920s and many reports of cannabis-induced psychosis date from those early days. Far fewer cases were reported after 1940, as users came to a better understanding of what to expect from cannabis intoxication. Pam from Detroit told me that her cocaine use became a problem when she lost control over it, but she also said that the problem was exacerbated by the incomprehension of those around her. 'My dad came to visit one time, and the friends that I was living with sat him down and said "hey, this girl's got a real problem." I was full of stories about why I was so skinny and why I was so depressed, but he was not a person who had a lot of emotional skills, so he didn't really do anything. He just freaked out and didn't say much.'

Having realistic and well-informed expectations of a drug's effects also explains why some cultures seem able to use drugs that others are ruined by. There are hill tribes in Thailand and Burma that are entirely dependent on growing opium. Precisely because it is widely available, opium consumption has had to be regulated and codified, and is generally reserved for old, unproductive members of the community. In less homogenous and cohesive societies, it is more difficult to set ground rules for who can and cannot take drugs, which makes it all the more important that drug users are well informed. The majority of Britain's primary and secondary schoolchildren are taught about drugs and the dangers associated with using them. Students are shown hard-hitting anti-drug videos and treated to lectures by former heroin addicts. Teachers promote a 'drug-free lifestyle' and stress the importance of personal responsibility. Young people are taught how to resist peer pressure and encouraged to seek 'alternative highs' such as pot-holing and abseiling.

Drug education in schools has been shown to have little impact on young people's decisions to use drugs.[22] Some teachers argue that the best that can be expected of drug education is that it restrains drug users' escalating use once they've started using drugs, and reduces some of the harm that those drugs can potentially do. An evaluation of the 'Know the Score' campaign in Scotland, which was designed to warn young people off trying cocaine through a campaign of ads on TV, radio and in the press, found that existing cocaine users, those most likely to be exposed to cocaine and females were all less likely to use cocaine after seeing the advertisements. But the majority of respondents could not remember specific campaign themes. They knew that taking cocaine was wrong, but they didn't know why it was wrong.[23]

Ted rolled his eyes skywards when I asked him about the role of education in warning young people of the harm done by drugs. 'Efforts by well-meaning authority figures to stop people taking drugs only make drug-taking more glamorous, exciting and desirable. Most of the governments propaganda campaigns about drugs are in fact advertisements, because the only genuine warning signs are those based on reality and experience.' But this approach is unnecessarily defeatist.

Drug education is important, but its effectiveness depends on the credibility of the educators. Many educators are loth to admit that the pursuit of pleasure might be a valid reason for drug use, or to recognize young people's curiosity, their need to experiment, to take risks and define their own boundaries. There are plenty of police officers, ex-addicts and theatre companies eager to tell young people 'the facts' about drugs, but the use of outsiders only sensationalizes drugs and reinforces the idea that teachers are unqualified to talk about them. Drug education in schools would be better grounded if it adopted the same aims that underpin the teaching of other subjects: to increase young people's knowledge and understanding, so that they can arrive at their own, informed views.

In the absence of credible education, young people have to draw the lessons that need to be learnt from their peers and from personal experience. Liverpool has experienced explosions of both heroin and crack use. Both have slowed of their own accord, as the informed opinions of one generation have been bought at the cost of the painful experience of the preceding generation. The harm done is much increased. But generations of drug users, whether dabblers or devotees, do learn from one another. It may be true that 50 per cent of the young people in Liverpool took cocaine in 2008, but there has been no corresponding rise in use of crack cocaine in the city.[24]

Jorge Hurtado, in his book *Cocaine: the Legend*, quotes a doctor from La Paz, Bolivia, as saying that 'cocaine is a safe drug, provided that it does not get into the hands of unbalanced people that can use it with self-destructive aims'.[25] Most drugs, whether legal or illegal, create problems for a minority of their users. In the United States, 0.3 per cent of drinkers are in treatment for their alcoholism, whereas 2 per cent of drug users are in treatment for their drug use.[26] But the criminalization of cocaine use has made it harder to distinguish problematic users, who might need treatment, from recreational users, who don't. In chapter 3, Russ a former narcotics detective, described the danger he ran in trying to pierce the inner workings of drug-dealing organizations. He also told me that after leaving the narcotics unit of the police department in San Jose, California, he spent the next ten years working with people in court-mandated drug-treatment programmes. 'Eighty-five per cent of them have been arrested because they've been caught with a small amount of cocaine in their wallet. But they don't have a cocaine habit and they're only in a rehabilitation programme because the court told them to go there. That is the same ratio that we have for alcoholics today. Eighty-five per cent of everybody who drinks alcohol drinks responsibly. They come home to their wife, children and the family dog, and they have a Margarita with their enchiladas. What most people don't understand is that most cocaine users do the same thing.'

Carl too was at pains to make the distinction between recreational and compulsive drug use when I spoke to him in London. 'I've grown up with people who've destroyed themselves with crack and heroin. They're on a ride and they're not going to get off until the drug's finished with them. No ifs or buts about it, I like cocaine. I like the feeling, I like the buzz. Me and a friend were seeing this Colombian guy on a regular basis. He had really good stuff and we got right into it for about a month. But I never felt like it had a hold on me. Some people are more-ish with it, because, like any good experience, you don't want it to finish. If I've got some cocaine, most of the time I've also got some weed, some drink, some fags, and it blends well with them, but when the charlie's gone, I accept that it's finished. I've still got the rest and the night carries on. I'm an average working man, in the 25- to 30-grand bracket, so I couldn't afford to be a victim of it. It's a treat like going to a restaurant, and I can't afford to go to a restaurant every night of the week either. If you're rich enough to get fucked up on it, you can probably afford to go to a proper rehabilitation centre place as well and get yourself sorted out.'

The authors of a study published in Toronto in 1989 found that the most frequent pattern of cocaine use over time, far from being an inexorable descent into drug addiction, was 'up-top-down'. Most of the 100 cocaine users they looked at had taken larger amounts of cocaine over time, but they didn't lose control of how much they were consuming and only a minority progressed to really heavy use.[27] Research done in Amsterdam in 1987 found that 21 per cent of cocaine consumers reached a high level of use at some point during their cocaine-consuming careers.[28] An American study which followed twenty-seven cocaine users over an eleven-year period concluded that 'the tendency for use to escalate to abuse was neither inexorable nor inevitable. Most never came to use cocaine daily or regularly in heavy amounts. The majority of our subjects had used cocaine for more than a decade, usually in a controlled fashion.'[29]

The typical career of a cocaine user lasts between three and six years, and peters out with age, experience and changing lifestyles. This is much shorter than the typical career of alcohol and heroin users, who can be dependent on one or the other for their whole lives.[30] Four years after the first interviews were conducted in Amsterdam in 1987, almost half of the respondents had stopped taking cocaine. Of the rest, over 90 per cent reported periods in which they hadn't used cocaine for at least a month. These reports and studies suggest that far from being blindly led down a road to ruin, most cocaine users take increasing amounts, realize that the effects are self-limiting, and soon tire of them. It is a pattern confirmed by the anecdotal evidence of users like Alan. 'Coke is running out of usefulness in my life. Five years ago, I used to take it every two weeks, whereas now it's once every three months, if that. I don't want to go out like I used to. Now it's all about the day and not the night. I'm older, I've got a family and I get joy from being out in the country, looking after the house and family and messing around with the dog.'

Gabrielle and her husband Steve are in their thirties. They still take cocaine from time to time, but not in the quantities and with the frequency that they once did. 'Most people seem to have a three-year phase and I think my three years are up,' Steve told me. 'I used to smoke weed and I've given that up and I've learnt from experience that it's not worth the bother of doing a pill to have a good time on Friday night, only to feel horrible for three days next week.' 'And you're not sharing that horrible experience with everyone else,' Gabrielle added. 'When we used to take pills, we'd spend the weekend with our friends, but now everyone has got families and other commitments, so you're breaking up the party before it's even started.'

The notion that the charm of cocaine is such that it destroys the user's powers of self-control just doesn't stand up to scrutiny. As Alan said, 'what limits my intake of cocaine is that I don't want to get off my face that often, the same reason that I don't want to get drunk every day. I want to be in control of my life 95 per cent of the time and 5 per cent of the time I want to let myself go and forget about the other 95 per cent.' What then, of the 5 per cent of the time that users like Alan want to let themselves go? Doesn't bingeing on large quantities of cocaine inevitably lead users to become addicted? A Dutch study of 1993, entitled *Ten Years of Cocaine*, found that 6 per cent of cocaine users had run into difficulties with cocaine, meaning that they considered asking for assistance to help them control or stop using it. All but one of them either quit cocaine without seeking help or continued using it at more moderate levels.[31]

Plenty of Britons enjoy bingeing on cocaine (partly because it helps them to binge on alcohol), but few of them develop a daily habit, if only because most of them have to go to work on Monday morning. For those so inclined, a true intoxication marathon can last for days, and pave the way for a drug experience quite different to that produced by snorting a couple of lines. The pulses of euphoria experienced by participants in a cocaine binge can create vivid long-term memories, which for some will become a fount of craving for stimulants. Large doses of cocaine can also lead to severe psychosis while the user is still on the drug, with symptoms including powerful cravings, escalating doses, inability to eat or sleep, chaotic mental processes and paranoid hallucinations.

Pam, the former cocaine addict from Detroit, described the terrible fear that would overcome her after taking too much cocaine. 'One night Steel Pulse were in town. I'd gone to the sound-check, and some of the road crew wanted coke, so that gave me an excuse to go cop a bunch. I went back to my house to do some before I had to go back with the backstage passes and the list of people who were supposed to get in for free. I got so jacked up and paranoid, I was staring out of the window, convinced that there were people in the trees watching me, then crawling around on the floor, and hiding behind the curtains. I told my assistant to come over and get the passes, because I was way too messed up to even go over there.' Doris, who had told me what she remembered of the free-base phenomenon in Harlem, had, like Pam, been injecting large doses of cocaine. 'The cocaine would have me up all night, picking on myself. I'd look in the mirror and everything would be magnified. I'd see these big bumps on my face and I'd start squeezing and digging. Later my mother would say "What is wrong with you? You're losing your mind." That cocaine is nothing to play with. It ruins you for days.'

The doctor cited in *Cocaine: the Legend* had treated some of the first problematic cocaine users of La Paz and offered an explanation for the tendency of regular cocaine users to keep taking the drug. 'The intervals of abstinence from chronic use are invariably followed by a rebound effect, manifested in bad humour, irritability, and permanent tiredness. This in turn deepens the exhaustion, closing the circle and establishing the psychological drug dependency.' Ted's explanation of escalating use echoed the doctor's. 'Cocaine is like spending your whole pay cheque on Friday night. It feels great on Friday night, but it sucks to wake up broke on Saturday morning. That's what cocaine does to your dopamine levels. You've used up your capacity to feel pleasure for the foreseeable future. Like Freud says in *The Cocaine Papers*, cocaine is not addictive. It's just that discontinuing the dose produces a feeling of lethargy and ennui that is immediately relieved upon repeating the dose.'

'As soon as I'd get high, I'd want some more,' Doris told me. 'Heroin is more physical, but that cocaine, it's a psychological addiction. The desire is so strong, when you run out, you feel desperate. It makes you think "man, I'd do *anything*." I never killed anybody, but I'd prostitute myself, steal, lie, manipulate, whatever it took to get the money. The mind is a powerful thing, and it can have us do things that we don't want it to.' Yet as the user starts to take cocaine on a habitual basis, what was once a completely engaging experience ultimately becomes a boring one. 'With all this stuff, the longer you use it, you don't get the same high any more,' Pam said. 'You spend a lot of time trying to get that same high back, and you just can't.' Unrealistic expectations lead to inevitable disappointment, yet habitual users seem to have a perverse need to experience that disappointment, perhaps to puncture expectations they know to be unreal.

The feelings that accompany withdrawal from heroin or the delirium tremens of the recovering alcoholic set in hours or days after the user has stopped taking the drug. Because the physical symptoms of withdrawing from a cocaine habit are minor, many doctors initially classified cocaine as a non-addictive drug, or at least one which all but the pathologically pathetic could resist. Habitués of cocaine were not thought to be addicted to the drug, but to pleasure itself. The problem lay not so much with the drug, as with its users, who saw no reason to cease gratifying their basest instincts. As a result, compulsive cocaine users were generally given shorter shrift than heroin addicts, with enforced abstention being the typical means of breaking the habit. Ted disparaged the very idea that people become addicted to cocaine. 'People who talk about their addiction to cocaine are basically weak-minded pussies. With heroin you get physically sick, you're vomiting, you're shitting in your pants as you walk down the street. With coke, you feel like shit and life sucks, but what exactly is the difference between that and real life? If you can't handle the shit that's around you, you should go and get a heroin habit or something.'

Asa Hutchinson was head of the DEA between 2001 and 2003. In a speech he made on accepting his new job, he echoed the notion that drug addiction is essentially a character flaw. 'I will bring my heart to this great crusade. My heart will reflect a passion for the law, a compassion for those families struggling with this nightmare, and a devotion to helping young people act upon the strength and not the weaknesses of their character.'

There was a time when 'addiction' was used exclusively to refer to compulsive use of alcohol or class A drugs like heroin. These days, we can be addicted to just about anything, from pornography and chocolate to shopping and love. The advocacy group Action on Addiction claims that one in three British adults suffers from some form of addiction.[32] So in what sense is cocaine 'addictive'? Repeated use of a substance is no indication of addiction (if it were we would all have to admit to an addiction to toothpaste). Compulsive use would be a better description, and a substance's potential for being used compulsively seems to depend on several factors. The first is how intoxicated the user feels after taking it. In terms of intoxication, alcohol is an even stronger drug than heroin, which is in turn stronger than cocaine, which is stronger than marijuana. Reinforcement is a measure of how often users dose themselves with the substance. Alcohol tops the list, followed by heroin, then nicotine, then cocaine. The third factor is withdrawal. Nicotine has the severest withdrawal symptoms, followed by heroin, then cocaine, then alcohol. The factor that best highlights the potential dangers of cocaine use is dependence, which refers to the likelihood that users will continue using the drug even after it has started to do them harm, how hard they find it to stop using the drug and, having stopped, how easily they relapse into using the drug again. Cocaine is more likely to attract dependants than heroin, alcohol, nicotine or marijuana.[33]

But the physical qualities of any substance only go so far in explaining why people become dependent on it. Compulsive internet use is reported to be a problem all over the world, but it became an issue in South Korea when young people started dropping dead from exhaustion after playing online games for days on end. South Korea claims to be the most internet-savvy country in the world. Ninety per cent of homes have broadband internet connections. There are 140 internet-addiction counselling centres and 250,000 of the country's under-eighteen year olds are said to show signs of internet addiction, a syndrome characterized by an inability to stop using computers, rising levels of tolerance that drive users to seek ever longer sessions online, and withdrawal symptoms like anger and craving when prevented from logging on. Dr Jerald J. Block, a psychiatrist at Oregon Health and Science University in the United States, estimates that up to nine million Americans may also be at risk of developing the disorder.[34]

What Dr Block calls 'pathological computer use' cannot be explained by scrutinizing South Korea's computers or the online games that users play. It has its roots in an intensely competitive society that regularly sacrifices the rounded self-development of its young people to a conformist, target-driven education system. The 'compulsive escapism' that this has created might also be a better explanation for problematic drug use. The law and the medical profession generally focus on the drug, rather than the life and mind of the drug user, when trying to explain why people lose control of their drug use. But if young South Koreans can suffer withdrawal symptoms when deprived of online entertainment, in what sense can it be said that drugs are more dangerous than computers? Ted is critical of the pharmaco-centric approach to understanding compulsive drug use. 'It's an easy cop-out from personal responsibility to blame the drugs. Skiing is a dangerous activity involving a white powder. It involves starting up real high and then coming down real fast. And it takes all sorts of effort, like a ski-lift, to get back up to the top. Is that an addiction? Is it pernicious? Should ski lifts be banned?'

Pain and intoxication are intimately bound, as the doctor from La Paz, Bolivia, made clear. 'In almost all cases where there is this type of abuse of cocaine, I have found in the user's previous history depressive states of the most varied origins: losses in life, dependent personalities, low tolerance for frustration, etc. These states in turn create conditions for easy dependency. Really, [drug abuse] is a desperate and intuitive search for treatment, an uncontrolled self-medication, which only results in the worsening of the previous depression.'

A verse from Proverbs 31: 6 advises the reader to 'give strong drink unto him that is ready to perish, and wine unto those that be of heavy hearts'. Popular iconography of the drug addict suggests that social deprivation and self-destructive drug abuse go hand in hand. While there is a lot of truth to this, this materialistic focus on poverty masks the many, more familiar instances in which depression leads to substance misuse, as in the case of Gabrielle. 'I'd come home having worked really hard all day and I'd have a line to give me the energy to do the things that I needed to do at home, to feel like I could have my spliff, to feel like I'd earned it. I had to earn everything. Cocaine was very linked to my working pattern, being on my own at work and being on my own at home. The cocaine use was easy to keep hidden, but it was also completely miserable because I'd have a lot more time to consider what I was doing and to feel shit about it the next day. I was coping really well with the rest of my life. But when there's no one to stop you, you just keep going. I ended up going deeper and deeper into it to try to escape. I'm quite frightened of cocaine now.'

'Oftentimes, the issues underneath drug use aren't the issues that people expect them to be,' Pam told me. 'I had all the intellectual, material and physical things you could ever need. I was a state finalist in gymnastics and finished 11th in a class of 700 people. The way I saw it, as long as I was getting good grades, the drug use didn't really matter. A lot of my coke use was about procrastinating for as long as I could on my assignments, and then using cocaine for the last six weeks of term to get them all done. I didn't have any major trauma as a child, but my parents were pretty much emotional and spiritual zeros. They threw a lot of money at me to try to make up for other things and I spent most of it on coke and pot. Our society puts so much emphasis on the physical, the trivial and the intellectual, and a lot of people completely short-change the spiritual and the emotional. I really believe that drug abuse is just a symptom of a spiritual and emotional disease.'

Intoxication by any substance offers an escape from circumstances. It follows that the most dissatisfied people tend to take the most intoxicating drugs. The most marginalized and isolated among them continue to take hard drugs in spite of the harm it does them because all too often there is nobody to stop them. Crack cocaine is not a drug that appeals to many people. Less than one in a hundred British people have tried it, and most of them never smoke it again. One in five hundred Britons used it in 2005, and only half of them had used it in the past month.[35] Whether in London, Los Angeles or Lima, crack is generally consumed by people suffering from trauma or depression, who find themselves with few resources to ease the burden of either. Louis is a crack user from New York City. He told me that he first started using drugs as a form of pain relief. 'I'd left home at a very early age. I'd lost a very close friend, and there was some other trauma that occurred, so I was going around with these feelings, not knowing where to put them. I was hanging around with a gang, so sometimes those feelings showed up in violent ways. I did my first institutional bid when I was eighteen, but I knew that violence wasn't going to lead me to freedom. With speed and crystal meth I discovered that I could alter how I felt. The depression that I was feeling lifted. So drugs weren't just experimentation. They were an escape.'

Most crack users begin using drugs in adolescence and most use the drug compulsively. Nine out of ten of London's crack users have been found to suffer from depression and a third have attended a mental health service. These people don't develop crack habits because they try the drug and become addicted to it. Most of them were so damaged before they even picked up a crack pipe that it's hard to know how much responsibility for their frazzled state should be borne by the drug, and how much by the lives they led before they found the drug. In London, the average age of first arrest for a crack user is sixteen, well before they ever started taking crack.

Crack is not the sort of drug that you can indulge in at leisure. It picks you up and runs with you, all the while convincing you that you are more in control of your life than you have ever been. Many of the people interviewed by the authors of *On the Rocks: A Follow-Up Study of Crack Users in London* spoke in glowing terms of the pleasure they got from 'running about' and being 'on a mission'.[36] The pleasure of crack might be lost on the average Londoner, but the motive for taking the drug is a familiar one. For every City of London stockbroker with a weekend cocaine habit, smiling with satisfaction at the pace and excitement of his life, there is a compulsive crack user smiling for the same reason. But since most Londoners have a barely restrained contempt for 'crack-heads', compulsive crack users tend to flock with those of their feather. Half of London's crack users have at least one family relation with a drug or alcohol problem and over two thirds of them say that most of their friends also have problems with drugs or alcohol.

But crack use is not necessarily compulsive. A crack user can stop using rocks, and experience no physical withdrawal symptoms. In many ways, wealthy former crack users, such as the magazine publisher Felix Dennis, are surer guides to the harmful effects of crack because their wealth insulates them from much of the chaos that regular use of such a powerful stimulant brings in its wake. To suggest that the drug is responsible for the dependent relationship that many users develop is to gloss over the deprivation and neglect that many of them have experienced. Far from facing up to the origins of problematic drug use, it would seem that the greater society's reluctance to confront mental illness and depression, the more strictly it prohibits the use of certain drugs.

The settings in which users of criminalized drugs congregate are always likely to be furtive. This makes it easier for their dealers to adulterate their product. Much of the physical damage done by crack is a consequence of its poor quality. For example, crack that has been washed in ammonia can cause permanent lung damage, a condition known as 'crack lung'.[37] Crack users have on occasion organized themselves to improve matters. Crack Squad is a users' group that has taught East London GPs how to make crack pipes with a glass stem, so that the doctors can then teach users how to avoid burning their fingers and lips, which is the main cause of the high rates of transmission of hepatitis C among crack users. Unfortunately, most efforts to reduce the harm done by crack smoking are dismissed as only encouraging a habit that should be prohibited. This moralizing approach to drug policy is irrelevant to most drugs users and does nothing to protect their health.

'Hell is of this world,' wrote the French theatre critic and opium smoker Antonin Artaud in 1934, 'and there are men who are unhappy escapees from hell, escapees destined *eternally* to reenact their escape.'[38] In discussing the prohibition of opium, Artaud wrote that nobody can stop another from intoxicating himself. But he also insisted on a much broader definition of intoxication, to mean something more akin to immersion. He described the intoxicating effects of solitude, reading and anti-sociability. People value intoxicants, not just for the immediate pleasure they give, but for the measure of independence from the outside world that they supply. Most people enjoy that independence in small doses, but those buckling under the pressure exerted by the outside world will crave it. Sigmund Freud defined drugs as 'painkillers'. It is precisely because painkillers offer refuge from external pressures that they will always be potentially dangerous.

Why some people enjoy cocaine from time to time while others let their drug intake define the course of their lives, is a question of what sobriety means to the drug taker. Mass drug addiction is a recent phenomenon that has flourished in a specific culture, one notable for the stresses that many of those who live in it have to bear and the solitude that many of them bear it in. But modern city dwellers don't just take drugs to escape the world. They also take drugs in a misguided attempt to kick-start their participation in it. They are actively encouraged to believe that there is a product that can be bought that can satisfy their every desire, including their desire to participate more fully or escape entirely. The market for escape is partially fed by our notions of success, many of which are as prohibitive and exclusive as our favourite goods. Those deemed unsuccessful will always be tempted to alight on drug-taking as a pursuit (in the original sense of the word, as a flight from reality). Many of them will use drugs as part of a compulsive quest for some imagined state of grace; and some will use them in greater quantities as they realize the ultimate futility of the quest.

I asked Ted who he thought was most likely to develop problems with drugs. 'Stockbrokers basically play Monopoly for a living. Most people past the age of seven find that boring. If you're a guy with a healthy Wall Street income, you almost certainly have no emotional or psychological centre, so when you plug into the main circuit of pleasure, you're fucked. Brokers are a drug dealer's dream customers. They value things that are expensive and showy. Big tits! Porsche! Coke! So of course they get all fucked up on cocaine and are out selling pencils six months later. But to extrapolate from that sample something about the substance? No. I would certainly be in favour of criminalizing stupidity, but criminalizing something because stupid people might like it is not a very productive approach, is it?'

Dealing with other people's stupidity, as well as their depression, means facing up to the destructive qualities inherent in personality traits that we prefer to celebrate, such as competition, individualism and self-denial. It requires that we accept drug abuse as an attempt to self-medicate conditions beyond the aegis of most doctors, who are trained to focus on physical well-being. Regular, compulsive crack use is symptomatic of deeply rooted obsessive or compulsive psychological disorders. Such disorders can also manifest themselves through torturous relations with other substances (like alcohol) or activities (like sex, or even the internet). The pharmacological properties of cocaine can only go a short way in explaining why there are so many compulsive crack users in America's inner cities. Far more telling is the price and wide availability of drugs like cocaine in communities of deeply troubled people.

*

Doris told me how she finally reached ground zero. 'I'd come into work late and say the lock broke off the door, or the dog just died, or my aunt is sick. Every kind of excuse you could think of. I was looking for a way out but I didn't know a way out. I felt like I was going to die strung out on drugs. I never prided myself on being suicidal, but one day I just got tired of the living. "God," I started to think, "I just don't want to live no more."'

It can take many years for compulsive drug users to decide to quit. I remember asking Louis what he did when he hit rock-bottom. He told me that he found a trapdoor. In the early stages of a drug epidemic, there isn't much that can be done to reduce drug use because users have yet to develop serious problems. But as the crack epidemic in the United States waned, its last embers proved susceptible to intervention, not by law enforcement, but by treatment providers. It is not easy to reduce or stop the compulsive drug use of long-term heroin, crack or methamphetamine users. A study conducted in the United States in 1994 found that only 13 per cent of hard-core drug users who received help were able to reduce their use substantially, or kick it entirely.[39]

This may seem a demoralizingly low success rate, but it is far higher than that achieved by arresting, jailing, disenfranchising, and un-employing drug addicts. A study by the RAND Corporation in 1994 found that to achieve a 1 per cent reduction in cocaine consumption in the United States, the government could spend an additional $34 million on drug-treatment programmes, or twenty-three times as much ($783 million) on trying to eradicate the supply of cocaine from Colombia.[40] Despite this vindication of the efficacy of drug-treatment programmes, provision in the United States is woefully inadequate. Over a million Americans were thought to need treatment for cocaine abuse in 1998, but in the previous four years only 250,000 of them had actually received it.[41]

America's problematic drug users are more likely to find themselves drying out in prison than in a treatment programme. Drug courts have been heralded as an effective alternative to incarceration, but they put users who want to get help in the Kafkaesque position of having to get themselves arrested in order to be treated. This is a bitter irony considering the vehemence with which the United States government has prosecuted its war on drugs. The drug treatment mandated by the courts is often a throw-back to the twelve-step programme first devised by Alcoholics Anonymous, a method based on repenting for the harm the user has done to other people, finding a substitute for drugs in spiritual belief, and abstaining from drugs entirely. 'I had twenty years of programmes,' Doris told me. ' "Heal! Demon, come out!" I had all that, and none of it worked. You can't make people do anything. They have to be ready. One day I surrendered to what they call "the high cost of low living", and decided that I wanted to change my life. My boss helped me get clean, and once I saw the clean side of living, I started to think "hey, maybe it's not so bad." '

Drug treatment has come a long way from its origins in exorcism. Contemporary programmes focus less on the drug itself, and more on encouraging drug users to question their compulsive behaviour, so as to recognize and resist 'the euphoric recall'. 'Narcotics Anonymous tell you to stay away from "people, places and things", Doris explained. 'Don't go to places where you know drugs are. Get a watch. When I first came back to the neighbourhood after getting clean in a programme, people would say "Doris! How ya doing?" They thought I was going to say "alright, where's the red cap? Where's the coke?" But I'd look at my watch and say "aw shit! I gotta go!" It works if you work it, but even now, with twenty years clean, I still make meetings. It's where my friends are, people like me. They say that baseball players dream of baseball. Well, I'm a drug addict, so I dream of drugs. But I'm not like a newcomer to it, you know? The obsession has been lifted.'

Jerry, a former methamphetamine user and treatment programme graduate from Chico, California, told me where he thought the roots of compulsive drug use lay. 'A lot of people feel lonely, you know? So they seek companionship, sometimes in a very unhealthy way, via drugs and alcohol. You have to ask yourself "OK, what can I do?" First off, I can change the way I perceive being lonely. It's not such a bad thing. How can I develop some support, some friendships, so I feel a part of things, and have some purpose in my life? We treat drug dependency as a symptom of a lack of coping skills. You start to learn how to deal with anger and frustration without having to run and numb yourself with drugs and alcohol. How to deal with loss and grief, and relationship issues. How to communicate effectively. A lot of the guys have never had to manage money or be responsible for their actions. So we focus on changing thinking patterns, changing our environment, and really developing some sober living skills.'

But as Louis told me, drug treatment can only work when its providers recognize the drug user's right to define their problem for themselves. 'It is one thing to be using recreationally, another thing to be self-medicating, and another thing to be on a suicidal track.' For the many people whose drug-taking is a response to trauma, depression or hopelessness, being told to stop taking drugs is not always the best way to reduce the harm they are doing to themselves. 'Crack users are stigmatized, marginalized and criminalized, but really, the harm is caused more by society's attitudes than by the drug in and of itself. My drug use has changed as I've realized that it is possible to be a productive member of society and still be a drug user. You need some kind of base, a sense of responsibility for yourself and your relationships. The self has to be in place, and then the self can make choices. Once you have that, you can enjoy the experience of smoking crack, without the would-have-beens, could-have-beens or should-have-beens. If you fail to plan, you plan to fail. It's a quaint saying, but I believe there's some truth to it.'

Kenneth is a former crack user and dealer from Dothan, Alabama. 'While I was inside God gave me a vision of the Ordinary People's Society, to go out to the ordinary people who were overlooked or outcast, the homeless, the drug addicts and the prisoners who were despondent just like me, and to clean up where I had messed up. I thought about how my mother would always leave me a key, no matter how bad I was, and how she would always have food prepared for us. When I got out of prison, I went back to the same 'hood in Dothan where I had sold drugs. There was a pizza shop across from the mall where my mother used to work and the Puerto Rican guy there would give me the pizzas that he was going to throw away at the end of the night. I would go to the crack-houses that I knew in the area and I would pass the pizzas out, because I knew that when we were out there doing drugs we didn't eat and that if they ate, it would diminish their drug use, and stop them from robbing and stealing and shooting people.'

The Ministry of Health of the Netherlands has said that 'the Dutch policy assumes that it is not possible to completely quash drug consumption through government policies. Partly because of this belief . . . government policy discourages drug consumption. For those who continue to consume drugs, there is a wide range of measures in place to manage potential social and health problems associated with drug use.' The Netherlands has only a quarter of the UK's population and considerably fewer drug users, but its government spends twice as much as Westminster on preventing and treating drug abuse.[42] Of the 30,000 opiate addicts in the Netherlands, 15,000 receive some kind of treatment.[43] In terms of drug use per head, the Netherlands is in the same league as Germany and France, at a considerably lower level than the United Kingdom, and half or even a third of the levels seen in the United States.[44] That the Netherlands is famously liberal in its attitudes to drug use, while the United States is among the most punitive of all countries, suggests that drug policy has very little influence on the number of people who use drugs. In fact, cannabis consumption in the Netherlands went *down* after the laws were liberalized, which could be taken to mean that forbidden fruit loses its taste once we're allowed to eat it.

The Dutch approach is to be commended, but real change will only come when people develop a more nuanced understanding of what propels compulsive drug use. Drug-treatment professionals have long said that the best drug abuse prevention programme ever invented is gainful employment. It is all too easy to imagine that a crack or cocaine addiction is a curse to be exorcized, when it is usually only an accomplice to existing chaos. Doctors, health visitors and social workers try to limit the damage to individuals and communities, but they are clearing up the mess rather than getting to the root of the problem, which is invariably nourished by long-neglected social and personal problems.[45]

In the absence of public understanding and political will, the vacuum is being filled by improvements in medical technology. A new treatment for compulsive cocaine users is expected to become available in 2009, what might be called the *Clockwork Orange* approach to breaking stubborn thought-patterns. The biotechnology company Xenova has developed a therapeutic vaccine for the treatment of cocaine dependence which induces antibody responses to the drug. In trials, most drug users who took cocaine within six months of being given Xenova's vaccine reported a reduction in the euphoric effects of cocaine. The drugs had finally stopped working.[46]

IO

Legalization

Not that which goeth into the mouth defileth a man; but
that which cometh out of the mouth, this defileth a man.

Matthew 15: 11

The demand for cocaine comes from two sources: recreational users and problematic users. At present, neither seems amenable to intervention by law enforcement or drug education specialists. Those most likely to be put off drugs by a spell in prison face minuscule odds of being arrested.[1] As Alan said, 'the police have to worry about the bigger things going on. Let's face it – a couple of ad agency twats taking a bit of coke are not doing any harm to anybody, are they?'

Meanwhile, those least likely to be dissuaded from using drugs by a prison term are those most likely to be given one. Most regular crack users are unable to hold down a job, much less one that allows them to indulge a £100-a-day crack habit. As a result, nearly all crack users finance their drug-taking through crime. Up to 80 per cent of America's thieves are thought to be hard-core drug users, and every year they steal goods worth £3.75 billion. The illegal market in drugs also binds compulsive drug users to other criminal activities. Most crack users are poor, many are in debt to their dealers, and are either threatened or beaten when they cannot pay those debts. Half of the women who regularly use crack in London are prostitutes. Almost two thirds of heavy crack users have spent time in prison, and more than half of prison inmates report that they used drugs while there.[2]

But the links between hard drugs and crime, however stubborn, can be broken if the drugs can be made cheaper and more accessible. In Switzerland, prescription programmes that have been doing just that for the past ten years have been instrumental in reducing the number of crimes committed by drug addicts by up to 90 per cent and doubling the numbers able to sustain full-time employment.[3]

In thinking about the crimes committed by compulsive drug users, and the extent to which police and public health officials can do anything about them, it should be clear that the illegal marketplace is the worst possible arena for affecting change. The prohibition of drugs actually sustains problematic drug use and creates drug addicts. One reason is that the heaviest and most troubled drug users prove to be the best customers. Twenty-two per cent of cocaine users in the United States account for 70 per cent of total consumption. Their suppliers have every interest in encouraging compulsive consumption, and much less interest in supplying occasional, recreational cocaine users. Consequently, ambitious drug dealers congregate wherever there are likely to be compulsive users – in other words, where the poorest, most neglected and hopeless people live.[4]

Drug abuse is assumed to make people criminally violent, but a closer look shows most instances of drug-related violence to be a consequence not of drug use, but of the criminalization of drug use. In 1988, at the height of the crack epidemic that swept through New York City, there were 414 murders in the city. In police reports, more than half of those killings were described as 'drug-related'. This might lead one to think that being high on cocaine played a big role in making people murderous. Mental health problems, social deprivation and strong pharmaceuticals will always be a potent brew, but in fact none explain the violence of the drugs business. Just eight of those murders were committed by people under the influence of crack or cocaine; 85 per cent of drug-related killings would be better described as 'money-related': committed in order to get money to buy drugs, in disputes between drug dealers and their customers or in territorial disputes between rival dealers.[5]

The prohibition of drugs has created drug neighbourhoods, drug dealers and drug violence. Steven Soderbergh's film Traffic, released in 2000, was the first time that Hollywood had tried to get to grips with the failures of the war on drugs. The action moves between Mexico, where corruption stymies the government's attempts to curtail the smuggling business, and Washington D.C., where the drug tsar is forced to reconsider his belligerent anti-drugs talk when he realizes that his daughter has developed a heroin habit. One scene in particular brilliantly encapsulates the process by which drugs have become such a major employer of young men in the United States. The drug tsar appears to blame the (black) inner city for (white) suburban drug problems, but is quickly pulled up short by a friend of his daughter, who tells him that 'right now, all over this great nation of ours, 100,000 white people from the suburbs are cruising around downtown, asking every black person they see "you got any drugs? You know where I can score some drugs?" Think about the effect that has on the psyche of a black person. Bring 100,000 black people into your neighbourhood, and they're asking every white person they see "you got any drugs?" Within a day everyone would be selling: your friends, their kids. Here's why: it's an unbeatable market force, man. A 300 per cent mark-up. You can go out on the street, make $500 in two hours, come back and do whatever you want to do with the rest of your day. You're telling me that white people would still be going to law school?'[6]

Drug use, whether light or heavy, is common to all classes and ethnicities in the United States, but middle-class and suburban abuse of drugs, whether legal or illegal, is more readily concealed so it is easier to disregard. The difference between uptown and downtown drug markets is one of economics. Suburban drug dealing is more likely to be part of a partying lifestyle, in which drugs are mainly sold by word-of-mouth through contacts at work, in pubs and bars, and at gigs and raves. In the suburbs, there are no stable, drug-selling locales, and drug dealers are much less likely to have employees. Inner-city drug dealing will always be more chaotic than suburban drug dealing because dealers and buyers are less likely to know one another, there is more through traffic and turnover is higher. Dealers have to take to the streets to attract customers, where they are more likely to run into the police and rival dealers, which only increases the likelihood that events will turn violent. People who don't live in inner-city neighbourhoods might equate visible drug-dealing with actual drug use, but rates of drug dependency are only slightly higher in the inner-city than elsewhere, and many who live there see drug dealers, rather than users, as the primary problem.[7]

Eighty per cent of the cocaine in the United States is consumed by white people, yet police operations and drug-treatment programmes have focused on poor, inner-city neighbourhoods, typically inhabited by minority populations.[8] This focus on visible drug sales rather than actual drug abuse has turned the campaign for a drug-free America into a daily struggle for control of neighbourhoods in which drug sales have become a mainstay. Although black Americans make up just 12 per cent of the population and 13 per cent of drug users, and arrest rates for other crimes are pretty similar for minorities and whites alike, African-Americans make up 38 per cent of those arrested for drug offences and 59 per cent of those convicted for drug offences.[9]

In fact, young white Americans are more likely to take illegal drugs than young black or Hispanic Americans. Seventeen per cent of young whites report having tried drugs, mainly marijuana, compared to 13 per cent of black Americans. Only 2.6 per cent of teenagers had tried cocaine in 2003, but the rate was four times higher for white teenagers than it was for black teenagers.[10] Ted tried to explain why this might be. 'Rates of drug use are considerably higher among affluent white folk than among poor minority folk because drugs cost money. Black and Hispanic drug users are much more likely to be in touch with their families, and vastly more likely to go to church, so they're more likely to hear that drug use is bad, degrading and sinful, and much less likely to hear that drug use is liberating or rebellious. There is no black Keith Richards, you know?' So why should it be that despite such abstemious beginnings, 9.7 per cent of adult African-Americans use illegal drugs compared to 8.5 per cent of adult Caucasian-Americans?[11] When you look at who is smoking crack, you see that 46 per cent of them are white, 36 per cent of them are black and 11 per cent of them are Hispanic. Crack has never found a following outside the most run-down inner cities of the world, and the breakdown of the racial origins of crack smokers tallies closely to the racial mix of the most neglected neighbourhoods of the United States.

The British Crime Survey last asked questions about ethnicity in 1996, so there is no way of knowing whether black Britons are more or less likely to use drugs than their white counterparts, but if the 1996 survey is anything to go by, black people are marginally less likely to use illegal drugs than white people.[12] The number of black people serving prison sentences for drug offences is disproportionately high, but there are disproportionately high numbers of black people serving time for all kinds of offences in the UK's prisons because black communities are subject to much higher levels of policing than other neighbourhoods. Black Britons are less likely to be cautioned, more likely to be charged with an offence and, once in court, more likely to be sent to prison than the white majority. The linchpin for this racial bias is the stop and search powers that Parliament ceded to the police under the Misuse of Drugs Act 1971.

In the film *Layer Cake*, which was released in 2004, Daniel Craig's character advises the viewer to 'always remember that one day all this drug monkey business will be legal. They won't leave it to people like me, not when they finally figure out how much there is to be made. Not millions. Fucking billions!' Despite its obvious appeal, the legalization of the drugs trade has long been the elephant in any room in which the future of drugs policy comes up for discussion. Until recently, most advocates of legalization were to be found working in drug users' organizations, in the provision of front-line treatment, or among those who have experienced the war on drugs in transit countries such as Colombia, Brazil and Mexico. But now, many war-weary police officers in the United States are also arguing for a fundamental change in the law.

Jack Cole is executive director of Law Enforcement Against Prohibition and spent most of his career working as an undercover narcotics police officer. 'Let's legalize these drugs like we did alcohol in 1933. The day after we got rid of that law, Al Capone and all his smuggling buddies went out of business. They were no longer out there killing one another, or killing us cops. They were no longer killing our children, caught in drive-by shootings. We could take all the violence out of the equation by legalizing drugs.' If cocaine were legalized, the millions of people around the world who work in the cocaine business would lose their jobs. Some might enter legal drug production, transport and distribution. Pound and ounce men would become regional sales managers. Runners and jugglers would become shop assistants. Fences, money launderers and hit-men would be no more.

'Then we could do two very important things,' Jack went on. 'We could keep drugs out of the hands of our children, who have been telling us for the past ten years that it's easier for them to buy illegal drugs than it is legal beer and cigarettes. They go to buy cigarettes, and someone is going to ask them "hey, are you old enough to buy these?" All the unregulated market is going to ask is "where's the money?" We could take drugs off the streets. We could also stop overdose deaths. People don't die of overdoses because they shoot more and more dope. They die because they don't know how much of that little packet of powder is the drug and how much of it is the cutting agent. Once we start treating drug abuse as a health problem instead of as a crime, we can actually start helping some of those 38 million people that we've arrested. We can bring them back into society. And we can save $69 billion a year by doing it!'

Kurt Schmoke, the former mayor of Baltimore, Maryland (or as viewers of *The Wire* have come to know it, 'Body More, Murderland'), has seen the flaws inherent in the war on drugs at first hand. He is convinced that the legalization of drugs is a vital first step in developing effective treatment for problematic drug users. 'I would change the law to allow physicians to be certified as drug treatment providers, so that I could walk into a doctor's office and have my substance abuse treated as a health problem. I'd also let doctors make the decision as to what legal drugs to give you to help you get over the problem and I'd even let doctors provide cocaine, if they thought that it was necessary, as they step you down from your addiction. Our experience of needle exchange in Baltimore was that when addicts out on the streets thought they had an opportunity to get help without arrest and without stigma, they came forward. As a society, there are ways of communicating that we don't support the use of these substances, without making it a crime.'

Sir Keith Morris, once the British government's most senior representative in Colombia, is another convert from the war on drugs, now convinced that legalization is the only viable way of drawing the venom from the drugs trade. 'The majority of people who use illegal drugs cope with them pretty well, but in the UK we have something like 250,000 people who are problematic users of various drugs. These are people with problems – problems that are being exacerbated by the fact that what they want to do is illegal. They very often have to resort to illegal and violent means to meet that need, and the costs of this run to many billions of pounds. It seems inconceivable to me that we couldn't produce a system which would have lower costs in lives and money than the present one. I think society could look after those with a problem, instead of stuffing them in jail, where they're only going to get even more drugs. Disastrous!'

Politicians of all loyalties have recognized the failure of prohibitionist drug policies. In 2005, David Cameron, the leader of Britain's parliamentary opposition, showed the extent of the dissatisfaction with the status quo, when he admitted that 'politicians attempt to appeal to the lowest common denominator by posturing with tough policies and calling for crackdown after crackdown', and that 'drugs policy has been failing for decades'.[13] As a member of the Home Affairs Select Committee inquiry into drug misuse in 2002, Cameron voted in favour of the recommendation that 'the Government initiate a discussion within the Commission on Narcotic Drugs of alternative ways, including the possibility of legalization and regulation, to tackle the global drugs dilemma'.[14] 'I think all drugs should be decriminalized,' former mayor of London Ken Livingstone has been quoted as saying. 'Addicts could register with their GP so organized crime could be driven out of drugs.'[15] In 2001, Lord Ramsbotham, the retired Chief Inspector of Probation, told the BBC that 'there is merit in legalizing and prescribing [drugs] so that people don't have to go and find an illegal way of doing it. The more I think about it and the more I look at what is happening, the more I can see the logic of legalizing drugs.'[16]

The patience of even the United States' most loyal allies in the war on drugs seems to be wearing thin, as demonstrated by an editorial in Colombia's leading daily, the otherwise conservative *El Tiempo*, in March 2006. 'After several years, billions of dollars and thousands of Colombian lives lost, the same quantities of cocaine reach the United States, while our country is more deforested and more hampered by the conflict, and the narco-traffickers more buoyant than ever. In an editorial of October 2000, we said that should the recently launched Plan Colombia fail, "the United States would have the historic responsibility to find and travel the road to the legalization of drugs." Isn't it time to reconsider a strategy that is clearly failing? Legalization is unpopular, but perhaps it's time to start thinking about it seriously.'[17]

Legalization is what American pundits term 'a third-rail issue', meaning that it is judged to be politically suicidal for anyone in public office to openly advocate it. Once away from the scrutiny of the international press, however, cities and states around the world have been decriminalizing drug use. Back in 1994, Colombia's Constitutional Court decriminalized the personal possession of up to 20 grams of marijuana, and/or a gram of cocaine. Judge Carlos Gaviria argued that it made no sense to penalize drug users but not drinkers, who were much more likely to commit acts of violence. He reasoned that 'legislators can proscribe certain forms of behaviour towards others, but not how a person behaves towards himself, as long as this doesn't interfere with the rights of others'.[18] His ruling went against a century of legislation which took for granted that drug users were by definition either delinquents or deviants. In his place, Judge Gaviria posited the free individual, sovereign of his own body. The onus was now on Colombia's citizens to accept responsibility for their new rights, and on the authorities to ensure that drug users' decisions were well informed.

Judge Carlos Gaviria went on to become the leader of Colombia's main opposition party. He has since been cited as saying that the United States is the principal obstruction to the international community committing itself to the legalization of drugs.[19] While there is no reason to think that the legalization of cocaine would benefit the poor, usher in land reform, challenge the extreme concentrations of money and political power in Colombia, or end its fratricidal conflict, it would certainly make it easier for the state to regulate supplies, enforce contractual obligations, and decide where the coca fields should be. Thousands of poor farmers would have legal work, and pristine jungle could remain pristine. The police would be able to focus on enforcing laws other than those that ban cocaine production, and Colombia's Mafia, paramilitaries and guerrillas would be deprived of their principal source of funds. Politicians would no longer need to be bribed, and the whole sorry façade of strong-arm posturing veiling sly back-handers could be pulled down.

In June 2005, Brazilian Minister of Culture Gilberto Gil also came out in favour of legalization. 'I believe that drugs should be treated like pharmaceuticals,' he said. 'They should be legalized, although under the same regulations and monitoring as medicines.' Sérgio Cabral, the Governor of the state of Rio de Janeiro, has also come out of the drug war closet, saying of the sea change that legalization represents, 'I know that people are very conservative in Brazil, but I'm willing to engage in this fight. I'm not a coward.'[20]

Legalization is regarded as a modern-day heresy by many, but it is probably the least radical of the viable, long-term solutions to the chaos engendered by the cocaine trade in Caribbean and Latin American countries. It would be far more radical were their governments to create professional police forces and judiciaries and pay them professional salaries. A second option might be to invest in making their rural economies viable so as to offer productive employment to far more of their people. Or perhaps the United States could tighten controls on gun sales, fund the rebuilding of poor neighbourhoods and provide education and decent healthcare to all its citizens. Compared to such utopian prospects, the legalization of the drugs trade looks like a pragmatic response to a multi-faceted problem that has outlived all the solutions that have been tried to date.

Unfortunately, those suffering the collateral damage of the war on drugs also happen to be those with the least power to challenge it, a conundrum encapsulated by Colombian psychiatrist Luis Carlos Restrepo, when he said that 'if the people of the United States had lived through the war on drugs that we've lived through, they'd already be pushing their government to change its stance'.[21] Francisco Santos, the current Vice-President of Colombia, echoed this widely held perception that producer countries are carrying the can for European and American governments' failure to address the demand for drugs. 'Look five years ahead, and you see that this cancer is going to spread to other countries in Latin America and the Caribbean,' he told me. 'But for developed countries drug production is a footnote. It is a security problem, but one that poses a minimal threat to the state and one with a relatively low cost. Frankly, until the problem becomes less manageable for the developed countries, the debate is not going to change much.' To date, Western cocaine consumers have been unmoved by the Colombian government's efforts to raise awareness of the environmental damage caused by the cocaine trade. 'My generation is going to be reaching for the mirror after a dinner party for the next twenty years,' Bridget told me. 'Maybe we'll all be demanding fair-trade coke, but our society is not too concerned about fucking up the environment. The loss of a tree frog is not going to faze me.'

The appeals of Third World governments fall on deaf ears because Washington regards even the most timorous reforms as the thin end of a wedge that ends with crack cocaine being as readily available as Krispy Kreme doughnuts. In April 2006, the Mexican Congress approved a law that would have decriminalized the possession of small quantities of drugs for personal use. The law was backed by then-President Vicente Fox, but under intense pressure from the United States he vetoed it the following month. A spokeswoman for the US Embassy in Mexico City confirmed that officials had urged the Mexican government to re-examine the law 'to ensure that all persons found in possession of any quantity of illegal drugs be prosecuted or sent into mandatory drug treatment programmes'.[22] Defending his back-tracking, President Fox argued that 'the day that the consumption of drugs is freed from punishment, it will have to be done all over the world. We are not going to win anything if Mexico does it, but the production and traffic of the drugs to the United States continues.'[23]

Like prohibition, legalization can only work if it is accepted at the highest levels. While the United States government enforces the global ban on cocaine, the law-makers responsible for any future move to legalize the drugs trade are to be found at the United Nations. No human behaviour is governed by such comprehensive and severe global treaties as drug use and drug trafficking, and few treaties are as impervious to revision. The UN's Single Convention suffocates any local autonomy or inventiveness in solving problems associated with drug use. The United Nations General Assembly Special Session (UNGASS) of 1998 was supposed to consider how the Single Convention might be made less onerous to the producer and transit countries. Instead, the United States and its allies smothered UNGASS in a stifling embrace. Far from revising the Convention, the Special Session reaffirmed its commitment to 'eliminating or significantly reducing the illicit cultivation of coca bush, the cannabis plant and the opium poppy by the year 2008', under the rallying cry of 'A Drug-Free World: We Can Do It'. Their self-imposed deadline has since been extended to 2009, when a new UNGASS is due to meet to measure progress. It is hard to avoid speculating that they will have failed to have made any.[24]

The United Nations' promise of a drug-free world is as illusory as that of the forty virgins waiting for Islam's martyrs in heaven.[25] Indeed, the best way to understand the respect that the UN's Single Convention continues to command is to regard it as a religious text. It has acquired a patina of unquestioned value, protected by a clique of true believers, hired not for their knowledge of sociology, pharmacology or epidemiology, but for their conformity.[26] The vocabulary they use to address drug-related problems is unimaginative, belligerent and depressingly repetitious.

In 2002, the House Government Reform Committee convened a hearing to consider ways to improve Plan Colombia. Republican Congressman Dan Burton asked the sixty-four-million-dollar question. 'What would happen if they couldn't make any money out of selling drugs? Would [the number of people addicted to drugs] go up or down?'[27]

In struggling to answer that question, proponents of legalization have long been lampooned for having fallen for a superficially attractive, but dangerously naive proposal. Mark Kleiman, author of *Against Excess: Drug Policy for Results*, has argued that 'freely available cocaine is likely to give rise to self-destructive habits for an unacceptably large proportion of users'.[28] Opponents of legalization argue that because drugs like crack are highly addictive, making them legally available and thereby cheaper would inevitably lead to huge increases in drug use. More drug addicts would support themselves by committing more crimes and claiming more welfare. The accumulation of violence and destruction in the United States, Jamaica, Mexico and Colombia would surely be as nothing compared to the chaos that would follow the legalization of drugs. It is a fear that overwhelms all comers. As Gabrielle told me, 'cocaine won't be legalized because there are too many people with too much control to lose, or what they think is control. They have no idea what would happen. There would certainly be casualties along the way and I don't think anyone is willing to have that on their hands. "It was your decision and now my son is dead" is reason enough to chuck someone out of office.'

This is a maddeningly trite conclusion to an increasingly shop-worn debate. It assumes that were it not for anti-drugs laws, the people of the world would launch themselves into a collective frenzy of nasally induced self-destruction. In reality, the law is regularly flouted by anyone who wants to buy cocaine. David is a former police officer with South Bureau Narcotics in Los Angeles. When I met him, he made it plain that 'anybody who wants to use crack is already using crack, because it's so available now. But once you allow people to go to the hospital, or wherever it's regulated, to get their crack, then they can have more stable lives.' I thought that this solution might be overly optimistic, but in fact David's suggestion was based on hard-won experience. 'We worked a lot of heroin addicts down in Wilmington, and a lot of them were dock workers on methadone. They'd get their methadone a couple of times a day, and they'd work the docks. They were productive, they could work a job without having to hustle or burglarize, or whatever else they have to do to get money for drugs. If drugs were legalized, I don't think drug abuse would deviate much from that 1.3 per cent that is going to be addicted no matter what.'

Government regulation of the distribution of class A drugs would make it easier to monitor problematic users and provide effective health services. But that still leaves the question of how to supply the market for recreational drug use, and how much it might expand if cocaine were legal. Wouldn't people currently dissuaded from trying cocaine by its illegality inevitably regard legalization as a green light? Opponents of legalization argue that for all its failings, the prohibition of drug use has at least restricted access to drugs by keeping prices relatively high. 'I don't think they should legalize drugs,' Alan told me. 'There are a lot of vulnerable people who don't take cocaine because they perceive it as socially unacceptable. If you legalize it, they'd end up taking it as well. Everyone would try it.'

But would they? A poll conducted in Arlington, Virginia, asked respondents: 'If cocaine were legalized, would you consider buying it?' Only 1 per cent of them said they would.[29] Admittedly, this finding might just as easily be taken as proof of the coyness of the people of Arlington as of their love of drug-free living, but in the few instances in which cocaine use has been depenalized, its popularity has remained essentially unchanged. Police in Amsterdam have adopted a policy of not intervening in individual cocaine use or small-scale distribution. This hasn't created a large group of cocaine consumers unable to control their use. In fact a survey of cocaine use in the city found that price had little bearing on how many people used cocaine or how much they chose to use. When asked whether a substantial drop in price would increase their consumption, a majority of cocaine users said it would have no bearing.

Alan had initially been dismissive of legalization, saying that 'if it was for sale next to the cigarettes in the off-licence, I'd have a line now. I'm three pints down and I'd say "what the hell?"' But if he went for a drink three days later, would he do it again? He had to admit that he probably wouldn't. 'It would be so easy to have that it would no longer be a surprise.' Alan's mixed feelings on the subject also surfaced in responses to the Amsterdam survey. There, too, a majority thought that while lower prices wouldn't affect their cocaine use, it *would* encourage others to use cocaine. In the run-up to the liberalization of the licensing laws in England and Wales in 2005, journalists and pundits speculated that by extending the right to sell alcohol, naive politicians were paving the way for an orgy of twenty-four-hour boozing. These fears proved unfounded: having been granted the right to drink into the early hours, most Britons exercised that right no more or less responsibly than they had prior to liberalization.

Rusty, the former narcotics officer with the Department of Corrections in Arizona, insisted that legalization would bring more, not less, control over drug consumption. 'When I talk about legalizing drugs, people say "you can't mean heroin and crack, right?" But after thirty years of the drug war, spending a trillion dollars and locking up 1.6 million people a year, the bad guys still control the price, purity and quantity of every drug. Knowing that they control the drugs trade, which drug are you going to leave in their control? Regulation and legalization is not a vote for or against any drug. It's not about solving our drug use problem. It's solely about getting some control back.' Paradoxically, by denying its citizens the right to take drugs, the United States government has lost rather than gained control over drug use.

Unfortunately, the war on drugs thrives on ignorance of drugs and misplaced faith in the power of the law to regulate human vice. The less people know about drugs, the more concerned about them they tend to be. The 2006 British Crime Survey found that older people were particularly concerned about the risks that drugs pose to young people, but were often unable to distinguish the risks involved in injecting heroin from the risks involved in smoking cannabis.[30] Twenty-seven per cent of respondents to a survey of attitudes to drug use in deprived neighbourhoods of the United Kingdom reported that people using and dealing drugs was a problem in their local area and admitted feeling bewildered by the inability of the police to put a stop to it.[31] One local resident told the BCS that 'there is a feeling in this community that the police know there is drug dealing going on all around but they just don't do anything.'[32] The survey found only one example of collective action against drugs, a case in which the residents' association had considered establishing a 'mothers against drugs' campaign but had been put off doing so because they were worried about reprisals from local dealers.

But the unpopularity of legalization cannot solely be attributed to the association of drugs with crime and violence in the popular imagination. The prospect of cocaine being legally available also stirs up deep-seated fears of intoxication itself. The Victorian middle class saw intoxication by sexual passion as a force that took its victim in its grip and stripped her of her precious self-control. Sexuality posed a constant threat to the probity of every decent Victorian and could only be managed by rigorous self-denial. The Victorians believed that by sheer strength of will, they could send their genitalia into functional, manageable exile and maintain the restraint, diligence and deference upon which their standing in society was founded. Instead of acknowledging human desire, including the desire to alter or temporarily dull one's consciousness, the Victorian corralled his desire into a recess of his mind and pretended that it didn't exist. In moments of weakness, he would succumb to temptation, and guiltily embrace what he once had banished. This to-ing and fro-ing between formal refusal of and secret dalliance with drugs and sex, has kept the British tabloids in fascinated incredulity for as long as they have existed.

'I come from a generation that was educated in the '50s,' former British ambassador to Colombia Sir Keith Morris told me. 'We did national service, and started out in life at a time when drugs were very remote and very esoteric. The social structure of family, church and trade unions was tremendously strong, there was much greater social cohesion and much greater conformity. Drugs were illegal. Homosexuality was illegal. Abortion was illegal. Off-course betting was illegal, and almost all Sunday trading was illegal. Almost everything has gone in the other direction, except the laws on drugs, which have become harsher in this country than they were then.'

Having conceded ground to more liberal attitudes in the course of the past fifty years, the righteously indignant seem to be making a last stand. Their stoic pose is one that conservatives are accustomed to striking in times of rapid change. The patriarchs of the Italian establishment and the papal state stood fast against the legalization of divorce well into the 1960s, long after it had become a grudgingly accepted fact of married life across much of Europe. Roman Catholic ideology was so embedded in the Italian political system that in spite of the increasing numbers of separated couples and the enormous social costs of denying them a legal divorce, the conviction that divorce was wrong was overpowering. It was a question of right and wrong. As such, it was not susceptible to reasoned debate.

Since he helped to draft the United States' Anti-Drug Abuse Act of 1986, Eric Sterling has spent many of the intervening years examining the rationale that has been put together to defend what is at root a moral objection to certain psychoactive substances. 'Prohibitionists will say "Well, yes, none of the usual tests of a just law apply. No one has been wronged, no rights have been abridged and no duty has not been carried out. So we're going to construct a new order, which is that if you harm yourself, we can punish you." ' This injunction against self-harm was a novel one, and Eric has been hard pushed to find similar instances. 'The law against suicide was a crime because you were depriving the king of a loyal subject,' he conceded, 'but that is not a doctrine in a democracy.'

Law-makers argue that because drug users are deluded by the drugs they take, they are in no position to recognize the harm that they do to themselves. Society has a moral obligation to intervene, against the will of the drug user if need be, to save him from his own worst impulses. Legislators then go a step further, arguing that the prohibition of those drugs provides the best framework for dispensing medical treatment to those who want to stop taking drugs, and managing those who can't or won't stop taking drugs. But the assumption that the power of these drugs is such that they take away the individual's power of autonomy and self-determination is unsustainable. Most people simply do not behave that way when they use these drugs.

Writers such as Peter Cohen and Harry Levine have tried to trace the origin of the modern concept of a 'drug' over which the 'addict' is unable to exercise control. They point to the birth in the mid-eighteenth century of individualism, a new ideology centred on the free individual, the precious fruit of long struggles against colonial dependence, slavery and the aristocracy. Where humanity's defining purpose had until then been to acquire God's grace for the salvation of the soul, from the Enlightenment onwards, the quest for God's grace was replaced by the independent individual's exercise of free will. In modern times, this has been supplanted by a new quest for and duty to a healthy body. The confusion that results from this clash of the paternalist impulse and the need to respect the free choice of the free individual is apparent in polls conducted in France in 1999. Eighty-five per cent of respondents agreed that criminal penalties should be imposed on consumers of heroin and cocaine; 70 per cent of them thought that cannabis smokers should face penalties too. But when the question was reframed to emphasize the rights of the user, one third of interviewees agreed that the prohibition of cannabis was an infringement of the right to use one's body as one sees fit.[33]

To mete out punishment as part of a duty of care seems contradictory. Even compulsive drug users are aware of and responsible for their drug use, to an extent that paternalists find hard to admit. It might appear easier to ban the drug with which the users hurt themselves, but this allows wider society to avoid confronting the reasons for self-harm. All the interest falls on the weapon, and none on the motives of the wielder. Besides, the debate is academic unless paternalists can impose their ban effectively, which, as the preceding chapters have shown, they can't.

Although more than five hundred years have passed since Europeans first encountered the coca plant, cocaine is arguably the last botanical extract to be traded in large quantities and at an accessible price on a global scale. Alcoholic drinks, the most widely consumed and accepted of all drugs, are produced in Britain and most Britons are aware of the production process. But most psychoactive drugs are imported and not produced nationally, so there is also a fear of foreign substances. Despite the long history of cocaine use in the West, the drug is still new and exotic. Heroin likewise remains an exotic drug, despite archaeological evidence of opium poppy drinks being consumed for their pain-killing properties in northern Europe since Neolithic times. Medieval medical books expounded the medicinal properties of opium, but also made plain that regular heavy use could lead to dependency.[34] Opiates have been regarded as familiar to one generation, and exotic to the next, only to have once again become familiar, and the same might be said of tobacco. When tobacco was first introduced to Japan, the authorities would regularly cut off the fingers and lips of smokers as punishment. These days, the Japanese get through 336 billion cigarettes a year.[35]

It takes some time to learn how to use a new drug, to find out what it is good for, the negative effects to avoid, and then to decide whether on balance it is worth taking. The learning curve is slowed by a lack of education about mind-altering substances, which will not be remedied as long as teachers disapprove of drug use and the law bans it. Drug education as it is currently taught is destined to become ridiculous as more people who have grown up in drug-taking cultures join the teaching profession. Instead of devising effective public health policies to manage widespread, limited-risk drug consumption, and a minority of compulsive, usually deranged hard drug users, the parameters for the debate have been set by politicians and law-makers, who find it expedient to pander to fear of foreigners, fear of black violence and fear of crime.

Understandably, the prospect of cocaine being legally available is a daunting one, but past experience provides a model for a legal, regulated market in cocaine and other drugs. The period at the end of the nineteenth century showed both the highest levels of availability and the lowest levels of abuse. Reverting to that legal market would be an incremental process, mirroring in reverse the way in which drugs such as cocaine were banned in the first place. The first step would be to restore doctors' rights to prescribe drugs like cocaine and heroin to chronic users. This is already happening in Switzerland, where 5,000 heroin users and 50 cocaine users receive their supplies on prescription from a doctor. The scheme has been judged a success, and Swiss medical authorities want to expand it.

Dr E. K. Rodrigo, the former drug tsar of Sri Lanka, has conjectured that 'legal availability of drugs would work in the same way as alcohol. People would apply for a licence to sell cannabis, coke and heroin. The government would be freed from chasing these people and it would be a controlled legal trade. You would still have the problem with health, but you have that anyway. At least this would take away the criminal aspect and we could concentrate on reducing the health problem as much as possible.' In a legal market, those who develop problematic cocaine use would benefit from services similar to those that already exist for problem drinkers. This would in essence be a case of facilitating a cycle that tends to occur spontaneously anyway, and compulsive cocaine users would in all likelihood need those services for a much shorter period of time than most alcoholics.

Legalizing drugs is not a popular proposal because most people imagine a scenario in which crack cocaine would be sold next to the super-strength lager in the supermarket. But Dr Rodrigo also made a vital stipulation. 'No drugs should be allowed to be marketed. Make all of them available, but no promotion.'[36] The commercial context in which legal drugs are made available is of fundamental importance. Alcohol control policy in North America has historically swung from one extreme to the other, from strict prohibition to a free and highly commercialized market. When alcohol returned to the over-ground of American life, it was soon subjected to the incantations of advertising gurus and marketing executives like any other product. But blanket prohibition and unfettered legal commerce are the extremes at either end of a wide spectrum of possible control. At present, powerful interest groups keep psychoactive substances at one extreme or other of that spectrum. On the one hand, the police support the blanket prohibition of illegal drugs and generally oppose any proposal they regard as loosening their control of access to illegal drugs, such as needle exchange programmes, supervised injection sites or medical prescription of heroin. On the other, big multinational alcohol and tobacco manufacturers support unfettered legal commerce and often oppose further government controls on their products.

Allowing cigarettes to be freely traded and consumed created a situation in which more than half of the adult population of Europe and the United States smoked. In spite of the terrible harm caused by their product, tobacco corporations have done all they can to defend the interests of their shareholders over those of the public at large. Nevertheless, lung cancer, heart disease and emphysema are not taken to be sufficient grounds for a legal ban on tobacco. Governments have instead opted for a middle way in managing the distribution of potentially harmful tobacco and alcohol. They allow commerce in malt whisky, but mitigate against the harm it can do by restricting advertising. Many governments also insist on training programmes for people who serve alcohol, designated driver schemes and courses to educate drinkers about the risks of drinking too much.

In the United States, 16 per cent of high school seniors smoked cigarettes in 2004, a huge drop from the 27 per cent that did so in 1975.[37] The catalyst for this change has been credible scientific evidence of the harm done by long-term tobacco smoking and government control over how tobacco is marketed, where it is sold, and who is allowed to buy it. These controls have led to a fundamental shift in public attitudes to smoking. The lesson to be learnt from the enormous harm done by tobacco in Europe and the United States is that handing supply of such a noxious habit to profit-driven corporations is not the most appropriate of the regulatory approaches available. Their advertising and marketing only stimulate the demand for tobacco products. But making cigarettes illegal would be entirely counter-productive. High taxation, honest education and effective treatment programmes are what count. As Sir Keith Morris says, 'people would take drug education much more seriously if drugs were legal, as they've taken tobacco campaigns seriously. Some people ignore it, but large numbers of people have taken it to heart, because they believe the evidence.'

Judge James Gray of Orange County, California, agrees that the commercial setting for drug sales is of paramount importance. 'If you want to talk legalized drugs, talk aspirin. Aspirin can be advertised, there are trade names, there are no age restrictions, you can buy as much as you want to, and the price is set by the free market. I wouldn't do that. I would have strictly regulated and controlled government-packaged stores for adults. I would not want it to be advertised. I wouldn't want someone to go into the drug store and say "I heard on the radio that you're having a special on six-packs of Great Kick Cocaine."'

Aside from its commercial setting, let's assume that price would have a considerable bearing on the popularity of cocaine in a future, legal market. Alcoholic drinks were about three times more expensive during the Prohibition Era in the United States than they were before alcohol production was outlawed in 1922. It has been suggested that if cocaine were legalized, it could retail at prices twenty times lower than those of today.[38] On the assumption that compulsive users will pay practically any price for their drug of choice, it follows that cheaper drugs would obviate their need to commit crime to raise the money to buy them. But cheaper drugs would also invite more consumption by more recreational users. The most effective way of reducing demand for recreational drugs would be by raising a sales tax. The current tax regime for beer, wines and spirits has been successful in making milder alcoholic drinks more popular than the stronger forms. It has been estimated that a legal market in drugs in the United States could bring an additional £2 billion in taxes into state coffers every year,[39] which could then be used to fund comprehensive drug education programmes.

Establishing a workable tax regime would be a careful balancing act. If taxes were too high, people would certainly try to find cheaper supplies, creating a black market that would leach off the legal market. This is just what has happened to the tobacco market in the United Kingdom, as criminal organizations exploit varying tax regimes by illegally importing huge quantities of cigarettes from the European Union. But black markets are not inevitable. Legal cocaine that retailed at anything less than £40 a gram would wipe out the illegal competition. There is no black market in selling alcohol to minors because off-licencees and pub landlords have a strong incentive to obey the law that prohibits the sale of alcohol to minors. Some teenagers find ways of getting their hands on alcoholic drinks, but a survey of American teenagers conducted in 1996 found that 42 per cent of them find marijuana easier to buy than either beer or cigarettes.[40]

The distinction between legal and illegal drugs is arbitrary and increasingly hard to maintain. Its main purpose seems to be to support a façade of nominal abstention behind which the United States dopes itself up to its collective eyeballs. The actor Heath Ledger died in New York City on 22 January 2008 of acute intoxication by the combined effects of oxycodone, hydrocodone, diazepam, temazepam, alprazolam and doxylamine. Commercial names for these legal drugs include the anti-anxiety medications Valium and Xanax, the painkillers Oxy-Contin and Hydrocodone, and the sleeping aids Restoril and Unisom.[41] The abuse of legal sedatives is not a crime, and perhaps as a result the press treated the death of Heath Ledger as a tragedy brought on by anxiety and insomnia.

Across the developed world, children grow up in an environment in which mood-altering, pain-killing, sleep-inducing substances are accepted and widely marketed. Aspirin, tranquillizers, caffeine, anti-depressants, alcohol, tobacco and a welter of other psychoactive substances are part of modern urban life. Eleven million Americans use illegal marijuana every month, but the second most abused class of drugs in the United States is legal prescription drugs.[42] Between 2000 and 2004, the commercial distribution of pharmaceuticals in the United States more than doubled. By 2006, one in ten teenagers admitted to non-medical use of painkillers such as OxyContin and Hydrocodone.[43]

In the United Kingdom, the Home Office says that the misuse of benzodiazepines has caused 17,000 deaths since their introduction in the 1960s. A parliamentary inquiry into misuse of prescription drugs warned that 'although the reclassification of some substances from prescription-only to over-the-counter has resulted in often significant cost savings for consumers, the abuse of these substances can result in dependency, addiction, hospitalization and potentially even death'. A total of 1,135 Britons died as a result of an adverse reaction to legal drugs in 2007, including 25 who overdosed.[44] By any reckoning, this makes legal drugs more dangerous than illegal drugs like cocaine, which killed 147 people in England and Wales in 2004. Furthermore, 'death by cocaine' is open to interpretation because cocaine is often used in conjunction with other drugs, there are no instructions on the side of the packet and its contents are often cut with phenacetin, ketamine or whatever other white powder the dealer happens to have to hand.[45]

The drug of choice among adolescents and adults in the United States is alcohol, a fact that no drug tsar can afford to address fully because of the huge financial and political clout wielded by the drinks industry. The United Kingdom's Misuse of Drugs Act of 1971 stipulates that drugs be separated into classes A, B or C to indicate the potential danger they pose to their users, with class A being the most harmful and class C the least. Neither alcohol nor tobacco is even classified as a harmful drug. The health, social and crime-related costs of drug misuse in the United Kingdom have been estimated to be between £10 billion and £16 billion a year.[46] Most arise from the use of *legal* drugs. Tobacco and alcohol account for about 90 per cent of all drug-related deaths in the UK. Forty per cent of all hospital illnesses are estimated to be caused by tobacco smoking. Every year, half a million Britons go into hospital suffering the long and/or short term effects of alcohol abuse, and every year that abuse kills 25,000 of them.[47]

Even in the United States, where there has been a terrible epidemic of hard drug abuse for over twenty years, the £49 billion bill for dealing with the consequences of illegal drug use in 1992 was far outweighed by the £74 billion cost of alcohol abuse.[48] In 2007, an article in the *Lancet* admitted that there was no justification for the current classification of drugs. Its authors wrote that if the classification were to be revised according to their findings, alcohol would be reclassified as a class A and tobacco as a class B drug.[49]

How can the physical harm done by cocaine be used to justify its prohibition, when the mortality rate among tobacco smokers in the United States is one hundred times that of cocaine users?[50] Indeed, how much of a concern can the physical health of its people really be to the United States government, when fifteen times as many Americans die from illnesses associated with poor diet and lack of exercise than from the use of illegal drugs?[51] Would the harm done by alcohol, tobacco or even fast food be reduced by making them illegal? As Judge Jim Gray has said, 'we're doing a pretty effective job in the court system today, of holding people to account for their actions with regard to another highly dangerous, sometimes addictive drug, namely alcohol. You don't have to make drugs illegal to be able to make people accountable for their actions.'

Plato recognized as much 2,400 years ago. 'We are not going to vilify Dionysus' gift. It is enough that wine is banned for those under the age of eighteen and that, until the age of thirty, men drink it in measure and avoid excessive drunkenness.'[52] The French philosopher Michel de Montaigne went a step further when he asserted, in a series of essays published in 1580, that the law had no business interfering in excessive drunkenness either. 'I would wish that even in debauchery a man outdid his companions, so that when he refused to indulge in vice, it was not because he lacked the knowledge or the power but simply the will. A man should be ashamed not to dare or to be able to do what he sees his companions doing. Such a one should stick by the kitchen fire.'[53]

At its worst, drug use is a vice, but it is not a crime. A vice is an act by which a man damages himself, or his possessions. Nobody practises their vice with criminal intent: they are motivated by their pleasures, however unconventional they may be, not by wishing pain on others. The distinction between a vice and a crime is the bedrock on which individual freedom rests. 'To this day, I still believe that drugs are bad,' Rusty, the former Arizona Department of Corrections narcotics officer, told me. 'But that's my personal opinion, and I don't have the right to force you to live by my beliefs. What about "mind your own business"? That works real good for me.' Shortly before meeting Rusty, I had heard an ominous definition of freedom from former Mayor of New York City Rudy Giuliani. 'Freedom is about authority. Freedom is about the willingness of every single human being to cede to lawful authority a great deal of discretion about what you do.' When I asked Rusty what he made of this mind-bending oxymoron, Rusty said that 'if that was true, we'd still be speaking the Queen's English. I'm an old American, I guess. I believe in freedom and I refuse to live in fear. Nor will I have my laws based on fear.'[54]

The right to life, liberty and the pursuit of happiness precede whatever obligations Americans might have vis-à-vis the state. Those rights have to include the right to ingest whatever substances we like. When governments tell us what drugs we can and cannot take, they intrude on an interior affair. When the state takes the lead in questions of public morality or public health, it implicitly asserts our weakness and the need to protect us from ourselves. As Gabrielle said, 'the government doesn't trust us to buy a cup of coffee without having to be told on the side of the cup that it might be hot. There are a lot of things that we're not trusted to do, and it has created a generation of people who *can't* be trusted, because "somebody should have stopped me".'

Mountaineering, scuba diving and rugby are all dangerous activities, but because they only harm consenting adults, their practitioners are left to climb, dive and jump head-first into scrums, whatever the risks to their safety. The danger associated with illegal drugs, however, is tied to the ultimate human fear: of madness and the end of reality, from which we are gratefully rescued by our law-makers. Mike Jay has written that 'just as the pioneering journeys of nineteenth-century explorers have become today's popular travel destinations, so the inner worlds first colonized in the nineteenth century are now visited by more people than ever before'.[55] The wide expanse of the oceans, the distant peaks of mountains and the remotest peoples have all inspired fear in the past, but through enlightened exploration we have transformed our relationship to the world around us. 'Who's to say you can go up Mount Everest, but not have a line of charlie?' Steve asked. 'It's pushing at the boundaries of human experience and who's to restrain you from doing that?'

Kenneth, founder of the Ordinary People Society, in Dothan, Alabama, pastor and former crack dealer, warned me that 'we have to be very careful not to be judgemental when we consider what is holy and what is not. Only God can do that, and we all fall short of the Glory. In Jesus' time, he was speaking to drunkards, but in our time, it may be crack cocaine users. He invited everybody to come into the Kingdom, to come and get cleaned up. Jesus didn't do a criminal background check on nobody. Jesus said "drink wine for the stomach's sake". If you start drinking to get drunk, that's a sin. If you overeat to the point of gluttony, that's a sin too. Are we going to say that food is bad? No! We're going to say that over-eating is bad.' The pastor's words carry the same staunch morality and duty of care as those of the most hard-line prohibitionist, but he made no mention of banning anything. The closest he came to censure was in his parting words. 'But crack cocaine? I ain't seen nothing good come from it.'

11

Prospects

The more prohibitions you have, the less virtuous people will be. Try to make people moral, and you lay the groundwork for vice.
Lao Tzu, *Tao Te Ching*

One of the few legal buyers of coca leaves outside the Andes is the Coca-Cola Company.[1] The world's most popular soft drink is the last vestige of an age in which coca-infused tonics were both legal and popular. When first marketed, 'the pause that refreshes' owed its potency to the 60 mg of cocaine in every eight-ounce bottle.[2] These days, coca is used only as flavouring. The company's annual consignment of coca leaves is shipped to New Jersey under armed guard, where it is de-cocainized for use by Coca-Cola bottlers around the world. In recent years, the makers of 'the real thing' have taken umbrage at Bolivian companies' marketing of coca-infused soft drinks, and forced the real 'real thing' off the market in the name of copyright infringement. In March 2007, Bolivian bottlers struck back, demanding that Coca-Cola drop the word 'coca' from its name, on the grounds that the stuff doesn't have enough coca in it to warrant the name.[3]

While I was in Bogotá, I spoke to a young Colombian called David Curtidor. He had started marketing a coca-based carbonated energy drink called Coca-Sek and was keen to tell me about the campaign to restore the good name of coca. 'When I was a kid, if I had an upset stomach, my mum would prepare some tea with coca, rosemary and camomile. In Cali, you used to find coca bushes growing at the side

of the road and people used to grow them in their front gardens. Coca
is a very beautiful plant, but as it became demonized, people pulled
up their coca bushes. These days, when you have a stomach ache, you
reach for the paracetamol or the anadin. Fabiola Pinaque was the first
to get things moving. She told me that at her university she was taught
that coca was the root of all Colombia's problems. It offended her
that coca should be seen as a poison, so she started brewing up coca
tea for her classmates. We clubbed together $100 and started a little
company, making and selling coca teas. We started producing
Coca-Sek two years ago, and we were soon selling 40,000 cans a
month in Popayán. In September 2006, we registered the trademark
of Coca-Sek at the government patent office but Coca-Cola opposed
us, saying that we couldn't use the word "coca" in a soft drink. We
won the case, but the Colombian government says that commerce is
not culture, and that once you bottle coca as a drink, or make teabags
out of it, it's no longer traditional or cultural. But what is the difference
between coca in a gourd, and coca in a can? It's the same plant,
and the same custom. They're such fascists. They'll be prosecuting
indigenous people for wearing shoes next, or for travelling in buses and
aeroplanes, saying that they are not cultures traditional to indigenous
people!'

In 1995, a World Health Organization study of coca and cocaine
concluded that the coca leaf has practically no adverse effects on
human health. The study was pulled after the United States' ambassador to the United Nations threatened to withdraw all funding for the
WHO if its findings were published. David Lewis was one of the
authors of the study. He told me that while the report's findings were
not news, 'there was great concern that we were not pointing out all
the dangers involved in cocaine use, and that the WHO would be seen
as permissive. They said that we had no business comparing cocaine
to alcohol or tobacco. The discussion that I heard was that you
couldn't say anything good about chewing coca leaf because it's
a source of crack cocaine. I thought "Are you people stupid?"'

Ironically, tests have suggested that coca tea can be an effective
substitute for those weaning themselves off habitual use of cocaine,
heroin, tobacco or alcohol.[4] The many coca products to be had in

the marketplaces of La Paz, Bolivia, have also been shown to be effective in treating arthritis, diabetes, asthma, stomach ulcers and period pain. Among Bolivians, coca leaves, coca chewing gum and coca tea are more popular than cocaine. This may be because they are cheaper or it may be down to Bolivians' suspicion of new-fangled tinkering with ancient plants. But plenty of urbane Peruvians take cocaine at the weekend and stick to coca tea during the week. In the last ten years, mild coca products have become popular in Buenos Aires, a city with no history of coca consumption, which shows that milder variants of the coca high can take hold outside Andean countries.

Unfortunately, coca was swept up in the same wave of prohibitionist zeal that confined all the products of the coca bush to the margins of society. Plenty of people in the Andes, indigenous and otherwise, say that Western cocaine consumers are missing out on the true value of the coca plant and that Western governments are wilfully ignorant of the plant's potential. Stigmatized coca growers began to find a voice on the international stage after 1988, when a revision of the Single Convention made some allowance for traditional use of coca by the indigenous peoples of the Andes. Many Andeans would like to go a step further and commercialize coca production as a way of providing coca farmers with outlets other than the cocaine market for their crop. Coca products, say the farmers, could become a globally recognized health product along the lines of Korean ginseng.

Emboldened, Bolivian President Jaime Paz Zamora started on a round of 'coca diplomacy' in the early 1990s, chewing coca leaves in public and shipping coca leaves to the Bolivian pavilion at Expo '92 in Seville, where Spanish customs agents, in compliance with the Single Convention, promptly impounded the shipment. A wave of national outrage swept through Bolivia, assuaged only when Queen Sofia of Spain made an official visit to La Paz to apologize and drink coca tea for Bolivian television cameras. This 'Andean fundamentalism' proved to be a vote-winner in La Paz, but before long, the American ambassador started making threatening noises about debt repayments and aid. Sensing a need to backtrack, the Bolivian press began running stories of corruption in the presidential palace. Paz Zamora was forced to back down, and a series of more conservative governments took over for the remainder of the 1990s.

Bolivia's coca farmers came back with a vengeance when the leader of the coca farmers' union, Evo Morales, was elected president in 2005. Morales had made the commercialization of coca products for export a key part of his manifesto, but once in power, Morales too found it very difficult to mount an international lobbying campaign to challenge the Single Convention. Even if the International Narcotics Control Board, the World Health Organization and the United Nations Economic and Social Council were amenable to the revision, it would take at least three years to negotiate the labyrinthine bureaucracy, by which time any politician backing the revision would most likely be out of office. So Morales has chosen to 'save his breath to cool his porridge'. He knows that his rhetoric is what wins votes at home, and the United States knows that his rhetoric, however discomforting, is ultimately harmless.[5]

Were coca derivatives to become globally recognized health products, they would doubtless appeal to western consumers. Once introduced, they might be shorn of their exotic cultural connotations and assimilated into daily life. Legalization and regulation would be the first steps in making people more aware of the milder, less harmful forms of those products, how to use them and the potential dangers of their most concentrated versions. As the Colombian psychiatrist Luis Carlos Restrepo has said, 'Colombia has a cultural heritage that goes back thousands of years, which you can see today in the socialized consumption of psychoactive substances by its indigenous peoples. I'm not suggesting that we try to return to indigenous rituals, but we should look at their experiences and draw conclusions that can be applied to modern, market-based societies, so we can find alternatives to compulsive consumption. Drugs are a mirror: they reflect back our inner conflicts. What we have to do is not break the mirror, but face up to those conflicts wisely.'[6]

Over the past twenty years, the financier George Soros has spent almost £1 billion in support of the many organizations that are encouraging the former Soviet Union's transition from a closed to an open society.

Soros has also funded drug reform movements in the United States, because he sees in the war on drugs a resurgence of the very traits that he opposed in the ex-Stalinist bloc: political indoctrination that passes for education, a self-serving bureaucracy that twists scientific advances to suit its own ends and thousands of state and police agents employing thousands of informants in ever more intrusive ways. 'Drug warriors' create 'enemies within' and build vast prisons to house them. Certain lifestyles are criminalized, along with the free market that supplies them.

Seven years have passed since an editorial in the *Economist* suggested that drugs might be legalized by the second decade of the new millennium. Yet the campaign for the legalization and regulation of the drugs trade remains marginal. In the cities of the developed world, a denouement of sorts has been reached between drug users and the police. Users find it relatively easy to circumvent the law and moralists get to vent their spleen. The anti-prohibitionist movement, if it warrants such a name, has always been a strange amalgam of interests. It strays outside left–right political lines, attracting everyone from authoritarian Colombian senators to libertarian ecologists. Its affiliates argue over whether drugs should be legalized or only depenalized, whether the global ban on drugs should be repealed or just reformed, and never agree on any other issue.

Policy makers in Washington D.C. have been quick to nip any talk of legalization in the bud. United States Congressman Larry Smith once said that 'the most dangerous people in America are those who believe in legalizing drugs. They're traitors.'[7] As Judge James Gray was at pains to stress, 'you have to understand that our policy of drug prohibition includes a policy of debate prohibition. The people in the drug tsar's office will not appear for a debate.' Calls for legalization are seen as a non-starter by nearly all political parties, even in countries where the prohibition of drugs threatens to make some regions near ungovernable. In Jamaica, Mexico, Colombia and many other countries on the supply routes, smugglers, traffickers, *capos* and cartels show up the state. They challenge its physical and political power, make a travesty of its commitment to the lawful protection of its citizens and corrupt its officials. And they pay better. At best, this encourages careers in crime, at worst it makes the police, the law and the state look irrelevant. Unless there is a fundamental reassessment of the problem and a willingness to consider novel solutions, prohibition can only make for bigger problems in the future.

Thankfully, most of the real work of dealing with mass drug abuse in the United States takes place at city level, and many city and state governments have moved away from a punitive approach to the illegal drug economy. In 2000, voters in California passed a 'treatment-not-incarceration' initiative known as Proposition 36. Rather than being sent to prison, more than 150,000 Californians have been given places on state-funded, community-based drug treatment programmes, thereby saving state taxpayers more than $1.5 billion over seven years.[8] Encouraged by the success of Proposition 36, law-makers proposed a Nonviolent Offender Rehabilitation Act (NORA) to transform California's dysfunctional, $10 billion-a-year prison system by developing a comprehensive public health approach to substance use. NORA was projected to save at least $2.5 billion on future prison construction costs by rendering new prisons unnecessary, but in the elections of 2008, NORA was voted down by Californians, largely thanks to an advertising campaign that was heavily subsidized by the prison guards union.[9]

Police and public health officials in many of Europe's largest cities have also come round to the idea that instead of trying to create a drug-free society, they should limit their ambition to reducing the negative consequences of drug consumption, like acquisitive crime, blood-borne illnesses and overdoses. In the Netherlands, individual drug use and small-time drug dealing are never prosecuted. But the increasing involvement of the medical profession in dealing with drug problems has not undermined the official policy of total drug prohibition. In fact, there has been a substantial increase in drug arrests all over Europe since 1985. In the UK, drug offence arrests went from 44,000 in 1990 to 104,000 in 2000. In France they've gone up threefold over the same period, and in Germany they've gone up fourfold. In all three countries, more than half of those arrests were for possession of cannabis. Europe is clearly caught between the prohibitionist model and the harm reduction model, and is failing to resolve the contradictions implicit in both.[10] The pressure to break this stalemate is coming from cities with large drug-using populations, where the local authorities are straining at the leash to reform their drugs policies.

In 2001, Portugal introduced a pioneering law which decriminalized the possession of all illicit substances for personal use.[11] Law 30/2000 did not legalize drug use or possession, but it did put an end to the use of penal sanctions. Some users face fines, others are recommended for treatment through Commissions for the Dissuasion of Drug Addiction. The thinking was that if the authorities could divert problematic users into treatment, police resources would be freed up to tackle the traffickers. Prior to decriminalization, Portuguese courts were overburdened, there were long delays in processing cases, and the prisons were overcrowded. Since 2001, overcrowding rates have fallen and there have been crucial reductions in drug-related health problems. Until 2001, the Portuguese authorities usually had little to suggest to anyone who wanted help in overcoming their dependence on drugs, aside from abstinence. Now health workers have a better understanding of who the users are, and how and why they take drugs. Drug users feel less stigmatized, and are more willing to turn to treatment services for help when they want it.

Some Portuguese say that decriminalization has encouraged young people to use hard drugs. Cannabis use has certainly gone up in Portugal since 2001, but the same trend is evident in neighbouring Spain and Italy too. Seizures of all drugs have doubled since passage of Law 30/2000, but cocaine trafficking was likely to rise with or without decriminalization because Portugal is the European country closest to Colombia and cocaine seizures have gone up across European countries with quite different drug laws. The extent to which increases in occasional use can be attributed to decriminalization remains unclear, but it might be ventured that decriminalization has reduced problematic use of drugs like heroin, while it has increased recreational drug use.

The decline of religion, the spread of democratic market-based economies, the integration of global trade, mass education and access to information are all likely to corrode national peculiarities in the twenty-first century. The ideology of the drug warriors of the United States is one such peculiarity. To say that drugs should be legalized, or that prohibition can never work would be to trade in abstractions. What is easier to assert is that, given the world in which cocaine production, distribution and consumption has found a home, prohibition is unworkable and counter-productive. Jack Cole told me 'to just think about what a terrible metaphor a "war on drugs" is for policing in a democratic society. When you train your police to go to war, they've got to have an enemy. In 1970, 4 million Americans had tried an illegal drug. By 2003, 112 million Americans had tried an illegal drug. That's the majority of the adults in the United States. So it's not a war on drugs, it's a war on us.' Criminalizing drugs has not reduced drug use. It has only made criminality as widespread as drug use, and made a mockery of the law.

Those in authority are unwilling to admit their addiction to control, or the illusion of control. The United States government should face up to its inability to devise a workable response to the demand for drugs. It should concede that some countries are making progress and that their own zealous defence of prohibition is constraining further progress. That would open the way for repeal of the United Nations' Single Convention. Individual countries would then be free to draw up new legislation in response to the particular demand for drugs in their country. The scape-goating and demonization of drugs would doubtless continue, but there are many activities that meet with the approval of the law yet the disapproval of much of society, including abortion, atheism and homosexuality. They are all in the process of being normalized, as is drug use. Assuming this normalization process takes place in a context in which drugs remain illegal, cocaine will eventually go the way of cannabis. The law will become irrelevant, at which point it will probably be quietly dropped.

Legalization will not solve the ongoing crisis of compulsive drug use. Only when nations produce responsible citizens with stakes in conventional society and in their communities will they truly have pulled up the roots of compulsive consumption. In *The Post-American World* (2008), Fareed Zakaria says that 'America has become a nation consumed by anxiety, worried about terrorists and rogue nations,

Muslims and Mexicans, foreign companies and free trade, immigrants and international organizations. The strongest nation in the world now sees itself as besieged by forces beyond its control.'[12] In this intoxicating atmosphere of all-pervading fear, it becomes all the more difficult to persuade Americans that the legalization of drugs would supply more, not less, peace and order.

However dramatic the failure to prohibit the use of certain drugs, the lack of a sober appraisal ensures that prohibition is unlikely to be repealed on the grounds of health, ethics or human rights. As countering terrorism, preventing illegal immigration and staving off economic decline come to dominate the political agenda, all three are going to demand greater resources and manpower. The war on drugs will most likely be abandoned for financial reasons, as the United States government is forced to accept that it doesn't have the resources to prosecute this war to its logical conclusion.

It is just a week since the election of Barack Obama to the White House. The hope that he embodied was not just that white Americans might be prepared to vote for a man of mixed race. It was also the hope that the concerns of the black electorate might, for the first time, be comprehensively addressed. Since 1970, when the war on drugs was launched by Richard Nixon, its principal targets have been black Americans and its gravest consequence has been to cement the poverty and neglect on which the cocaine trade thrives. The chorus of calls for renewal, honest appraisal and perspicuity that greeted Barack Obama as he campaigned for the Presidency should now be addressed to the authors and directors of the United States' war on drugs. Their paranoia, gnat-like attention span and general indifference to the consequences of their actions are more characteristic of crack addicts than of officials responsible for managing public health. Finding a workable alternative to prohibition has to begin in the United States, because it is the ultimate guarantor of the United Nations' conventions on drug use. So it rests with young Americans to ensure that future drug policies are grounded in science and the protection of public health and to recognize that knowledge is the prerequisite for free choice. Once made, we have no choice but to respect it.

Notes

Introduction

1. Richard Ford and Adam Fresco, 'UN condemns Britain's celebrity cocaine culture', *The Times*, 5 March 2008.

2. Marek Kohn, 'Cocaine Girls: sex, drugs and modernity in London during and after the First World War', in Paul Gootenberg (ed.), *Cocaine: Global Histories* (London: Routledge, 1999), p. 108.

3. Ford and Fresco, 'UN condemns Britain's celebrity cocaine culture'.

4. Stewart Tendler, 'Police chief clamps down on dinner party cocaine', *The Times*, 2 February 2005.

5. Leo Benedictus, 'Cocaine, Anyone?', *Guardian*, 3 February 2005.

6. Cited in Alexander Cockburn and Jeffrey St Clair, *White Out: the CIA, Drugs and the Press* (London: Verso, 1999), p. 76; also accessible through the Ronald Reagan Presidential Library at <http://www.reagan.utexas.edu/archives/speeches/1988/022988a.htm>.

7. The last figure refers to 2001 prices; United Nations Office on Drugs and Crime, *World Drug Report 2006*, Vol. 2, *Statistics* (Vienna, Austria: UNODC, 2006), pp. 369–70; Calvani estimates wholesale prices per kilo in the US in 2006 to be between £7,700 and £9,200, see Sandro Calvani, *La Coca: pasado y presente, mitos y realidades* (Bogotá: Ediciones Aurora, 2007), p. 125.

8. Ibid., p. 119.

9. By the UNDCP and the *Washington Post*, among others; see Peter Reuter, 'The Mismeasurement of Illegal Drug Markets: The Implications of Its Irrelevance', in S. Pozo (ed.), *Exploring the Underground Economy: Studies of Illegal and Unreported Activity* (Kalamazoo, MI: Western Michigan University, W. E. Upjohn Institute for Employment Policies, 1996).

10. The author of the report was Peter Reuter. This anecdote is cited in Francisco Thoumi, 'The Numbers Game: Let's All Guess the Size of the

Illegal Drugs Industry,' *Journal of Drug Issues*, Winter 2005, pp. 185–200.

11. The larger number comes from B. Freemantle, *The Fix: Inside the World Drug Trade* (New York: Tom Doherty Associates, 1986); the smaller number comes from Ricardo Rocha García, *La Economía Colombiana tras 25 Años de Narcotráfico* (Bogotá: Siglo del Hombre Editores, 2000).

12. Max Singer, 'The Vitality of Mythical Numbers', *Public Interest*, Spring 1971.

13. Ivan Rios, 'Fenómeno y efectos del capitalismo salvaje: El narcotráfico', in *Conversaciones de paz: Cultivos ilícitos, narcotráfico y agenda de paz* (Bogotá: Mandato Ciudadano por la Paz, la Vida y la Libertad, 2000), pp. 153–7.

14. *Guardian*, 20 November 2007.

15. The estimates are based on prison interviews with 222 convicted high-level drug dealers. S. Pudney, 'Estimating the size of the UK illicit drug market', in N. Singleton et al. (eds.), *Measuring different aspects of problem drug use: methodological developments* (London: Home Office Online Report, 16 June 2006). The assumptions and calculations that follow are mine.

16. Non-tax evasion crimes included trafficking in illicit drugs, human trafficking, burglary, larceny-theft, motor vehicle theft, robbery, fraud, arson, non-arson fraud, counterfeiting, illegal gambling, loan sharking and prostitution. Tax evasion crimes included federal income, federal profits and excise tax evasion.

1. From Soft Drink to Hard Drug

1. Hugh Trevor-Roper, *The European Witch-Craze of the 16th and 17th Centuries* (London: Pelican, 1969), p. 78.

2. From the documentary, *Coca Mama: the War on Drugs*, an Icaro and Jan Thielen production, 2001.

3. Cited in Andrew Weil, 'The New Politics of Coca', *New Yorker*, 15 May 1995.

4. 'Colombian Coca Trade', Trade and Environment Database paper 136, American University, 1997.

5. Sandro Calvani, *La Coca: pasado y presente, mitos y realidades* (Bogotá: Ediciones Aurora, 2007), p. 20.

6. Anthony Henman, *Mama Coca: un estudio completo de la coca* (Lima: Juan Gutemberg Editores, 2005), p. 115.

7. Anibal Prado, cited in Jorge Bejarano, *Nuevos capitulos sobre el cocainismo* (Bogotá: Editorial Iqueima, 1952).

NOTES

8. Cited in Weil, 'The New Politics of Coca'.

9. *Coca Cultivation in the Andean Region: A Survey of Bolivia, Colombia and Peru* (Vienna: United Nations Office on Drugs and Crime, June 2006).

10. David F. Musto, 'Opium, Cocaine and Marijuana in American History', *Scientific American*, July 1991, pp. 20–27.

11. Cited in Weil, 'The New Politics of Coca'.

12. Calvani, *La Coca: pasado y presente, mitos y realidades*, p. 63.

13. '7X' refers to the seven ingredients of Coca-Cola: caffeine, vanilla extract, aromatizing substances (orange, lemon, nutmeg, cinnamon, coriander and citron blossom), citric acid, lemon juice, sugar, water and 'X', which is liquid coca extract; as revealed in Mark Pendergrast, *For God, Country and Coca-Cola: the history of the world's most popular soft drink* (London: Orion Business, 2000).

14. Alonso Salazar, *Drogas y Narcotráfico en Colombia* (Bogotá: Planeta, 2001), p. 30.

15. Joseph Spillane, 'Making a Modern Drug: the manufacture, sale, and control of cocaine in the United States 1880–1920', in Paul Gootenberg (ed.), *Cocaine: Global Histories* (London: Routledge, 1999).

16. Cited in Musto, 'Opium, Cocaine and Marijuana in American History'.

17. Salazar, *Drogas y Narcotráfico en Colombia*, p. 31.

18. Eric Sterling, 'Beyond Just Say No', *Sojourners* magazine, May 2003, p. 40.

19. Mike Jay, *Emperors of Dreams: Drugs in the Nineteenth Century* (Sawtry, Cambs: Dedalus, 2000), p. 181.

20. Ibid., p. 178.

21. Charles B. Towns, 'The Peril of the Drug Habit', *Century Magazine*, 84 (1912), p. 586.

22. Cockburn and St Clair, *White Out: the CIA, Drugs and the Press*, op. cit., p. 71.

23. Musto, 'Opium, Cocaine and Marijuana in American History'.

24. Philip Guy, 'Race and the Drug Problem: more than just an Enforcement Issue'; available online at <http://www.drugtext.org/library/articles/PDG Race.htm>.

25. *Daily Mail*, 22 July 1901, cited in Kohn, 'Cocaine Girls: sex, drugs and modernity in London during and after the First World War', in Gootenberg (ed.), *Cocaine: Global Histories*, p. 107.

26. *World's Pictorial News*, 26 April 1926.

27. *Daily Express*, 14 March 1922.

28. Data from 1933 comes from Gary F. Jensen, 'Prohibition, Alcohol, and Murder: Untangling Countervailing Mechanisms', *Homicide Studies*, Vol. 4,

No. 1 (Thousand Oaks, CA: Sage, February 2000), p. 31. The data for 1980 comes from US Census Data and FBI Uniform Crime Reports.

29. Jeffrey A. Miron and Jeffrey Zwiebel, 'Alcohol Consumption During Prohibition', *American Economic Review*, vol. 81, No. 2, Papers and Proceedings of the Hundred and Third Annual Meeting of the American Economic Association, May 1991, pp. 242–7.

30. W. A. Niskanen, *Economists and Drug Policy*, Carnegie-Rochester Conference Series on Public Policy 36, 1992, p. 234.

31. St Clair Drake and Horace Roscoe Cayton, *Black Metropolis* (New York: Harcourt Brace, 1970).

32. Jay, *Emperors of Dreams*, p. 239.

33. Sterling, 'Beyond Just Say No', p. 40.

34. Musto, 'Opium, Cocaine and Marijuana in American History'.

35. Cited in Rick Curtis, 'Crack, Cocaine and Heroin: Drug Eras in Williamsburg, Brooklyn 1960–2000', *Addiction Research and Theory* 2003, vol. 11, No. 1, p. 50.

36. Ibid.

37. *Drug Enforcement Agency: A Tradition of Excellence 1973–2003*, US Department of Justice, Drug Enforcement Agency, 2003.

38. Harry Levine, 'The Secret of Worldwide Drug Prohibition: the varieties and uses of drug prohibition', *Independent Review*, Fall 2002.

39. Cited in Cockburn and St Clair, *White Out*, p. 291.

40. Cited in Hugh O'Shaughnessy and Sue Branford, *Chemical Warfare in Colombia: the Costs of Fumigation* (London: Latin American Bureau, 2005), p. 21.

41. Cited in Sterling, 'Beyond Just Say No.'

42. Available online at <http://www.csdp.org/publicservice/nixon06notes.htm>.

2. Building a Hard Drug Economy

1. Edward M. Brecher and the editors of the Consumer reports, *Licit and Illicit Drugs: the Consumers Union report on narcotics, stimulants, depressants, inhalants, hallucinogens, marijuana* (Mount Vernon, NY: Consumers Union, 1972).

2. *Drug Enforcement Agency: A Tradition of Excellence 1973–2003*, US Department of Justice, Drug Enforcement Agency, p. 38; and Michael Agar, 'The Story of Crack: Towards a Theory of Illicit Drug Trends', *Addiction Research and Theory*, Vol. 11, No. 1, 1 January 2003, p. 15.

3. Cited in Agar, 'The Story of Crack:', p. 15.

4. Cockburn and St Clair, *White Out: the CIA, Drugs and the Press*, p. 299.

5. Ibid., p. 310.

6. Ibid., p. 309.

7. Admittedly this statistic dates from 1991, but it is the only one I have been able to locate. See P. Reuter, R. MacCoun and P. Murphy, *Money from Crime: A Study of the Economics of Drug Selling in Washington, D.C.* (Santa Monica, CA: RAND, 1990).

8. David Henderson, 'A Humane Economist's Case for Drug Legalization', *University of California at Davis Law Review*, 1991, Vol. 24, p. 655.

9. Cited in Rick Curtis, 'The Improbable Transformation of Inner-City Neighbourhoods: Crime, Violence, Drugs and Youth in the 1990s', *Journal of Criminal Law and Criminology*, Vol. 88, No. 4, 1988, p. 1243.

10. Steven D. Levitt and Sudhir Alladi Venkatesh, 'An Economic Analysis of a Drug-Selling Gang's Finances', *Quarterly Journal of Economics*, August 2000, p. 755.

11. Kurt Schmoke, 'Forging a New Consensus in the War on Drugs: Is It Possible?', *Temple University Political and Civil Rights Law Review*, Spring 2001, p. 354.

12. *Baltimore 1999: A Transition Report*, Office of the Mayor of Baltimore, 1999.

13. James Scott, *Weapons of the Weak: Everyday forms of Peasant Resistance* (New Haven: Yale University Press, 1985).

14. The Jay Z lyric that Marc quotes is from the song 'Can I Live?'.

15. Some say that Pryor made the story up to explain the burns he received after pouring a bottle of rum over his head and setting himself alight after a night spent free-basing.

16. For those chasing the ultimate high, the speedball may well be it. Whereas dopamine levels in the brain increase by about 380 per cent with cocaine, and 70 per cent with heroin, when injected together dopamine levels shoot up by 1,000 per cent. The data is from a study by Gerasimov and Dewey from 1999, cited in Agar, 'The Story of Crack', p. 15.

17. Cited in Curtis, 'The Improbable Transformation of Inner-City Neighbourhoods', p. 1249.

18. Ainsley Hamid, 'The Developmental Cycle of a Drug Epidemic: the Cocaine Smoking Epidemic of 1981–1991', *Journal of Psychoactive Drugs*, Oct–Dec 1992.

19. The DEA says that before the crack epidemic, 75 per cent of crack users in New York City were typically white and middle class: 'Drug Enforcement

Agency 1973–2003: 25 Years of Excellence', US Department of Justice, Drug Enforcement Agency, p. 60.

20. Ainsley Hamid, 'From Ganja to Crack : Caribbean Participation in the Underground Economy in Brooklyn, 1976–1986. II, Establishment of the cocaine (and crack) economy', *International Journal of the Addictions*, 1991, Vol. 26, No. 7, pp. 729–38.

21. F. H. Gawin and E. H. Ellinwood Jr, 'Cocaine and Other Stimulants: Actions, Abuse, and Treatment', *New England Journal of Medicine*, 5 May 1988, pp. 1173–82.

22. Available online at <http://www.vandu.org/vrockgroup.html>.

23. 'Drug Enforcement Agency 1973–2003', p. 60, citing statistics from Department of Health and Human Services National Household Survey.

24. According to police testimony in Congressional hearings in 1986; see Agar, 'The Story of Crack', p. 21.

25. National Drug Intelligence Center, 2005.

26. William Adler, *Land of Opportunity: One Family's Quest for the American Dream in the Age of Crack*, (Atlantic Monthly Press), 1995, p. 220.

27. Cited in Curtis, 'The Improbable Transformation of Inner-City Neighbourhoods', p. 1272.

28. See Bruce Johnson, Andrew Golub and Elaine Dunlap, 'The Rise and Decline of Hard Drugs, Drug Markets and Violence in Inner-City New York', in Alfred Blumstein and Joel Wallman (eds), *The Crime Drop in America* (Cambridge: Cambridge University Press, 2000), p. 177.

29. D. Hatsukami and M. Fischman, 'Crack Cocaine and Cocaine Hydrochloride', *Journal of the American Medical Association*, 20 November 1996, p. 1585.

30. Reuter, MacCoun and Murphy, *Money from Crime*, p. xii.

31. Faisal Islam, 'Class A Capitalists', *Observer*, 21 April 2002.

32. Salazar, *Drogas y Narcotráfico en Colombia*, p.135.

33. International Crisis Group, 'Latin American Drugs I: Losing the Fight', *Latin America Report*, No. 25, 14 March 2008, p. 28.

34. International Crisis Group, 'Colombia's New Armed Groups', *Latin America Report*, No. 20, 10 May 2007, p. 18.

3. A Rush to Punish

1. Howard S. Becker, 'History, Culture and Subjective Experience: An Exploration of the Social Bases of Drug-Induced Experiences', *Journal of Health and Social Behavior*, Vol. 8, No. 3 (September 1967), pp. 163–76.

2. Dan Baum, *Smoke and Mirrors: The War on Drugs and the Politics of Failure* (Boston: Back Bay Books, 1997), p. 225.

3. Quote attributed to Bill Rhatican of the Ad Council in Baum, *Smoke and Mirrors*, p. 226.

4. Cited in ibid., p. 226.

5. Craig Reinarmann and Ceres Duskin, 'Dominant Ideology and Drugs in the Media', *International Journal on Drug Policy*, 3(1) (1992), pp. 6–15.

6. Katherine Greider, 'Crackpot Ideas', *Mother Jones*, July/August 1995.

7. Quoted in Carl Williams, 'Consequences of the War on Drugs for Transit Countries: The Jamaican Experience', *Crime and Justice International*, September/October 2007.

8. Presidential address, 5 November 1989, cited in W. A. Niskanen, *Economists and Drug Policy*, Carnegie-Rochester Conference Series on Public Policy, 36, 1992.

9. Cited in *ABC Special with Jon Storsel*, 30 July 2002, my transcription.

10. Baum, *Smoke and Mirrors*, p. 200.

11. Interviewed in *ABC Special with Jon Storsel*.

12. Richard Dennis, 'The Economics of Legalizing Drugs', *Atlantic Monthly*, November 1990.

13. Musto, 'Opium, Cocaine and Marijuana in American History', pp. 20–27.

14. Harry Levine, 'The Secret of Worldwide Drug Prohibition: the varieties and uses of drug prohibition', *Independent Review*, Fall 2002.

15. Philippe Bourgois, 'Crack and the Political Economy of Social Suffering', *Addiction Research and Theory*, Vol. 11, No. 1, 2003.

16. George Bridges and Sara S. Streen, 'Racial Disparities in Official Assessments of Juvenile Offenders: Attributional Stereotypes as Mediating Mechanisms', *American Sociological Review*, Vol. 63, 1998; cited in *The Vortex: the Concentrated Racial Impact of Drug Imprisonment and the Characteristics of Punitive Counties*, Justice Policy Institute Report 2007, p. 8.

17. Harry Levine, 'Are Cannabis Arrests Increasing in Europe?', unpublished paper, August 2007.

18. Ben Wallace-Wells, 'How America Lost the War on Drugs', *Rolling Stone* magazine, 13 December 2007.

19. It went from $362 million to $769 million; see *Drug Enforcement Agency 1973–2003: A Tradition of Excellence*, US Department of Justice, Drug Enforcement Agency, p. 59.

20. P. Kraska and V. Kappeler, 'Militarizing American Police: The Rise and Normalization of Paramilitary Units', *Social Problems*, Vol. 44, No. 1 (February 1997), p. 10.

NOTES

21. Ibid.

22. California, Connecticut, Kentucky, Oklahoma and Rhode Island have enacted statutes that prohibit 'stopping a person based solely on race or ethnicity instead of an individualized suspicion arising from the person's behavior'. See Bureau of Justice Statistics, *Traffic Stop Data Collection* (Washington, DC: US Dept. of Justice, December 2001), p. 1.

23. David Cole, *No Equal Justice: Race and Class in the American Criminal Justice System* (New York: New Press, 1999), p. 36.

24. Ibid., p. 50.

25. See *Hearne, Texas: Scenes from the Drug War*, a documentary produced by ACLU, Texas, in 2005.

26. E. Blumenson and E. Nilsen, 'Policing for Profit: The Drug War's Hidden Economic Agenda', *University of Chicago Law Review*, 65: 35–114 (Winter 1998), p. 5.

27. Ibid., p. 4.

28. 'Assets Forfeiture Fund and Seized Asset Deposit Fund Annual Financial Statement Fiscal Year 2006', Office of the Inspector General, Audit Division, US Dept. of Justice (Audit Report 07–15, January 2007), p. 6.

29. Blumenson and Nilsen, 'Policing for Profit', p. 10.

30. Ibid., p. 8.

31. Ibid., p. 9.

32. Ibid., p. 2.

33. Andrew Schneider and Mary Pat Flaherty, 'Government Seizures Victimize Innocent', *Pittsburgh Press*, 27 February 1991.

34. Cole, *No Equal Justice*, pp. 23–4.

35. 'Urban League in Los Angeles Asts Police Chief Suspension', *The New York Times*, 12 May 1982.

36. Interviewed for *ABC Special with Jon Storsel*.

37. These statistics are from 'The Wire's War on the Drug War', an article written by the creative team behind the HBO TV series *The Wire* (Ed Burns, Dennis Lehane, George Pelecanos, Richard Price and David Simon) and published in *Time*, 5 March 2008.

38. Cockburn and St Clair, *White Out: the CIA, Drugs and the Press*, p. 78.

39. *Cracks in the System: Twenty Years of the Unjust Federal Crack Cocaine Law* (Washington DC: American Civil Liberties Union, 2006).

40. The first part of this excerpt is from an interview Daniel Rostenkowski gave to host Ira Glass on episode 143 of the radio programme *This American Life*, National Public Radio, 22 October 1999. The second part is from a speech Rostenkowski gave to lawyers shortly after his release, which Glass quotes from in the same radio programme.

41. 'Clinton's Crack Cocaine Apology: Too Little Too Late?', *Huffington Post*, 4 March 2008.

42. 'Judges Given Leeway in Crack Sentencing', Associated Press, 1 December 2007.

43. Schmoke, 'Forging a New Consensus in the War on Drugs: Is It Possible?', p. 356.

44. Rosie Cowan, 'Fourteen jailed as police smash global crack cocaine network', *Guardian*, 28 February 2006.

45. Michael Isikoff, 'Penal Colonies for Drug Criminals', *Washington Post*, 17 September 1990.

46. Blumenson and Nilsen, 'Policing for Profit', p. 12.

47. Johnson, Golub and Dunlap, 'The Rise and Decline of Hard Drugs, Drug Markets and Violence in Inner-City New York', in Blumstein and Wallman (eds), *The Crime Drop in America*, p. 184.

48. Howard Campbell, 'Drug Trafficking Stories: Everyday forms of Narco-Folklore on the US-Mexico Border', *International Journal of Drug Policy*, 16, 2005, p. 327.

49. 'Clinton's Crack Cocaine Apology', *Huffington Post*.

50. Johnson, Golub and Dunlap, 'The Rise and Decline of Hard Drugs', in Blumstein and Wallman (eds), *The Crime Drop in America*, p. 184.

51. Craig Haney and Philip Zimbardo, 'The Past and Future of US Prison Policy: Twenty-five Years after the Stanford Prison Experiment', *American Psychologist*, Vol. 53, No. 7 (July 1998), p. 716.

52. Marc Maurer, *Race to Incarcerate* (New York: New Press, 1999), p. 185.

53. Observatoire Géopolitique des Drogues, 'The World Geopolitics of Drugs 1998/1999' (Paris, France: OGD, April 2000), p. 133.

54. According to Maia Szalavitz, a senior fellow at the media watchdog STATS who has written extensively about drug policy.

55. National Research Council, *Informing America's Policy on Illegal Drugs: What We Don't Know Keeps Hurting Us* (Washington DC: National Academy Press, 2001), p. 1.

56. Wallace-Wells, 'How America Lost the War on Drugs'.

57. Ryan S. King, 'A Decade of Reform: Felony Disenfranchisement Policy in the United States', Sentencing Project, 2006, p. 2. Also see Jamie Fellner and Marc Mauer, 'Losing the Vote: The Impact of Felony Disenfranchisement Laws in the United States', Human Rights Watch and The Sentencing Project, 1998, p. 8.

58. According to Students for Sensible Drug Policy, Washington DC.

59. *AMA 2004 Workplace Testing Survey: Medical Testing*, American Management Association, New York, 2004, p. 3.

60. Edward M. Shepard and Thomas J. Clifton, 'Drug Testing and Labor Productivity: Estimates Applying a Production Function Model', Institute of Industrial Relations, Research Paper No. 18 (Syracuse, NY: LeMoyne University, 1998), p. 8.

4. Cutting off the Lizard's Tail

1. James Fox, *Trends in Juvenile Violence: A Report to the United States Attorney General on Current and Future Rates of Juvenile Offending* (Washington DC: Bureau of Justice Statistics, 1996).
2. 'Clinton Unveils Flurry of Plans to Fight Crime', Allpolitics, 1997; available at <http://images.cnn.com/ALLPOLITICS/1997/02/19/clinton.crime/>.
3. Levitt and Venkatesh, 'An Economic Analysis of a Drug-Selling Gang's Finances', *Quarterly Journal of Economics*, August 2000, pp. 755–89.
4. Steven D. Levitt, 'Understanding Why Crime Fell in the 1990s: Four Factors that Explain the Decline and Six that Do Not', *Journal of Economic Perspectives*, Vol. 18, No. 1, Winter 2004, pp. 163–90.
5. Todd Clear, 'The Problem with Addition by Subtraction: the Prison–Crime Relationship in Low Income Communities', in Marc Mauer and Meda Chesney-Lind (eds.), *Invisible Punishment: The Collateral Consequences of Mass Imprisonment* (New York: New Press, 2003).
6. This was part of a national trend away from cocaine use among the young in the late 1980s. The rate of lifetime cocaine use among high school seniors declined from 17 per cent in 1985 to 6 per cent in 1992. See Johnson, Golub and Dunlap, 'The Rise and Decline of Hard Drugs, Drug Markets and Violence in Inner-City New York', in Blumstein and Wallman (eds), *The Crime Drop in America*, p. 170.
7. Cited in Curtis, 'The Improbable Transformation of Inner-City Neighbourhoods: Crime, Violence, Drugs and Youth in the 1990s', p. 1258.
8. Office of National Drug Control Policy, *National Drug Control Strategy: Budget Summary* (Washington, DC: US Government Printing Office, 1992), pp. 212–14. Office of National Drug Control Policy, *The National Drug Control Strategy: 2000 Annual Report* (Washington DC: US Government Printing Office, 2000), p. 94, figure 4–1. L. Johnston, J. Bachman and P. O'Malley, *Monitoring the Future: National Results on Adolescent Drug Use Overview of Key Findings 1999* (Washington, DC: NIDA, 2000), pp. 3–6, p. 48, Table 6.
9. Interview conducted in 1996, cited in Curtis, 'The Improbable Transformation of Inner-City Neighbourhoods', p. 1264.

10. Cited in ibid., p. 1265.

11. Cited in Curtis, 'Crack, Cocaine and Heroin: Drug Eras in Williamsburg, Brooklyn 1960–2000', p. 60.

12. Rick Curtis, 'The New York Miracle: Crime, Drugs and the Resurgence of Gangs in the 1990s', unpublished.

13. Interview conducted in 2001, cited in Rick Curtis, Travis Wendel and Barry Spunt, *We Deliver: The Gentrification of Drug Markets on Manhattan's Lower East Side* (Washington DC: National Institute of Justice, 2002), p. 51.

14. Interview conducted in 1997, cited in Curtis, Wendel and Spunt, op. cit.

15. John Hagedorn, *The Business of Drug Dealing in Milwaukee*, Wisconsin Policy Research Institute, 1998.

16. Interview conducted in 1995, cited in Curtis, Wendel and Spunt, *We Deliver*, p. 51.

17. Reuter, MacCoun and Murphy, *Money from Crime: A Study of the Economics of Drug Selling in Washington, D.C.*

18. Peter Reuter and Michael Levi, 'Money Laundering', *Crime and Justice*, 2006, Vol. 34, pp. 289–375.

19. Campbell, 'Drug Trafficking Stories: Everyday Forms of Narco-Folklore on the US–Mexico Border', p. 326.

20. Hagedorn, *The Business of Drug Dealing in Milwaukee*.

21. Curtis, Wendel and Spunt, *We Deliver*, p. 105.

22. Levitt and Venkatesh, 'An Economic Analysis of a Drug-Selling Gang's Finances', p. 781.

23. Noah Mamber, 'Harm Reductive Drug Legalization', *Cornell Journal of Law and Public Policy*, Summer 2006, p. 628.

24. Recounted by historian John C. Burnham in the *Columbus Dispatch* on 30 June 2006. Attendees at the program included Jerome Jaffe, Robert L. Du Pont, Dr Peter G. Bourne, Lee I. Dogoloff, Donald Ian Macdonald, Lee Brown and retired US Army General Barry R. McCaffrey. William Bennett and current drug tsar John Walters were among those absent.

25. Beckley Foundation/Drugscope, *Assessing Drug Policy Principles and Practice*, Beckley Park, Oxford, 2004.

26. R. Lupton, A. Wilson, T. May, H. Warburton and P. Turnbull, *Drugs in Deprived Neighbourhoods*, Home Office Research Study, 240, 2002.

27. Office of National Drug Control Policy, *Reducing Drug Abuse in America: An Overview of Demand Reduction Initiatives*, Chapter II (Washington, DC: Executive Office of the President, January 1999); available to view at <http://www.whitehousedrugpolicy.gov/drugabuse/2a.html>.

28. The number of Americans who used an illegal drug in the past year

started falling from 16 per cent in 1986, but was back to 14.5 per cent by 2005; see Wallace-Wells, 'How America Lost the War on Drugs'.

29. Andrew Golub and Bruce Johnson, 'Crack's Decline: some surprises across US cities', National Institute of Justice Research in Brief, July 1997.

30. Evan Wood, Patricia M. Spittal, Will Small, Thomas Kerr, Kathy Li, Robert S. Hogg, Mark W. Tyndall, Julio S. G. Montaner, Martin T. Schechter, 'Displacement of Canada's Largest Public Illicit Drug Market in Response to a Police Crackdown', *Canadian Medical Association Journal*, 11 May 2004: 170 (10), p. 1554.

31. Peter D. A. Cohen and Hendrien L. Kaal, *The Irrelevance of Drug Policy: Patterns and Careers of Experienced Cannabis Use in the Populations of Amsterdam, San Francisco and Bremen* (Centrum voor Drugsonderzoek: University of Amsterdam, 2001).

32. Brecher et al. (eds), *Licit and Illicit Drugs*, p. 52.

33. C. A. Youngers and E. Rosin, 'The US "War on Drugs": its Impact in Latin America and the Caribbean', in Coletta Youngers and Eileen Rosin (eds), *Drugs and Democracy in Latin America: The Impact of US Policy* (Boulder, CO: Lynne Rienner, 2004), pp. 1–13.

34. Peter D. Hart Research Associates, for Police Foundation and Drug Strategies, *Drugs and Crime Across America: Police Chiefs Speak Out*, 2004.

35. According to Coletta Youngers of the Washington Office on Latin America.

36. Michael Hardy, 'Five to Vie for Counter-Narco-Terrorism Work', *Washington Technology*, 10 September 2007.

5. Smugglers

1. United Nations Office on Drugs and Crime, *World Drug Report 2006, Volume 1: Analysis* (Vienna, Austria: United Nations, 2006), p. 16.

2. The UN Office for Drug Control notes that estimates of production and total supply are probably understated by reporting governments, so they are probably seizing a lower percentage than they report (see United Nations Office for Drug Control and Crime Prevention, *Global Illicit Drug Trends 1999* (New York, NY: UNODCCP, 1999), p. 51.

3. National Anti-Narcotics Agency, *Colombian Drug Observatory Report 2005* (Bogotá: DNE, 2005), p. 173.

4. That is, between leaving the factory in the producing country and being sold in retail markets in the consuming country; from R. Fritter and

R. Kaplinsky, 'Who gains from product rents as the coffee market becomes more differentiated? A value chain analysis', Institute of Development Studies Bulletin Paper, 2001.

5. Matrix Knowledge Group for the Home Office, *The Illicit Drug Trade in the United Kingdom* (London: 2007), p. 46.

6. Ibid., p. 51.

7. Ibid., p. 51.

8. Dan McDougall, 'Ghana to UK: the new trail of misery', *Observer*, 11 November 2007.

9. *International Narcotics Control Board Annual Report 2006*, p. 38.

10. United Nations Office on Drugs and Crime, *World Drug Report 2006, Volume 1: Analysis*, p. 17.

11. Colombia's Deputy President Francisco Santos told me in October 2007 that he would be very surprised if coca were not being grown in West Africa in the next five years. But then, it is in his interests to make Colombia's problem appear to be an international problem.

12. Ed Vulliamy, 'How a tiny West African country became the world's first narco state', *Observer*, 9 March 2008.

13. Ibid.

14. According to Hibiscus, there were 105 Jamaican women in prison in the UK in 2007.

15. *Crime, Violence, and Development: Trends, Costs, and Policy Options in the Caribbean*, a joint report by the United Nations Office on Drugs and Crime and the Latin America and the Caribbean Region of the World Bank, March 2007, p. 96.

16. Ibid., pp. ix, 103.

17. According to Hibiscus, 124 foreigners and 79 Jamaicans were arrested for cocaine offences at Jamaican airports in 2004.

18. *Jamaica Gleaner*, 16 May 2007.

19. Jeremy McDermott and Colin Freeman, 'Prince William set for show-down with drugs baron on Royal Navy patrol in Caribbean', *Daily Telegraph*, 8 June 2008.

20. *Crime, Violence, and Development: Trends, Costs, and Policy Options in the Caribbean*, p. 21.

21. Ibid., p. 19, citing statement of Rogelio E. Guevara, Chief of Operations of the US Drug Enforcement Administration, before the House of Representatives Committee on International Relations, 10 October 2002.

22. International Crisis Group, *Latin American Drugs I: Losing the Fight*, Latin America Report, No. 25, 14 March 2008, p. 27.

23. United Nations Office for Drugs and Crime, 2004.

24. International Crisis Group, *Spoiling Security in Haiti*, Latin America/ Caribbean Report, No. 13, 2005.

25. According to a poll conducted in 2006.

26. *Crime, Violence, and Development*, p. 43.

27. *Jamaica Gleaner*, 17 January 2002.

28. This is not as far-fetched as it might at first appear. The Americans were ready to intervene wherever they saw fit. In 1983 Grenada was invaded by US troops. In 1989 Panama was invaded.

29. The term was coined by University of the West Indies at Mona, Jamaica, Professor Carl Stone. A fire on Orange Street made the front cover of the papers because one of the arsonists had taken a baby from the arms of its mother as she was fleeing the flames. He had thrown the baby back into the burning house, supposedly while 'high on cocaine'. The emotional numbness that cocaine can produce makes it well suited for carrying out acts of great violence.

30. A local journalist told me that a popular and effective PNP minister who served for eighteen years from 1989 got his start in the ganja business.

31. Quoted in an article by Elaine Cole in the *Independent*, 9 October 2000.

32. Laurie Gunst, *Born Fi' Dead: a Journey through the Jamaica Posse Underworld* (New York: Owl Books, 1995), p. 22.

33. According to the US Bureau of Alcohol, Tobacco and Firearms, as cited in Gunst, *Born Fi' Dead*.

34. *New York Times*, 8 December 1990.

35. Cited in Dunst, *Born Fi' Dead*, p. 11.

36. *Jamaica Gleaner*, 18 June 2007.

37. Carl Williams, 'Consequences of the War on Drugs for Transit Countries: The Jamaican Experience', in *Crime and Justice International*, September/ October 2007, p. 36.

38. Jamaican Ministry of Finance and Planning, cited in Williams, 'Consequences of the War on Drugs for Transit Countries: The Jamaican Experience', p. 36.

39. *Crime, Violence, and Development*, p. 83.

40. 'Raid in MoBay: Two men held for alleged involvement in smuggling, (*Jamaica Gleaner*, 23 June, 2004).

41. Commissioner of Police, Lucius Thomas, in *Jamaica Gleaner*, 7 May 2007.

42. *Jamaica Gleaner*, 3 March 2007.

43. Bernard Headley, *A Spade is Still a Spade: Essays on Crime and the Politics of Jamaica*, (Kingston, Jamaica: LMH Publishing, 2002), p. 66.

44. According to Commissioner of Police Lucius Thomas in *Jamaica Gleaner*, 7 May 2007; also *Jamaica Gleaner*, 15 January 2007. There were 1,139 murders in 2001, 1,805 murders in 2004, 1,674 in 2005, and 1,340 in 2006.

45. *Crime, Violence, and Development*, p. 87. In 2003, Jamaica's prison population was 4,744; cited in ibid., p. 85.

46. I am grateful to Barry Chevannes, Professor of Social Anthropology at the University of the West Indies at Mona, for his insights on the origin of violence in Jamaica.

47. *Crime, Violence, and Development*, p. 71, citing a World Bank report from 2003.

48. See Anthony Harriott, *Police and Crime Control in Jamaica* (Kingston, Jamaica: University of the West Indies Press, 2000).

49. Headley, *A Spade is Still a Spade*, p. 44.

6. The Mexican Supply Chain

1. Cited in Mark Cameron Edberg, *El Narco-Traficante: Narcocorridos and the Construction of a Cultural Persona on the US–Mexico Border* (Austin, Texas: University of Texas Press, 2004), pp. 56, 156.

2. Figures refer to flights in 2004, according to the United States Interagency Assessment of Cocaine Movement, cited in United Nations Office on Drugs and Crime, *World Drug Report 2006, Volume 1: Analysis* (Vienna, Austria: United Nations, 2006), p. 88.

3. According to the US State Department, cited in *At a Crossroads: Drug Trafficking, Violence and the Mexican State*, Beckley Foundation and Washington Office on Latin America, November 2007.

4. *El Pais*; see <http://www.elpais.com/articulo/internacional/Mexico/eleva/5400/muertos/narcotrafico/doble/hace/ano/elpepuint/20081209elpepuint_5/Tes>.

5. United Nations Office on Drugs and Crime, *World Drug Report 2006, Volume 1: Analysis*, p. 87. Also *Crime, Violence, and Development: Trends, Costs, and Policy Options in the Caribbean*, joint report by the United Nations Office on Drugs and Crime and the Latin America and the Caribbean Region of the World Bank, March 2007, p. 20.

6. BBC News online, 'Mexico in record cocaine seizure', 2 November 2007.

7. Howard Campbell, 'Drug Trafficking Stories: Everyday Forms of Narco-Folklore on the US–Mexico Border', *International Journal of Drug Policy*, 16, 2005, p. 327.

8. Corrido de los Bootleggers is cited in Edberg, *El Narco-Traficante*, pp. 41, 149.

9. International Narcotics Control Board Annual Report 2006, p. 48.

10. According to the president of Mexico's Supreme Agricultural Court, cited in Beckley Foundation, *At a Crossroads*. As far back as 1999, Thomas Constantine, then head of the US Drug Enforcement Agency, told Congress that the power of Mexican drug traffickers had grown 'virtually geometrically'. The DEA can be relied on to match topsy-turvy policies with topsy-turvy syntax.

11. James Siegel, cited in Campbell, 'Drug Trafficking Stories', p. 328.

12. International Crisis Group, *Latin American Drugs I: Losing the Fight*, Latin America, Report No. 25, 14 March 2008, p. 25.

13. Beckley Foundation, *At a Crossroads*.

14. *The Economist*, 25 October 2007.

15. US Department of Justice, Drug Enforcement Agency, *DEA 1973–2003: A Tradition of Excellence*, p. 144.

16. See Ted Galen Carpenter, 'Mexico is Becoming the Next Colombia', Cato Institute Foreign Policy Briefing, No. 87, 15 November 2005.

17. Jorge Fernández Menéndez, 'Mexico: the traffickers' judges', in *Transparency International Global Corruption Report 2007* (Cambridge: Cambridge University Press, 2007), p. 77.

18. Quoted in 'Bishop's Admission on Drug-Tainted Donations Causes Uproar'; available online at <http://www.cnn.com/2005/WORLD/americas/10/04/mexican.church.ap/index.html.; cited in Carpenter, 'Mexico is Becoming the Next Colombia'.

19. From the song 'El Tarasco' by Los Tigres del Norte, cited in Edberg, *El Narco-Traficante*, pp. 51, 151.

20. See Luis Astorga, 'Cocaine in Mexico: a prelude to "los narcos"', in Paul Gootenberg (ed.), *Cocaine: Global Histories* (London: Routledge, 1999).

21. For a short time after the Bolshevik Revolution of 1917, Moscow and St Petersburg had small but significant cocaine scenes.

22. Cited in Manuel Roig-Franzia, 'Surge in Violence Shocks Even Weary Mexico: Drug Killings Nearly Doubled in Past Year', *Washington Post*, 29 November 2006.

23. Cockburn and St Clair, *White Out: the CIA, Drugs and the Press*, p. 361.

24. Cited in Carpenter, 'Mexico is Becoming the Next Colombia'.

25. Brian Winter, 'Fox Is Victim of Own Success in Mexico Drug War',

Reuters, 15 February 2005, cited in Carpenter, 'Mexico is Becoming the Next Colombia'.

26. From Reporters Without Borders Annual Report 2007, Reporters Without Borders, Paris, pp. 59–61.

27. *The Economist*, 25 October 2007.

28. 'Can the army out-gun the drug lords?', *The Economist*, 15 May 2008.

29. Lennox Samuels, 'Fox Says Mexico Will Prevail In War Against Drug Cartels', *Dallas Morning News*, 17 August 2005.

30. 'Analizarán México y Estados Unidos la violencia fronteriza', Notimex, *La Jornada*, 4 June 2005.

31. Quoted in Danna Harman, 'Mexican Drug Cartels' Wars Move Closer to US Border', *USA Today*, 18 August 2005.

32. Terrence Poppa, 'Quién Está Manejando la Plaza?' in Luis Humberto Crosthwaite, John William Byrd and Bobby Byrd (eds), *Puro Border: Dispatches, Snapshots and Graffiti from La Frontera* (El Paso, Texas: Cinco Puntos Press, 2003), pp. 93–4.

33. James Pinkerton, 'Corruption Crosses the Border with Agent Bribes', *Houston Chronicle*, 31 May 2005.

34. Department of Justice, 'Three More Plead Guilty as Operation Tarnish Star Nets 13 Current, Former Soldiers of Conspiracy to Take Bribes', press release issued 25 April 2006.

35. Department of Justice, 'Three Current and Former US Soldiers Plead Guilty to Participating in Bribery and Extortion Conspiracy', press release issued 24 April 2006.

7. 'Cocaine is the Atomic Bomb of Latin America'

1. A remark attributed to pioneering cocaine smuggler Carlos Lehder.

2. 'La Caína' by Rubén Blades. 'Te agita y te enreda, pecadora/después que la abrazas, te devora/ no se puede querer a la Caína, no se puede creer en la Caína/ tú crees que la tienes controlada, pero tú sin ella no eres nada/ no se puede querer a la Caína, no se puede creer en la Caína.'

3. Figures from the Shared Responsibility website; <http://sharedresponsibility.gov.co>. Francisco Santos came to the United Kingdom in November 2008 to warn of the environmental impact of cocaine production; see Sandra Laville, 'Cocaine users are destroying the rainforest – at 4m squared a gram', *Guardian*, 19 November 2008.

4. UNODC, *Colombia Coca Cultivation Survey*, June 2007, p. 64; cited in

Washington Office on Latin America, 'Chemical Reactions: Fumigation: Spreading Coca and Threatening Colombia's Ecological and Multicultural Diversity', February 2008, p. 23.

5. Interview for Underground Online, March 2006; available online at <http://www.ugo.com/channels/filmtv/features/16blocks/bruce.asp>.

6. The White House, 'Report on US Policy and Strategy Regarding Counter-narcotics Assistance for Colombia and Neighboring Countries', 26 October 2000, cited in 'Chemical Reactions: Fumigation', p. 11.

7. Office of National Drug Control Policy, Cocaine Smuggling in 2006, August 2007.

8. UNODC, Colombia Coca Cultivation Survey, p. 40.

9. Ibid., p. 58.

10. Ibid., p. 47.

11. UN World Drug Report 2006, pp. 49, 82.

12. Salazar, Drogas y Narcotráfico en Colombia, p. 112.

13. Washington Office on Latin America, 'Chemical Reactions: Fumigation', p. 13.

14. United States Senate, Senate Appropriations Committee Report 107–219 on S. 2779 (Washington: Library of Congress, 24 July 2002); <http://ftp://ftp.loc.gov/pub/thomas/cp107/sr219.txt>, cited in Center for International Policy, The War on Drugs Meets the War on Terror, February 2003, p. 10.

15. Colombian National Anti-Narcotics Agency (DNE), Colombian Drug Observatory Report 2005, p. 81.

16. Salazar, Drogas y Narcotráfico en Colombia, p. 114.

17. UNODC, Colombia Coca Cultivation Survey, p. 78.

18. Transnational Institute Drug Policy Briefing, 'The Politics of Glyphosate', June 2005.

19. Inter-American Drug Abuse Control Commission (CICAD), 'Study of the Effects of the Program of Eradication of Illicit Crops by Aerial Spraying with the Herbicide Glyphosate (PECIG) and of illicit crops on human health and the environment', Washington DC, 2005.

20. International Crisis Group, 'Guerra y Droga en Colombia', Latin American Report, No. 11, 27 January 2005, p. 28.

21. Washington Office on Latin America, 'Chemical Reactions: Fumigation', p. 4.

22. Cited in Angela Maria Puentes Marin, El Opio de los Taliban y la Coca de las FARC (Bogotá: Universidad de los Andes, 2006), p. 74, my translation.

23. International coffee prices fell from 168 cents a pound in 1997 to 67 cents a pound in 2000.

24. Washington Office on Latin America, 'Chemical Reactions: Fumigation', p. 4.

25. House Appropriations Subcommittee on Foreign Operations, 10 April 2002, cited in 'The War on Drugs Meets the War on Terror', Center for International Policy, February 2003, p. 7.

26. Quoted in Salazar, *Drogas y Narcotrafico en Colombia*, p. 69, my translation.

27. Ricardo Vargas, 'A View from a Producer Country: The Impact of Drugs Control Policies at the National Level in Colombia', *Drugs Edition*, April 1996.

28. I am very grateful to Francisco Thoumi for his insights into the origins of Colombian illegality; interview, October 2007.

29. House Government Reform Committee hearing on 'How We Can Improve Plan Colombia', 12 December 2002, cited in *Sojourners* magazine, May 2003, p. 23.

30. Trade and Environment Database (TED), TED Case Studies, *Colombia Coca Trade* (Washington DC: American University, 1997), p. 4.

31. £1 = 3,800 COP Colombian pesos, correct at 4 February 2008.

32. 'El Computador de Chupeta', *Semana*, 1 October 2007, p. 30.

33. For more on the origins of bandits and mafiosi, see Eric J. Hobsbawm, *Primitive Rebels: Studies in Archaic Forms of Social Movement in the 19th and 20th Centuries*, (New York: Norton, 1965).

34. Agar, 'The Story of Crack: Towards a Theory of Illicit Drug Trends'.

35. According to Congressman Wilson Borja, the Colombian Congress debated legalization in August 2001, but has never looked into the economic impact of the drugs trade, the links between the legal and illegal sectors or the best way to treat drug consumption.

36. Salazar, *Drogas y Narcotráfico en Colombia*, pp. 44–8.

37. According to Salomon Kalmanowitz, cited in ibid., pp. 81–2.

38. Ricardo Rocha Garcia, *La Economia Colombiana Tras 25 Anos de Narcotrafico* (Bogotá: Siglo del Hombre Editores, 2000), p. 18.

39. International Crisis Group, 'Guerra y Droga en Colombia', p. 30.

40. *UN World Drug Report 2006*, p. 91.

41. Camilo Echandia, *Geografía del Conflicto Armado y las Manifestaciones de la Violencia en Colombia* (Bogotá: Centro de Estudios sobre Desarrollo Económico, 1999), p. 78; also Francisco Thoumi, 'The Numbers Game: Let's All Guess the Size of the Illegal Drugs Industry', *Journal of Drug Issues*, Winter 2005.

42. Statement before the House Committee on Government Reform, 17 June 2004.

43. Colombian National Anti-Narcotics Agency (DNE), *Colombian Drug Observatory Report 2005*, p. 67.

44. Interview with Francisco Thoumi, September 2007.

45. US Library of Congress statistics.

46. Salazar, *Drogas y Narcotráfico en Colombia*, pp. 86–7.

47. UNODC, *Colombia Coca Cultivation Survey*, p. 69.

48. Comisión Internaciónal de las FARC-EP, San José, Costa Rica, *Narcotráfico en America Latina y el Caribe*, 1997; available online at <http://six.swix.ch/farcep/Documentos/tallernarcotrafico.html>.

49. International Crisis Group, 'Guerra y Droga en Colombia', p. 9.

50. See Pino Arlacchi, *The Mafia Ethic and the Spirit of Capitalism* (Oxford: Oxford University Press, 1994) for the sociology of narco-traffickers in Italy, how the Mafia emerged from rural communities, and was transformed by the drugs trade.

51. The M-19 were urban guerrillas, formed in protest at what they considered to be fraudulent elections in 1970 and disbanded in the late 1980s. The M-19 movement was responsible for the siege of the Palace of Justice in 1985. The government's attempt to lift the siege resulted in the deaths of over 100 people.

52. Congressional testimony of DEA head James Milford in 1997, House International Relations Committee, Subcommittee on the Western Hemisphere, 16 July 1997.

53. For some examples of official exaggeration and falsehood, see International Crisis Group, 'Guerra y Droga en Colombia', p. 12.

54. 'United States charges 50 traders of narco-terrorist FARC in Colombia with supplying more than half the world's cocaine', DEA press release, 22 March 2006.

55. International Crisis Group, 'Latin American Drugs I: Losing the Fight', Latin America Report, No. 25, 14 March 2008.

56. 'Armas siguen llegando a FARC, pese a estrictos controles en área de operaciones del Plan Patriota', *El Tiempo*, 7 June 2005.

57. Joaquín Villalobos, 'FARC: un amenaza transnacional, de Robin Hood a Pablo Escobar', *El País*, 24 March 2008.

58. According to Alfredo Rangel, director of Fundación Seguridad y Democracia, cited in Marin, *El Opio de los Taliban y la Coca de las FARC*, p. 63.

59. Daniel Pecault, *Guerra Contra la Sociedad* (Bogotá: Espasa Hoy, 2000).

60. *Jamaica Gleaner*, 16 March 2007.

61. Center for International Policy, 'Plan Colombia: Six Years Later', November 2006. Plan Colombia has been a boon for defence contractors, albeit nothing compared to what they get from supplying US forces in Iraq

and Afghanistan. See 'The Lost War,' *Washington Post*, 19 August 2007, citing data from the Government Accountability Office.

62. Cited in 'Nos daban cinco días de descanso por cada muerto', *Semana*, 26 January 2008 (my translation).

63. 'Corrupcion hasta el tuétano', *Semana*, 13 August 2007.

64. Salazar, *Drogas y Narcotrafico en Colombia*, pp. 83–4.

65. According to Professor Jenny Pearce, who visited Sincelejo in 2005, and described her time there in 'The crisis of the Colombian state', *Open Society*, 14 May 2007.

66. Interview published as 'El Hombre del Cartel', *Semana*, 16 June 2007, my translation.

67. According to a study, Mauricio Romero (ed.), *Para-politíca: la ruta de la expansión paramilitar y les acuerdos políticos* (Bogotá: Corporacion Nuevo Iris, 2007).

68. The scale of his production was confirmed by fellow trafficker Fabio Ochoa Vasco in an interview published as 'El Hombre del Cartel', *Semana*, 16 June 2007.

69. According to Gustavo Gallon of the Colombian Commission of Jurists, cited in 'Ex paras podrian vivir en tierras que AUC usurparon', *El Tiempo*, 14 February 2006. The figures on the total number of demobilized paramilitaries come from Washington Office on Latin America, 'Chemical Reactions: Fumigation', p. 8.

70. Pearce, 'The crisis of the Colombian state'.

71. International Crisis Group, 'Colombia's New Armed Groups', Latin America Report, 20, 10 May 2007, p. 5.

72. His conviction was overturned on a legal technicality, but in May 2009, a fresh warrant for his arrest was issued, this time in connection with the murders of a politician, a journalist and a trade union official. 'Ex-director del DAS Jorge Noguera Cote, a juicio por crimen de colrea de Andreis', *El Tiempo*, 14 May 2009.

73. Fabio Castillo, *Los Jinetes de la Cocaína* (Bogotá: Editorial Documentos Periodísticos, 1987), p. 225.

74. 'La Fibra Íntima', *Semana*, 23 April 2007.

75. 'Because both the source of the report and the reporting officer's comments section were not declassified, we cannot be sure how the DIA judged the accuracy of this information,' said Michael Evans, director of the National Security Archive's Colombia Documentation Project, 'but we do know that intelligence officials believed the document was serious and important enough to pass on to analysts in Washington.' See 23 November 1991 (Date of Information 18 March 1991), Narcotics – Colombian Narco-

trafficker Profiles, Defense Intelligence Agency, Intelligence Information Report, Confidential, 14 pp. Declassification Release Under the Freedom of Information Act, May 2004.

76. Castillo, *Los Jinetes de la Cocaina*, p. 72.

77. 'Free Trade in Thugs', *The Economist*, 15 May 2008.

78. Interview published as 'El Hombre del Cartel', *Semana*, 16 June 2007.

79. Salvatore Mancuso, for example, sold his South of Bolivar front to drug lords in Putumayo. For more on this, see International Crisis Group, 'Colombia's New Armed Groups', p. 4. Also Marin, *El Opio de los Taliban y la Coca de las FARC*, p. xv.

80. 'Asi siguen mandando los paras', *El Tiempo*, 5 March 2006.

81. Salazar, *Drogas y Narcotráfico en Colombia*, pp. 75–6.

82. Center for International Policy, 'Plan Colombia: Six Years Later'.

83. Cited in International Crisis Group, 'Guerra y Droga en Colombia', p. 25.

8. Globalization

1. C. Mackay, *Extraordinary Popular Delusions and the Madness of Crowds* (New York: Crown Trade Paperbacks, 1980, reissued), preface to the edition of 1852.

2. United States House of Representatives, speech by Rep. Mark Souder (R-Indiana), Congressional Record, Washington, 23 May 2002, H3001; also available online at <http://thomas.loc.gov/cgibin/query/B?r107:@FIELD(FLD003+h)+@FIELD(DDATE+20020523)>, cited in Center for International Policy, 'The War on Drugs Meets the War on Terror', February 2003, p. 12.

3. Cited in Daniel Scott-Lea, 'Descubriendo Petróleo debajo de la Guerra contra las Drogas y el Terror', Masters degree thesis in Latin American Studies, Universidad Javeriana, Bogotá, unpublished, October 2005.

4. Interview conducted in 2002; cited in Doug Stokes, *America's Other War: Terrorizing Colombia* (London: Zed Books, 2005), p. 90.

5. Francisco Ramirez Cuellar, *The Profits of Extermination: How US Corporate Power is Destroying Colombia* (Monroe, Maine: Common Courage Press, 2005), p. 73.

6. Ethan A. Nadelmann, 'The DEA in Latin America: Dealing with Institutionalized Corruption', *Journal of Interamerican Studies and World Affairs*, Vol. 29, No. 4, Winter 1987–88, pp. 1–39.

7. Jamie Dettmer, 'Family Affairs: Mexican businessman and politician

Carlos Hank Gonzalez allegedly involved in drug trade', *Insight on the News*, 29 March 1999.

8. Frank Smyth, 'The Untouchable Narco-State: Guatemala's military defies the DEA', *Texas Observer*, 8 November 2005.

9. See his autobiography, Celerino Castillo III, *Powderburns: Cocaine, Contras and the Drug War* (Oakville, Ontario: Mosaic Press, 1994), p. 124.

10. Cockburn and St Clair, *White Out: the CIA, Drugs and the Press*, p. 289.

11. Nadelmann, 'The DEA in Latin America', pp. 1–39.

12. *Crime, Violence, and Development: Trends, Costs, and Policy Options in the Caribbean*, March 2007, p. 23.

13. Cited in Nadelmann, 'The DEA in Latin America', pp. 1–39.

14. 'Rio governor says legalize drugs to fight crime', Reuters, 2 March 2007.

15. *Jamaica Gleaner*, 13 May 2007.

16. Adriano Oliveira, 'Trafico de drogas e crime organizado, pecas e mecanismos', in M. O. Campos, *Estado Bandido e as Mulheres no Trafico*, fazendomedia.com.

17. Tijuana also has ten times the number of pharmacies you would expect to find in a city of its size; see National Drug Intelligence Center, 'National Drug Threat Assessment 2007', US Department of Justice.

18. Interview with Benito Azcano Roldán of La Carpa Hogar Integral de Juventud, Mexico City, March 2008.

19. According to the US Justice Department's National Drug Intelligence Center, cited in *The Economist*, 25 October 2007.

20. National Drug Intelligence Center, 'National Drug Threat Assessment 2007'.

21. Peter Andreas, 'Free market reform and drug market prohibition: US policies at cross-purposes in Latin America', *Third World Quarterly*, Vol. 16, No. 1, 1995.

22. Williams, 'Consequences of the War on Drugs for Transit Countries: the Jamaican Experience', p. 34. The author was once Jamaica's Chief of Narcotics Police; the Colombian cartels offered a $1 million bounty to anyone who would kill him. He stayed alive long enough to leave his post.

23. *Jamaica Gleaner*, 21 September, 2007, reports that from January to August 2007, the authorities destroyed 387 hectares of ganja.

24. Medical cannabis refers to the use of the cannabis plant as a physician-recommended herbal therapy. Cannabinoids have been found to be useful in the treatment of a wide variety of oxidation associated diseases, such as ischaemic, age-related, inflammatory and autoimmune diseases. They can be used as neuroprotectants, for example in limiting neurological damage

following stroke and trauma, or in the treatment of neurodegenerative diseases such as Alzheimer's disease, Parkinson's disease and HIV dementia.

25. Center for International Policy, 'Below the Radar: US Military Programs with Latin America 1997–2007', 2007, p. 6.

26. Brecher et al. (eds.), 'The Consumers Union Report on Licit and Illicit Drugs', 1972.

27. Office of National Drug Control Policy, *The Price and Purity of Illicit Drugs: 1981 Through the Second Quarter of 2003* (Washington DC: Executive Office of the President, November 2004), Publication Number NCJ 207768, p. 58, Table 1 and p. 59, Table 2.

28. United Nations Office for Drug Control and Crime Prevention, *Global Illicit Drug Trends 1999* (New York, NY: UNODCCP, 1999), p. 86. Also Office of National Drug Control Policy, *The Price and Purity of Illicit Drugs*, p. 62, Table 5 and p. 63, Table 6.

29. C. P. Rydell and S. S. Everingham, 'Controlling Cocaine' prepared for the Office of National Drug Control Policy and the United States Army (Santa Monica, CA: Drug Policy Research Center, RAND, 1994), p. 6.

9. The Demand for Cocaine

1. Data from the 2001/2002 sweep of the *British Crime Survey 2001/02*.

2. European Monitoring Centre for Drugs and Drug Addiction, *Annual Report 2005: The State of the Drugs Problem in Europe* (Luxembourg: Office for Official Publications of the European Communities, 2005), p. 12.

3. 'Spain Drug Situation 2000', Report to the European Monitoring Center on Drugs and Drug Addiction by the Reitox National Focal Point of Spain, Plan nacional sobre drogas (Madrid, Spain: Ministerio del Interior and EMCDDA, November 2000), pp. 18–19. (DGPNSD 2000a: Delegación del Gobierno para el Plan Nacional Sobre Drogas, Encuesta Domiciliaria Sobre Use do Drogas 1999, Ministerio del Interior. 2000d: DGPNSD, Encuesta Sobre Drogas a Poblacion Escolar, Ministerio del Interior.)

4. European Monitoring Centre for Drugs and Drug Addiction, *Annual Report 2005: The State of the Drugs Problem in Europe*, p. 17.

5. BBC News, 'Half City's Youth Take Cocaine', 9 May 2008; study conducted by Professor Mark Bellis at the Centre for Public Health at Liverpool John Moore's University.

6. *UN World Drug Report 2006*, from p. 24.

7. In 1993, among those who had used cocaine in the last year, 77 per cent

had snorted it, 26 per cent had smoked it and 7 per cent had injected it; see National Drug Intelligence Center, 'National Drug Threat Assessment 2007', US Department of Justice, citing National Survey on Drug Use and Health (NSDUH) and Monitoring the Future (MTF) data.

8. See the Serious Organized Crime Agency website.

9. Niskanen, *Economists and Drug Policy*, p. 237, citing Gill and Michaels, 'Drug Use and Earnings: Accounting for the Self-Selection of Users', Working Paper 11–90, California State University at Fullerton, 1990.

10. See <http://news.bbc.co.uk/go/pr/fr/-/2/hi/uk_news/7142413.stm>; published 14 December 2007.

11. E. Joël and F. Fränkel, *Der Cocainismus: Ein Beitrag zur Geschichte und Psychopathologie der Rauschgifte* (Berlin: Julius Springer, 1924), p. 18.

12. Cited in Ernest Jones, *Sigmund Freud: Life and Work* (London: Hogarth Press, 1953–7), Vol. I, p. 91.

13. R. A. Johnson and D. R. Gerstein, 'Initiation of use of alcohol, cigarettes, marijuana, cocaine, and other drugs in US birth cohorts since 1919', *American Journal of Public Health*, 88, 1997, pp. 27–33.

14. J. Schedler and J. Block, 'Adolescent Drug Use and Psychological Health', *American Psychologist*, 45, May 1990, pp. 612–30.

15. P. Clifford, 'Drug Use, Drug Prohibition and Minority Communities', *Journal of Primary Prevention* 12 (4), 1992, pp. 303–16.

16. *UN World Drug Report*, p. 96.

17. Harry Levine, citing data from http://www.nida.nih.gov/infofacts/cocaine.html.

18. This was the conclusion reached at an international conference on municipal cannabis policies, organized by the Dutch Minister of Justice in 2001 and attended by 120 participants from 50 European cities from 20 countries; Trimbos Institute, *Report to the EMCDDA by the Reitox National Focal Point, The Netherlands Drug Situation 2002* (Lisbon, Portugal: European Monitoring Centre for Drugs and Drug Addiction, November 2002), p. 23, citing Ministerie van Volksgezondheid, Welzijn en Sport, 2002a, pp. 17–18.

19. Patricia G. Erickson, *The Steel Drug: Cocaine and Crack in Perspective* (Lexington, Mass.: Lexington Books, 1987).

20. Noah Mamber, 'Harm Reductive Drug Legalization', *Cornell Journal of Law and Public Policy*, Summer 2006, p. 629.

21. Ibid., p. 630.

22. J. O'Connor and B. Saunders, 'Drug Education: an appraisal of a popular preventive', *International Journal of the Addictions*, 27, 1992, pp. 165–85; also N. Dorn and K. Murji, *Drug Prevention: A Review of the English*

Language Literature (London: Institute for the Study of Drug Dependence, 1992); Julian Cohen, 'Drug Education: Politics, Propaganda and Censorship', *International Journal of Drug Policy*, Vol. 7, No. 3, 1996.

23. Ian Binnie et al., 'Know the score: cocaine wave 3: 2005 post-campaign evaluation: summary', Scottish Executive, 2006, based on 466 interviews.

24. Interview with Anthony Henman, Chepstow, August 2007.

25. Van Dyck and Robert Byck, as cited in Jorge Hurtado Gumucio, *Cocaine, the Legend: About Coca and Cocaine*, 2nd revd edn (La Paz: Editorial Hisbol, 1995).

26. Niskanen, *Economists and Drug Policy*, p. 229.

27. Patricia Erickson and Glenn Murray, 'Cocaine and Addictive Liability', *Social Pharmacology*, 3, 1989, pp. 249–70.

28. Peter Cohen, *Cocaine Use in Amsterdam in Non-Deviant Sub-cultures* (Amsterdam: University of Amsterdam, 1989).

29. Sheila Murphy, Craig Reinarman and Dan Waldorf, 'An 11-year follow-up of a network of cocaine users', *British Journal of Addiction*, 84, 1989, pp. 427–36.

30. Mike Jay, 'A Snapshot History of Coca, Cocaine and Crack', on the Transform Drug Policy Foundation website: <http://www.tdpf.org.uk/Policy_General_Cocaine_MJay.htm>.

31. Peter Cohen, Peter and Arjan Sas, *Ten years of cocaine: a follow-up study of 64 cocaine users in Amsterdam* (Amsterdam: Department of Human Geography, University of Amsterdam, 1993), p. 24.

32. Cited in Ken McLaughlin, 'This Case Could Make Losers of Us All', 20 February 2008; available to view at <http://www.spiked-online.com/index.php?/site/article/4564/>.

33.

Substance	Withdrawal	Reinforcement	Tolerance	Dependence	Intoxication
Nicotine	6	4	5	3	2
Heroin	5	5	6	5	5
Cocaine	4	3	3	6	4
Alcohol	3	6	4	4	6
Caffeine	2	2	2	1	1
Marijuana	1	1	1	2	3

Withdrawal: Presence and severity of characteristic withdrawal symptoms.

Reinforcement: A measure of the substance's ability, in human and animal tests, to get users to take it again and again, and in preference to other substances.

Tolerance: How much of the substance is needed to satisfy increasing cravings for it, and the level of stable need that is eventually reached.

Dependence: How difficult it is for the user to quit, the relapse rate, the percentage of people who eventually become dependent, the rating users give their own need for the substance and the degree to which the substance will be used in the face of evidence that it causes harm.

Intoxication: Though not usually counted as a measure of addiction in itself, the level of intoxication is associated with addiction and increases the personal and social damage a substance may do.

Source: Dr Jack E. Henningfield for NIDA National Institute on Drug Abuse, cited in Philip J. Hilts, 'Is Nicotine Addictive? It Depends on Whose Criteria You Use', *New York Times*, 2 August 1994.

34. Martin Fackler, 'In Korea, a Boot Camp Cure for Web Obsession', *New York Times*, 18 November 2007.

35. S. Roe and L. Mann, 'Drug Misuse Declared: Findings from the 2005/06 British Crime Survey England and Wales', *Home Office Statistical Bulletin*, 2006.

36. Criminal Policy Research Unit, 'On the Rocks: A Follow-up Study of Crack Users in London', South Bank University, 2003.

37. Interview with Tony D'Agostino of Coca, a London charity working at an international level to increase knowledge and understanding of cocaine and crack use, August 2007.

38. Antonin Artaud, 'Appeal to Youth: Intoxication-Disintoxication', reproduced in Susan Sontag (ed.), *Selected Writings*, pt. 24 (Berkeley, CA: University of California Press, 1988).

39. C. P. Rydell and S. S. Everingham, *Controlling Cocaine*, prepared for the Office of National Drug Control Policy and the United States Army (Santa Monica, CA: Drug Policy Research Center, RAND Corporation, 1994), p. xvi.

40. Ibid.

41. Abt Associates, *What America's Users Spend on Illegal Drugs 1988–1998* (Washington, DC: ONDCP, Dec. 2000), p. 9, citing data from the Substance Abuse Mental Health Services Administration.

42. See Ministry of Health, *Drug Policy in the Netherlands*, September 2003.

43. Canadian Senate hearing from Peter Cohen in 2001. Proceedings of the Special Committee on Illegal Drugs, Issue 3, Evidence for 28 May, Morning Session, Ottawa, Canadian Senate; available online at <http://www.parl.gc.ca/37/1/parlbus/commbus/senate/Com-e/ille-e/03eva-E.htm>.

44. Trimbos Institute, *Report to the EMCDDA by the Reitox National Focal Point*, p. 8.

45. As reported in *Drugs in Deprived Neighbourhoods*, Home Office Research Study 240, 2002.

46. Katherine Griffiths, 'Xenova sees hope for cocaine treatment', *Independent*, 18 June 2003; also see the company's website at <http://www.xenova.co.uk/dctacd.html>.

10. Legalization

1. British police arrested 4,400 people on charges of possessing cocaine in 2000, up a third from the previous year, but that still left 745,000 cocaine users who escaped all censure.

2. Criminal Policy Research Unit, 'On the Rocks: A Follow-up Study of Crack Users in London', South Bank University, London, 2003. And from Beckley Foundation/Drugscope, *Assessing Drug Policy Principles and Practice*, London, 2004, p. 5.

3. Eric Sterling, *Eleven Ways the Drug War is Hurting Your Business* (Silver Spring, MD: Business Council for Prosperity and Safety, 2007).

4. S. Everingham and P. Rydell, *Modeling the Demand for Cocaine* (Santa Monica, CA: RAND, 1994).

5. Based on data from New York City in 1988. Out of a total of 414 murders, 218 were described as drug-related. P. J. Goldstein, H. H. Brownstein, P. J. Ryan and P. A. Bellucci, 'Crack and Homicide in New York City: A Case Study in the Epidemiology of Violence', in Craig Reinarman and Harry Levine (eds), *Crack in America: Demon Drugs and Social Justice* (Berkeley, CA: University of California Press, 1997), pp. 113–30. Also J. Miron and J. Zwiebel, 'The Economic Case Against Drug Prohibition', *Journal of Economic Perspectives*, Fall 1995, p. 179.

6. Quotes from *Traffic* can be viewed at the Internet Movie Database; <http://www.imdb.com/title/tt0181865/quotes>.

7. Saxe et al., 'The Visibility of Illicit Drugs: Implications for Community-Based Drug Control Strategies', *American Journal of Public Health*, Vol. 91, No. 12, December 2001.

8. *National Survey on Drug Use and Health* (Rockville, MD: Substance Abuse and Mental Health Services Administration (SAMHSA), June 2007).

9. Schmoke, 'Forging a New Consensus in the War on Drugs: Is It Possible?'

10. Center for Disease Control, 'Youth Risk Behaviour Survey', quoted in *Morbidity and Mortality Weekly Report*, Vol. 49, No. SS-5, p. 66.

11. 0.3 per cent of whites, 1.6 per cent of blacks, and 0.6 per cent of Hispanics reported having used crack in the past month. These figures are cited in the documentary *Letter to the President*, directed by Thomas Gibson, QD3 Entertainment, 2005.

12. Philip Guy, 'Race and the Drug Problem: More than Just an Enforcement Issue'; available online at <http://www.drugtext.org/library/articles/PDG Race.htm>.

13. Marie Woolf, 'Tory contender calls for more liberal drug laws', *Independent*, 7 September 2005.

14. Available online at <http://www.parliament.thestationeryoffice.co.uk/pa/cm200102/cmselect/cmhaff/318/31814.htm>.

15. IRC on VirginNet, 12 November 1997.

16. BBC News, 9 July 2001; available online at <http://news.bbc.co.uk/1/hi/uk/1429694.stm>.

17. *El Tiempo*, 7 March 2006.

18. Salazar, *Drogas y Narcotráfico en Colombia*, pp. 51–2.

19. RCN Colombian radio programme, August 2002, directed by Juan Gozain.

20. 'Rio governor says legalize drugs to fight crime', Reuters, 2 March 2007.

21. 'El Siglo XXI será el siglo de la legalización', *Cambio* magazine, Issue 408, April 2001, p. 28.

22. David Fickling, 'US asks Mexico to reconsider "stupid" drug law', *Guardian*, 4 May 2006.

23. John Rice, Associated Press, 19 March 2001. A slightly different translation of some of this quote (from the original Spanish article in the newspaper *Unomasuno*, 7 March 2001) appeared in the *Village Voice* ('Dream of a Worldwide Truce', 5 June 2001).

24. Beckley Foundation/Drugscope, *Assessing Drug Policy Principles and Practice*, p. 14.

25. Salazar, *Drogas y Narcotrafico en Colombia*, p. 132.

26. Peter Cohen, 'The drug prohibition church and the adventure of reformation', *International Journal of Drug Policy*, Vol. 14, Issue 2, April 2003, pp. 213–15.

27. House Government Reform Committee hearing on 'How We Can Improve Plan Colombia', 12 December 2002, cited in *Sojourners* magazine, May 2003, p. 23.

28. Mark Kleiman, *Against Excess* (New York: Basic Books, 1992), p. 307.

29. Dennis, 'The Economics of Legalizing Drugs'.

30. Home Office, *Drugs in Deprived Neighbourhoods*.

31. A. Walker, C. Kershaw and S. Nicholas, *Crime in England and Wales 2005/6*, Home Office Statistical Publication 12/6 (London: Home Office, 2006), cited in *United Kingdom Drug Situation*, Annual Report to the European Monitoring Centre for Drugs and Drug Addiction (EMCDDA), 2006.

32. Home Office, *Drugs in Deprived Neighbourhoods*.

33. *France Drug Situation 2000*, Report to the European Monitoring Center on Drugs and Drug Addiction by the Reitox National Focal Point of France, l'Observatoire français des drogues et des toxicomanies (OFDT) (Paris, France: OFDT and EMCDDA, December 2000), p. 18.

34. 'Fear of Drugs', a translation from the Dutch by Mario Lap of DrugText of an article by Dr Erik van Ree called 'Angst voor Drugs', published in *Vrij Nederland*, 18 May 1996.

35. The *Wall Street Journal* interactive edition, 8 December 1999.

36. James Whittaker, 'Let's Talk about a Revolution', *Bermuda Sun*, December 2005.

37. L. D. Johnston, P. M. O'Malley, J. G. Bachman, J. E. Schulenberg, *Monitoring the Future: National Results on Adolescent Drug Use* (Bethesda, MD: National Institute on Drug Abuse, 2004).

38. Miron and Zwiebel, 'The Economic Case Against Drug Prohibition', p. 176.

39. Niskanen, *Economists and Drug Policy*, p. 244.

40. The National Center on Addiction and Substance Abuse (CASA), *National Survey of American Attitudes on Substance Abuse II: Teens and their Parents*, New York, 1996, p. 2.

41. *Guardian*, 7 February 2008.

42. These figures are from Abt Associates, *What America's Users Spend on Illegal Drugs 1988–1998* (Washington, DC: ONDCP, Dec. 2000), p. 61. The data on prescription drugs is from the International Narcotics Control Board annual report 2006, p. 46.

43. International Narcotics Control Board annual report 2006, p. 49, citing National Survey on Drug Use and Health in the United States data. Between 2002 and 2005, OxyContin abuse increased by almost 40 per cent among students in their final year of secondary school to an annual prevalence rate of more than 5 per cent. In 2005, 7 per cent of college students abused Hydrocodone.

44. Denis Campbell, 'GPs have got Britain hooked on painkillers', *Observer*, 10 February 2008.

45. Available online at <http://www.drugscope.org.uk/resources/faqs/faq pages/how-many-people-die-from-drugs.htm>.

46. D. Nutt, L. A. King, W. Salisbury, C. Blakemore, 'Development of a rational scale to assess the harm of drugs of potential misuse', *Lancet*, Vol. 369, 24 March 2007.

47. Salazar, *Drogas y Narcotrafico en Colombia*, p. 125.

48. Various sources, cited in 'A Public Health Approach to Drug Control in

Canada: Health Officers Council of British Columbia', Victoria, British Columbia, October 2005, p. 7.

49. 'Development of a rational scale to assess the harm of drugs of potential misuse', *Lancet*.

50. Dennis, 'The Economics of Legalizing Drugs'.

51. Department of Health and Human Services, *Substance Abuse and Mental Health Statistics Source Book 1998*, p. 218, citing statistics from 1990.

52. Cited in Salazar, *Drogas y Narcotráfico en Colombia*, p. 136, my translation.

53. Marvin Lowenthal (ed.), *The Autobiography of Michel De Montaigne: Comprising the Life of the Wisest Man of His Times: His Childhood, Youth, and Prime; His Adventures in Love and Court, and in Office, War . . .*, (Jaffrey, New Hampshire: Nonpareil Books, 1999), p. 28.

54. 'Freedom is about Authority: Excerpts from Giuliani Speech on Crime', *New York Times*, 20 March, 1994.

55. Jay, *Emperors of Dreams: Drugs in the Nineteenth Century*, p. 244.

11. Prospects

1. It is worth mentioning that like cocaine, Coca-Cola has been sullied by association with Colombian paramilitaries. In both cases, the context in which the product is manufactured is more at fault than any quality intrinsic to either product.

2. Calvani, *La Coca: pasado y presente, mitos y realidades*, p. 47.

3. *Jamaica Gleaner*, 21 March 2007.

4. Sandro Calvani cites a letter written by four doctors and published in the *Journal of the American Medical Association* purporting to demonstrate the effectiveness of coca as a substitute for cocaine (*JAMA*, No. 1, January 1986), cited in *La Coca: pasado y presente, mitos y realidades*, p. 20.

5. From an interview with Anthony Henman, August 2007.

6. Luis Carlos Restrepo, 'El Siglo XXI será el siglo de la legalización', *Cambio* magazine, Issue 408, April 2001, p. 26. Luis Carlos Restrepo is currently Colombia's High Commissioner for Peace, and played a key role in negotiations with the AUC paramilitaries that led to their demobilization in 2006–7.

7. Cited in Baum, *Smoke and Mirrors: the War on Drugs and the Politics of Failure*, p. 202.

8. Gabriel Sayegh, 'Justice Reform should begin with drug laws', *Albany Times Union*, 22 August 2007.

9. 'Our Most Important Legislation Ever', Drug Policy Alliance email newsletter, 14 March 2008; 'Prop. 5 Falls to Prison Guards' Millions', Drug Policy Alliance email newsletter, 5 November 2008.

10. Tukka Tammi, 'Medicalizing Prohibition: Harm Reduction in Finnish and European Drug Policy', PhD dissertation; available at <http://www.stakes.fi/EN/Julkaisut/Kirjakauppa/bookshop_research_reports/t161_en.htm>.

11. For more on this, see Alex Stevens and Kaitlin Hughes, 'The Effects of Decriminalization of Drug Use in Portugal', Beckley Foundation, December 2007.

12. Fareed Zakaria, *The Post-American World* (London: Allen Lane, 2008).

Permissions and Acknowledgements

Every effort has been made to trace all copyright holders, and the authors and publishers will gladly rectify in future editions any errors or omissions brought to their attention.

p. 107: Bounty Killer, 'Down in the Ghetto' © Greensleeves Records, Courtesy of Greensleeves Records.

p. 134: Los Tucanes de Tijuana, 'Mis Tres Animales', from 'El Narcotraficante: Narcocorridos and the Construction of a Cultural Persona on the US–Mexico Border', by Mark Cameron Edberg, translation © University of Texas Press 2004.

p. 138: 'Corrido de los Bootleggers', from 'El Narcotraficante: Narcocorridos and the Construction of a Cultural Persona on the US–Mexico Border', by Mark Cameron Edberg, translation © University of Texas Press 2004.

p. 141: Los Norteños de Ojinaga, 'Los Tres de la Sierra', from 'El Narcotraficante: Narcocorridos and the Construction of a Cultural Persona on the US–Mexico Border', by Mark Cameron Edberg, translation © University of Texas Press 2004.

p. 146: Los Tigres del Norte, 'El Tarasco', from 'El Narcotraficante: Narcocorridos and the Construction of a Cultural Persona on the US–Mexico Border', by Mark Cameron Edberg, translation © University of Texas Press 2004.

p. 251: Traffic: NBC Universal © 2000.

p. 254: *Layer Cake*: © 2004 Columbia Pictures Industries, Inc., All Rights Reserved, Courtesy of Columbia Pictures.

Index

assets:
  forfeiture 73–5, 109
  freezing 207–8
atheism 282
Atlanta 18, 76
Atlantico 190
AUC *see* Autodefinsas Unidas de
  Colombia
authoritarian governments 147,
  172
Autodefensas Unidas de Colombia
  (AUC) 169, 183, 188–90,
  192–4, 197, 317

babies, drugs and 63–4
Bahamas 51, 116, 118, 204
'balloon effect' 159
Baltimore 23, 44–5, 77, 255
  crack in 23, 42, 44–5, 54, 65
banana trade 184
Bank of Commerce and Credit
  International (BCCI) 93
banks 5, 178, 209
  and money-laundering 208, 209
Barbados 126
Barcelona 110
'barrel children' 114
Barry, Mayor Marion 63
basuco 176
Baugh, Kenneth 299
BCCI *see* Bank of Commerce and
  Credit International
Bedford-Stuyvesant 44, 54
Beijing 207
Bejarano, Diego Fernando Murillo
  ('Don Berna') 193–4
'Belica' 155–6, 161, 163
Belize 204
Belushi, John 49
Benedict XVI, Pope 205

Bennett, William 65–6, 96, 296
benzodiazepines 271
'Berna, Don' *see* Bejarano, Diego
  Fernando Murillo
Berrellez, Hector 201
Betty Ford clinic 101
Bias, Len 61–2
bingeing 3, 21, 53, 235–6
bio-diversity 153
birth defects 64
Black Panthers 32
black people:
  cocaine scare stories 20–1, 63
  discrimination against 68–9, 98,
    283; *see also* racism
  and drugs 62–4, 71, 83, 137,
    252, 253–4, 283, 314
  and education 83
  fear of 20–1, 63
  and job opportunities 95
  journalists 63
  in poverty 45
  and suburbs 45, 64
  see also African–American
  people
Blackwater (company) 103
Blades, Rubén 152, 302
Blair, Sir Ian 3
Blair, Tony 97
Blake, Vivian 124
Blandon, Danilo 40–1
'Bling Bling' gang 81
Block, Dr Jerald J. 239
Bloods 55, 59, 92
Bogotá (Santa Fé de) 111, 115,
  135, 154, 167, 194–5, 227,
  275
Bolivia 209–10
  anti-drug programmes 210
  coca/cocaine production and use

Economist 279
ecstasy 81, 218, 219–20, 226, 229
Ecuador 108, 159, 161, 198–9,
    204
Edison, Thomas 17
education 20, 45
    see also drug education; students;
    teachers
Edwards, Delroy 'Uzi' 54
Egypt 155
Eighteenth Amendment (US) 26
Eisenhower, President Dwight D.
    34
Elizalde, Valentin 140
ELN *see* National Liberation Army
El Paso-Ciudad Juárez 82, 138,
    141, 142, 143
El Salvador 40, 48, 137, 141, 207
emphysema 268
employers and drug testing 87,
    101, 221
employment issues:
    and prohibition 20
    and young people 95
    see also unemployment
Enlightenment 265
environmental issues 152, 161,
    164, 259, 279, 302–3
escape/escapism 19, 53, 220, 229,
    239–41, 243–4
Escobar, Pablo 124, 134, 165, 169,
    171, 172–4, 178, 191, 193,
    195
ethnicity *see* racism/race issues
'euphoric recall' 246
Europe:
    and Africa 109–10
    cocaine in 109–10, 212, 218–19
    decriminalization debate
    280–81, 311

European Union:
    anti-drug policy 164
    drugs entering 108–10, 112
    and Jamaica 127
'Everybody Against Coca' 162
exorcism 64, 246, 248
explorers 11–13, 274
Expo '92 277
Extraditables, Los 173
Exxon 200

FARC (Revolutionary Armed
    Forces of Colombia) 5, 154–5,
    161, 164, 167, 168, 176,
    177–8, 179–86, 195, 196,
    197, 199
farmers *see* agriculture
favelados 205–6
FBI 124, 125, 151, 203
fear:
    all-pervading 200–1, 283
    of drugs and users 20–1, 28–9,
    34, 63, 65, 66–7, 102, 200, 219
felony disenfranchisement 85–6
festivals (UK) 220
'Fighting 69' 119
film industry 29, 37
    see also Hollywood
Financial Action Task Force 4
Flatbush 50
Fleischl von Marxow, Ernst 223
'flipping the freaks' 58
Florida 38, 85–6, 135
Fonda, Peter 37
Ford, Betty 101
Ford, President Gerald 38
Foreman, Geoff 199
forfeitures 73–5
formication 53
Fox, Professor James Alan 88

law enforcement agencies:
  and money-laundering 209
  self-financing 74
  and targets 75
  and war on drugs 102
laxatives 4
Leal, Jaime Pardo 181
Lebanon 43
Ledger, Heath 270
legalization/decriminalization
    (depenalization) of drugs 35,
    38, 65, 97–8, 101, 212,
    254–74, 279–84, 304, 311
  advocates of 35, 38, 65, 97–8,
    254–8, 261–3, 279–84
  and compulsive drug use 281,
    283
  de facto decriminalization 226,
    257, 259, 262
  likely benefits of 254–5, 255–6,
    263
  opposition to 35, 65, 101,
    257–9, 263–8, 279–80
  regulation and monitoring after
    256, 258, 261, 263, 278–9,
    280
  US and 35, 38, 101, 212, 257,
    279–84
Lehder, Carlos 202, 302
Leon XIII, Pope 17
Levine, Harry 31, 67, 265
Levitt, Steven 89, 96
Lewis, David 276
liberals:
  and drugs 36, 264
  vs. conservatives 39
Lima 47, 241
Lincoln, Abraham 17
Lipotevsky, Gilles 188
Lithuania 112

liver damage 3
Liverpool 233
  John Moores University 218–19
Livingstone, David 18
Livingstone, Ken 256
local/state authorities and drug
    reform 280–81, 310
London 127
  City professionals 221, 242
  cocaine and crack in 2–3, 25, 81,
    112, 176, 220–1, 227, 241–2
  drugs smuggled to 81, 112–14,
    123
Long, James 81
Los Angeles:
  cocaine and crack in 40, 42, 51,
    55–6, 93, 139, 241, 261
  gangs and drugs 33, 59–60, 69,
    137
  policing and law enforcement 76,
    77
lotteries 48
'Louis' 241, 245, 247
Lower East Side 50, 94
LSD 33, 38
Luciano, Lucky 42
lung damage 243, 268

M-19 181, 305
McAfee, Marilyn 201
McAllen, Texas 142
McCain, John 101
MacDonald, Dr Donald 86
McGregor Gully, Kingston 125
McGriff, Kenneth 'Supreme' 83
Machu Picchu 12
Mackay, Charles 198
madness, fear of 273
  see also mental health
Maestre, Daniel 14–16

PENGUIN HEALTH

FAST FOOD NATION: WHAT THE ALL-AMERICAN MEAL IS DOING TO THE WORLD
ERIC SCHLOSSER

'A shocking exposé ... *Fast Food Nation* could make a difference to the way we eat. For ever' *Evening Standard*

'*Fast Food Nation* has lifted the polystyrene lid on the global fast food industry ... and sparked a storm' *Observer*

Do you *really* know what you're eating when you tuck into that juicy burger?

Britain eats more fast food than any other country in Europe. It looks good, tastes good, and it's cheap. But the real cost never appears on the menu.

Eric Schlosser's explosive bestseller, by turns funny and terrifying, tells the story of our love affair with fast food. He visits the lab that re-creates the smell of strawberries; examines the safety records of abattoirs; reveals why fries taste so good and what really lurks between the sesame buns – and shows how fast food is transforming not only our diets but our world.

'Has wiped that smirk off the Happy Meal ... Thanks to this man, you'll never eat a burger again' *Evening Standard*

'Startling ... Junk food, we learn, is just that ... left this reader vowing never to set foot in one of these outlets again' *Daily Mail*

'This book tells you more than you really want to know when you're chomping that hamburger ... Have a nice day? Listen – you should live so long' *The Times*

PENGUIN POLITICS

THE RIGHT NATION: WHY AMERICA IS DIFFERENT
JOHN MICKLETHWAIT & ADRIAN WOOLDRIDGE

'Conservatism's 40-year climb to dominance receives an examination worthy of its complexity in *The Right Nation*, the best political book in years' George Will, *Washington Post*

What makes America seem so different from the rest of the world? *The Right Nation* **is the definitive portrait of a United States that few outsiders understand: the nation that votes for George Bush, that supports the death penalty and gun rights, that believes in minimal government and long prison sentences, that pulled out of the Kyoto Protocol.**

America, argue John Micklethwait and Adrian Wooldridge, award-winning journalists at the *Economist*, has always been a conservative country; but over the past fifty years it has built up a radical conservative movement unlike any other. The authors examine how these right-wing radicals took over the Republican Party, and deconstruct the Bush White House, examining its many influences from neo-conservatism to sun-belt entrepreneurialism. Their quest to understand the mindset of the overlooked and often disdained, but crucial, Middle America takes them from young churchgoers in Colorado Springs to gay gun clubs in Massachusetts to black supporters of school vouchers in Milwaukee.

The Right Nation drives to the heart of a question that is relevant to us all: why is America – increasingly, and often frighteningly – different, and what does this mean for the world?

'A remarkable achievement … *The Right Nation* is authoritative, entertaining and astonishing in its breadth and objectivity. It can perhaps make claim to an extraordinary boast as the best book on modern America in print' Graham Stewart, *Spectator*

BUSINESS

THE WORLD IS FLAT
THOMAS FRIEDMAN

Winner of the *Financial Times*/Goldman Sachs Business Book of the Year 2005

Three-times winner of the Pulitzer Prize

> The world is changing, the future is flat.

Thomas Friedman's international bestseller is the most up-to-date and exciting view yet of today's new era of globalization. He draws on this travels to India, China and the Middle East, and on the explosion of new technologies including blogging, online encyclopedias and podcasting, to show how knowledge and resources are connecting all over the planet as never before. This 'flattening' of our world, he argues, can be a force for good – for business, the environment and people everywhere.

'Truly amazing ... an essential read' A. C. Grayling

'A great book ... makes you see things in a new way' Joseph Stiglitz

PENGUIN POLITICS

THE SHOCK DOCTRINE
THE RISE OF DISASTER CAPITALISM
NAOMI KLEIN

'Impassioned, hugely informative, wonderfully controversial, and scary as hell'
John le Carré

In this groundbreaking book, the bestselling author of *No Logo* exposes the gripping story of how America's 'free market' policies have come to dominate the world – through the exploitation of disaster-shocked people and countries.

Based on breakthrough historical research and four years of on-the-ground reporting in disaster zones, *The Shock Doctrine* explodes the myth that the global free market triumphed democratically.

As Klein shows how the deliberate use of the shock doctrine produced world-changing events from Pinochet's coup in Chile in 1973 to the Tiananmen Square Massacre in 1989 and the collapse of the Soviet Union in 1991, she tells a story radically different from the one usually heard. Once again Naomi Klein has written a book that will reframe the debate.

'Naomi Klein has written a brilliant, brave and terrifying book. It should be compulsory reading' Arundhati Roy

'There are very few books that really help us understand the present. *The Shock Doctrine* is one of those books' John Gray

'A book to be read everywhere' John Berger

PENGUIN ECONOMICS

THE ACCIDENTAL THEORIST AND OTHER DISPATCHES FROM THE DISMAL SCIENCE
PAUL KRUGMAN

'Probably the most creative economist of his generation' *Economist*

'Everything Mr Krugman has to say is smart, important and even fun to read...he is one of a handful of very bright, relatively young economists who do everything well' Peter Passell, *New York Times Book Review*

Paul Krugman has made a reputation for himself by telling us the truth about economics, however unlikely it may seem and however little we want to believe it.

In this wonderfully cohesive set of sharp, witty essays, Krugman tackles bad economic ideas from across the political spectrum, giving us clear-eyed insights into unemployment, globalization, economic growth and financial speculation among other topics. The writing here brilliantly combines the acerbic style and clever analysis that has made Krugman famous. Some of the articles have been written in response to particular economic events, but there is no particular orthodoxy in them, only rational common sense.

'Paul Krugman is the heir apparent to Galbraith. Some of these essays will make you smile, some will make you wince, all will make you think. Krugman's words are as sharp as his mind' Alan S. Blinder, Princeton University

'You can learn a great deal, about economics and otherwise, by reading these delightful essays' Robert M. Solow, Nobel Laureate, Massachusetts Institute of Technology

'[Paul Krugman] writes better than any economist since John Maynard Keynes' Rob Norton, *Fortune*

He just wanted a decent book to read ...

Not too much to ask, is it? It was in 1935 when Allen Lane, Managing
Director of Bodley Head Publishers, stood on a platform at Exeter railway
station looking for something good to read on his journey back to London.
His choice was limited to popular magazines and poor-quality paperbacks –
the same choice faced every day by the vast majority of readers, few of
whom could afford hardbacks. Lane's disappointment and subsequent anger
at the range of books generally available led him to found a company – and
change the world.

*'We believed in the existence in this country of a vast reading public for intelligent
books at a low price, and staked everything on it'*
Sir Allen Lane, 1902–1970, founder of Penguin Books

The quality paperback had arrived – and not just in bookshops. Lane was
adamant that his Penguins should appear in chain stores and tobacconists,
and should cost no more than a packet of cigarettes.

Reading habits (and cigarette prices) have changed since 1935, but
Penguin still believes in publishing the best books for everybody to
enjoy. We still believe that good design costs no more than bad design,
and we still believe that quality books published passionately and responsibly
make the world a better place.

So wherever you see the little bird – whether it's on a piece of
prize-winning literary fiction or a celebrity autobiography, political tour
de force or historical masterpiece, a serial-killer thriller, reference book,
world classic or a piece of pure escapism – you can bet that it represents
the very best that the genre has to offer.

Whatever you like to read – trust Penguin.